The Transition from Command to Market Economies in East-Central Europe

Published in cooperation with
The Vienna Institute for
Comparative Economic Studies

The Transition from Command to Market Economies in East-Central Europe

The Vienna Institute for Comparative Economic Studies
Yearbook IV

EDITED BY
Sándor Richter

Routledge
Taylor & Francis Group
LONDON AND NEW YORK

First published 1992 by Westview Press, Inc.

Published 2019 by Routledge
52 Vanderbilt Avenue, New York, NY 10017
2 Park Square, Milton Park, Abingdon, Oxon OX14 4RN

Routledge is an imprint of the Taylor & Francis Group, an informa business

Library of Congress Cataloging-in-Publication Data
The transition from command to market economies in East-Central Europe
/ edited by Sândor Richter.
p. cm. — (The Vienna Institute for Comparative Economic Studies yearbook ; 4)
ISBN 0-8133-8559-8
1. Europe, Eastern—Economic conditions—1989- . 2. Europe, Eastern—Economic policy—1989- . I. Richter, Sândor. II. Series: Yearbook (Wiener Institut für Internationale Wirtschaftsvergleiche) ; 4.
HC244.T6987 1992
330.947—dc20 91-45237
CIP

ISBN 13: 978-0-367-29669-8 (hbk)
ISBN 13: 978-0-367-31215-2 (pbk)

In honor of Kazimierz Laski,
who celebrated his seventieth birthday
on December 15, 1991. To mark the occasion,
his colleagues at The Vienna Institute
dedicate this volume to him.

CONTENTS

FOREWORD

In its fourth yearbook published by Westview Press, The Vienna Institute for Comparative Economic Studies presents a selection of publications written during 1991 by staff researchers and invited scholars. Some of the chapters presented in this volume appear for the first time, others are updated and revised versions of working papers previously published at the Institute. The focus of the chapters are the first results of the stabilization and transformation policies of East- and Central-European countries on their way from command to market economies. The great hopes at the start of the process gave way to some disenchantment and even, as it has been termed, a postrevolutionary hangover in these countries. The hardships of the transition are in part an unescapable heritage of the communist past and are partly related to policies chosen by the present governments. These policies, their theoretical background, and the results are the main topic of the chapters presented in this book.

My special thanks are due to Sándor Richter, who compiled and edited this volume.

Kazimierz Laski

ACKNOWLEDGMENTS

Without doubt 1991 will be seen as a turning point in contemporary history. The communist system collapsed in the Soviet Union after the abortive military coup, and by the end of the year the dissolution process of the earth's biggest state entered its final stage. The successor states of the Soviet Union will soon have to face the same or very similar dilemmas of transition to a market economy that the East European countries have faced recently. This made the compilation of this book a challenging task.

My special thanks go to the contributors of this volume. The book could not have been prepared for publication without the editing help of Fred Prager and the skills of Renate Szumilowski who prepared the camera ready copy. Both have performed their tasks with the usual precision and speed. Carolyn Richards of Westview Press helped to ensure that the yearbook was published within the shortest timespan possible under the circumstances. To all of them, I wish to express my gratitude. The shortcomings and remaining errors are my responsibility.

Sándor Richter

INTRODUCTION

Sándor Richter

Transition from command to market economy has no fully developed theory as yet; and the experiences of modernization and stabilization that have been compiled in other spheres of world economy are hardly applicable under the peculiar conditions of the former socialist countries. Certainly this is not the time to wait for the adequate theory: transition progresses at full speed in the former GDR, in the Czech and Slovak Republic, in Poland, and in Hungary. The other East European economies and the successor states of the Soviet Union follow the former group of countries at a smaller or bigger time lag. However, the search for the adequate theory of transition remains still one of the most powerful intellectual challenges for the social sciences in the 1990s. The stake is very high: the welfare and social stability of countries populated altogether by hundreds of millions, depends directly or indirectly on the success, or failure, of transition. That is the reason why contributions to the emerging theory of transition were placed in the focus of the WIIW's fourth yearbook. These essays make up the contents of Part One.

When theory is missing, analysis of experiences of transition in individual countries or in certain sectors of the countries concerned has special significance. Transition is a typical "learning by doing" process, where the lessons learnt from other countries, coping with similar problems, may save expensive blind alleys of development. Part Two provides contributions dealing with the specific experiences of transition.

Although main issues of transition are more or less identical in all economies concerned, the internal conditions under which the individual programs are drafted, vary substantially. Foreign debt is one of those issues which set limits to any economic program in the former socialist countries. The correct assessment of the actual economic strength of the countries concerned is another necessary precondition of viable economic programs. The essays of Part Three analyze, besides these issues, aspects of the external environment of transition and the lessons to be learned from the spectacular development of some Far-Eastern economies.

The Economics of Transition

Relations with the international financial institutions are of vital importance for all countries in transition. The International Monetary Fund has (or in the case of the successor states of the Soviet Union is going to have) decisive influence on economic policy in former socialist countries. All the more important is the question whether the policy recommendations of the International Monetary Fund help to stabilize the economies concerned and promote the smoothest possible way of transition. In his essay A. Bhaduri provides a critical analysis of the concept on which stabilization policy measures recommended by the IMF seem to rest. He points out that it is necessary to discuss the basic concept of the IMF, namely the so called financial programing, since it is being applied – with some country specific features – across countries with different major economic and structural features. Important elements of macroeconomic policies for Eastern Europe even bear a striking similarity with "conditionalities" negotiated by the IMF with developing countries for stand-by loans. That suggests that a more or less uniform conceptual scheme or model is assumed to be applicable across a variety of countries and economic situations. Bhaduri describes and criticizes the cornerstone of this general scheme as specified in Polak's famous 1957 paper, and finally proposes an alternative approach.

Shock therapy or gradualism? Of the three leading reform countries (the Czech and Slovak Republic, Hungary, and Poland) Hungary followed its cautious, gradual transition policies that had been launched still under the last (reform-)communist government. Poland and the Czech and Slovak Republic opted for the radical solution. Gradualism or shock therapy: this crucial dilemma of politicians and economists of the countries in transition is addressed in the papers of K. Laski and F. Levcik. In his sharply critical overview of the Polish case Laski demonstrates that the goals of the radical stabilization plan were not met; moreover, that the costs of the program were much higher than anticipated. He identifies several important explanations for the negative features of the Polish development. As the most important one he mentions the excessive concentration on monetary and fiscal policy, coupled with neglect of the non-monetary sphere of the economy. He also draws attention to two serious mistakes made in the domain of monetary policy: first the drastic rise of the interest rate in early 1990 which gave an initial impetus to the decline of production; and second, the excessive devaluation of the zloty leading to an initial acceleration of inflation. Addressing general problems of stabilization in Eastern Europe, Laski believes that the crucial problems for the post-stabilization economies is the replacement of the vicious circle of stagnation by the virtuous circle of growth. Recession caused by a stabilization program comes sooner or later to an end. If it is successful, inflation is also pushed down to a tolerable level. However, the achieved equilibrium will be characterized by a low level of employment and output, by low profitability of firms and low utilization of capacities; and also by the continuance of an unfavorable climate for investment. One can not exclude that all these problems will be solved by spontaneous market forces, but one has to wait for years, and success is not certain. Examples of the more successful countries, like Mexico and Chile, where the road from stabilization to recovery lasted for about a decade, should be a warning. In Laski's perception some external factor to launch the cumulative tendencies towards growth may be helpful, if not absolutely necessary; and the first candidate to take over this task may be the state.

Big state-owned enterprises in a monopolistic position on the domestic market survived the first two years after the political changes in Central and Eastern Europe more or less untouched. In his essay F. Levcik devotes special attention to the problems originating from missing competition in the countries of transition. Price liberalization without a competitive milieu, coupled with more expensive imports due to gross currency devaluation, must initially lead to substantial price increases. Serious efforts are to be made to promote competition. Free market access for new private enterprises, privatization measures, the freeing of foreign trade from administrative impediments, and the threat of bankruptcy are necessary institutional prerequisites, already realized in part. Levcik thinks that more has to be done: encouraging competition ought to be a day-to-day task of the government and of the representatives of enterprise and labor interests. In economies where the public sector, like it or not, is going to remain an influential factor for a longer period, competition policy is to encompass state enterprises as well. Beside anti-trust and demonopolization policy Levcik urges offensive competition policies, too. Viable enterprises could be reconstructed by temporary, conditional stand-by alleviations and supportive actions to enable them to compete. He warns that such policies may not always prove successful: bankruptcies and failures will occur; but the majority of the enterprises could be refloated by such supportive policies. This could also improve the chances of privatizing them later under better conditions.

In the last essay of Part One, R. Dietz provides an unconventional approach to the problem of transition. In his system theoretical analysis exchange is the central category. According to Dietz the systemic rationality of Western societies originates from exchange, the basic communicative element from which all modern economic institutions (money, prices, property, organizations) emanate. Since exchange is responsible for the high-grade rationality of modern economy, the question arises how exchange communication can be revived in the former command economies. The disappointingly slow pace of privatization in Eastern Europe is examined in Dietz's approach, who maintains that only functioning markets can render identity and autonomy to firms. At the stage of transition a systemic vacuum appears, in which neither the old command nor market (exchange) communication fulfills its task. This vacuum blocks the emergence of the market economy. Unfortunately it can not be eliminated by traditional economic policy measures or by institutional reforms. Therefore Dietz regards the involvement of Western capital as a sine-qua-non for the development of capital markets in the region concerned. Macroeconomic stabilization under the conditions of transition cannot mean anything but the increase of the opportunities for investment. Consequently, he stresses, and here Dietz shares the view of the other three authors of Part One, that for these economies a shock therapy is dangerous.

Specific Issues of Transition

Privatization is a fundamental element of transition in all economies concerned. Nevertheless, initial plans for a rapid privatization proved to be over-simplistic everywhere in Eastern Europe. Confusing terms in discussions about privatization still hinder a clear insight into the problem. To introduce the notion of different levels of privatization, G. Hunya, in his essay, provides analytical tools for clarifying advantages and disadvantages of alternative privatization strategies. According to Hunya's scheme the identification of property rights occurs at the first level of privatization; this is quite difficult, as public ownership often means no specified owners in the countries concerned. At the second level "surface privatization" takes place, which covers ownership transfers to some transitional owner. This concerns the cases of mutual cross ownership of state owned companies, the issuance of free or almost free privatization vouchers to the population and, the transfer of property into property management funds, holdings and other institutional owners established by the state. The third, final stage is "deep privatization", after the completion of which private physical or legal persons attain a dominant position among the owners. Hunya points out that at present a mix of these different levels of privatization coexists in each East European country. After reviewing several further aspects of privatization he provides a case-study of privatization in Hungary.

Agriculture is an especially difficult terrain of transition, where only few of the experiences accumulated in other sectors of the economy are applicable. Z. Lukas presents an analysis of the challenges facing Czechoslovak agriculture in the process of transition. After reviewing the development of the sector under the former regime, the problems of trade in agricultural products, and of subsidization policy, the author pays special attention to the issue of restitution: its outcome will have a decisive influence on the further development of this sector. Dealing with the perspectives of Czechoslovak agriculture, Lukas assumes that the currently oversized state and cooperative farms will be subdivided into smaller units; however, a splitting up into family businesses (under 100 ha) is unlikely to take place. A rise of productivity and profitability is urgently needed. But Lukas thinks that the speed of transition in agriculture should be secondary to the rule that costs involved for the whole economy should be kept at a minimum. The danger that many of the redundant farm workers will be unable to find employment in other sectors of the economy is imminent. Lukas argues that if subsidies were increased from the present level, which is relatively much lower than that in Western Europe, some comparative advantages of the Czechoslovak agriculture could be retained. That way unemployment in the sector and migration to the urban areas could be kept under control, and furthermore, the country could thus continue to be a self-sufficient producer of basic foodstuffs and a moderate exporter of some agrarian specialties.

While developments in Poland, Hungary, and Czechoslovakia are permanently in the focus of attention of Western observers, Romania, and perhaps even more so, Bulgaria, have been "stepchildren" of Western media and research in this respect. I. Grosser's paper thus provides one of the rare insights into the transition process of the latter mentioned Balkan country. Her essay makes it clear that the economic transition is in an early phase yet in Bulgaria; it started under exceptionally unfavorable internal and external conditions, and its political and social background is characterized by many uncertainties. In Grosser's perception the currently pursued transition policy, based on liberalization, radical stabilization, and an abrupt opening of the up till recently heavily isolated economy under conditions of deficient market structures and weak competitiveness, bears the risk of a deep and prolonged depression. The Bulgarian blueprint of "shock therapy", which is comparable, but in its details not identical, with the Polish and the Czechoslovak cases, threatens to destroy many basically viable enterprises. This danger has been enhanced by the loss of important former COMECON markets, the very limited access to Western capital in the wake of Bulgaria's debt moratorium, and last but not least by the severe delay in the implementation of institutional reforms. In attempting to reduce the role of the state to a minimum, extreme restraint has been exercised in industrial policy. Although up till now the population proved to be ready to accept the massive real income losses, such patience may not last for ever.

Internal and External Environment of Transition

An evaluation of the economic development level of the former socialist countries is a critical issue, which has substantial influence on the modalities of any Western contributions, promoting the process of transition to market economy in the countries concerned. Financial contributions to international organizations, access to various forms of foreign aid, ranking among the potential foreign direct investment targets by global investors, have traditionally been dependent upon the outcome of such comparisons. In his essay P. Havlik reviews the enormous difficulties researchers have to face when trying to compare crucial categories like GDP, productivity, income, wages, etc. of the East European countries with the respective Western counterparts or even within the former Eastern Bloc. Wide divergences in data availability and reliability mostly prohibit the use of more sophisticated estimation methods which could be uniformly applied for such comparisons. Havlik, evaluating the generally used estimation methods and their results, introduces alternative estimates obtained by the so called "physical indicators global" (PIG) method. The concept makes use of the relationship between various physical indicators and the level of per capita GDP observed in market economies. These estimates form an approximation for the assessment of an inter-country ranking of real output levels, but, as the author warns, disregard important systemic and qualitative differences between market and command economies. Nevertheless these estimates might more properly reflect the real economic potential of a country than the alternative approaches. Until reliable purchasing power estimates for all former centrally planned economies become available, the PIG method provides a more complete and realistic picture for a ranking of relative economic development levels in individual countries, even if not for comparing absolute levels of per capita GDPs measured in US$.

In 1991 the Union of Socialist Soviet Republics ceased to exist, together with the seven decade long rule of the communist party in that region. Since the thwarted military coup in August of that year the world has been preoccupied with the possible outcomes of the accelerated disintegration process of the multinational Soviet state, the future of the nuclear arsenal dispersed across the huge country, and with the search for appropriate aid programs to avoid mass starvation and consequent social explosions in the successor states. P. Havlik's second essay in this volume gives an insight into the developments of the last six months prior to the military coup. He reviews, first the official stabilization program of early 1991 in which the central government still demanded unspecified extraordinary powers, then the efforts of a group of Soviet economists to elaborate an alternative, more radical reform program for transition to market economy linked to massive Western financial assistance. A detailed description of the rapidly deteriorating economic situation over the first half of 1991 follows, with special attention to the collapse of foreign trade. Finally, in his assessment Havlik draws attention to the enormous and unavoidable economic difficulties the successor states of the Soviet Union will have to face. Nevertheless he is cautiously optimistic concerning the medium and long term economic prospects.

Cartographers will be busy in 1992, not only redrawing the map of the former Soviet Union; there is no solution as yet in sight of an end to the civil war in Yugoslavia, and the state the world knew under that name, practically no longer exists. Although states may disappear from one day to the other, most of the economic problems these states were coping with remain. Foreign debt is exactly such an issue. There have been serious discussions how to distribute foreign debt obligations evenly among the successor states of the former Soviet Union, where the disintegration of the state took place, at least up to recently, surprising peacefully. All the more difficult will it be to allocate foreign debt among the entities emerging on the ruins of former Yugoslavia. F. Štiblar's effort to provide the clearest possible picture about the indebtedness of Yugoslavia thus deserves special attention. He reviews the history of the Yugoslav indebtedness from the mid-1960s and compares its main indicators with the World Bank indebtedness criteria and respective indicators of the East European and Third World countries respectively. Certainly the most interesting part of his analysis addresses the attribution of federal debt to federal units (the six republics and the two autonomous republics). According to Štiblar's findings Slovenia, Croatia, and to a lesser extent Voivodina can be classified as lightly indebted federal units, while Kosovo is found at the other extreme as the only severely indebted federal unit. 85% of the US$ 4.6 billion hard currency reserves of Yugoslavia (in the fall of 1991) was deposited at the central bank in Belgrade. Massive western financial assistance will be needed, despite the relatively low level of indebtedness, to enable an independent Slovenia and Croatia to service their foreign debts.

The international context was crucial with the fall of the old system in Eastern Europe and it will be by no means less important for the successful completion of the transition in Eastern Europe. H. Gabrisch's essay is devoted primarily to the analysis of the external environment of transition and the related challenges the East European economies have to face. He critically analyzes, mainly by the example of Poland, the attempts to generate export-led recovery by massive devaluation of the national currency. Further he reviews the development of foreign direct investment in the region and provides a detailed overview of the Western financial assistance programs for the economies in transition. The author emphasizes the importance of promoting the concept of "help towards self-help" instead of endless transfers of emergency aid. Paying special attention to Eastern Europe's relations with the EC, Gabrisch also addresses the delicate issue of the future role of reunited Germany in the region. Finally, various solutions are reviewed that could revitalize the vanishing trade relations within the former COMECON region.

After decades of central planning, autarchy, biased prices and rule of almighty, nevertheless inefficient bureaucracies, it is no wonder that the new East European regimes have a vision of an economic system where the above mentioned features are missing. The target is just the opposite: free prices, opening up of the economies to foreign competition, the removal of subsidies, the quickest possible privatization. However, as W. Urban's essay demonstrates, Korea and Taiwan in many respects did not follow this liberal strategy in their long march from poverty stricken Third World countries to economic success stories. For a long time both countries maintained a combined system of export promotion and import controls. But protection was only transitional for individual sectors, and it was its final purpose to achieve international competitiveness of the selected sectors as soon as possible and then immediately to start to penetrate significant foreign markets. None of the two countries used undervaluation of their currencies as a means of export promotion: thus relatively cheap imports played an important role in upgrading the quality of exported commodities with high import content. Exporters were compensated for loss of price competitiveness by other export promoting measures. The role of foreign direct investment in capital formation was relatively modest, compared with other successful Far Eastern countries, which were massive importers of foreign capital. However, again a very important lesson for Eastern Europe, as foreign involvement was concentrated in few crucial branches, its impact was substantially positive on the economic development of both economies. Urban points out the similarities in the field of privatization. When the Japanese left the two countries after World War Two, 80 to 90 % of industrial assets came into national property and had to be privatized. In both countries it took more than ten years to reach the projected level of privatization. The author draws attention to the numerous cultural, social and political differences separating the two Far Eastern countries from the former centrally planned economies. Notwithstanding, she leaves no doubt that there are many lessons to be shared.

Part One
The Economics of Transition

1

CONVENTIONAL STABILIZATION AND THE EAST EUROPEAN TRANSITION

Amit Bhaduri

1. Introduction

It is the purpose of this chapter to analyze some possible pitfalls in the IMF-style stabilization program in East Europe, and then, to suggest some policies which might possibly avoid them. At the very outset it should be emphasized that, unlike many developing market economies in the Third World which turned recently to the IMF to tackle a difficult balance of payments situation, the formerly centrally planned economies of East Europe have an additional reason for undertaking IMF-style stabilization. In order to facilitate the transition from the command to the market-oriented system, it is widely believed that the IMF-style stabilization is a necessary step in the right direction in the short run. And, at least in this respect, the objective underlying the stabilization programs in East Europe seems to be more ambitious in scope than that of a typical developing country.

It would have been meaningless to discuss IMF-style stabilization in general, if these economic programs were highly country-specific, and differed substantially across countries according to their major economic and other structural features. However, this is hardly the case. On the contrary, the hard core macroeconomic policies in the stabilization programs tend to be rather uniform and stereotyped, and even bear a striking degree of similarity with "conditionalities" imposed by the IMF on developing market economies for "stand-by" loans. In other words, a more or less uniform conceptual scheme or "model" is assumed to be applicable across a variety of countries and economic situations. It may be helpful to begin a discussion of IMF-style stabilization programs by identifying the central features of the underlying model, and the policy implications that follow from it.

2. The Model Underlying Conventional Stabilization

At the intellectual core of the IMF stabilization program lies the procedure of financial programing, which derived from the influential work of Polak (1957). Perhaps the most important feature of such financial programing is its supposed ability to suggest policy measures, based exclusively on the double entry accounts of external trade and banking. Note, this also implies that Keynesian national income accounting with its emphasis on the centrality of effective demand is treated as less important, a sort of fifth wheel to the coach of financial programing.

Financial programing starts from an identity: "money" supply as the liability of the financial sector must be matched by assets held by that sector. Thus, increase in "money" supply (ΔM_S) ≡ increase in the liabilities of the financial sector ≡ increase in the assets of the financial sector ≡ increase in international reserve (ΔR) + increase in credit to the private sector (ΔB), normally from the commercial banks + increase in credit to the public or government sector (ΔG), normally from the Central-Bank/monetary authority, i.e.

$$\Delta M_S \equiv \Delta R + \Delta B + \Delta G \quad (1)$$

The increase in international reserve (ΔR) is related to the external trade and payments accounts through the following identity:
Increase in international reserve (ΔR) ≡ Export (E) – Import (Z) + Net capital inflow (F), i.e.

$$\Delta R \equiv (E - Z) + F \quad (2)$$

Note, net capital inflow (F) must include not only foreign concessional inflows, but various net factor income, e.g. emigrant workers' remittances, interest payments on account of servicing external debt etc. in order to complete the accounting picture (see endnote 8).

Finally, use is made of the celebrated "exchange identity" which, with some modification, can be interpreted later as the "quantity theory of money", i.e. the demand for money (M_d) times velocity of circulation (V) ≡ price level (P) times output level (X).

Thus, the familiar expression,

$$M_d \equiv k.P.X, \quad k \equiv (1/V)$$

can be written in its first order approximation (neglecting second and higher order terms) as,

$$\Delta M_d \equiv PX.\Delta k + k.P.\Delta X + k.X.\Delta P \quad (3)$$

Since the increased supply of money must equal its demand[1], i.e.

$$\Delta M_s \equiv \Delta M_d,$$

we can substitute (2) in (1), and then equate it with (3) to obtain

$$(E-Z)+F+\Delta B+\Delta G \equiv PX.\Delta k+k.P.\Delta X+k.X.\Delta P \qquad (4)$$

Note that up to this point, i.e. up to identity (4) there is little scope for logical disagreement, simply because we are dealing with definitions. Disagreement or doubt may begin to creep in only when special assumptions are made to modify identity (4) for the purpose of financial programing. There are two special assumptions:

1. The crucial postulate of the quantity theory of money that the velocity of circulation of money is roughly constant, which yields $\Delta k = 0$
2. The assumption that the level of output (X) and its increase (ΔX) can be exogenously fixed from the supply side, i.e. in terms of supply considerations. This would make $\Delta X = \Delta \bar{X}$, as exogenously given.[2] Thus, the whole term $k.P.\Delta X$ becomes a constant on the right hand side of identity (4), but only on the strength of assumptions 1 and 2 above.

Given $\Delta k = 0$ and $k.P.\Delta X = C_1$, an exogenous constant by assumptions, identity (4) becomes equation (5) below:

$$(E-Z)+F+\Delta B+\Delta G = k.X.\Delta P+C_1 \qquad (5)$$

or, dividing throughout by the nominal value of output, PX (note, $X = X_{-1}$, output of the previous period)

$$\left[\frac{(E-Z)+F}{PX}\right] + \left[\frac{\Delta B+\Delta G}{PX}\right] = k.\frac{\Delta P}{P} + C_2 \qquad (6)$$

where $C_2 = k(\Delta X/X)$ = constant by assumption.

Equations (5) or (6) are capable of suggesting policy conclusions, closely in conformity with some typical recommendations of IMF stabilization. For instance, assuming net capital inflow to be exogenous (F), a stricter financial discipline interpreted as a lower increase in credit advanced by the financial sector to the government (ΔG) and/or to the private sector (ΔB), would tend to reduce left hand side of equation (5) or (6). To balance the equation, either the rate of price increase ($\Delta P/P$) i.e. inflation must slow down correspondingly, and/or the trade balance (E–Z) must improve. However, note that, even on the rather heroic assumptions made, the case for financial discipline in terms of (5) or (6) is not unambiguous from a purely logical point of view. Since we have only one equation (5) or (6) in three variables, it is still conceivable that lower public and private borrowing as a proportion of GNP, i.e. lower $(\Delta G+\Delta B)/PX$ in (6) may be associated with higher (lower) inflation $(\Delta P/P)$ but a larger (smaller) trade surplus, $(E-Z)/PX$ to balance the equation. In brief, greater financial discipline alone need not necessarily reduce both inflation and trade deficit even in terms of the conceptual framework used by the IMF. It may, e.g., drastically improve the trade balance in the short period, but with a sharp rise in the inflation rate. Such a situation is not altogether uncommon in several countries which recently undertook IMF style stabilization.

3. The Conventional Policy Package for Stabilization

The package of policies usually recommended under the stabilization program goes beyond financial discipline of credit restraint, but is supposed to reinforce the basic thrust of reducing inflation and balance of payments deficit. Thus, the package typically consists of:

(a) restriction of credit made available through the domestic financial system, especially to the government/public sector. The case for discriminating against the government sector is partly the general bias towards a private sector oriented market philosophy. But it may be supported also from extending the "reduced equation" (5) or (6) of financial programing, if it is assumed that the central bank's additional lending to the government (ΔG) acts as "high-powered" money, i.e. as a credit base for commercial banks' additional lending to the private sector (ΔB). In this case,

$$\Delta B = n.\Delta G, \; n > 1 \tag{7}$$

where n can be interpreted as the "credit multiplier" of the commercial banks.[3] Using (6) and (7),

$$\left[\frac{(E-Z)+F}{PX}\right] + \left[\frac{(1+n)}{PX}\right] \Delta G = k.\frac{\Delta P}{P} + C_2 \tag{8}$$

so that any reduction of credit to the government (i.e. lower ΔG) has a magnified effect in reducing either inflation or trade deficit or both, and thus reinforcing the basic objective of financial programing.

(b) Equation (8) could also be used to justify the need to reduce the "fiscal deficit" of the government or reducing the "public sector borrowing requirement". Thus, cuts in government subsidies and increase in administered prices of basic public utilities usually constitute another typical element of the IMF-style stabilization package.[4]

(c) In addition to "quantity rationing", i.e. restraint on the amount of loan advanced by the financial sector $(\Delta G+\Delta B)$, the typical IMF package also recommends "price rationing" of credit, i.e. a higher interest rate. This is designed to serve as a double-edged weapon. On the one hand, it is supposed to encourage (private) savings and thus reduce total borrowing requirement from the banking sector. And, on the other hand, it is expected to reduce the demand for loans from the banking sector due to the higher cost of borrowing finance through the price mechanism in the money market. This aspect of financial liberalization, interpreted as a general movement from quantity to price rationing of credit, is encouraged by the IMF's general philosophy of relying on the price mechanism, even in the financial markets.

(d) As already indicated in the reduced equation (6), the restriction on credit from the financial sector as a proportion of GDP, i.e. $(\Delta B+\Delta G)/PX$ in (6), must either reduce the inflation rate $(\Delta P/P)$ or improve the trade balance, $(E-Z)/PX$, in order to balance both sides of equation (6). However, because of three unknowns in one equation, there is a crucial indeterminacy – credit restriction may improve balance of payments so much as to permit even higher inflation rate. Obversely, it may reduce inflation rate so much as to accommodate even higher trade deficit for balancing equation (6). It is therefore necessary to go beyond equation (6) and introduce an additional instrument of policy, apart from domestic credit rationing.[5] Thus, the IMF-style policy package also recommends devaluation of the domestic currency in the hope that this will directly improve trade balance by making export cheaper to foreigners and import dearer to domestic residents. As is well-known, provided, (i) exports and imports are sufficiently price sensitive (to satisfy the Marshall-Lerner condition) and (ii) domestic supply for export is sufficiently elastic, devaluation can become an effective instrument to deal with adverse balance of payments problems. In this respect, the IMF stabilization package seems to reinforce two interdependent objectives: while devaluation increases international price competitiveness by reducing the export price to foreigners, domestic credit restriction tends to achieve the same target by reducing the domestic rate of inflation. Nevertheless, the critical element in this argument remains the (absolute) magnitude of the price elasticity of demand for exports. Because a lower value of the elasticity makes it more difficult on the one hand to satisfy the Marshall-Lerner condition for improving trade balance; but on the other hand, a lower value of this elasticity also dampens the unfavorable impact of domestic price inflation on export as a result of lower international price competitiveness.[6]

(e) The final element in the typical IMF policy package to be discussed in this context is the liberalization of the trade regime. This consists of two elements. First, moving away from bureaucratically controlled quantitative restrictions and quotas to price-induced restrictions in the form of a more uniform tariff structure. Second, dismantling of the protectionist trade regime to a more liberal regime with lower tariff (and quota) restrictions. The movement from quantitative restrictions to price (tariff) restrictions seems to be associated with the view that more transparent rules based on more or less uniform tariff are better than a maze of bureaucratic discretions in the form of detailed quantitative restrictions. In this sense, it touches on the familiar debate on rule versus discretion in macroeconomic management, with IMF-style stabilization generally favoring the former.

However, the sustainability of a liberalized trade regime is possible only if this does not tend to continuously widen the current account deficit. The support for trade liberalization is often sought on the ground that a more liberal import structure would not only help export promotion, but higher export would outweigh quantitatively higher imports to improve the trade balance in the longer run.

The issue of sustainable trade liberalization is thus intimately connected with success in export promotion. Consequently, liberalization of capital accounts of the balance of payments, especially for attracting foreign investment and technology as well as attaining convertibility of the domestic currency, assumes special significance in this context. However, these are issues which relate primarily to the longer term growth potential of the economy and not strictly to short-term stabilization scheme (underlying equation 6). Consequently, these and other issues related to longer term growth potential and structural adjustments will be dealt with separately in Section 5 of this paper, which also focuses on some more specific issues of the "transition to the market economy" in East Europe.

4. Pitfalls of the Conventional Stabilization Program

The policy recommendations of a model are as good as the assumptions made to construct the model (assuming no logical errors). Therefore, the soundness of the policy proposals contained in the typical IMF-style stabilization program can best be judged by more closely examining the implications of the two central assumptions made, for deriving reduced equation (5) or (6) from identity (4). To recall, these two assumptions are: (a) constant velocity of circulation of money, implying $(1/V) = k$ is constant or at least predictable, and (b) the change in output, ΔX, can be exogenously specified, so that $k.(\Delta X/X) = k.g = C_2$, is also a constant in equation (6).

To begin with, consider more closely the latter assumption (b). It not only implies that output is entirely supply-determined, but also that changes in the level of output (ΔX) are independent of changes in the instruments of economic policy, e.g. in this case, changes in the degree of credit restriction do not affect the level of output. These implications of assumption (b) are simply untenable, as we argue below.

First, there is no reason to accept that output is always supply-determined. As already pointed out, the basic (reduced) equation (5) or (6) can be derived by using balance sheets of banks (the financial sector) and balance of payments statistics in a double entry format. Thus, it does not assign a central role to the Kalecki–Keynes double entry national income accounting framework for developing the underlying model.[7] Since Keynesian national income accounting has been the essential intellectual framework for exhibiting the central role of demand in the determination of the level of output, i.e. how output can become demand – and not supply – determined, neglecting this national income accounting framework boils down to neglecting the possibility of seriously considering demand-determined output. Further, we hardly need to remind ourselves that supply-determined output basically postulates in some sense full employment/utilization of resources (including labor) – an assumption which flatly contradicts at least recent experiences of stabilization in East Europe.

Following Kalecki (1971), the possibility of demand-determined output is derived from expenditure – income equality in the form[8] Private investment (I_p) + Government budget deficit (D) + Current account surplus (A) = Private Savings (S_p)

$$\text{or, } I_p + D + A = S_p \tag{9}$$

Assuming private savings to be a constant fraction (i.e. marginal and average propensity to save are the same for simplicity) of gross national income, i.e.

$$S_p = s.PX,$$

the demand-determined level of output (X^d) is obtained through the multiplier mechanism as

$$X^d = \frac{1}{s}\left[\frac{I_p + D + A}{P}\right], \quad \text{i.e. in constant prices.} \tag{10}$$

To incorporate the possibility of either demand- or supply-determined (X^s) output, the actual or observed level of output (X) has to be constrained correspondingly either by the demand or the supply side, i.e.

$$X = \text{minimum of } (X^d, X^s) = \text{Min } (X^d, X^s). \tag{11}$$

Moreover, it is easy to see that a greater restraint on domestic credit would affect the demand-determined level of output (X^d) adversely by restraining government deficit, and possibly also by discouraging private investment.[9] At the same time, quantity-rationing as well as price rationing in the form of higher interest rate in the market for domestic credit may lead to reduced availability of working capital, especially for the smaller producing units in the economy, and for sectors with long production period as e.g. in agriculture. Thus, for different reasons, both the demand-determined and the supply-determined output levels are likely to decrease with greater degrees of credit control. This, of course, implies that changes in the level of output – either from the demand or from the supply side – are not independent of changes in the degree of credit restriction imposed. In symbols,

$$X(\alpha) = \min\,[X^d(\alpha), X^s(\alpha)], \quad \frac{dX^d}{d\alpha} > 0, \quad \frac{dX^s}{d\alpha} > 0 \tag{12}$$

where, α = index of the degree of credit availability, which can also be defined from equation (6) as $[\frac{\Delta B + \Delta G}{PX}] = \alpha$.[10]

The problem with IMF-style conventional stabilization through financial programing, mainly restriction on domestic availability of credit (i.e. α-index), should now be apparent. Note, first from equation (5) and (6), that C_1 or C_2 are no longer constants, if the degree of credit availability $[\frac{\Delta B + \Delta G}{PX}] = \alpha$ is reduced. Because, $C_1 = k.P.\Delta X$ or equivalently, $C_2 = k.(\Delta X/X)$ decreases, i.e. X decreases as credit availability is reduced. As a result, IMF policy recommendations become open to serious doubt. More explicitly, rewrite (6) as,

$$a + \alpha = k(p + g) \tag{13}$$

where $a = \frac{(E-Z)+F}{PX}$, $\alpha = \frac{\Delta B + \Delta G}{PX}$, $p = \frac{\Delta P}{P}$ and $g = \frac{\Delta X}{X}$.

Clearly, a reduction in credit availability, i.e. lower α on the left hand side of (13) can be matched simply by a lower, even negative, growth rate of output g on the right hand side, leaving the inflation rate $(\frac{\Delta P}{P})$ or the trade balance unaffected. Alternatively, equation (13) also shows how a lower availability of credit (i.e. lower α) may be associated with high inflation as well as reduction in output with (possibly) some improvement in trade balance – a situation of stagflation with trade surplus, not an unknown configuration in East Europe (especially Poland) under recent stabilization.

Once it is recognized that both aggregate demand and aggregate supply may tend to fall as a result of lower availability of credit, the basic objective of IMF-style stabilization through financial programing may be lost. Figure 1 clearly displays this possibility by contrasting the "pro-stabilization" with the "anti-stabilization" case. So long as aggregate demand responds more strongly than aggregate supply to credit availability, starting from an initial situation of excess demand – recall, the initial situation is characterized by the economy of scarcity in the former centrally planned economies – the lowering of credit availability due to stabilization (financial programing) will reduce the excess demand gap, because demand will fall more sharply than supply, as credit is reduced in conformity with Case A, Figure 1. Such lowering of excess demand gap will, in turn, be helpful for containing inflation and/or improving the current account position. However, as the anti-stabilization Case B in Figure 1 demonstrates, if supply falls more sharply than demand, the excess demand gap keeps increasing as a result of more severe credit restriction through stabilization. This may fuel both inflation and deterioration in trade balance, and conventional stabilization fails unambiguously in this case.[11]

This analysis identifies one of the fundamental problems of achieving successful stabilization in general. Problems arise and the economy may even get destabilized increasingly (see Case B, Figure 1) due to the failure of adequate synchronization between adjustments on the demand and on the supply side. The fundamental theoretical mistake – how important it is in practice depends on each individual case and economic sector – of blindly following conventional stabilization, rests on an untenable position. This position, as we have seen, in effect suggests (see identities/equations 1 to 6) that the impact of financial programing on output would be relatively small, because output change can be treated as exogenous. Thus, the main impact would be felt on price change (lower inflation rate) and on trade balance.

It is even less clearly understood that instruments of stabilization like financial programing affect output change by influencing both the demand and supply side at the same time. And the consequence of this in the more extreme cases (e.g. Case B, Figure 1) may be further destabilization in the name of stabilization!

Three comments are in order in this context. First, a usually implicit assumption underlying demand and supply elasticities/responses is that they are defined with respect to a given time period. This also holds for Figure 1, where the outcome of stabilization depends critically on the relative response of demand and supply to (say) credit squeeze. In general, supply responses in terms of output expansion (as a result of, say, easier credit conditions) is likely to be considerably slower than demand responses, e.g. supply may hardly

Figure 1

Two Cases of Stabilization Policy

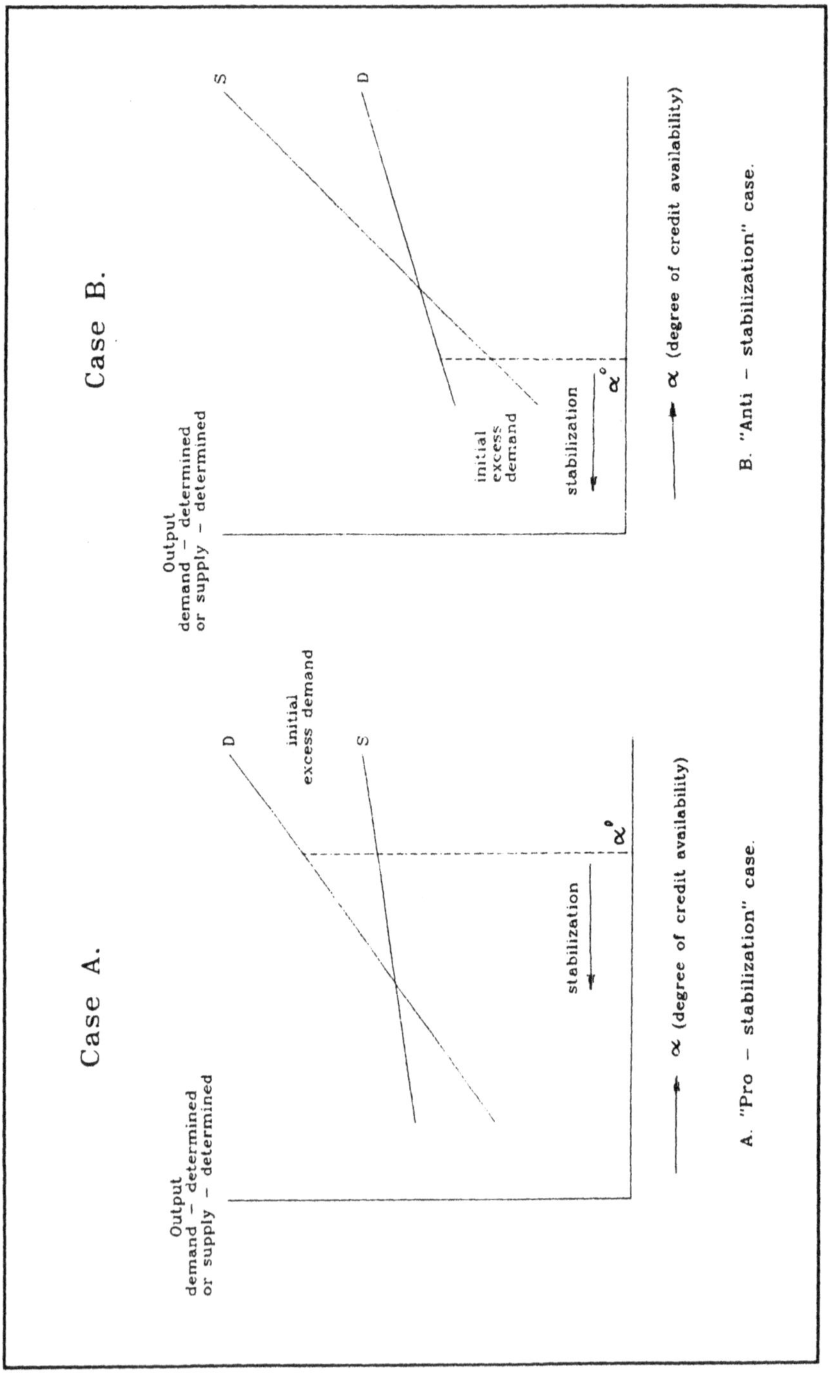

increase if the time period considered is short enough. Nevertheless, supply response in terms of output contraction (as a result of, say, tighter credit conditions) may be more or less as fast as demand contraction in some cases, e.g. lower supply due to working capital non-availability. This asymmetry – i.e., supply usually expands considerably more slowly than demand, but may contract almost as fast as demand – makes the simple analysis in Figure 1 not too misleading in the case of downward adjustment of demand and supply in the course of stabilization. As we shall later see (Section 5), it also makes the transition from stabilization to growth much more problematic, because the expansion of demand is usually governed by a much faster dynamics than that of supply.

Second, although the argument has been illustrated only with respect to restriction on the availability of domestic credit – a centerpiece of conventional stabilization program – the argument applies also to some other major instruments used in stabilization. For instance, with liberalization of import (i.e. a more liberal trade regime), aggregate domestic demand may fall through a widening of the current account deficit (see equation 9). At the same time, domestic supply may also fall as inefficient, domestic firms go out of business due to competition from superior and/or cheaper foreign products. As already pointed out (Case B, Figure 1), if supply declines faster than demand, the excess demand gap may widen to aggravate problems for the trade balance. Without repeating the argument, it is easy to see how a higher interest rate – usually an important aspect of financial liberalization – may create similar destabilizing dynamics, if higher interest leads to reduction in both demand and supply.[12] Thus, the central point deserves emphasis: Several of the important instruments of conventional stabilization, e.g. domestic credit control, trade liberalization, financial liberalization, lead to downward adjustment both on the demand, and on the supply side. Unless these adjustments are well synchronized (i.e. Case A, Figure 1), the stabilization program may actually contribute to destabilization (i.e. Case B, Figure 1).

Finally, note that general policies like greater restraint on the availability of domestic credit, higher interest etc., without further discretion and fine-tuning can create contradictory and awkward problems in different sectors. Thus, in some sectors demand and supply responses may be such as to reduce the excess demand gap (Case A, Figure 1), while in other sectors the same gap may increase (Case B, Figure 1) as a result of applying the same general policy. To illustrate the point with an important example, supply may typically decrease more slowly than demand in the agricultural sector to make excess supply a typical outcome of stabilization (see Case A, Figure 1). However, at the same time, supply may fall more sharply than demand in some manufacturing sectors due to non-availability of working capital, closing down of inefficient domestic firms in face of foreign competition etc., so that in these sectors "stabilization" would result in even greater excess demand (see Case B, Figure 1). While fine-tuning and bureaucratic discretion are admittedly unpleasant, the problematic nature of general policy rules without discretion should not be minimized either, especially in the context of stabilization.

We may turn now briefly to the other major assumption underlying the IMF-style stabilization which derives from the quantity of money, namely that the velocity of circulation of money is a rough constant.[13] In so far as it is postulated as an empirical constant, the constancy needs to be demonstrated rather than assumed in the context of the economies of East Europe.

Leaving aside the problem of empirical demonstration, the postulate of constant velocity allows changes in money supply to be transmitted directly into quantities (X) and commodity prices (P), without worrying about the "speculative demand" for money as a "store of wealth". This would also make the velocity of circulation relatively insensitive to variations in the rate of interest.[14] And further, when both the velocity of circulation (V) and the output level (X) are exogenously fixed (as the quantity theory as well as conventional stabilization seem to assume, see equations (1) to (6)), a direct link between the quantity of money and the price level is established through these assumptions.

Perhaps the most important point not recognized in this context is that, if the supply of money determines the price level (assuming velocity of circulation and output level exogenous), then no scope is left for cost-determined prices, because we would be in an over-determined system with one equation too many! From the point of view of stabilization, this may lead to serious omissions, as very many elements of cost-push inflation have to be neglected. For instance, a higher interest rate has been argued to increase the unit variable cost of production, and therefore price, in many instances (Cavallo, 1977; Taylor, 1988, 1991). Similarly, devaluation of the home currency can also erode international price competitiveness for certain products by sharply raising the price of imported raw materials and thus unit production cost. The point lies not in these specific examples, but in realizing that the quantity theory/monetarist framework is particularly ill-suited to deal with the problem of cost-determined prices. The task of price stabilization is certainly not going to be made easier by ignoring the various cost push aspects that may be set in motion by the conventional stabilization program.

5. The Relation Between Stabilization, Economic Dynamism, and Growth

In conventional stabilization schemes, it is generally assumed that stabilization is the first step in a sequence to be followed later by greater economic dynamism and growth. In the context of East Europe, the economic dynamism is supposed to be imparted by the "restructuring" in favor of the market economy and the private sector. Thus, one of the implicit assumptions of stabilization is that it must simultaneously stimulate the development of the private sector, through programs such as privatization, transfer of technology through multinational/foreign investment etc., which would ultimately strengthen the private sector to compete successfully in an international environment. The basic policy dilemma of stabilization in the context of East Europe seems to arise from its two rather contradictory objectives, i.e. how to reconcile the restrictive policies of conventional stabilization which are believed to be needed to improve trade balance, and to lower the inflation rate (see Section 3) with stimulative or expansionary policies which will help the private sector/private enterprise to grow at a sufficiently rapid pace to take over the task of growth. There is no unambiguous answer to this question either in stabilization theory or in the recent stabilization experiences of the developing countries (e.g. Taylor, 1988). Nevertheless, one could perhaps identify at least three central themes or propositions in the conventional view of stabilization, which are supposed to help in rapid transition from stabilization to growth, mostly through the dynamism of the private sector. First, there should not only be expenditure reduction by the government, but also expenditure switching in favor of the private sector, e.g. cut of subsidies to the general public (in the form of higher price for public utilities, food etc.), while providing various price and tax incentives (e.g. accelerated depreciation, lower corporate tax rate etc.) to private business.

Second, greater reliance on the price mechanism to deal with balance of payments problems by shifting the relative price in favor of tradables against non-tradables. Devaluation of the home currency is an instrument specifically favored for this purpose; but liberalization of the trade regime is also expected to help in achieving the same target perhaps in the long run.

Third, greater flexibility of the labor market. In essence, this means allowing the real wage rate to fall drastically in order to improve the profitability of private business. It would also mean liberal exit policies for inefficient firms, i.e. allowing inefficient domestic (especially public sector) firms to go out of business, usually as a consequence of trade liberalization, which would also create unemployment in the short term.

However, this unemployment is to be tolerated in the hope that the economic dynamism of an efficient and competitive private sector would create enough jobs to overcompensate the employment loss in the longer run. The Schumpeterian view of the process of "creative destruction" under capitalism is often invoked in this context to justify such a liberal exit policy for existing enterprises.

These policies do not form a coherent whole. Intellectual honesty demands that we recognize these three policy propositions as "open-ended", i.e. neither side – those who favor these policies as well as those who oppose them – have adequate theoretical or empirical reason to come to firm a priori conclusions about the effectiveness of these policies to bring about the transition from stabilization to sustainable economic growth.[15] Economic reasoning can only caution us regarding why and how these policy propositions may fail under certain conditions, and thus point to new and/or different policies that may be needed.

A central idea underlying apparently diverse policies like expenditure switching, relative price shift in favor of the tradable sector through devaluation, and labor market flexibility, is that it will promote also the profitability of private investment, which must be considered crucial for a successful process of transition. For instance, various tax concession measures in favor of private business that may be encouraged by expenditure switching would increase post-tax profitability directly. Similarly, at constant labor productivity and lower real wages would increase the profit margin per unit of sale, while devaluation of the home currency would also tend to push up that margin of profit in domestic currency for domestic exporters.[16]

Nevertheless, most of these measures increase profit margin per unit of sale, while total profit depends not only on that margin per unit of sale, but also on the volume of sales. In other words, the rate of profit, i.e. profit per unit of invested capital (in accountants' book value) depends both on the profit margin and on the degree of capacity utilization (which may be assumed equal to the volume of sales, assuming no change in inventories). In symbols, we have definitionally,

$$\frac{\text{Total Profit}}{\text{Book Value of Capital}} \equiv \text{Rate of profit (r)}$$

$$\equiv \frac{\text{Total Profit}}{\text{Volume of production (=sales)}} \cdot \frac{\text{Volume of Production}}{\text{Capacity Output}} \cdot \frac{\text{Capacity output}}{\text{Book value of Capital}}$$

≡ profit share (h) times degree of capacity utilization (u) times technologically given output – capital ratio ($\bar{v}$), i.e.

$$r \equiv h.u.\bar{v} \qquad (14)$$

Thus, the rate of profit realized (r) may even go down if the increase in the margin of profit (which is an increasing function of profit share (h)), is quantitatively outweighed by a decrease in the degree of capacity utilization (u) in (14).[17] The problem with conventional stabilization package – its insistence on government expenditure reduction as well as government expenditure switching, lower real wage through wage restraint etc. –, intended mostly to increase the profit margin per unit of sale, may now be obvious. It may increase the profit margin, but decrease capacity utilization and the volume of sales far more (proportionately) through government budget deficit reduction and decline in private consumption due to lower real wage, so that the rate of profit realized, as well as that expected, may decline in the process. The result would be a worsening, not an improvement in the climate for private investment due to stabilization.

The preceding analysis (equation 14) points to the importance of maintaining a high degree of capacity utilization in the economy, if only for the sake of maintaining a favorable climate for private investment.[18] Therefore, this argument does not depend on the social and economic costs of stabilization, but on the ultimate purpose of stabilization, i.e. whether stabilization can make possible the transition to growth through adequate private investment. It would therefore seem to follow that maintaining a high degree of capacity utilization is advisable, not only for minimizing the social cost of stabilization, but for making the transition to sustained growth easier. It also deserves to be pointed out here that the optimistic view, at times encouraged by IMF in-house research (cf. Khan and Knight, 1985), that conventional stabilization would more or less automatically lead to growth within a reasonably short time-span, often bases itself merely on the assumption that private investment is exogenous to the model.[19] With such assumptions, there is of course no need to discuss whether high capacity utilization (or any other measure) is necessary to induce more private investment for making the transition to growth.

From a policy point of view, maintaining a high degree of capacity utilization is a complex problem, as it involves arguments on the demand side as well as on the supply side in rather different ways, especially in the context of East European stabilization. On the demand side, as equations (9) and (10) show, policies to reduce government budget deficit would invariably have a negative effect, which needs to be compensated simultaneously by either current account surplus, or/and private investment. Since stimulation of private investment is the issue under discussion, it follows that on the demand side drastic reduction in government budget deficit is advisable only if more or less equally drastic increase in current account surplus can be achieved.

Unless such counter-balancing factors keep the volume of aggregate demand reasonably high and stable, the degree of capacity utilization would go down due to insufficient demand, and along with it private investment may also decline through the "acceleration effect", as it reduces the realized as well as expected profit rate (equation 14). Thus, as a policy rule the extent of budget deficit should be closely monitored in terms of performance on current account and the behavior of private investment for the management of aggregate demand in an intelligent way. There is simply no economic virtue in always asking for continuously lower budget deficits in all circumstances!

On the supply side, a reduction in the degree of capacity utilization may mean two different things. Low capacity utilization may either mean that reserve capacity exists, which in response to suitable market incentives, e.g. higher price or higher demand, would adjust and increase rapidly. This is the usual economic meaning of upward (or downward) movement along a "supply curve". However, especially in the context of stabilization in East Europe, an alternative meaning of downward movement along the supply curve must also be considered. It means not capacity kept in reserve, but capacity more or less permanently destroyed, e.g. firms may close down due to liberalized import or "credit crunch", but they would not spring back to life again in response to higher price or demand. This irreversible downward movement along a supply curve results in a phenomenon often described as "hysteresis", which may be interpreted in the present context as the crucial influence of "history" or "initial conditions" on economic policy. Thus, if demand restriction and import liberalization during conventional stabilization results in a large number of enterprises being destroyed, and labor deskilled permanently, then a new initial condition comes into existence, characterized by reduced productive capacity in the economy. This new initial condition would make any demand expansion in the next round more problematic, because a kind of downward "ratchet effect" is set in operation on the supply side.

It is unlikely that such irreversible downward adjustment in supply in the formerly centrally planned economies of East Europe can be simply overcome "in the long run" through relying blindly on the "market forces". There is no such automatic transition from stabilization to growth on the supply side, and the problem may become even insurmountable if free import of products is allowed to simply meet, as long as feasible, the falling supply. Unless a conscious domestic industrial policy is formulated, coordinated, and implemented by the government to encourage and initially protect domestic private investors and attract suitable foreign investors, the market forces will only exhibit their destructive side, not their creative side. While an exclusively defensive industrial policy will basically be directed at moderating the downward adjustment on the supply side (e.g. through some import restriction, subsidies, and protection to selected domestic enterprises etc.), and is not even intended to achieve spectacular success in making the transition to a market economy, an aggressive industrial policy emphasizing export promotion and penetration into foreign markets could at least in some cases yield spectacular results. Since Japan has been the show-piece of this latter strategy, it is worth quoting Vice Minister Ojimi's rationale for the industrial policy formulated by the Japanese Ministry of International Trade and Industry (MITI):

> The MITI decided to establish in Japan industries which require intensive employment of capital and technology, industries that in consideration of comparative cost of production should be the most inappropriate for Japan, industries such as steel, oil-refining, petrochemicals, automobiles, aircraft, industrial machinery of all sorts, and electronics, including electronic computers. From a short-run, static viewpoint, encouragement of such industries would seem to conflict with economic rationalism. But, from a long-range viewpoint, these are precisely the industries where income elasticity of demand is high, technological progress is rapid, and labor productivity rises fast. It was clear that without these industries it would be difficult to employ a population of 100 million and raise their standard of living to that of Europe and America with light industries alone; whether right or wrong, Japan had to have these heavy and chemical industries. According to Napoleon and Clausewitz, the secret of a successful strategy is the concentration of fighting power on the main battle grounds; fortunately, owing to good luck and wisdom spawned by necessity, Japan has been able to concentrate its scant capital in strategic industries.[20]

The choice of the appropriate mix of defensive and aggressive industrial policy must depend on particular circumstances and countries (recall, Japanese agriculture even today exhibits a partly defensive strategy). Our purpose here is not to formulate the parameters relevant for such an industrial policy, but only to remind that industrial policy by the government needs to act as a support for private investment in any successful transition to a market economy. Stabilization alone cannot be expected to do this job automatically.

Notes

1. Supply of and demand for money are equal, as long as we assume that people are willing to hold money in any case. Thus, with a large monetary "overhang" – common in some formerly centrally planned economies – money may be hoarded as idle cash which lowers the velocity of circulation (V) correspondingly. Unless either the velocity of circulation or the price level (P) adjusts freely, it is difficult to sustain that the demand and supply of money are equal.

2. Alternatively, the output growth rate (g) may be exogenously projected, as is common in most IMF financial programing exercises. Because, $\Delta X_t \equiv gX_{t-1}$, where $g = \tilde{g}$ and X_{t-1} is given historically.

3. Note equation (7) is from the supply side of credit creation by commercial banks. It implies that credit to the private sector is governed by the ability of the commercial banks to extend loan, but not by the demand for loan by the private sector. In the latter case of demand determined credit or "endogenous money" equation (7) must be replaced by the inequality, $\Delta B \leq n.\Delta G$.

4. Cutting subsidies rather than raising taxes (except for administered prices) seems to be the preferred alternative of the IMF. In particular, taxes on private business/profit are discouraged.

5. Such problems arise due to too few policy instruments (e.g. credit rationing) in relation to economic targets (e.g. inflation and trade balance). This is familiar from Tinbergen's view of matching the number of instruments with targets for the design of economic policy (Tinbergen, 1952). Note from later equation (9) that an increase in current account surplus (A) increases demand which may fuel inflation and still satisfy equation (6) as indicated.

6. Assuming export and domestic price level are the same (i.e. no distinction is made between tradables and non-tradables), $P_x = P$ and price elasticity of the volume of export (X_e) is given by

$$\Delta \log(X_e)/\Delta \log(P/r) = -n_x, \; n_x > 0$$

where r = domestic currency per unit of foreign currency (P = price in domestic currency).

Similarly price elasticity of the volume of import is

$$\Delta(\log X_z)/\Delta \log(P_z r) = -n_z, \; n_z > 0$$

P_z = import price in foreign currency.

Assuming international price P_z to be constant, simple manipulations yield the revised Marshall-Lerner condition for improvement in trade balance as proportion of export value (E) as

$$\frac{\Delta(E-Z)}{E} = (1-n_x)\ (\Delta P/P) + [n_x + u(n_z-1)]\ (\Delta r/r)$$

where Z is the import value, $(Z/E) = u > 1$, i.e., there is an initial trade deficit. Note, without domestic price inflation ($\Delta P/P = 0$) and initial trade balance, (u = 1), the familiar condition, $n_x + n_z > 1$ emerges. The interesting point in the formula is, a lower price elasticity of export (in absolute value) reduces the ability to improve the trade deficit (shown by the second square bracketed term) but it helps in so far as domestic inflation has a lower unfavorable impact on export (shown by the first term on the right hand side).

7. This was probably a virtue of the Polak model at the time of its publication (1957), as many developing countries did not then have systematic and reliable statistics. But this pragmatic justification no longer holds, and certainly not in the context of East Europe.

8. Note, GDP = C+I+(E–Z). And, GNP – (NFP) + (NTR), where NFP is net factor payment NTR is net unrequited transfer, e.g. grants. From this follows, (S–I) = = (E+NTR)–(Z+NFP) = (A), where (A) is current account surplus (see p. 380, Dornbush and Helmers for further details) and the equation in the text is derived by breaking up both saving and investment into government and private categories.

9. Either directly through quantity-rationing of credit to the private sector or through price-rationing, i.e. a higher interest rate as cost of borrowing finance by the firms.

10. Note $\alpha = [\frac{\Delta B+\Delta G}{PX_{-1}}]$, where X_{-1} = last periods output, a historically given constant and X = current periods output, $X_{-1}+\Delta X$. We ignore these tedious notations to keep the exposition in the text simple.

11. If aggregate demand and supply are also functions of price with usual signs (a big assumption), the market may stabilize, but at higher price.

Thus, $D(\alpha, P) = S(\alpha,P)$ so that, by total differentiation and rearrangement of terms,

$$\frac{dP}{d\alpha} = \frac{(\delta D/\delta\alpha) - (\delta S/\delta\alpha)}{(\delta S/\delta P) - (\delta D/\delta P)}$$

Since the denominator is positive for usual signs of demand and supply curves, price rises, i.e. $dP/d\alpha$ positive if supply increases less strongly than demand, as credit availability, α goes up.

12. Higher interest may reduce demand by discouraging hire-purchase consumption and investment, especially in residential housing and inventories. It may also discourage supply by making working capital more expensive, and by diverting investment efforts from production to financial/trading gains over a longer period.

13. There are serious problems of defining the "quantity of money", and also determining whether it is supply – or demand – determined (i.e. exogenous or endogenous). These problems increase with the level of financial sophistication in the economy. They are likely to be less serious therefore in the East European economies, although these economies have their peculiar problems, e.g. inter-enterprise loans outstanding.

14. A main empirical contention of "modern" quantity theory following Friedman.

15. It deserves emphasis that these policies have gained appeal in the current situation, because the centrally planned economic system failed miserably, while market-oriented economies succeeded in some cases. Nevertheless, it needs to be remembered that not all market economies, especially in the developing world, have succeeded; indeed, some failed equally miserably. Hence the need for caution and intellectual honesty in facing these issues (see also Dornbush 1990).

16. This is subject to erosion of profit margin due to higher cost of imported raw materials as well as higher labor cost due to higher money wage that may result from devaluation (e.g. due to higher cost of living index).

17. For details see Bhaduri and Marglin (1990), where the exact mathematical link between profit share and profit margin is worked out along with the conditions for "profit squeeze" despite higher profit margin.

18. Several econometric studies for the OECD countries suggest that, in influencing private investment in fixed capital, the capacity utilization (i.e. acceleration) effect may be stronger than the profitability effect. However, this argument needs to be treated with caution because of the inherent problems of definining a suitable statistical measure of (expected) profitability.

19. See Dornbush (1990), especially pp. 9-12 for pointing this out clearly in terms of the equation structure of the Khan–Knight simulation exercise.

20. *OECD*, 1972. I owe this quotation to an unpublished paper by Ajit Singh.

References

Bhaduri, A., Marglin, S. (1990), "Unemployment and the Real wage: the Economic Basis of Contesting Political Ideologies," *Cambridge Journal of Economics*, December.

Cavallo, Domingo (1977), *Stagflationist Effects of Monetarist Stabilization Policies* (unpublished Ph. D. dissertation), Harvard University, Cambridge, Mass.

Dornbush, R., Leslie, Fand Helmers, C.H. (1988), *The Open Economy:* Tools for Policy Makers in Developing Countries, Oxford: Oxford University Press.

Dornbush, R. (1990), "From Stabilization to Growth," *NBER Working Paper 3302*, National Bureau of Economic Research, Cambridge Mass.

Kalecki, M. (1971), *Selected Essays on the Dynamics of the Capitalist Economy*, Cambridge: Cambridge University Press.

Khan, M. and Knight, M. (1985), "Fund Supported Adjustment Programs and Economic Growth," *IMF Occasional Paper*, No. 41.

Polak, J. (1957), "Monetary Analysis of Income Formation and Payments Problems," *IMF Staff Papers*, pp. 1-50.

Taylor, L. (1988), *Varities of Stabilization Experience*, Oxford: Clarendon Press.

Taylor, L. (1991), *Income Distribution, Inflation and Growth*, Cambridge Mass., MIT Press.

Tinbergen, J. (1952), *The Design of Economic Policy*, Amsterdam, North Holland.

All references to East European economies in transition have been omitted, although this paper was motivated by reading many of them.

2

TRANSITION FROM COMMAND TO MARKET ECONOMIES IN CENTRAL AND EASTERN EUROPE: FIRST EXPERIENCES AND QUESTIONS *

Kazimierz Laski

1. Introductory Remarks

The present situation in Central and Eastern Europe is characterized by the transition from totalitarian party-states and command economies towards democratic systems and market-oriented economies. The beginning of this process saw such events as the — partly — free elections in Poland, which brought about a humiliating defeat for the communist party, a clear victory for the Solidarity movement under Walesa, and the first non-communist government in this part of the world. Then followed the street demonstrations in Leipzig with citizens proclaiming "We are the people", leading to reunification of Germany. Shortly afterwards the Velvet Revolution in Prague raised Václav Havel, the symbol of spiritual resistance against the communist dictatorship, to

---

* The first drafts of this paper were presented at the conference on "Medium Term Economic Assessment" (CMTEA) in Vienna, October 14-16, 1991, organized by the Austrian Federal Chancellery in cooperation with the Federal Ministry of Finance, and at the conference on "The Evolution of Mixed Economies: East and West" in Vienna, November 7-9, 1991, organized by the European Association for Evolutionary Political Economy (EAEPE). The remarks made during discussions on both conferences were very helpful in writing the final draft. Special thanks for critical remarks are due also to Leszek Kurowski and Friedrich Levcik as well as to colleagues from WIIW.

cular, was the development in Hungary, which had been pursuing its own course for several years already. In Romania and Bulgaria a part of the old elites managed to maintain their power positions, but only after taking over the slogans of radical change in their countries as well. Last but not least a similar process started several weeks ago after the failed coup in the USSR, the center of the previous communist commonwealth.

All these changes, unimaginable only two years ago, triggered a real explosion of hope – and even enthusiasm – on the part of the population at large in the Central and East European countries. People believed that the removal of the odious communist dictatorship and of the indolent command economy would very soon bring about a viable democratic regime and a flourishing Western-type market economy. As soon as it became evident that democracy means more than just free elections, and that the way towards a market economy and prosperity would be rough and protracted, disappointment and disillusionment spread. Václav Havel and the famous Polish philosopher Kolakowski, independently of each other, have found the proper expression for the actually prevailing popular frame of mind, calling it the "post-revolutionary hangover". It is an important task of economic research to identify the causes of this hangover and to find out whether it could be avoided or at least reduced to a less intensive level.

The existing hardships in the Economies in Transition (EIT) are mainly a heritage of the communist past. Another important factor is the collapse of the COMECON, and related losses of markets for, and suppliers to, EITs almost from one day to the next. Although both factors play an undeniable role, they are very often overemphasized by ruling groups in order to divert attention from economic strategies and policies which, to a considerable degree, are responsible too for the present situation and lack of perspectives. It is the firm conviction of this writer that, if these policies were different and mistakes avoided, the situation would be better in the sense that hardships would not go beyond the level determined by the heritage of the past and by external circumstances.

We start this chapter by investigating the sequencing of the transition towards a market economy (the alternative of a shock versus a more gradual therapy). Then we go on to stabilization and recession as necessary phenomena during transition from a command towards a market economy. The relation between stabilization policy and growth is analyzed in the next chapter. Finally we will devote some thoughts to ideological matters.

2. Shock Therapy Versus Gradualism – A Partly False Alternative

The EITs are confronted with three main tasks: (a) stabilization and introduction of market clearing prices, (b) privatization, and (c) restructuring and growth. While the first goal should be tackled at the very beginning of the transformation process, the two remaining tasks require rather years than months or days. From this point of view the whole discussion concerning the sequencing of the transition is beside the point.

Proponents of a shock therapy frequently argue that gradual changes in the past were always absorbed and neutralized by the existing structure of command economies. But they forget that previous blueprints of change were reforms inside a socialist system (like the well-known NEM in Hungary since 1968, and the hesitant reform attempts in Poland, Czechoslovakia and other countries). These reforms were not aimed at abolishing central planning (and the prevalence of collective property of material production factors) but at improving it. Market coordination, mostly limited to current decisions, had to substitute for administrative coordination, and represented just a more efficient instrument of central planning (Brus and Laski (1989), Ch. 7). All these reforms failed, not because they were gradual, but because command economies proved to be incapable of being reformed. The present EITs are not confronted with reforms as in the past, but with a systemic transformation (Altmann et al. (1991), p. xi). Their target is the disbanding of the command economy, not its improvement; therefore the former arguments against gradual changes do not hold water.

It is simply out of the question at one stroke to introduce a market economy in countries that have lacked market institutions and environment as well as appropriate human attitudes for almost half, and in one case even for three quarters of a century (Oppenheimer, p. 59). This is somehow overlooked in numerous metaphors now so popular in some EITs. One of them says that the command and capitalist economies are separated by a kind of abyss, and that it is not advisable to try to leap across an abyss other than by one mighty jump. This sounds quite convincing. However, Peter Wiles draws our attention to the fact that the relation between the two systems should rather be described by a precipice with capitalism at the top and command economy at the bottom. To try to jump to the top instead of systematically climbing the hill would be both exhausting and fruitless (Wiles, p. 88). The road to a market economy will require much effort and much time, but stabilization and price liberalization have to start the process, and the sooner the better. This is our next topic.

3. Stabilization and Recession

3.1 From "Suction" to "Pressure"

To understand the reasons why a stabilization policy is necessary and why a related recession is unavoidable, we should start by a somewhat more general approach. It deals with an important asymmetry between the transition from a command towards a market economy and the reverse process, i.e., the transition from a market towards a command economy. This asymmetry is closely related to basic features of each system.

The market economy is a demand-constrained system. Given the production capacity and the price-wage relation, the actual national income is determined by effective demand. As a rule, effective demand stays behind the potential supply (or potential national income), resulting in some reserve production capacity and some unemployment. While some factors of production lie idle, the others are used in a rather efficient way. The economy under these conditions is said to work under "pressure" (Kornai), the market is characterized as a "buyers' market".

The command economy is a supply-constrained system. In this system factors of production, including labor, are utilized very intensively, although in a rather inefficient way. Indeed, effective demand can always be (and is) generated by a fiat of the Central Planning Board which in addition determines – at least in principle – the price-wage relation, adjusting it to the expected uses of final output. In a command economy, demand as a rule is ahead of potential supply, creating a permanent state of "suction" (Kornai). Under these conditions the market becomes a "sellers' market", and the economy is characterized by permanent, more or less intensive, shortages.

The passage from a market economy towards a command system, seen from the discussed point of view, implies a drastic increase in effective demand and the substitution of a "buyers' market" by a "sellers' market". The previously idle factors of production, especially labor, as proved by the experience of socialist countries, can – under these conditions – be activated, and the others, which were not fully utilized, more intensively employed. This leads to a quick increase in production, employment and consumption. These short- (or even medium-) term gains are overcompensated by losses in efficiency and creativity in the long run; however, they make the transition to a command economy rather attractive. They were quite an important factor in the initial successes of central planning, sustaining illusions concerning its alleged superiority over the capitalist economies.

The transition from a command economy to a market one requires the substitution of "pressure of supply" for "suction of demand". This substitution implies a limitation of effective demand to a level below that of potential supply, resulting in some reserve capacity and unemployment. They allow for a necessary degree of flexibility of production (in the sense of the ability to adjust the structure of supply to that of demand). Some decrease of actual national income caused by cuts in total demand is necessary, if the economy has to be exposed to the demand constraint. In this sense some recession, implying immediate losses in production, employment, and consumption, must be part and parcel of every program to transform a command economy into a market one. These short- (and even medium-) term losses should be overcompensated by an increase in efficiency and creativity in the long run, but they make the transition to a demand-determined market system quite difficult.

3.2 Controlling Effective Demand

The driving force of the market mechanism is the price mechanism. This mechanism requires scarcity prices equilibrating demand and supply. A seriously meant transition towards market coordination is thus bound to start with the suppression of price controls and administrative price fixing. This would, as a rule, cause substantial price increases because repressed inflation becomes an open one, and – additionally – because the lifting of price controls is usually coupled with the cutting of numerous subsidies. However, not all subsidies must and should be abolished at once (e.g. basic foodstuffs in some cases, rents in most cases, etc.). Thus the introduction of market clearing prices does not necessarily mean a full and immediate price liberalization. In that sense, elements of gradualism should be present even in the first phase of transition.

Whatever the policy chosen with respect to price liberalization, an acceleration of inflation may be expected. In order to avoid an uncontrolled inflationary process, the price liberalization must be accompanied by a stabilization program. As excess demand is the rule in a command economy, an internal equilibrium can in the short run be achieved only by reducing demand. The existing disequilibria mostly have their source in the sector of state enterprises, in the state budget, and in the monetary policy. The therapy must therefore start here.

The soft budget constraint of state enterprises must be hardened. Only in this way will it be possible to control and restrict their insatiable demand on resources (investment, labor, material inputs) and abolish the very cause of the shortage economy. At the same time the artificial concentration of production should be lessened. The dissolution of different associations of enterprises, representing true monopolies, is advisable in order to create better competitive conditions on the market. The creation of smaller units would also facilitate privatization.

Government budget deficits play a weighty part in creating excess demand. In order to cut these deficits to a tolerable level, expenditures (e.g. defence, subsidies) have to be cut and the revenues adjusted. As far as private households are concerned, their current incomes must be adjusted – at expected prices – to current consumer goods supplies. Therefore some kind of income policies restraining uncontrolled money wage increases seem unavoidable.

At the same time a solution must be sought to the problem of monetary overhangs (representing partly forced savings of the past), which exist everywhere, though to a varying extent in the individual countries. In countries with high inflation, or even hyperinflation, the real value of cash balances has been so strongly reduced that the monetary overhang may not exist anymore. Money has to fulfill its basic function not only as a medium of exchange but as a store of value, too. Thus an effective monetary and credit policy is everywhere a necessary – though not sufficient – precondition for a successful stabilization of the economy. The separation of commercial banks from the central bank, and the autonomy of the central bank in determining the money supply, are important elements of the reform of the banking system. Under existing circumstances a prudent monetary policy, clearly marking an end to the irresponsible monetary expansion of the past, cannot be avoided.

Internal stabilization should be accompanied by a gradual reintegration of the East into the world economy. The first important measure here is the introduction of a unified exchange rate (necessitating a substantial devaluation in most countries) linked with some internal convertibility of the currency, mainly for goods and services, and limited to firms only. A full currency convertibility, however, should be approached step by step – in concurrence with the transition to free market conditions in other fields. The arguments for a gradual approach to convertibility are forcefully presented by Levcik (1991). On the other hand, an internal stabilization of the economy without some liberalization of foreign trade and without taking account of world market conditions does not make sense, because the achieved internal equilibrium would not be adjusted to these conditions.[1]

All these measures should be started concurrently, giving a clear signal that a new market order is being introduced. In this sense, but only in this sense, they represent a shock therapy; it is necessary, especially in countries with high (open or repressed) inflation, in order to break the inflationary expectations of the economic actors – mainly enterprises and private households. This therapy is not free from dangers. The reduction of global demand together with a tight monetary and credit policy, as well as some opening to the outside world, would provoke a fall in production and employment. It may also create a heavy burden on the population in terms of reduced real wages. This policy can work, if the population is ready to accept sacrifices in the form of unemployment and lower standards of living, as a necessary price for abolishing the hated and inefficient communist regime. But the ability of the population to sacrifice the present for the sake of the future should not be overestimated, nor the duration of time during which the readiness to accept painful measures prevails. Thus even under propitious conditions the exposure of the economy to market forces should not exceed certain limits and must be accompanied by various government measures softening the blow of the shock therapy and creating general conditions for its success in the foreseeable future.

From the macroeconomic point of view the most important task is that of controlling and influencing total effective demand, and in the first place such factors as investment, budget deficit, and export surplus. Indeed, these three factors determine the savings of both the enterprise and private household sectors, and, given the share of savings in the gross domestic product (GDP), also its volume. It is known that *ex post* (gross) savings S, defined as above in the text, can be specified as follows:

$$S = I + E + D \tag{1}$$

where I denotes (gross) investment in the enterprise sector, E stands for the difference between exports and imports (trade surplus) and D represents the budget deficit, i.e. the difference between government expenditures (on goods and services) and revenues. Further, we define s the rate of savings, (the share of savings in GDP) as

$$s = S/GDP$$

or

$$GDP = (1/s)S. \tag{2}$$

From (2) we get: if s = constans

$$\Delta GDP = (1/s)\,\Delta S \tag{3}$$

and in general case: if s ≠ constans

$$\Delta GDP = GDP(gS - gs), \tag{4}$$

where all aggregates are measured in constant prices.

In (3) the term (1/s) denotes the multiplier measuring the impact of changes in savings S, i.e. of the sum of investment, deficit spending and export surplus upon the GDP. In (4) the terms gS and gs denote the rate of growth of S savings and of s the rate of saving, respectively. The formula (4) cannot be used when the yearly changes in S and s are not small. In the latter case we get from (2)

$$1 + gGDP = (1 + gS)/(1 + gs)$$

where gGDP denotes the rate of growth of GDP. By simple manipulations we get

$$\Delta GDP = GDP(gS\text{-}gs)/(1 + gs) \qquad (5)$$

the formula which can be used when yearly changes of S and s are not small.

Let us assume that before the stabilization plan is being started the economy was characterized by rather high deficit spending of the government and the plan intends to cut this deficit. Let us assume, on the other hand, that the plan does not foresee an increase in the sum of both investment and foreign trade surplus. Under these conditions the cuts in deficit spending should be adjusted to the expected changes in the saving propensity of the economy. If it is expected that, e.g., the overall propensity to save (which depends on the distribution of value added net of taxation between profits and wages, and specific propensities to save out of these incomes) would not decrease (i.e., remain constant or even increase), then cuts in deficit spending would cause a multiplied reduction of the GDP. Thus, the size of the cuts in deficit spending must be calculated so that the resulting drop of aggregate demand would not go beyond that necessary to create enough "pressure" on the supply side of the economy. A policy of "sound" finance aiming at balancing the budget (or even creating a budget surplus) as fast as possible would under these conditions provoke only a sterile recession, avoidable unemployment, and the danger of a cumulative process involving further cuts in investment and output. *Mutatis mutandis*, the same applies to monetary and credit policies. They should be adjusted to the existing situation and aims, and not blindly follow some dogmatic prescriptions.

3.3 The Polish Stabilization Plan 1990 – An Illustration of the Method

The stabilization plan for 1990 represented a completely new approach to the problems facing Poland, and the reaction of the economy to the measures envisaged was quite uncertain. Nevertheless, some estimates had to be made, and have been made, with respect to prices, output, employment, government budget, and foreign trade.

According to the stabilization plan the rate of inflation between December 1990 and December 1989 should not have exceeded 140 percent. The highest price increase, of about 45 percent, was expected in January 1990, to be followed by the slowing down of inflation in February and March. Already in the second quarter of the year inflation was to be reduced to about 1-2 percent per month.

The sharply limited increases in money wages, with anticipated inflation, were to lead to a reduction of real wages. According to the scenario of the plan, real wages should fall by about 15-20 percent between 1989 and 1990, with most of the reduction taking place in the first quarter of the year. At the same time real consumption was to fall only insignificantly, because it was assumed that part of money incomes in 1989 was not supported by adequate supplies of goods and services. Thus losses in real wages were to be mostly of a statistic nature.

The anticipated decline in industrial output amounted to about 5 percent, and in national income to about 3.1 percent. Unemployment was to reach the level of about 400,000, representing some 3 percent of total employment. The Government budget was to be balanced, at least towards the end of the year.

In foreign trade in convertible currencies, with exports more or less constant, an increase in imports of about US$ 1.0 bn was expected, thus changing the surplus in the trade balance of 1989 into a trade deficit of about US$ 0.8 bn in 1990. In trade with the CMEA countries the export surplus in the trade balance was expected to decrease to about 0.54 bn transferable rubles.

One of the main achievements of the stabilization plan in 1990 was the restoration of the basic money functions to the zloty. Hyperinflation was replaced by inflation. Prices reached the market clearing level, and most of the shortage phenomena, typical of a command economy, disappeared. There was some improvement in the structure of prices, caused by the cutting down on subsidies, and by their exposure to the demand constraint. The exchange rate of the zloty to the US dollar was kept constant over the whole year, the Government budget closed with some surplus, and in both convertible and non-convertible currencies a considerable trade surplus was achieved.

The goals of the stabilization plan, however, were not met and, what is more important, the costs of these achievements were much higher than anticipated (for more on this topic see Kolodko (1991) and Kolodko and Rutkowski (1991)). Table 1, in which some goals and results of the plan have been confronted, shows that in 1990 GDP fell by 12 percent, almost four times stronger than anticipated. The same applies to industrial output (including private industry), where the real

Table 1

Polish Stabilization Plan 1990: Goals and Results

(average rate of growth p.a. in percent, if not otherwise stated)

	Assumption (1)	Results (2)	(2):(1) (3)
1. GDP	-3.1	-12	3.9
2. Industrial output	-5.0	-23.3	4.7
3. Consumer prices			
December 1990 over December 1989	140	249	1.8
IV. quarter 1990	1.5[a)]	5.5[a)]	3.7
4. Real wages	-15 (-20)	-28.1	1.6
5. Unemployment			
in thousand	400	1,126	2.8
6. Trade balance			
in US$ billion	-0.8	2.2	-2.75
in TR billion	0.5	7.1	14.2

a) Average rate of growth per month, in percent.

Source: Kolodko (1991); Kolodko and Rutkowski (1991); GUS (1991).

decline was almost five times stronger than anticipated. Prices of consumer goods increased by 250 percent instead of expected 140 percent from December 1989 to December 1990. The monthly rate of growth of the CPI in the fourth quarter of 1990 was still 5.5 percent instead of 1.5 percent as fixed in the stabilization plan. Real wages decreased by 28 percent instead of 15-20 percent as assumed in the plan;[2] and unemployment reached 1,126,000 at the end of the year – almost three times the assumed number. Only in foreign trade the results were better than expected. In trade in convertible currencies exports expanded considerably, and although imports increased also, a significant trade surplus of US$ 2.2 billion was registered. A big surplus (of TR 7.1 billion) was registered too in trade in non-convertible currencies, especially with the Soviet Union. Here, however, exports decreased slightly while imports fell dramatically. It should be stressed that the large trade surplus, in face of a sharply declining GDP, additionally limited internal absorption. Indeed, private households' consumption decreased in 1990 by 24 percent against about 1 percent (sic!) foreseen the plan.

There are several important causes of the negative features of the development in 1990 and of the visible gap between the goals and the results of the stabilization plan. Perhaps the most important of them was the excessive concentration on monetary and fiscal policy with almost complete neglect of the real sphere. In the domain of monetary policy two serious mistakes have been made. The drastic rise of the interest rate at the beginning of 1990 gave an initial impetus to the sharp decline of production. The devaluation of the zloty was also higher than economically justified. Indeed the exchange rate could be kept constant although the internal price level increased by 250 percent from the beginning to the end of the year. This is the best proof that the devaluation was excessive, and it resulted in an initial acceleration of inflation. As far as fiscal policy is concerned, it was a serious fault to tolerate a sizeable budget surplus over most of the year. This factor additionally constrained the level of effective demand. Only at the end of the year was the budget surplus reduced.[3]

Table 2

Gross Domestic Product in Poland

(in trillion zloty, constant prices of 1989)

		1989 (1)	1990 (2)	(2)-(1) (3)	(3):(1) (4)	1990 (5)[a)]
1. Gross domestic product	Y	118.3	104.2	-14.2	-12%	
2. Investment of the business sector (including changes in inventories)	I	38.6	32.7	-5.9	-15.3%	-3.9
3. Export surplus	E	4.6	7.2	2.6	56.5%	-5.6
4. Budget deficit	D	3.6	-0.3	-3.9	-108.3%	-3.6
5. Savings of the business sector and private households	S	46.8	39.6	-7.2	-15.4%	-13.1
6. Rate of savings (5:1)	s	39.6%	38.0%	-1.6[b)]	-4.0%	

a) Changes in I, E and D as forecast in February 1990. – b) Percentage points.

Source: Own estimates based on data from the Central Planning Commission, Warsaw.

The main cause of the excessive recession, however, was the stabilization plan itself. If data implied in the plan concerning investment, export surplus, and budget deficit were aggregated, the resulting savings for 1990 could be approximated. If – additionally – an assumption were made concerning the propensity to save expected for 1990, the approximate level of GDP could be found. The resulting estimate could not but show that the recession administered by the plan had to go much further than anticipated in the same plan.[4]

The reduction of savings (in 1990 compared to 1989) implied in the plan was equal to Zl 13.1 trillion (see column (5) of Table 2). This reduction would provoke – at a constant saving rate – a dramatic decrease of the GDP amounting to

$$\Delta GDP = (1/0.396)(-13.1) = -33.1 \text{ trillion Zl}$$

or to a relative decline of about 28 percent. In reality the decline of savings was much smaller; they decreased by Zl 7.2 trillion against 13.1 adopted implicitly in the plan. As could be expected (because of the decline of the GDP and of the extreme devaluation of the zloty), the trade deficit (of Zl 1 trillion) did not materialize, and instead a quite important trade surplus was recorded (of Zl 7.2 trillion). Thus – in relation to 1989 – the export surplus increased by Zl 2.6 trillion instead of the expected decline by Zl 5.6 trillion. This factor alone corrected the savings foreseen in the plan by Zl +8.2 trillion. This was also the main cause of the gap between the factual and the implied decline of the savings, because investment and budget deficit declined more or less according to the assumptions of the plan.

We must, however, come back to the assumption concerning the constancy of s, the rate of savings. At the beginning of 1990 nobody knew for sure how the rate of savings would change and in what direction, if at all. However, factors which influence these changes were known and could and should have been analyzed. First, because the share of the sum of direct and indirect taxes in GDP in 1990 (according to the budget projections) was to increase by almost 4 percentage points, the share of value added after taxation would correspondingly decrease. Given the distribution between wages and profits, and the propensity to save out of these incomes, this factor should have diminished the coefficient s. Second, it could be expected that the propensities to save out of wages (and in the case of peasants, out of their earnings) would probably decrease, because forced savings would disappear and real income would decline. Under these conditions the second factor should have acted in the same direction as the first one, although it should be stressed that the private households' propensity to save in Poland was rather low. Third, it could be expected that the distribution of value added after taxation between wages and profits would change and the share of profits would probably increase. Indeed, when subsidies are strongly reduced, profits correspondingly increase, even if prices increase only by the amount of subsidies withdrawn. But it was known that prices would increase also in relation to unit labor costs, because real wages were expected to decline in absolute terms and in relation to labor productivity, creating room for additional profits. As the propensity to save out of profits is much higher than that out of wages – and out of profits in state-owned enterprises almost equal to one –, this redistribution of value added towards profits would increase the value of the coefficient s. Taking together the first two factors seemed to act in one direction, the third one in an opposite one. As there existed forces acting in different directions, it was safe to assume already in the plan that changes in the coefficient s would at least not be very large.

This proved to be the case. The rate of savings decreased by 1.6 percentage points, i.e. by 4 percent, reaching in 1990 the level of 38.0 percent. This decline somewhat softened the blow to the GDP provoked by the fall of S, but was too weak to play a more important role. The relative stability (or the change) of the rate of saving – if it can be estimated – means that there is a simple method of evaluating the joint influence of different measures affecting investment, export surplus, and budget deficit upon the GDP. The real problem is that this kind of calculation was not made at all by the authors of the stabilization plans, and they did not seem to be particularly interested in their results either. This applies not only to Poland, but to other countries starting or preparing stabilization plans as well. The theoretical basis of the stabilization policy practiced now in EITs is the quantity theory of money, and a complete neglect of the theory of effective demand.

4. Stabilization and Growth

Stabilization is not an aim in itself, it is required as a condition for the resumption of growth. Stabilization of the economy is principally a short-term goal; it has to be achieved at given production capacities. Growth of the economy is principally a long-term goal; it implies expanding production capacities, due mainly to investment. Growth following a successful stabilization is the more important, the greater the costs in terms of lost output of the stabilization program. It should be stressed that these costs are in the case of EITs much higher than in other countries that have undergone similar treatment.[5] Indeed, the negative growth rates p.a. in Central and East European countries have reached levels unknown elsewhere since the times of the great crisis of 1929-33.

An additional factor is the low level of GDP per capita in the EITs compared with other European countries. In the past six years the gap between Czechoslovakia, Hungary and Poland on the one hand, and Austria on the other, measured by GDP per capita, increased by about one third. The same conclusions apply for other Central and East European countries. Havlik's estimation (in Chapter 10 below, Table 12), based upon the Physical Indicator Global (PIG)-Method, gives a proper ranking, but seems to exaggerate the absolute levels of output of the Central and East European countries. More reliable from this point of view are the data in Chapter 10, Table 13, as estimated by the Purchasing Power Parities (PPP)-Method. According to this method the GDP per capita in Czechoslovakia, Hungary, and Poland in 1990 reached 55 to 27 percent of the Austrian level. Completely unreliable, on the other hand, are calculations based on exchange rates of national currencies against the US dollar. According to this method Czechoslovakia and Hungary in 1990 achieved about 15 percent and Poland only 8 percent of the Austrian level. These figures are rather an index of the intensity of the devaluation of national currencies than a measure of their output level.

This, however, is not our present topic. The important point for our further analysis is the fact that EITs remain far behind the average European level and that this lag becomes larger. The falling back of these countries means not only absolute and relative losses in their standards of living, but also increased difficulties in their efforts to join the European Community in the future. An enlargement of the community would quite certainly be opposed the more strongly by its rich members, the more the EITs become the poorhouse of Europe.

Thus, it is clear that EITs desperately need growth, the sooner the better. These countries are told that a successful stabilization, resulting in strongly reduced price inflation, a balanced government budget, and competitive real exchange rate would not only promote a more efficient static allocation of resources, but would also create a sound base for future growth. This is more or less the economic strategy of the IMF as exemplified e.g. in the paper by Khan and Knight (1985). In their model the most important factors that should bring about growth – and that rather quickly (in less than two years) – in the aftermath of the stabilization shock, are an increase in the export surplus due to real devaluation (and gains in competitiveness), and – foremost – an increase in investment. Dornbush (1990), analyzing these factors, reveals the weak points of the model: foreign demand is assumed to be perfectly elastic, reduced real wages would not affect the inflationary process itself (by provoking wage compensations which would start a vicious circle where devaluation brings inflation, and inflation necessitates further devaluation), investments are treated exogenously and are not linked to credit conditions, especially high interest rates advocated to mobilize savings. The model also completely disregards the issue of income distribution. Dornbush (1990, pp. 12-13), concludes:

> All the serious issues in stabilization are, in fact, glossed over, strategically assumed away or made exogenous. As a result one is left with a strikingly optimistic outlook. The reality, however, is that attempts to implement these measures fail more often than not. They fail either because the income distribution issues produce a serious inflation and recession problem, or because the financing for supply side policies that raise growth cannot be marshalled, or they fail because the trimming back of credit growth and the devaluation produce a deep recession and no investment boom, not in the first and not for many years ... In summary then, the IMF model fails to recognize critical empirical linkages and assumes away the key issues of what mechanism

> brings about the resumption of investment. Disappointingly, it does not teach us anything about adjustment and the return of growth.

Dornbush illustrates his criticism by the example of Bolivia. I am going to continue quoting him on this subject, not only because the case is interesting per se, but also because Jeffrey Sachs – the famous adviser to some EITs – has got his credentials, especially in Poland, as the author of the successful Bolivian stabilization:

> Bolivia has tamed hyperinflation, stabilized public finance and administered a heavy dose of supply side economics. The easy work is done, and now the country waits for recovery and growth: Per capita income ... is no longer plummeting, but it has fallen desperately low and there is no assurance, 4 years after stabilization, of a major turn of events. Per capita income continues to fall. Moreover, in November 1989, social conflict erupted into the open when the government declared a state of siege and once again jailed striking union leaders. The Bolivian government may have won the war on inflation, but they have now lost the peace. Bolivia's case is so important because there is consensus that the country implemented all those reforms that should be accomplished, did so firmly and by now many years ago. The case confirms the suspicion that stabilization may not be enough. (Dornbush (1990), (p. 4)

The basic problem in a market economy is its tendency to cumulative developments. In an economy in recession, employment is low, and so is output. Capacity is only partly utilized. Therefore investment is low and so are profits. Because of the poor outlook for the future, investment decreases further, and so do profits. Of course, recession caused by a stabilization program comes sooner or later to an end. If it is successful, also inflation is pushed down to a tolerable level. But the achieved equilibrium is characterized by a low level of employment and output, by low profitability of firms, by low utilization of capacity, and by lack of perspectives for the future resulting in continued low investment.

In a booming economy the cumulative tendency is present too, but now it works in an opposite direction. Employment is high, and so is output. Capacity is fully utilized, investment is high, and so are profits. Thus, perspectives for the future are good, and result in continued high investment.

The problem with stabilization is how to get from the former cumulative tendency to the latter, from the vicious circle of stagnation to the virtuous circle of growth. One cannot exclude that spontaneous market forces could in the end solve the problem, but one has to wait for years, and success is not certain. At the recent congress of the European Economic Association, the Minister of Finance of Mexico and an economist from Chile, both coming from countries where the economic situation has lately improved considerably, said that the experience of their countries proves that the lag between stabilization and growth amounts to about ten years. This is a terribly long period for EITs, especially in view of the losses in output and standards of living recorded till now.

One could object that all these examples are taken from developing countries. But in EITs, although their economic development level is higher, there exist additional factors which make their passage to growth even more, not less difficult. The main problems are the very high share of the public sector, unclear ownership relations, and the lack of entrepreneurs able to make responsible economic decisions, especially investment decisions. Under these conditions some additional factor to help start the cumulative growth tendency may be helpful, if not absolutely necessary, and the first candidate to take over this part is the state.

The general mood in the economic profession is rather against the state. It has become fashionable to call for the "minimal" state. It is said that state intervention rather harms than helps. Even if this were true in the case of "fine tuning", when the problem is limited to small deviations from full employment (but that is yet far from having been proved), the conclusion would not automatically apply to big problems, when large and persistent unemployment occurs. This point has been forcefully made by Assar Lindbeck (1991) in his Presidential Address at the Annual Congress of the European Economic Association:

> In the context of a non-market clearing labor market, it is certainly reasonable to regard unemployment, in particular highly persistent unemployment, as a major macroeconomic distortion. There is therefore a potential case for policy actions, provided such actions do not create more problems than they solve. Experiences in many countries suggest that the latter reservation is not a trivial one. ... For reasons like these, I am perfectly willing to subscribe to the prevailing skepticism about "fine tuning" of monetary and fiscal policy actions, if such policies are interpreted as very ambitious attempts to counteract even modest fluctuations in aggregate employment and unemployment. However, these objections to stabilization policy activism are less important when there are what may be called major macroeconomic "level problems", i.e. situations when the economy is either clearly overheated, as for instance in the US in the mid-1960s, or when unemployment is far above the long-run term trend, as in several EC countries in the mid-1980s. In cases like these, it does not matter much if the size and timing of the policy actions are far from perfect from a cyclical point of view. Thus, even though it may be advisable to avoid "fine tuning" in monetary and fiscal policy, there may be a strong case for "coarse tuning", e.g. policies designed to avoid serious macroeconomic "level problems".

Lindbeck had in mind Western countries and their big problems. But they are minor in comparison with big problems of the EITs. To require a "minimal" state under these conditions is more than irresponsible.

So far we have concentrated on global problems. But the need for state activities is created also by structural problems facing the formerly socialist countries on their way to a market economy. The share of services in total employment and output has to increase, that of agriculture must be diminished. The industrial sector must be basically restructured and modernized in order to reduce its high material- and energy intensity. The opening of the so far isolated economy towards the outside world, and the expansion of export capacities, are further fundamental requirements. Last but not least, the environmental situation, which is critical almost everywhere, must be dealt with. To believe that all these problems can be solved by spontaneous market forces is a dangerous illusion.

Foreign trade is a good example for an area where macroeconomic and industrial policies must work together. The structure of production inside command economies came into existence almost without any consideration for world market conditions and international division of labor. The abrupt exposure of such economies to world competition, as clearly illustrated by the example of the former GDR, may be quite a dangerous experiment. In this situation the introduction of a unique exchange rate and the liberalization of foreign trade should be accompanied by a selective tariff policy, sheltering those branches of production which can become competitive in the future, or those which will eventually be liquidated, but only gradually, after the necessary conditions have been created. Also different quantity restrictions, tolerated even in most developed countries, should be used when necessary.

The strengthening of the position of the former socialist countries in the world economy is a major problem on their way from a command to a market economy. These countries require an active policy, facilitating imports of modern technology, and promoting exports and changes in export structure towards manufactures, especially machines and equipment of an up-to-date technological standard. This policy cannot simply follow the conclusions of the conventional theory of comparative advantage of the Ricardo and Heckscher-Ohlin type, consisting in free trade policy. It should rather concentrate on a factor which is missing in all these static theories, namely on technical progress.

Luigi Pasinetti (1988) provides an example of two countries: one developed, the other one underdeveloped, but both having exactly the same structure of prices. Under these conditions, foreign trade in the pure form is not interesting for either country. Let us imagine, however, that labor productivity in the developed country is 10 times higher than that in the less developed one. From the point of view of the latter country, international trade linked with the process of learning from the former is an extremely interesting proposition. The main role of international interaction in this case lies not so much in the choice of an optimal point on the production possibility curve, but predominantly in the shift of this curve outward from the origin of the coordinate system. Pasinetti concludes that the major and primary source of international gains is international learning, not international trade (pp. 139-147). This is a rather fundamental proposition, not only for less developed countries, but particularly for the former socialist countries when they turn towards a more market-oriented economy, because it shifts their attention from pure static to dynamic problems, and from free trade policy prescriptions on to efforts of learning and adopting technical knowledge from abroad.

There is one important problem with this approach. In the case of static equilibrium theories there exists a well defined set of unambiguous policy prescriptions on what to do, and especially what not to do, in order not to hinder the benevolent action of the "invisible hand" of the market. What, however, should be done in order to break a lethargic industrial structure, to develop industries which do not yet exist, to teach skills which are not available in the country, to create a social climate propitious for entrepreneurship, innovation, and risk taking? These questions are much easier asked than answered. (Datta-Chaudhuri, pp. 76-77)

The action of market forces is absolutely necessary. Thus a sound policy may and should support (not replace) the market mechanism. It is known that Japan (and later on most of the NICs) followed two basic rules in their policy of selecting and supporting export-oriented industries: First, the selected industries should be those that are the most promising from the point of view of the expected rate of growth of labor productivity; as a rule these are young industries where the potential for further technical progress is still unexploited. Second, export promotion should concentrate mainly on goods that are characterized by an expected high income elasticity of demand. These two rules have not much in common with the traditional theory of comparative advantage and with the postulate of state abstention from foreign trade. They seem, however, to deliver the results, although mistakes could not be avoided either.[6]

Government intervention can be – but is not necessarily – benevolent. Import substitution (supported by import restrictions creating a climate favorable for private domestic and foreign investment) can make sense in well-chosen industries, first of all in larger countries. But this strategy is of limited applicability. If used indiscriminately for all industries and for all time, an artificial production structure would be created and ossified; consequently it could survive only as long as the protection lasts. Additionally vested interests of protected industries (usually within the state sector) would be articulated and would demand the perpetuation of protection, endangering the achievement of original policy targets of the whole maneuver. Thus, state support has to be strong enough to assist the development of promising firms, but not as strong as to let firms survive which cannot become self-supporting after a while. This is easier said than done. However, there exists no other solution.

The same applies to export promotion policy. Export capacities can develop only concurrently with an industrialization program. Nobody – and rare exceptions (e.g. transnational companies) only support the general rule – is going to invest in capacities oriented towards export only. Thus the creation and enlargement of the internal market is a precondition for successful export promotion. Efficient import substitution and export promotion must be flexible and selective; they must also be part and parcel of an integrated industrialization policy if they are to be successful.

Many professional economists and international institutions tend to think in terms of two standard concepts. "In the field of economic development, two mutually exclusive sets of associated ideas are often set against each other: one set consists of capitalism, free trade and export promotion and the other, socialism, State intervention and import substitution" (Datta-Chaudhuri, pp. 76-77). This opposition is simply wrong. On the one hand, socialist countries failed completely, not because they were interventionist, but because they killed private entrepreneurship, the very medium which their intervention should have moulded. On the other hand, Japan and the NICs are examples of highly interventionist states, promoting capitalist development through selective intervention in both export promotion and import substitution.

5. Some Ideological Considerations

Economics is a mixture of ideology and science intertwined. It is not at all easy to separate one from the other. Does the ideological attitude of an economist simply follow his scientific convictions, or are the latter rather no more than a scientific decoration of the former? In normal circumstances it is very difficult to say what prevails in a given case: ideology or science. Under special conditions, however, this is not impossible. Assume, e.g., the following proposition of Joan Robinson, that an economist changes his political attitude from one day to another. If after this change his previous economics disappears completely, we are entitled to conclude that there was nothing but ideology in it. If, conversely, our economist still supports some elements of his economics, this part is certainly non-ideological (although not necessarily true).

What Joan Robinson saw as an abstract experiment has become an experience of a whole generation of economists in the past years. Of course, I mean here the group of economists who were critical of capitalism and had more or less pronounced socialist inclinations. They were often influenced by Marx, but also by the theory of effective demand in its more or less radical version.

The collapse of the socialist experiment in the form of a command economy could not but shatter their economics. The great majority of them stopped perceiving socialism as a closed system transcending the institutional framework of capitalism, and accepted the idea that the continuity of economic development, broken by the revolution from which the "real socialist" economy emerged, should be restored. Thus their anticapitalistic attitude gave way to the acceptance of industrial capitalism as an unavoidable system, and the conditions of the experiment formulated by Joan Robinson were fulfilled for a number of them.

The results – as could be expected – are mixed. Part of previously radical economists revised important elements of their thinking. First of all they accepted the necessity of real markets, real money and real competition based, at least to a preponderant degree, on private ownership of economic resources. But they still believe in the existence of an overall interest of society that cannot be reduced to a sum of individual interests. They would also very often retain the basic assumptions of the theory of effective demand. They would argue that central planning was introduced as a remedy against the illnesses of capitalism, but this remedy proved to be worse than the malady itself. They would accept the fact that the medicine almost killed the patient and has been discarded, but they would reject the idea that the patient had been in perfect health in the first place. Thus it can be said that parts of economic thinking of this group contained more than pure ideology, in so far as it survived the change of political opinions.

The other group behaved differently. They made a full turn about and moved from Marx and Keynes–Kalecki directly to Mises and Hayek. They did not only accept the latters' criticism of orthodox socialism, which after all had been correct, but took over their extreme liberal position identifying any economic action of the state with socialism. Say's Law has become for them as solid as it was shaky before. Of the economics of this group nothing remained after the political turnabout; it had contained no scientific elements.

The transition from a command to a market economy is based on an anticommunist and uncritically procapitalistic ideology (Drewnowski,

1990, pp. 5-6). This is understandable, because ideology played a decisive role in the rise of central planning and in the destruction and suffering caused by its functioning; but it may become dangerous if it leads to a doctrinaire attitude in the practical reconstruction of the economies. The generation of economists which is now directing the transition in Eastern Europe has no immediate experience with the capitalist economy in their countries before the Second World War. They know capitalism mostly from microeconomic textbooks and from superficial visits in the most developed Western countries. Their consciousness has been moulded by the absurdities, of the Soviet-type economy in their countries, they are inclined to identify every economic activity of the state with these absurdities, and to promote a purely capitalistic system with a marginal role of the state in economic matters. The social climate is propitious for this attitude; it is supported also by foreign experts, mostly monetarists, who in the majority of cases have no knowledge of these countries, and – as a rule – by theoretical inclinations of such potent institutions as the IMF and the World Bank. It should be added, however, that these institutions do not have an official theoretical position. Thus they are often ready to discuss the problems with local economists and to look for solutions acceptable to both sides. A good example is Hungary, where – with full IMF approval – no shock therapy has been applied. The sad truth is that very often the ruling groups in EITs are "plus catholique que le pape" and use the prestige of the IMF as a cover for their own extreme liberal inclinations[7]. The situation is, however, much more complicated. The transition from socialism to capitalism is without any precedents (McCracken). Under such conditions it is not enough to decree the introduction of free markets and then wait for the market forces to do the job. What is badly needed is to analyze the situation, to look for new solutions and, most of all, not to neglect economic policy at a time when it is needed more than ever.

Notes

1. We come back to this topic on pp. 49-51.

2. Jeffrey Sachs (1990), an important designer of the Polish shock therapy, said: "... fears of plummeting take home pay abound, though the average industrial worker earned the equivalent of $ 131 in October (1990 – my remark, K.L.), compared with $ 108 in October 1989."

Indeed, between October 1989 and October 1990 monthly industrial wages in zloty increased by a factor of about 5, while the exchange rate of the US dollar measured in zloty increased only by a factor of about 4. Jeffrey Sachs forgot, however, to add that prices of consumer goods in the same period increased by a factor of about 6. Thus, the purchasing power of one US dollar on the consumer goods market in Poland decreased by about 50 percent.

3. In the first half of 1990 the budget registered a surplus of Zl 6.5 trillion, while in the second half of the year the budget closed with a deficit of Zl 5.6 trillion.

4. In February 1990 an estimate of the expected decline of GDP was undertaken by the present writer, using data for 1989 available at that time. The results were published in Laski (1990).

5. E.g., in Israel, between 1985 and 1989, GNP did not decrease at all during a successful stabilization. Mexico, between 1984 and 1989, registered a negative rate of GNP growth only in one year (-3.8% in 1986), and even Argentina, where the stabilization has failed, negative and positive rates of growth in the same period compensated each other more or less, resulting in a stagnation of GNP. (Blanchard et al., p. 9).

6. In Japan, in the 1950s and 1960s, the following "four priority industries" received preferential treatment: steel, coal, shipbuilding, and electric power. In addition – and partly later – several other industries were supported, too (e.g. cars, electronics, color films, computers, semiconductors), as growth industries. In the majority of cases the policy was most successful, in some cases, however, failures were registered (e.g. in coal industry and shipbuilding). Also aircraft industry failed to stand on its feet despite substantial government assistance.

7. Having in mind exactly those people, Wyczalkowski (1991), a retired senior economist who had worked in the IMF for dozens of years, was quoted recently as making a sarcastic remark in Warsaw that IMF stands for Internatinal Monetary Fund and not for International Market Fanatics.

References

Altmann, Franz Lothar, Clement, Hermann, Vacic, Aleksandar M. (1991), Introduction to "Reforms in Foreign Economic Relations of Eastern Europe and the Soviet Union," *ECE, Economic Studies* No. 2, United Nations, New York.

Blanchard, Olivier, Dornbusch, Rudiger, Krugman, Paul, Layard, Richard, and Summers, Lawrence (1991), *Reform in Eastern Europe*, The MIT Press, Cambridge, Mass.

Brus, Wlodzimierz, and Laski, Kazimierz (1989), *From Marx to the Market. Socialism in Search of an Economic System*, Clarendon Press, Oxford.

Datta-Chaudhuri, M. K. (1981), "Industrialization and Foreign Trade: the Development Experience of South Korea and the Philippines," in: *Export-Led Industrialization and Development*, edited by Eddy Lee, International Labor Organization.

Dornbush, Rudiger (1990), *From Stabilization to Growth*, NBER Working Paper No. 3302.

Drewnowski, Jan (1990), "Paradoksy polskiej gospodarki," in: *Trybuna*. Political Quarterly, London, No. 65/121.

Havlik, Peter (1991), "East-West GDP Comparisons: Problems, Methods and Results," *WIIW-Forschungsberichte*, No. 174, The Vienna Institute for Comparative Economic Studies (WIIW), Vienna, September.

Kolodko, Grzegorz W. (1991), *Transition from Socialism and Stabilization Policies. The Polish Experience*, Paper presented at the 32nd Annual Convention of the International Studies Association, "New Dimensions in Internal Relations", Vancouver, 19-23 March 1991, mimeographed.

Kolodko, Grzegorz W., and Rutkowski, Michael (1991), "The Problem of Transition form a Socialist to a Free Market Economy: The Case of Poland," in: *The Journal of Social, Political and Economic Studies*, Vol. 16, No. 2, Summer.

Kornai, Janos (1980), *Economics of Shortage*, North-Holland Publishing Company, Amsterdam.

Khan, Mohsin S., and Knight, Malcolm D. (1985), *Fund-Supported Adjustment Programs and Economic Growth*, IMF Occasional Paper No. 41.

Laski, Kazimierz (1990), "O niebezpieczenstwach zwiazanych z planem stabilizacji gospodarki narodowej," in: *Gospodarka narodowa*, Warsaw, No. 2/3, pp. 5-9.

Levcik, Friedrich (1991), "The place of convertibility in the Transformation Process", in: *Currency Convertibility in Eastern Europe*, edited by John Williamson, Institute for International Economics, Washington, D.C., pp. 40-44.

Lindbeck, Assar (1991), *Macroeconomic Theory and the Labor Market*, mimeographed.

McCracken, Paul W. (1990), "Thoughts on Marketizing State-managed Economies," in: *Economic Impact*, No. 71, 1990/2.

Oppenheimer, Peter (1991), "Economic Reforms and Transitional Policies: Summary of Discussion," in: Reforms in Foreign Economic Relations of Eastern Europe and the Soviet Union, *Economic Studies* No. 2, United Nations Economic Commission for Europe, edited by M. Kaser and A. M. Vacic, New York.

Pasinetti, Luigi (1988), "Technical Progress and International Trade," in: *Empirica*. Austrian Economic Papers, Vol. 15, No. 1.

Sachs, Jeffrey (1990), "A Tremor, Not Necessarily a Quake, for Poland," in: *International Herald Tribune*, 30 November.

Wiles, Peter (1991), "Die kapitalistische Siegessicherheit in Osteuropa," in: *Europäische Rundschau* 1991/3.

Wyczalkowski Marian (1991), quoted in ".... Rada ekonomiczna," in *Zycie gospodarcze*, No. 47 of Nov. 24, 1991, Warszawa.

3

THE THORNY PATH OF TRANSITION FROM COMMAND TO MARKET ECONOMY *

Friedrich Levcik

1. Point of Departure

Following the short-lived euphoria which, towards the close of the 1980s, in the wake of the popular revolutions in the countries of Central and East Europe, had swept through both East and West, a view we had voiced at an early stage finds general acceptance now: that the transformation of the formerly centrally planned autocracies into Western type market economies is going to be an arduous and long drawn-out process. The great expectations especially in the countries directly concerned are now supplanted not merely by a process of disillusion but – to quote President Havel of the CSFR – by a veritable hangover.

But why? Have not the past two years' developments in Central and East Europe surpassed, in some respects, the expectations then entertained? When the Soviet Union remained passive in Poland and East Germany, tolerating the escalation of popular wrath that swept away the established regimes there, most countries of the region promptly took decisive steps to initiate democratic institutions. Halfway through 1990 the traditional communist regimes in Poland, Hungary and the CSFR had been replaced by new, democratically elected governments. East Germany rapidly achieved unification with, and integration into the Federal Republic of Germany. Democratic trans-

---

* The above paper was presented at the International Symposium of the *French-Austrian Center* on May 21 and 22, 1991 in Paris.

formation took a more complicated course in Bulgaria and Romania. A section of the old power elite was able to cling to their former positions, and despite their avowal that they too would willingly go along with the transformation of their countries into market economies, the opposition is not reconciled to these leaderships; political discord impedes the inauguration of serious and radical reforms. In Yugoslavia it is strife among her nations that hinders the reform process, which might otherwise find fertile ground in this country, formerly oriented toward market socialism. It is only in the USSR that the path toward a market economy is still completely in the dark, despite the decisive weakening of the Communist Party's supremacy, and where a relapse into dictatorship and ruinous civil war is by no means banned.[1]

At the same time the collapse, or weakening, of communism has ended the former split-up of Europe into politically hostile and antagonistic economic blocs. The Warsaw Pact is virtually dissolved, COMECON is doomed to inactivity, and only disputes about settlement of old claims and liabilities have so far prevented its formal dissolution.[2] In most of the countries of the region the legislative and institutional foundations have been laid – though at disparate pace and varying intensity – for an historical, unique transformation towards market economism.

When we contemplate all the changes that have come to pass in such a brief space of time, it must be puzzling at first sight that discontent and disquiet are rife. The explanation can be found in the, so far predominantly negative, economic results, their social consequences, and the growing realization that, in the first place, the road to prosperity according to a Western pattern will be long and stony; and that, in the second place, it might be nearly hopeless without massive Western aid.

2. The Present Economic Situation

The year 1990, characterized in some of the Central- and East European (CEE) countries by the beginnings of economic transformation, was also a year of severe economic crisis for the region as a whole; that crisis befell those countries too, that had abandoned the central planning of their economies, without however having taken decisive steps in the direction of a market economy. The aggregate output of the region (including the "Länder" of East Germany) declined by more than 10 percent, with the highest drops recorded in East Germany (19%) and Poland (13%). Industrial production, predominantly still State owned, shrank by around 18 percent as against the preceding year, and agricultural output declined by 3 percent. Although prices in the CEE countries – excepting Poland, Hungary and East Germany – had still remained administratively set, inflation everywhere exceeded expectations, reaching two-digit figures.

This was followed by a perceptible decline of real wages and real incomes of the population. Mass unemployment, spreading rapidly, is a completely novel phenomenon for that region. Though still low by western standards, it grows to a disquieting degree, nor has it by any means reached its peak. Employment is declining at a similar pace, especially in the still dominant State sector. True, the new private sector is expanding, but its weight is still too little to make up for the slump in employment in the public sector.

All told, the welfare losses that make their appearance in connection with the collapse of the communist system in Europe, and which are characterized by economic shrinkage, massive real wage losses, inflation, and rising unemployment, are of a magnitude capable of destabilizing the delicate new democracies through social unrest and/or national conflicts. The populations, especially in Poland, Hungary and the CSFR, where the governments have promised speedy transition to market economy, are up to now still willing to undergo privation as a price that must be paid in return for being freed from the yoke of communism. But the governments there, and those in the West, with their counselors, ought to beware at their own peril of overtaxing the patience and endurance of the population.

The external economic conditions of the region, too, give cause for alarm. In the second half of 1990 supply stoppages of crude oil and other primary energy sources from the Soviet Union to Central and East Europe in the main, and the consequences of the embargo against Iraq, had damaging effects on the region: Some countries had compensation agreements pending with Iraq, promising crude oil supplies against unpaid credits (mainly for arms deliveries). Supply stoppages from that source caused energy bottlenecks in some countries, particularly in Bulgaria and Romania, contributing substantially to the drops in output. In addition, the CEE countries were forced to make supplementary crude oil and oil products purchases at rising hard currency spot prices, thus further burdening their already strained trade and payments balances. Both the trade balances and the balances on current account of the region deteriorated – excepting Poland's and Hungary's, who both achieved record trade surpluses with the West (both countries' greatly devaluated currencies acted as import barriers whilst facilitating rising exports). Especially the Soviet Union (trade deficit: US$ 4.8 bn) and Yugoslavia (US$ 3.4 bn), and the deficit resulting in intra-German trade (approximately US$ 8 bn) contributed to the deterioration of the trade balances, adding up to an aggregated regional trade deficit of almost US$ 14 billion (as compared with 1989: US$ 6.5 bn). We may estimate East Europe's deficit on current account for 1990 at US$ 4.5 bn, while the USSR's amounted to US$ 6.6 bn. The CEE countries' gross indebtedness reached US$ 87 bn (US$ 104 bn including Yugoslavia), the Soviet Union's was approximately US$ 53 bn. Thanks to the crude oil prices' rise in the second half of 1990, the Soviet gross debt was not much higher than in 1989, but the Soviet deposits in Western banks and their gold stocks were depleted to a perilously low level. The same applies to the bank deposits in the West of other countries of the region, boosting net indebtedness by US$ 17 billion, twice the total of gross indebtedness.

In 1991 the various CEE countries' external situation has further deteriorated. The virtual collapse of all intra-(ex)CMEA trade in face of the region's continuing dependence on Soviet crude oil and basic materials deliveries, and the USSR's inability (or unwillingness) to purchase (and pay for) their industrial goods was made complete by the newly determined price and payment modalities in intra-(ex)CMEA trade. In practice, trade among all these countries, and not only with the Soviet Union, has come to a standstill, because none of the countries is willing to obey the new rules and lay out scarce hard currency for East European goods.

Considering that intra-regional trade before 1990 had still accounted for fifty percent of all the region's foreign trade, it can be imagined how disastrously the failure of the bulk of that trade has affected the region's economic situation. Even that fact alone shows that the recessionary trends must be expected to deepen during 1991 (see Table and Graphs) and presumably also the next few years.

Moreover, the unfavorable foreign trade conditions are merely one – though an important – factor in assessing economic trends. Other causes, too, are rather indicative of further decline of economic activity.[3] Depending on the pace of transformation of the economic system, various elements exert their influence at varying degrees. A certain systemic vacuum is effective everywhere, since the old system of centrally planned economy has been more or less abandoned and the new system of market economy is coming into effect in a rudimentary form only. Where the old system has collapsed without being replaced by a new, more or less functioning market system, the money system has ceased to function, inflation can barely be controlled and the supply of basic necessities is no longer assured. Central allocation of raw materials, intermediate products, and foreign currency can no longer function, and the incipient chaos in the economy is compounded by political, social, and national conflicts. All this applies mainly but not solely to the Soviet Union. In these cases one may speak of a supply constrained economic crisis.

Table 1

Gross Domestic Product

annual changes in %

	1990	1991 estimated
Bulgaria	-11.8	-20 to -25
CSFR	-2.0	-15 to -18
Hungary	-4.3	-7
Poland	-12.0	-8 to -10
Romania	-7.3	-15 to -20
Yugoslavia[a)]	-7.6	-25
CEE Region	-8.4	-15 to -16
USSR	-2.0	-13
Total	-3.8	-13 to -15

a) Gross national product.

Source: WIIW-Databank.

At the opposite end of the range we perceive the economic situation of the former GDR. Under existing political circumstances the speedy unification within the framework of immediate adoption of the West German currency- and economic systems may well have been unavoidable. At any rate, the politically motivated 1:1 exchange rate of the former East-Mark to the Deutsch-Mark administered an insupportable shock to the totally unprepared economy of the (former) GDR. Exposed to unchecked competition by West Germany's far more productive economy, the majority of the former GDR enterprises had to capitulate. Their products became unsalable, consumers all over East Germany clamored for goods from the West. Money transfers from the West, far surpassing anything anticipated – and still unabated – are averting the worst. The West German social security network can make some amends; but this will not ban unemployment and misgivings about the future.

Further massive cash infusions are needed for the budgets of the five East German Länder, and resources of above two digit billion amounts, too, are required for the neglected infrastructure. Only when – and not before – the worst obstacles are cleared away with the help of public funds, is there any expectation of any major private investments becoming available to put the East German economy on a reasonably competitive footing. In view of the West German economy's enormous productivity and productive capacity, the transformation of the East German economy will, despite its present deep recessionary aspects, be accomplished much more easily and quickly than may be expected for the rest of the CEE countries, who cannot count on any remotely similar assistance from the West.

At any rate, the former GDR presents a warning example of what the total exposure of a formerly centrally planned economy to the highly developed world economy with its market determined prices can bring to pass, unless that sudden liberalization has been carefully prepared, and the transition been supported by additional structural policy measures. Nevertheless, it would appear that up till now Western mainstream economic thinking – uncritically accepted by the principal economic experts in the East – had nothing to offer but an ultra-liberal and strictly monetaristic concept. We shall deal with these policies in the next section of this chapter.

3. Diverse Starting Conditions, Similar Transformation Strategies

Here we deal with the CEE countries that have already entered unequivocally on the path to converting their economies into market economies. At the time of writing this chapter, they comprise Hungary, Poland, the CSFR, and to some extent Yugoslavia.[4] The basic conditions in the individual countries were, and still are, radically dissimilar.

Hungary, looking back on a long trek of economic reforms, which were already initiated by the old communist regime, was able to accumulate positive and negative experiences. At any rate, a private sector having been established years ago already, especially in commerce and in services, agricultural cooperatives had become accustomed to taking business initiatives without being hampered by major government interference, and the managers of State enterprises, too, were able to acquire some positive market experience. But the old regime has also burdened the country with a heavy load of debts, severely restricting the present government's scope for action. In contrast to some other CEE countries, however, despite carrying the highest per capita debt burden, Hungary has always met its obligations.

In entering upon its radical transition to a market economy, *Poland* set out from a fundamentally different starting position. Here the radical reformers were faced with a wrecked economy, a supply system in total collapse, uncontrollable inflation, and far-reaching dollarization of all money transactions. On the other hand, Poland was endowed with an agrarian sector largely based on peasant private ownership, and in the economy at large the gradually spreading private sector was able by legal and illegal means to make profitable use of the prevalent confusion in the economy. Poland, too, was deep in debt; but unlike Hungary, Poland was no longer able to meet its commitments.

Graph 1

GDP and Industrial Output Changes in Hungary

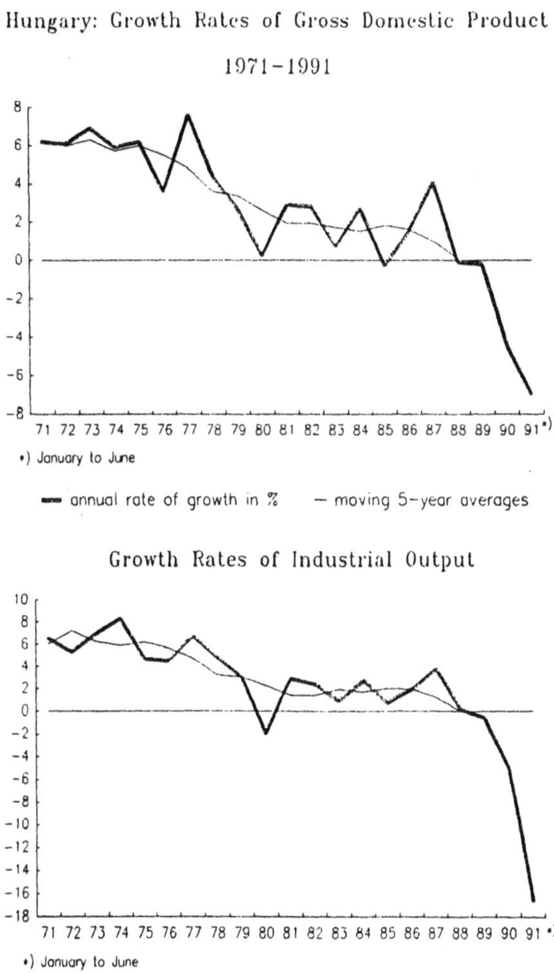

Source: WIIW-Database

In *Czechoslovakia*, after the fall of the old regime, the new government was left with an outmoded and antiquated, yet basically functioning economy. Indebtedness was moderate, and also the internal global equilibrium could be kept more or less intact. But the central administrative machinery had also remained basically intact, the obsolete monopolies in production and distribution continued to prevail in the economy. There was almost no private sector, and the agrarian sector, too, was almost totally dominated by oversized agricultural production cooperatives and State farms. However, a shadow economy throve, tolerated by a partly corrupt administration. The administratively controlled system of set prices was able to maintain the supply situation – though with numerous supports and subsidies – without any substantial inflationary developments.

Although – as set out in the foregoing – the initial situation differed widely from country to country, the economic strategy recommended by Western advisers (including IMF and World Bank) was confined to substantially identical macro-economic measures. However, bulk acceptance of this economic strategy was made virtually conditional for release to the CEE countries of emergency and stand-by credits (including assistance programs initiated by the EC and the G 24).

The center piece of the recommended transformation policy in Czechoslovakia consists of early, if possible total, decontrol of prices and quick introduction of currency convertibility, at least for the balance of payments on current account (some extremist liberal economists even want convertibility extended at once to capital transactions). Since price liberalization makes the withdrawal of existing price subsidies necessary, and the introduction of convertibility necessitates a massive devaluation of the country's own currency, the two operations are bound to cause a mighty jump in the price level and to expose the economy to enormous inflationary pressure. That pressure is to be counteracted by draconic restrictive macro-economic frame conditions. A preferably balanced budget, and a restrictive monetary policy, including the maintenance of a positive real rate of interest, even in the face of high rates of inflation, are to inhibit the upward trend of prices. Further, there is the need to install a minimal social security net to protect the redundant labor for a time from the worst. Thereafter it is proposed to privatize, as fast as possible, the predominantly State-owned sector, or to shut it down. Further State interference (of an import protecting, export promoting, structural or regional policy nature) is not wanted, and it is envisioned that the evolving market forces, after necessary, admittedly painful adjustments, will bring forth a new equilibrium, enabling the respective countries to set out on a steadily rising road of growth and prosperity.

Graph 2

GDP and Industrial Output Changes in Poland

Poland: Growth Rates of Net Material Product

1971–1991

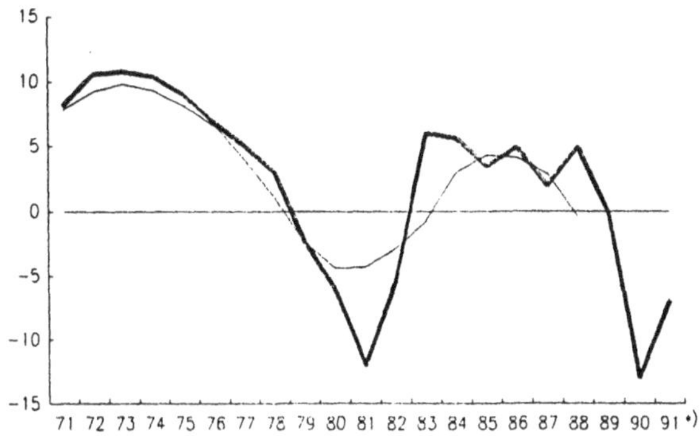

*) January to June

annual rate of growth in %   — moving 5-year averages

Growth Rates of Industrial Output

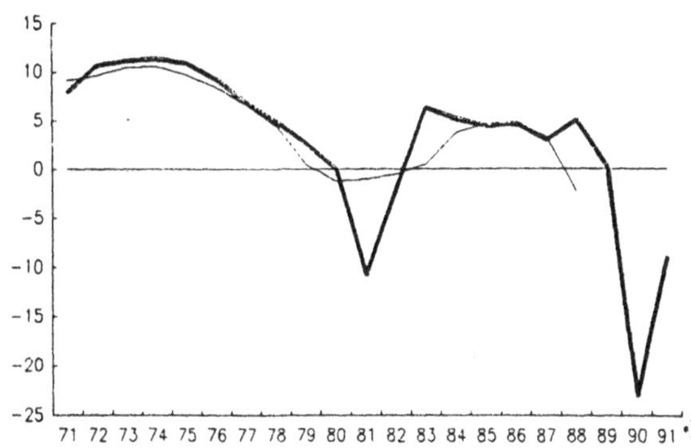

*) January to June

Source: WIIW–Database

Graph 3

GDP and Industrial Output Changes in Czechoslovakia

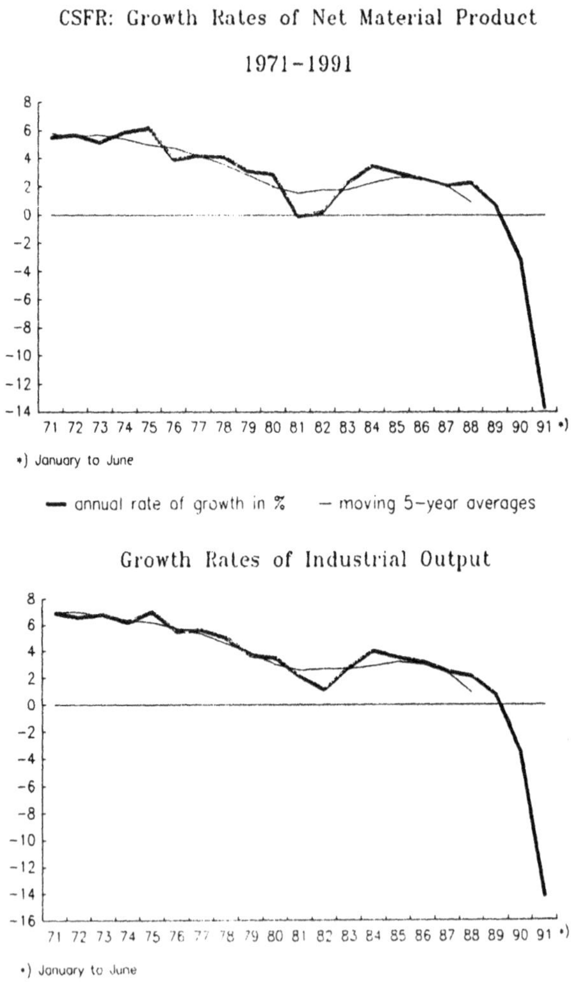

Source: WIIW-Database

The allure of this recommended strategy, sometimes simplistically termed shock therapy, consists in the relative ease of its launching by governmental and parliamentary decision, by the complete reversal of erstwhile prevalent general State interference with the government's total abstinence in all matters of the economy, and finally in the promise or at any rate hope of entering, as soon as possible, the haven of a free market economy. The initially widespread acceptance in the post-communist societies of such a radical program of transformation is quite understandable. In the countries where the old system has broken down, the supply of essentials is no longer assured, and inflation gone out of control, one can understand the impatience of the population, expectant of that "sanitary shock" bringing about the early end of its daily hardships. Besides, less drastic strategies may well prolong their miseries.

But also in those countries, where an alternative or at least a more moderate transformation policy would be feasible, a strong lobby exists that pushes public opinion in the direction of a "Big Bang". That lobby is made up of a strange mix of young, market economy oriented economists, mostly theoreticians without any practical experience of capitalist every-day life in Western industrial countries, further, of a new up-and-coming class of private entrepreneurs, heirs to capitalists of old, or would-be entrepreneurs, keen to acquire State enterprises up for privatization, which they would love to take over for free or buy for a handful of peanuts. They are types who want to become rich overnight, without much effort or ability, and who would not care much about what happens to the "losers". These types and their aspirations often find support from the ranks of government officials and media men, mostly settled in protected sectors, un-imperiled by the malignant consequences of the Big Bang.

Of a more complicated nature are the motivations of Western experts, backers too, predominantly, of a shock therapy. Some of them gained their experience in developing countries but have little direct experience of centrally planned economies with predominant State ownership. They do not comprehend the situation in countries without an adequate number of major independent market agents: where market signals such as prices or exchange rates do not evoke market-conforming adjustments but may trigger perverse reactions. With other Western economists one gains the impression that they propose to inflict on the new democracies in the CEE countries burdens they would not dream of insinuating, in the context of feasible economic policies, on their own countries or on the Western community of nations, without being laughed out of court as scatterbrains. Which sober economist, e.g., would dare suggest to the European Communities that they abolish all agrarian subsidies at one go? Nothing would come of that proposal but a shaking of heads at such artlessness. Or, again, who among Western economists would insist that the habitual multi-billion household deficit be straightaway replaced by a balanced budget, or more maybe even by a budget surplus? These expert opinions seem to apply the saying that *quod licet Jovi non licet bovi*, with the responsible actors in the CEE countries cast in the role of the oxen who are to take the dicta of Western textbooks and counselors all too literally.

Sure, subsidies ought to be cut, national budgets should be balanced and international free trade realized by dismantling protectionist trade barriers. But these laudable principles must be understood as desired ends – goals to be approached but which cannot be attained at short notice. In the 46 years since the end of World War Two the Western industrial nations have been able to achieve their present productive level and prosperity, treading a path plastered with good intentions – but also encumbered for many years with a multitude of subsidies, household deficits and not a few protectionist measures. Why should the CEE nations be expected to do away with all that at one fell swoop?

4. The Role of the International Monetary Fund

Let us now briefly examine the role and the possibilities of the International Monetary Fund in the context of introducing a market economy in East Europe. It is the IMF's main task to help countries to overcome temporary disequilibria and payments deficits, and to restore equilibrium. The means at the Fund's disposal can only be allocated by way of loans. The Fund is no development aid organization.

Its mode of operating comprises advice and the devising of programs elaborated in dialogue with the countries concerned. In this process the fund must, of course, keep in sight its overall objectives, viz the reduction of international imbalances.

Hence its special emphasis on budget discipline, on the establishment and maintenance of competitive exchange rates, and next also on the curtailment of subsidies and trade impediments. During the long years of its existence, the fund has become accustomed, when working out its assistance programs to come up against reservations and resistance, when the receiving countries object to harsh measures proposed, on grounds of consideration of their countries' overall economic and social situation. As a rule the program finally accepted represents a compromise aimed at solving the balance-of-payments problem without over-much harming the country's overall economic and social situation.

In its dealings with the CEE countries, however, it often happens that not merely no resistance is offered, but that the harsh demands are outbid by ultra-liberal partners. When, e.g., the IMF demanded budgetary discipline, the Czechoslovak Minister of Finance countered by offering a budget surplus, and was very pleased with himself when the surplus budgeted for was actually exceeded in the 1st quarter of 1991.

Quite the teacher's pet, he proudly announced to the public that the Fund had given his government "full marks" on examining the first months' results, because the drastically devaluated exchange rate is maintained and the balance of payments was not imperiled by the introduction of convertibility. That the prescribed medicine – household restraint resulting in a budget surplus, restricted money supply, and high taxation of wage increments – brought a 20 percent decline of total demand, he left cloaked in silence. As a consequence, a growing number of enterprises – not only the run-down, but also quite viable ones – went insolvent, unemployment is on the increase and far from its peak, and yet the population is subjected to the growing inflationary pressure that has boosted prices by nearly 50 percent in the first four months, contrary to optimistic official forecasts.[5]

This therapy, represented by Western main-stream economic thinking as being the sole feasible transformation policy, creates a situation that even lacks an appropriate label so far, since the epithet "stagflation" coined in the 1970s would be a grossly diminutive misnomer. What is about to happen may lead to South American conditions, where even inflation cannot be brought under sustained control, while depression may become a permanent feature, accompanied by glaring income disparities, with poverty and unemployment at one pole of society.

5. Competition – The Missing Link

I would pinpoint the central cause of this apparently perverse development – inflation in the face of declining demand – in the attempt to control, solely via market signals, an economy as yet still dominated by production and distribution monopolies. Price liberalization without a competitive milieu, and accentuated by dearer imports due to gross currency devaluation, must initially lead to substantial price increases. In such a situation, even the sales resistance then encountered by the monopolies will not lead to price cuts, as would happen under competition, but they will rather cut their output and default on commitments to their suppliers. These failures to pay will cause an upstream chain reaction of defaults, causing the previously mentioned insolvencies even of viable enterprises.

Speedier privatization is the customarily proposed panacea. But the so called small privatization of trading and service enterprises, which can be achieved comparatively quickly, say within one or two years, is of little avail, when the most important suppliers – mammoth enterprises – continue to stick to their monopolistic behavior.

However, the privatization of major production, trading, and service corporations will take more time. Even if novel methods are tried and a speeding-up of privatization is attempted by means of distribution of vouchers to the population, it will for a long time to come alter nothing in the behavior of the enterprises thus transferred into private ownership. These investment vouchers, to be acquired by risk inclined citizens at a nominal fee like in a lottery, will still have to be exchanged for stock in an enterprise of their own choosing, with the price of such stock dependent on the voucher holders' demand. If demand for a particular share is lively, then a booklet of vouchers might suffice only for the purchase of a fraction of a share; if demand is sluggish, a voucher may well buy several shares. In any case, it may be supposed that interest will be concentrated on a small number of enterprises expected to be able to survive the shock of transformation. The majority of State enterprises will presumably fail to tempt potential investors, meaning that these enterprises' fate will remain in balance. But even where the voucher method is going to create a widely scattered share holding, covering a rather small part of State enterprises, concentration of share holding in comparatively few hands can only be expected via a gradually emerging functioning capital market. Such concentration, however, is essential before managements can be replaced, by way of a "leveraged buy-out," at the future capitalist market actors' own pleasure and own interest. Even by this novel and non-traditional method of privatization an effective change of ownership, encompassing real influence on the enterprise's management, can only be achieved after years. Even while promoting all methods of privatization, the CEE countries will have to be resigned to State enterprises remaining part and parcel of their economies for many years to come. A reasoned policy vis-à-vis these enterprises is quite as important as all measures meant to promote the creation and rapid development of private enterprises. A hostile, even nihilistic attitude towards all that is of the State would result in the reconstruction of the economy being put off to the day when the last State enterprise has been privatized or has gone down the drain.

Up till now even the CEE countries that have already gone part of the way of transformation lack that milieu of competition capable of reacting to market signals in a truly market conforming manner. Free market access for new private enterprises, privatization measures, the freeing of foreign trade from administrative trade impediments, and, last not least, the threat of bankruptcy and elimination are necessary institutional prerequisites, already realized in part. But more is to be done. Encouraging competition ought to be a day-to-day policy task of government, of parliament and of enterprise and labor interests. In an economy where the public sector, for better, for worse, is going to remain an influential factor, competition policy must of necessity also encompass the State enterprises.

The monopolistic State enterprises must be deglomerated, redundant parts disposed of, and remaining new enterprises must be commercialized and converted into joint stock companies or other corporations. Beside such anti-trust and de-monopolization policy, offensive competition policies, too, are needed. Viable enterprises should in the first place be reconstructed by temporary, conditional stand-by and supportive actions to enable them to compete. Such a policy may not always be successful; bankruptcies and market failures will occur. But the majority of enterprises could be re-floated by such supportive policies. This will also improve the chances of privatizing them at a later date.

The widespread assumption that government is not well qualified to select the "winners and losers" is a prejudice, admittedly supported to some degree, yet disproved to a far greater extent by actual economic developments since the Second World War. Where would the economic super-power, Japan, be to-day without the influence exercised on its industry by the mighty MITI Ministry, and how ever could France have advanced to becoming a major power in the field of high technology without the helping hand of the public hand? The favorable development of the public Austrian Industries in recent years, too, exemplifies the ability of the State, as owner, even without interfering in operative management, to be of assistance in the enterprises' reconstruction and recovery. And, lastly, are not the joint exertions in science and research within the framework of EC, such as, e.g., the program Eureka, further proof of active structural policy by the community?

All the more are the new small and medium-size private enterprises in need of an active policy of competition promotion. Often the young entrepreneurs' firms lack the prerequisites for successful survival under competition. They need help in installing sound bookkeeping; needed R&D can only be tackled on a cooperative basis: there, their representative organizations may be of assistance. To obtain market access in foreign trade, too, a helping hand is needed.

6. The Western Community of Nations – Its Role and Tasks

There are no set patterns to be followed in the transition from command to market economies. Nor is there anything like an adequate theory. Under such circumstances, an approach colored by ideological prejudices is doubly dangerous. The results so far, mostly negative, seem to indicate that an economy basing itself on ultra-liberal paradigms, which would in effect leave everything to the self-healing forces of the market, could very easily lead to disaster. What is called for is a pragmatic, well considered economic policy that makes use of other countries' experiences.

The West, in a body, should lend support to such a policy. Apart from the technical and financial assistance under way the West ought to double its financial efforts. Further, the CEE countries need access, if possible unimpeded access, to the large Western markets. Much could still be improved in that direction, in particular as far as certain fields are concerned where the CEE nations are already competitive, e.g., in foods, iron and steel, and in textiles. I am well aware that these are sensitive spheres, but considering the small market shares held by the CEE countries, a more generous attitude should surely be possible. And, besides, I am convinced that, e.g., a large power like France, and our little Austria, have in their own history experienced lessons which do not quite correspond to to-day's ultra-liberal notions but which could be successfully applied in the CEE countries.

Notes

1. Since this paper was written, an unsuccessful coup attempt by reactionary Party and KGB forces occurred, followed by the disintegration of the Union, prohibition of Communist Party activities in most of the Republics, recognition of independence of the Baltic republics, and the attempt to coax the remaining republics into loose economic cooperation. However, real steps towards a rational economic reform are still in the offing. In Bulgaria, on the other hand, a democratic process of political transformation, integrating non-communist previously oppositional forces into the political establishment, and the commencement of transformation towards a market economy has been initiated.

2. The COMECON was thereafter also formally dissolved.

3. As may be seen from the Table and Graphs, the decline and crisis of the economy has deepened considerably in the course of 1991.

4. In the meantime Bulgaria could be added; on the other hand, Yugoslavia has to be omitted because of the undeclared war between its nations.

5. For the time being, current inflation has come to a standstill in the last few months of 1991; nevertheless, consumer prices are up by 60% compared with last year, and real incomes are down by 25%.

4

TEN PROPOSITIONS TOWARDS A THEORY OF TRANSFORMATION: FROM COMMAND TO EXCHANGE COMMUNICATION

Raimund Dietz

1. Neoclassical Orthodoxy Versus Theory of Communications

The collapse of the stalinist type of socialism will be an enigma, and theorizing on transforming command into modern money economies will be misguided, as long as there is no proper understanding of what the market really is, and on what its vitality rests (Hayek 1952, 1988).

The proper perception of the function of the market and money is inhibited by the substantive concept of rationality prevailing in economic sciences (Simon 1978). This concept assumes that for any society as a whole there is an hypothetical equilibrium, or optimum. In this view, co-ordination mechanisms of any kind whatsoever are given the function of effectuating this equilibrium, or optimum.

From this conception derives the idea of a symmetry or functional equivalence of central planning and the market. This idea does not only apply to pure but also to applied comparative economics. Pure theory treats market and centrally planned economies with the same models, and, assuming ideal conditions, stipulates identical criteria of economic welfare for centrally planned and market economies. Applied theory analyses the performance of economic systems from the viewpoint of static welfare criteria (Pareto-criterion). The difference between welfare criteria and real allocation is ascribed to market failures and cost of hierarchies respectively. With respect to systems policy these approaches lead to the proposal of a mixed economy, in which the advantages of both systems should be maximized while their respective disadvantages are to be avoided. This kind of comparing real economies with pure hypothetical states has been called a nirvana-form of analysis. The comparison is not a comparison between real type economies with stylized economies, but of real economies with commodity space models,[1] in which society is eliminated.[2]

But this approach – supported by the mainstream concept of rationality – comes to a dead end and prompts unsustainable positions. The decay of command economies and the dimensions of the transformation process will only be understood by radically departing from concepts of substantial rationality (commodity space models), and by modeling systemic rationality out of communicative procedures. Taking our lead from N. Luhmann's Systems Theory we propose to proceed not from conceptions about the existence of an equilibirum or optimum, i.e. from a solution of equations, but from a concept of communications as social events. To Luhmann, society is communication and only communication. Until people communicate there is neither society nor economy – except Robinson economies.

2. Exchange as the Basic Order Element of Modern Societies

The systemic rationality of modern (Western) societies derives from exchange – rationality cannot be modeled from ideal exchange conditions à la Walrasian Economics, but from exchange as real life communication. It is the basic communicative element from which all other modern economic institutions (prices, money, private property, organizations etc.) emanate. One of the greatest mistakes in economic sciences consists in neglecting or practically neglecting exchange as the basic element on which modern civil societies rest; or, what amounts to the same, to consider the neoclassical theory of allocation (Walrasian economics) a theory of exchange. Economies constitute themselves only through exchange. This is the basic hypothesis of the liberal philosopher Georg Simmel's main work: "The Philosophy of Money (1900)" – an opus that has been almost completely neglected by the economic theorists, even by the money theorists. Simmel's work is a reconstruction of the evolution of modern civilization. His work is of decisive importance especially for the formerly communistic countries in their striving to reconstruct the market. Civil (market) societies, according to Simmel, rest on exchange communication. Only exchange can bring about an objectivation of values (a primarily subjective phenomenon), generate money as the embodiment of exchange relations, making exchange the general principle of (world-wide) socialization in the economy. Money is the prerequisite of freedom (in the sense of choice from among dependences). Being man's most universal instrument, it becomes the goal of economic activity: money economy is capitalist money economy, it is exchange economy among private owners. ("Despite of" relying on a theory of exchange, Simmel's work essentially reconfirms and supports fundamental Keynesian ideas.)

3. The Asymmetry of the Plan-Market Mix

While substantive concepts of economic rationality lead to symmetric concepts of market and central planning – interpreting markets or government as alternatives (contingent choices), conceptualization of economies as communications shows that the relation of market and planning is asymmetrical. Of course, every modern society depends on the interplay between the market and bureaucratic (and central) control by the state. But these two forms of coordination cannot be mixed arbitrarily, if the mix is to function properly. The market must be the basis. State intervention, which is necessary – and may become even more so –, must depend on signals of the market as an autonomously working (sub-)system of society. In other words: plan and market are no mutually substitutable coordination mechanisms (if there are trade-offs then only at a very small margin) but they are systems which – comparable to the interplay between consciousness and bodily functions in man – execute completely different, yet mutually interdependent tasks. Man's mental activity must rely on the vital forces of the body, which can in no way be directed by strong will – otherwise neither the forces of digestion could function, nor his brain, center of his mental activities. Yet on the other hand it is decidedly advantageous if man acts consciously when ingesting his food: he can advance both his bodily and mental forces. Along the lines of this analogy we can proceed from an asymmetrical relation between plan and market.

If we press the relation of market and centrally planned economies into a short formula, we may say: market(s) – or market economies – mean economic vitality; planning on a central level means a more conscious dealing with this vitality. (This position does in no way imply that capitalist systems are ideal worlds).

4. Redefining Transformation

If exchange is responsible for the high speed of innovation, maneuverability, efficiency, in a word: high-grade rationality of economy, then the question arises, how can communication be gotten under way in a former command economy. That also defines the task of transformation in Eastern Europe and the USSR: it can be conceived as a transformation from command to exchange economies. This changeover is the change of the way by which society communicates in the economic subsystem. It is connected with a change of the logic, and in consequence, with the behavior of agents and with the material structure of the economy.

The logic of the command system is resource economics (Natural- or Güterwirtschaft), i.e., a process of relating scarce material means to virtually infinite ends, where means and ends formulated in material terms are conveyed within a hierarchical structure. In consequence, scarcities appear as material constraints, and the economy is a shortage economy (Kornai 1980). The logic of an exchange economy, in contrast, is the logic of a capitalist money economy.[3] In a money economy it is money that ultimately governs the economic decisions. Before the selective resource constraint becomes effective, the monetary constraint takes effect. Thus money economies are slack economies (Riese 1990). While customers queue for goods in command economies, goods queue for customers in market economies. Also the entrepreneurial behavior is different. In centrally planned economies entrepreneurial behavior is "paternalistic", the budget constraints are "soft". In exchange economies enterprises act autonomously and they are confronted by hard budget constraints. Their survival depends on earning a return on invested money, while the survival of enterprises in a planned economy depends on their subservience to superiors. While market economies organize themselves (i.e. are autopoietic systems) by producing information on scarcities by the process of exchange, command systems lack internally produced information on scarcities and must imitate market economies (by relying, e.g., on prices generated on the real markets abroad). Due to this systemic deficiency command economies are systemically inferior to market economies.

Different systems produce different results. Infrastructure in command systems is usually underdeveloped; industry, in particular heavy industry, absorbs, or absorbed, too high a share of investment and labor. Services are generally neglected. Production is "material extensive" (wasteful). Exports concentrate on energy, raw materials and semi-manufactures, prices per exported kilogram are very low.

5. Systemic Vacuum

During transition a systemic vacuum makes its appearance – for two reasons. The first concerns the type or character of transformation. The transition from a despotically organized society and command- to a market economy consists of two more or less seperate phases: a phase in which the old system is being demolished, and a phase in which the reconstruction of the civil society takes place. In between there comes into being a kind of no man's land, since communist systems defined themselves by, and are based on, the negation and destruction of civil socio-economic systems: collective ownership presupposes the confiscation of private property, and central commands were secured by prohibition or at least inhibition of contracting. Thus the market may self-organize itself only after the demolition of the despotic rule.

The second reason for the systemic vacuum refers to the relation between the complexity of the real system and the complexity of the communications (or control) system. These two dimensions, though not strictly comparable, should correspond to each other. The maturity (or level of development) of the first should fit the maturity of the second.[4] The development of capitalism may be visualized as an evolution wherein both dimensions evolved at about even pace, the speed of development being determined by the communications system. Conversely, communism, originally arisen claiming it would surmount the discrepancy between the stage of development of productive forces and production relations, did in actual fact create precisely that discrepancy – which has eventually led to its downfall. After the collapse of the command system its communicative system has broken down, plunging the East European countries into a systemic vacuum. Though there is no turning back, and whereas any continued struggling along under the command system would have led only deeper into the dead end, yet conditions are worse today than they were before the collapse.

It is obvious that relations between suppliers and customers established under the tutelage of central planners will only exceptionally survive the transformation of command to exchange communication. Not only have material relations between suppliers and customers often been imposed by force, and will therefore only exceptionally meet the requirement of voluntary exchange; but also the economic logic of decision making in command systems under shortage conditions was very different from considerations prevailing in modern money economies. Thus the network of purchases and sales will have to be tied almost from scratch.

The (re)construction of markets and fully monetarized economies is so difficult because two basic principles of evolution are violated:

- the correspondence rule
- the simultaneity requirement.

The corresponce rule is violated because East European economies are not primitive; they are, due to their degree of industrialization, highly complex worlds, which, in order to function, would require correspondingly complex communicative structures. The correspondence rule is closely connected with the simultaneity requirement, which makes sequencing so difficult, or even obsolete. In order to function, highly industrialized economies must consist of all elements characteristic of modern Western economies: In a modern economy there cannot be any functioning product markets without functioning capital markets, no development of intra-industry trade without the mutual penetration of firms' assets, no internationalization of commerce without internationalization of capital.

Markets organize themselves upwards from below, i.e. from simple to ever more complex systems, thereby consuming time. However, due to the high level of material structure in East European economies, markets are to perform a very complex assignment in former communist countries from the very beginning. They are infant and are being confronted with a task much too extensive and complex to be successfully tackled.

From the central idea that exchange is the basis for the evolution of rationality in society, follows the demand to set exchange communication into motion. To avoid misinterpretation, we would like to emphasise that by exchange communication we do not mean exchange just in the sense of barter or bazaar trading, but exchange operations appropriate to the complexity of Eastern European economies. Exchange operations would have to comprise all or virtually all markets necessary to deal with complex industrialized structures. This is the very meaning of the simultaneity requirement.

6. Some Further Developmental Blocks

While substantive concepts of rationality concentrate on how to secure equilibrium, whatever that may mean, from the systems theoretical approach one would be more interested in the question whether the system reproduces itself, i.e., whether exchanges (as communicative events) find follow-up events. Systems which – according to Luhmann (1984) – consist of communicational events, survive (i.e. reproduce themselves) by the latter being succeeded by other events. Command economies reproduce themselves by the periodic renewal of commands, exchange economies by ongoing exchange communication.

People participate in exchange only if they can expect gains from trade. However, the pattern of opportunities to trade is different in full-fledged market and transformation economies, mainly due to the still high frictions and/or transaction costs. The costs of exchange communication are several times higher in the transformation economies than in developed money economies. So we can speak of different system costs. We must remember in the first place that subjective assessments of opportunities concern not only the actual transaction but also the likelihood of successful follow-up events: what chances does the money price (revenue) promise to the seller, and what chances does the subsequent utilization of the good purchased offer to the businessman in his role as buyer? To evaluate this, one must come to an assessment of how "efficient" the "system" is. If "frictions" of the system are high, the seller (buyer) will be content only with a higher (lower) price, since frictions will probably eat up the advantages offered by the opportunities themselves.

Thus, badly functioning economies reduce the chances for exchanges, thereby blocking the evolution of the system. Not only must the network of exchange relations be tied almost from scratch, but also will the probability for each act of exchange be smaller than in established market economies. Transaction costs "consume" otherwise existing opportunities to trade. Higher transaction costs (or frictions) must be compensated by higher mark-ups on product prices, and by higher incentives for consumers. (If money doesn't buy, one must pay more to stimulate economic activity.)

In foreign economic relations economies can partly compensate the disadvantage of high system costs by undervaluating their currencies. The undervaluation can be interpreted as a general price discount, reflecting not only the lower quality of goods, to which undervaluation of currencies is mostly attributed, but also to compensate for systemic costs, i.e.

- the higher costs or frictions of each transaction,
- the higher risks and uncertainties with respect to the performance of the whole economy and also to the special business concerned,
- the narrower range of goods and assets which can be purchased.

Since it is the function of the exchange rate to secure "sufficient" employment, the exchange rate should be sufficiently undervaluated at any given time to allow at least 70-80% of the enterprises to survive. Too low a rate of exchange, on the other hand, would close the economy, instead of exerting steady pressure on it. From this follows that we may assume a "natural" rate of undervaluations for countries in transformation, implying, of course, the possibility for an overshooting undervaluation (case of Poland as to the first months of 1990).[5]

In turn, currency undervaluation may be partly compensated, or substituted by protectionist measures (as had already been demanded by F. List). His theory is as up-to-date today as it was 150 years ago. When economies are (fully) evolved (in the sense of high productivity or of a well functioning system), then liberalization has some advantages to offer; if their development is weak, complete liberalization will hinder their development rather than further it (Riese 1991).

As already mentioned, virtually all economic decisions in an economy are beset by uncertainty. Uncertainty increases exponentially with respect to the time for which the decisions are valid. Exchange transactions embracing investment activities (e.g. credit transactions, purchase of enterprises, large installations) are beset by worse uncertainty than those of so-called day-to-day business. But now, in the economies-in-transformation, the problem of uncertainty appears in a particularly acute form, because in them there's almost nothing that is "calculable": neither overall business cycle prospects nor inflation, neither exchange rate nor relative prices, least of all any other incidental risks. Clearly it is this uncertainty that has, on the one hand, led to the sharp decline of investments after the collapse of the planning economies, and that, on the other hand, can explain the trend to making a quick profit, to mere bazaar-fashion trading that transmits no impulse to production. Entrepreneurs appear ready, at best, by means of arbitrage transactions to draw a profit from existing bottlenecks, but are disinclined to invest, i.e., to enter into exchange operations which promise to bring a return for the money outlay only in years to come.

7. How Can Exchange Communication Be Set in Motion?

If exchange is responsible for the maneuverability, efficiency, in a word: high-grade rationality of modern economy, then the question arises, how the exchange communication can be gotten under way in a former command economy. Even when the exchange system is destroyed, it is easier to initiate exchange communication by means of units that have a "natural" identity. Whereas individuals or groups can more easily begin exchanges, because they possess at least a psycho-social identity, it is very difficult indeed for exchange to get under way within the state sector. This is because Socialism of the Soviet stamp rests precisely on the fact that the "businesses" had been replaced by one single economic organization.[6,7] The identity of enterprise(s) was thereby destroyed and the evolution of intra-economy environments (markets) was thwarted, obliterating the boundaries on which the rationality of modern money economies rests. The transformation consists in the restoration of the boundaries that make possible a clear differentiation of enterprises from their environment.

The disappointments from exaggerated privatization expectations prove that the key to the problem lies not in clarification of property rights as a legal act but in the evolution of exchange communication.[8]

A first institutional step would therefore be the transformation of state-etatist property into state owned joint stock companies to establish tangible ownership rights – sometimes referred to as "corporatization". Corporatization includes establishing a clear equity structure, vesting ownership of these shares in the government, and appointing suitable boards of directors to oversee the activities of the firms.[9] Commercialization means the thorough-going change from command and clientelistic relations between those corporations and the state to exchange communication. E.g., the state as the owner of the shares of the corporation ought to be interested only in profits (and therefore in the existence of the firm) but must not be allowed to instrumentalize its corporation for national goals. Monitoring of ownership rights should probably be exercised by a board of governors or a council rather independent from the minister in charge. The example of Austrian State banks and some Finnish State enterprises reveals, that these corporations would or could behave like private agents.

The formation of markets is supported by the opening of the East European economies to Western markets. The opening vis-à-vis the international product markets provides the economy of East European countries at one stroke with an "economy-internal environment" (as systems theory would call it), whereon the transactors can and must orient themselves. The foreign competition establishes transparent (or more transparent) criteria for the exchange communication of the enterprises; narrowing their price scope and enforcing quality improvements of output and trade; and thus reducing the power of the domestic monopolies. However, the opening must not be too radical, to allow domestic producers time to adapt to the new circumstances. Again, F. List is the proper reference in this context.

Due to complex logistics that is to be handled by large corporations, Western capital involvement is a sine-qua-non for the development of capital markets. Since markets are nothing but a network of exchange relations, and exchanges of complex bundles of assets (enterprises) will only be carried through between those partners who are able to organize and economize on these assets, capital markets will only come into being by the involvement of large Western corporations. The distribution or sale of vouchers or other titles as such will hardly generate a capital market.

8. Stabilization Versus Transformation?

According to our systems theoretical approach, stabilization of transformation economies in a broader sense can only mean securing the probability of follow-up exchange communications to give these ailing economies, with their inherent tendencies to collapse, some support or momentum. Therefore the economies in transformation need anything rather than a de-stabilization shock, such as, a sharp reduction of overall demand.

The rationale of stabilization in the sense of anti-inflationary policy derives from the fact that a liberalization of price formation translates the shortages inherited from the planned economy into price increases, possibly growing into a hyperinflation. That, however, imperils transformation as such; because high rates of inflation imperil not only the continuity of exchange communication in existing markets, but primarily they inhibit the evolution of markets. Therefore, anti-inflationary measures are needed. Of course, hyperinflation, or high inflation, must be brought under control. Though a certain reduction of demand to balance the state budget seems to be unavoidable, the appropriate measure would be a policy mix of a currency reform, fostering domestic competition, and launching an export drive on the basis of an undervalued currency; but reducing aggregate demand as little as possible.

However, it must be doubted whether the inhibition of inflationary tendencies by a reduction of overall demand is a suitable remedy to control inflation in an economy in transformation. That policy, advocated by monetaristically inclined economists (Lipton/Sachs 1990), and pursued by the Polish government, is clearly based on the theory that shortages are caused by overall excess demand, a thesis variously contested by Kornai (Kornai 1990). Shortages are not caused by overall excess demand in the economy, but are a consequence of commodity-based instead of monetary control of economic processes. Not until there are functioning money economies can shortages disappear, to be superseded by slacks. True, the degree of shortages may be lessened by reducing overall demand in the economy (just as, conversely, shortages may make their appearance in overheated market economies).[10] But a reduction of demand cannot eliminate "shortages" as syndromes of underdeveloped and therefore disturbed markets, overcoming the pathological manifestations of a centrally controlled planning economy. They persist below the surface, and only slowly can they be eliminated with the evolution of a money economy, while demand reduction in the short run leads to a downwards adjustment of supply and a resultant new shortage equilibrium with high inflationary tendency, demanding further restrictions. In other words: under the pretext of saving the market, stabilization foils the emergence of the market. The cure kills the patient, as Nuti (1991) puts it quite correctly.

Therefore, what is needed for economies in transformation is not a reduction of demand but measures aimed at strengthening the follow-up probabilities of the economic transactors' activities. Very disturbed and apprehensive economic actors will enter into follow-up transactions only if the expectations of profits are appropriate. But in the economy profits are assured not by reduction of demand but by a rise of demand after investments, and by increased exports. Seeing that production increase cannot be expected in the phase of "systemic vacuum", one should at least refrain from measures that further restrain investments.

In the long term, inflationary propensity caused by shortage situations cannot be checked by demand-side restrictions but only by supply-side expansion. Only when the actors engage in follow-up actions will the market evolve a constantly renewing and expanding network of exchange events, and only along this road can the price margin be narrowed by competition (i.e., by opportunities for exchange). The general conditions, though, must be circumscribed by a monetary policy that keeps money in short, but not too short supply. The (real) rate of interest in particular must be kept sufficiently low as not to inhibit investment activities in favor of monetary capital investments: profit expectations should be substantiated by gains obtained from current investments in the overall economy (Riese 1991, p. 13).

Unchecked expansion of the money supply will have to be inhibited mainly by the instrument of ordo-political measures. These include cuts of subsidies, which will compel the enterprises to restructure their communications away from paternalistic relations onto the market, i.e. to exchange communication – and that may be expected to lead to a hardening of the budget constraint – , and rigid credit control to foil corporatism, typical for planned economies, between (state) commercial banks and (state) corporations (Riese 1991, p. 3).

9. Country-Specific Conditions

Each country has its specific conditions of transformation. The systemic vacuum is the more menacing

– the higher its economy's already attained development. This is so because the discrepancy to be overcome between the complexity of the material structure and that of the system of communication is that much greater. At a primitive stage of technical development it is easier for people to find ways of muddling through;

– the more centrally organized the country, i.e., the further removed the economic system be from the institutions of a market economy, the more drastic is the separation of the phases of demolition and of reconstruction; and the more painful are the processes of demolition and of reconstruction;

– the more distorted the material structures, i.e., the more the structures in an East European country differ from those that would have developed under conditions of a market economy;
– the longer the duration of the communist regime. For the less is the accumulated experience and information concerning market economic institutions and behavior, and the less realistic is the public's picture as visualized by the market. That much about the socio-psychological dimension.
– The systemic vacuum grows with the cultural distance from the West. The less also the help and the degree of penetration to be expected from the West. Cultures once subject to the influence or in the penumbra of the Osman empire or of Russian Orthodoxy are mostly less Western oriented than those formerly under the influence of the Roman Catholic Habsburgs or of Protestant Prussia. And in addition, the further removed in space these countries are, the less will be the relative significance of interchange for their internal development, and the less may they count on Western direct investments.
– Finally, there is the consideration of the factors of overall economic skeleton (or "frame") conditions such as the degree of indebtedness, the present state of the balance of payments, of excess money supply, rate of inflation, and the question of the probity of economic, and transformation policy. However, the discussion of these factors must be left to more competent authors in this volume.

These are some of the aspects, by which the countries' chances for transformation may be evaluated. One may thus assess Hungary's institutional proximity to the Western system as "asset" per se, which might well counterbalance the burden of that country's relatively high indebtedness. Other countries start off with zero indebtedness; yet their position seems much less favorable.

Now, the more unfavorable the conditions just enumerated, the more likely will a dual economic structure, of bazaar type markets on the one hand, and rigid central control structures on the other, persist. The more difficult will it be to encourage the State enterprises to develop market-conform behavior and to generate the conditions for the emergence of a capital market. And, of course, the more painful will be the opening for a country, and the poorer its chances for attracting foreign capital.

10. Methodological Remarks

I am aware that my approach is quite unconventional. The attempt to define or deal with the problems of formerly socialist countries to the elimination of exchange communication, the objective of transformation as a resuscitation of such exchange communication into motion, must provoke opposition at any rate among academics; because in the academic tradition exchange stands for anything but a principle that might explain the dynamics, or the viability of economic systems. All else but not exchange is seen as the source of the market economies' vitality and superiority as against the planned economies. The negligent treatment of exchange in economic theory has a long tradition – which we cannot enter into here but have dealt with elsewhere. By elevating exchange to the role of key element we switch the problem of economy (of trading) and the whole issue of economics from the commodity-relatedly conceived (understood) ends-means sphere to society understood as communicative sphere; because society is communication. The author proceeds from the assumption that the modern economy is a self-organizing, highly complex, and reflexive system whose basic element is exchange communication. This methodological premise should be comprehensible: because the external conditions of the economy – preferences, production functions and furnishings, are not outwardly discernible as such. The sphere wherein economic actors act, and the media through which scarcities are (in a simplified manner) perceived, only comes into being through communication (and not before). The much quoted symbol of the invisible hand is a mere paraphrase, intended to save the economists from pondering on what is "market".

Acknowledgement

The author gratefully acknowledges financial support given by the Fritz Thyssen-Foundation (Germany).

Notes

1. We use the term Commodity Space Model to describe models of general equilibrium or neo-classical pure economics; these models are fully characterized by assumptions of convexly organized bundles of goods (preferences and production functions), and endowments.

2. " ... all 'social' content is squeezed out of individual behavior ... . The basic flaw in this model of perfect competition is not its lack of correspondence with observed reality; no model of predictive value exhibits this. Its flaw lies in the conversion of individual choice behavior from a social-institutional context to a physical-computational one. .. Frank Knight has consistently stressed, that, in perfect competition, there is no competition. He is, of course, correct, but, and for the same reason, there is no "trade", as such" (Buchanan 1987, 27/28).

3. Of course, one single act, or a few acts of exchange constitute capitalism as little as one swallow makes a summer. But the economic system of developed capitalism is founded on (world-wide) exchange communication, since only exchange is responsible for the emergence of money as a universal medium. Capitalism is the

"Gestalt" of modern economies; exchange is the basic element on which the system rests and from which it emanates in an evolutionary sense.

4. In a similar context Marx spoke of production relations and productive forces; Adam Smith emphasized that division of labor finds its limits in the extent of the market.

5. The present undervaluation of the Hungarian Forint, e.g., is less pronounced than that of the Polish Zloty or of the Czech Crown. As the reform proceeds, and frictions become less, currencies may revalue (in real terms) step by step.

6. For the distinction of society as organism and as organization, see N. Luhmann (1984).

7. If this replacement and the idea of communism was not fully realized, then because reality was too complex to make it possible for the whole economy to be organized under the roof of one giant enterprise.

8. It has become highly fashionable to demand privatization and to point out its beneficial effects for a modern society. But: what is private property without the simultaneously made assumption that such private property is an object of exchange communication, i.e., of exchange economy? In all economies a major part of private property is withheld from exchange communication (in that it is kept for personal use), and thus is of no relevance for the "economy". Thus one may doubt the usefulness of this approach, because, in a modern capitalist economy, property is primarily the property of values; and values result solely from exchange communication. In terms of Marx: in modern economies property (wealth) is not use value but value.

9. International Bank for Reconstruction and Development, 1991, p. 32.

10. To use Kornai's terminology: With existing "normal degree of shortages" "the almost insatiable demand" is repressed to the point that a shortage situation is turned into a slack in the economy. But that does not do away with the system-inherent causes of shortages in the sense of frictions.

References

Baecker, D. (1988), *Information und Risiko in der Marktwirtschaft*, Suhrkamp Verlag, Frankfurt a.M.

Hayek, F.A. (1952), *Individualismus und wirtschaftliche Ordnung*, Eugen Rentsch Verlag, Erlenbach-Zürich.

Hayek, F.A. (1988), *The Fatal Conceit: The Errors of Socialism*, The Collected Works of F.A. Hayek, Vol 1, Routledge, London.

Kornai, J. (1980), *Economics of Shortage*, 2 Vols., North-Holland, Amsterdam, New York, Oxford.

Lipton, D., Sachs J. (1990), "Creating a Market Economy in Eastern Europe: The case of Poland," *Brookings Papers on Economic Activity*. Vol. 1, pp. 75-133.

Luhmann, N. (1984), *Soziale Systeme. Grundriß einer allgemeinen Theorie*, Suhrkamp Verlag, Frankfurt a.M.

Luhmann, N. (1988), *Die Wirtschaft der Gesellschaft*, Suhrkamp Verlag, Frankfurt a.M.

Lüken-Klaßen, M. (1991), *Währungskonkurrenz und Protektion, Peripherisierung und ihre Überwindung aus geldwirtschaftlicher Sicht*, manuscript, Free University Berlin.

Mises, L. (1920), "Die Wirtschaftsrechnung im sozialistischen Gemeinwesen," in: *Archiv für Sozialpolitik*, Vol. 47, pp. 86-121.

Nuti, D. (1988), *Perestroika: The Economics of Transition Between Central Planning and Market Socialism*, Paper presented to the Conference on Plan and/or Market at the Institut für die Wissenschaften vom Menschen, Vienna, Dec. 15-18.

Nuti, D. (1991), *Sequencing and Credibility of Economic Reform*.

Riese, H. (1990), *Geld im Sozialismus – Zur theoretischen Fundierung von Konzeptionen des Sozialismus*, Transfer-Verlag, Regensburg.

Riese, H. (1991), *Transformationsprozeß und Stabilisierungspolitik*, manuscript, Wirtschaftwissenschaftliches Seminar Ottobeuren, September.

Simmel, G. (1900/1907), *Die Philosophie des Geldes*, Duncker & Humblot, 6th Edition, Berlin 1958.

Simon, H.A. (1978), "Rationality as Process and as Product of Thought," in: *American Economic Review*, Papers and Proceedings, Vol. 68, No. 2, pp. 1-16.

Streissler, E. (1980), "Kritik des neoklassischen Gleichgewichtsansatzes als Rechtfertigung marktwirtschaftlicher Ordnungen," in: E. Streissler und Ch. Watrin (Eds.), *Zur Theorie marktwirtschaftlicher Ordnungen*, Tübingen, pp. 38-69.

Part Two
Specific Issues of Transition

5

PRIVATIZATION OF BIG ENTERPRISES IN CENTRAL AND EASTERN EUROPE – GENERAL CONCEPTS AND THE HUNGARIAN EXPERIENCE

Gábor Hunya

The break-through of the idea of privatization in Central and Eastern Europe was achieved during 1990. As the discussion about fundamental questions tended to be rather time-consuming, there is still very little practical experience concerning the privatization of big state-owned enterprises. The legal framework of a market economy could not be created overnight. Initial plans for a rapid privatization proved to be over-simplistic, questions of procedure have put a rather big burden on inefficient bureaucracies. Most of the governments forecast an acceleration of the privatization of large industrial enterprises only for 1992, and this does not mean that all the conceptual questions will be settled by that time. As a matter of fact, advantages of learning by doing could already be greater than fruitless debates of an often more political than theoretical nature. Practical implementation is overdue, while the discussion on the coupon method in Czechoslovakia or on the role of the State Property Agency in Hungary deepens instead of making room for temporary compromise.

Confusing terms still hinder a clear insight into the problem of privatization. This chapter proposes to introduce the notion of levels of privatization in order to clarify advantages and disadvantages of alternative strategies. Scientific and political discussion on privatization in recent times has shifted towards favoring overall (wholesale) privatization as opposed to direct sale or case-by-case privatization. We shall argue that, if a government takes privatization seriously, advantages of a case-by-case solution can be considerable.

This paper will rely on familiarity with privatization strategies described elsewhere and does not aim to give a detailed analysis of national programs.[1] The case of Hungary will be discussed at greater length to show how initially simple concepts improved in the process of privatization based essentially on direct sale.

1. Conceptual Considerations

1.1 Privatization and Capital Accumulation

Privatization proper tackles the transfer of state (public) property into the hands of other, "private" actors. The broader sense of the term includes the emergence of new private firms as well, because new firms also diminish the relative share of state-owned actors in the economy. In fact; setting free private entrepreneurial initiative has led to the most manifest development of privately owned business in Eastern Europe. Some private firms in Poland or Hungary are already well established medium size companies. Although this paper will deal with privatization in the narrower sense, it is necessary to keep in mind, that from the viewpoint of systemic transformation, the dominance of private property is of vital importance, no matter whether achieved by new firms or by the transformation of old ones. As for privatization proper, its speed is determined to a considerable extent by the speed of domestic capital accumulation and spread of managerial skills.

There is a rather fast capital accumulation in the hands of those using all possible means for going into private business. Political stakeholders of the old regime as well as black marketeers might make up a considerable portion of new entrepreneurs, although their real share may be smaller than believed. If new businessmen make their business grow and establish legal corporations, they develop managerial skills and are subject to the general rules of the economy in their environment. Privatization strategies usually overlook that privately founded firms, if getting strong, can play a growing role in taking over state-owned assets. Privatization in the broad sense helps in solving the problem of deficient purchasing power for state assets, a central issue in the debate on privatization in the narrow sense. Let us mention two examples from Hungary. The state agricultural farm of Nyirlugos, after going bankrupt, was sold for Ft 400 mn (US$ 5.3 mn) to a private businessman.[2] Four major private industrialists made an offer to the State Property Agency to take over Hungary's electronics mini-giant, Videoton, for Ft 3 bn (US$ 40 mn).[3] The business success of these businessmen allows them to raise enough credit in addition to their private capital to finance a major takeover. (It is a different point that the government demands a price double of this offer.) The problem of lack of purchasing power for taking over state-owned assets is thus smaller than suggested by advocates of free distribution of shares or vouchers.

1.2 Depth of Privatization

Privatization in its narrower sense can be specified along two lines: the kind of property to be privatized, and the depth of privatization. As for the object of privatization, it is useful to differentiate between (1) small units in services, trade and production, (2) big industrial companies, (3) land, and (4) housing. These categories of property usually call for different privatization techniques, attract different types of investors, and their privatization takes different lengths of time. This paper deals only with the most difficult task, the privatization of big companies, "large-scale privatization". The amount of state assets and their concentration in big companies deters individual investors, who dominate the privatization process of the other three categories of assets. Therefore a more complex technical device is necessary.

It is large privatization where the depth of privatization can be considered a central issue. Most authors use the term privatization for a multitude of operations: transferring state property into investment funds, distributing vouchers to the population, public and private offering, etc. These steps call into being owners with different scopes of independence from the state, at different levels of direct control over property and management. It means that the depth of privatization achieved by these actions differs. Reorganizing state-owned companies into corporations is an even lesser degree of privatization, because in many cases the state remains the sole owner. Privatization is completed in depth, when private investors exercise control over the management. Artificially induced transfers of property achieve a lesser level of privatization than sales to risk-taking owners. Levels of privatization can be defined as follows:

1. Identification of property. A considerable confusion of property rights exists in a post-socialist economy. Public ownership means no specified owner: central and local state administrative units, workers' councils and enterprise management can hold some of the rights. Legal clarification is a necessary and mostly not a very simple prerequisite of transferring property to new owners.

2. Surface privatization is a possible term for ownership transfers to some transitional owner. This can include several possibilities.

(a) Mutual cross-ownership of a company by other companies, all state-owned in the final instance.

(b) Issue of privatization vouchers. This means free or almost free distribution of property to the population. They function as real property only if changed for shares subject to capital market operation.

(c) Transfer of property into property management funds, holding companies and other institutional owners established by the state. Even if founded as private corporations, they can be under a considerable state influence at the initial stage, as a matter of fact they could be similar to former ministries. Even if their stocks are broadly spread, like those of funds managing freely distributed shares of the population, shareholders will not have effective control.

3. Deep privatization, or privatization proper is achieved when private physical or legal persons obtain a dominant position. A capital market develops where some of the capital is constantly evaluated. Takeover by a private firm or introduction on the stock exchange with listed securities are the possible forms.

At present, a mix of these levels of privatization as well as socialist type enterprises co-exist in each East European country. Traditional enterprises themselves can be at various levels of legal and political autonomy. It is widely suggested that an end be put to this situation by transferring property into funds and vouchers, that is, privatization on the surface.

The place of "corporatization" needs special attention in our analysis. This is the process of transforming traditional socialist enterprises into corporations. Identification of property and formal evaluation of assets (based on book value) take place at this stage, but also some forms of surface privatization can be introduced. If corporatization changes only the legal status of the enterprise and leaves all the property with the state, this action falls under identification of the owner in our classification. This was the case in Czechoslovakia and in Romania, where enterprises were transformed into corporations, the state being the only shareholder. The transformation law in Hungary on the other hand gave way to corporatization including some surface privatization, usually cross-ownership, but also real transfer of property into joint ventures with foreign firms. Corporatization is a generally necessary step in order to increase the autonomy of companies in relation to state organs in countries where earlier reforms did not take place. It is also necessary to give state-owned and private economic agents an equal legal standing. It is for the latter reason that corporatization on a massive scale must be carried out sooner or later. If it is done step by step, conditions of value assessment can be developed and de-monopolization and internal reorganization can be carried out.

As corporatization identifies the state as the only owner of the company, the rights of workers' councils in Poland and Hungary cease to exist. An important political task of corporatization in these countries is in fact the dismantling of the over-powerful workers' councils. Preferential access to part of the shares (10-20%) in the course of privatization is offered to workers as a compensation. In countries with formerly strict central planning, Czechoslovakia and Romania, corporatization increases the influence and the responsibility of managers. They become more powerful, enabling them to resist centrally initiated programs (e.g. privatization), but they are also left holding the inherited financial and technological burden. In Czechoslovakia, the big drive for corporatization died both because ministries saw managers grow too powerful and because the Slovak government stopped it when seeing that most of the Slovak military industry would go bankrupt if traditional channels from the budget go dry.

The distinction between active and passive owners is rather important in the East European context. Both surface and deep privatization can lead to dispersed and to dominant owners. In the case of surface privatization (dispersed vouchers, dominant funds) both tend to be passive. Deep privatization calls into being active owners. Having in mind that Central and East European economies are not yet market economies, privatization itself should foster the transformation of the whole economic system. Therefore privatization by broad distribution of shares, like in an American public company[4], would not suffice to change the companies' behavior: a major partner with business experience is usually necessary. Only dominant owners can provide companies with improved production and sales strategies.

The distinction between surface and deep privatization is useful also to develop the discussion on wholesale versus step-by-step privatization.[5] The speed of privatization is usually considered to be the main issue in this debate, without taking account of the different levels of privatization the two methods can achieve. Accelerated privatization can only aim at some surface solution, whereas patience can result in deep privatization. If surface privatization is aimed at on a massive scale, it must be kept in mind that it is only an interim solution. The final, basically the active owner is not yet found, and it must be made sure that the process is carried on.

If mass-scale surface privatization is not aimed at, primary state property dominates rather long; and solutions must be found for its interim management. It would certainly hinder the transformation process if these assets were kept under the control of traditional state institutions. In this respect, criticism of case-by-case privatization by the advocates of wholesale privatization is well founded. Until case-by-case privatization reaches a company, it must prepare privatization strategies, and its assets must be managed by independent organizations. The forms of assets management of state property can actually take rather similar forms, e.g. holdings, as surface privatization. Asset managing organizations can have the task of managing property, and privatize it mainly by public or private offering. This solution is included in the recent privatization program of the Hungarian government. (See 2.3.) A useful distinction can be made between etatist and private forms of asset management. The Hungarian solution with several competitive asset managers conforms more to marketization than the big monopoly funds to be established in Czechoslovakia and Romania according to these countries' laws on privatization. The mass privatization program being introduced in Poland calls into being asset managers with a status between the competitive and the etatist solution.

It can be concluded at this stage that neither the wholesale, nor the case-by-case method will lead to active ownership on a mass scale very rapidly. Transitional solutions are necessary and unavoidable. The fierce debate between strategies based on wholesale versus piecemeal privatization is not justified, taking into consideration the level of privatization they achieve.[6] Privatization is not an overnight act, but there are certain economic developments capable of accelerating this process.

1.3 Changing Economic Environment

The present state of the economy, political debates and social demands influence privatization strategies beyond economic considerations. The economic environment is determined by the level of transformation, macro-economic stability, and the performance of the given economy. It is not the aim of this paper to prove that Central and East European economies are in a rather tense situation in all three respects.[7]

Stabilization policies as well as external shocks have led to declining performance, high inflation, and growing unemployment. For most countries, debt servicing puts a major burden on the balance of payments. Under these circumstances, the market value of firms to be privatized can decline and be below the level possibly achieved in a healthier economic situation. (This is why the State Property Agency of Hungary could not yet sell any of the twenty companies included in the first privatization program. See 2.1.) Lowering the price, wholesale surface privatization, and company initiated privatization are the possible answers of policy-makers. At the same time, widespread efficiency problems and the need for new enterprise strategies have fostered the recognition of the need for privatization both among state agencies and companies.

Most of the written discussion on privatization quoted in our references is based on the experience of 1989 and early 1990, when economic transformation was at a rather early stage in Central and Eastern Europe. The massive decline of production witnessed in 1991 had not yet set in. An everyday pressure of economic survival was not obvious at the enterprise level. The legal environment of a market economy was also much less developed than at present. A rather slow pace of privatization, giving enough time for individual and social learning (Kornai 1990), was just as much justified, as the criticism of the behavior of enterprise management and the fear of workers' councils (Lipton and Sachs 1991) as obstacles of privatization.

In 1991 companies have been exposed to rather harsh shocks all over Eastern Europe. The loss of the Soviet market as well as ongoing austerity policies have put them under considerable pressure to undertake major reorganization in order to survive. The need for new markets and for additional capital has increased. Traditional solutions via state interference having mostly come to an end, managements had to take their own initiatives. Corporatization carried out in Czechoslovakia and Romania have created the necessary legal frameworks for enterprise autonomy also in formerly centralized countries. In some cases, certainly more widely in Hungary, workers' representatives have also learned that wages and work-place depend on the survival of the company, demanding major sacrifices on their part. Politicians hesitant about the merits of privatization have changed their attitudes, seeing the pressing necessity for making the economy more efficient. An interest in speeding up privatization in 1991 can be observed all over the region. Still, there are questions to be answered concerning the sequence of policy measures.

1.4 What to Do First: Restructure or Privatize?

A major argument for general surface privatization is, that it includes all companies, no matter whether good or bad.[8] True, direct, deep privatization strategies prefer economically sound companies, because those needing major restructuring or even rescue operations can only be privatized for a rather low or no price. State agencies interested in maximizing revenues of privatization would try to sell the better companies first. Nevertheless, the problem of inefficient companies must be solved sooner or later, either by restructuring via investing and/or contraction, or through bankruptcy. If privatization agencies were not hesitant in selling inefficient firms at no price to investors ready to carry out the necessary restructuring, privatization could get momentum and the state could get rid of a task it is generally unable to solve. The state must of course get guarantees from the buyer that restructuring will be implemented, and the amount of investment and the number of jobs to be saved must be included in the deal.

In case of most forms of surface privatization, the responsibility for restructuring is shifted, together with property management, to institutional investors. The problem remains, but it will not be a burden for government agencies. One can doubt that assets managing organizations will possess the management skills necessary to solve the problems of unsound companies. They can, of course, rely on the services of management advisors and consulting firms, but then their way of operation would be even less different from a state privatization agency and its property managing subcontractors. The capitalization of ownership funds is another problem. They will own good and bad firms simultaneously, which provides a considerable risk to the funds' creditors. There is also some danger that they try to keep inefficient firms alive to the detriment of good ones, just as former branch ministries did.

State organs have repeatedly tried to invest and restructure first and sell later in order to increase earnings from sale, and dictate reorganization in order to save jobs. Many such attempts failed, because new state authorities were just as incapable of guiding efficient transformations as were the former branch ministries. The Treuhandanstalt (Trustee Corporation) in East Germany changed its strategy early in 1991, allowing more sales at low prices and let the new owners make the necessary restructuring. In Hungary the recent failure of state agencies to save the prominent electronics firm Videoton or the steel mill Ozd can lead to similar conclusions. It is actually up to the privatization authorities to apply a strategy of selling bad companies at a low price. Not doing so is not an inherent shortcoming of case-by-case privatization strategies. Advocates of wholesale privatization on the other hand do not say how institutional investors, or widespread public owners, would manage the reorganization of inherently inefficient, loss-making companies.

Consultant firms usually suggest making companies profitable first and selling them afterwards.[9] They usually fail to pay due consideration to the fact that East European public agencies lack the experience and funds to do this and are forced to get rid of companies at a lower price.

Problems with administrative restructuring of firms are considerable in an economy in transition. There is no functioning market which in the West sets the functional environment for public decision-making. The danger of voluntary decision is even higher, taking into consideration the inherited personnel and structure of state organs in former socialist countries. All this does not necessarily mean that restructuring should take place only in the course of privatization. Corporatized state-owned companies must be given the freedom and the incentive to take steps to improve their efficiency. Property managers must in turn see to it that this restructuring is not done to the detriment of the value of property. Government organs will have a crucial role in setting up a friendly environment for company initiated reconstruction. Unfortunately, they dream more of maintaining their outdated influence over companies than they care to learn methods of market-conforming industrial policy.

1.5 Managers in the Process of Privatization

Politicians have to win workers and managers as well as the most active part of the population for the transformation of the economic system and for privatization. The need for politically viable privatization strategies has dominated the debate on privatization for over a year now. Much of the discussion between advocates of gradual, but deep privatization and proponents of general, surface privatization use in the main political arguments.

In the process of systemic transformation, managers and workers share the common interest of maintaining the existence of their workplace, and there are other issues where they oppose each other. Transformation is a personal shock for both managers and workers. Both are exposed to a possible loss of their job. Managers must develop very different skills from those they could rely on in the former system. And, even if they are able to do so, they can lose their jobs for political reasons. In countries with no past de-etatization process, the low level of managerial skills, the lack of personnel for these positions is a major obstacle to systemic change. (Most obvious examples are Romania and the Soviet Union, but East Germany and Czechoslovakia also face the problem to a more serious degree than Hungary.)

Liberalization and privatization in an economy makes sense only if lower level actors of the economy are able to use their autonomy and take the initiative themselves. The transformation imposed from above should be slow enough to make managerial adaptation (by learning or by replacement) possible. It must of course be rather quick also, to come to a more efficient economic system in a relatively short time. The actual speed of transformation cannot be prescribed, but a favorable condition for the social learning process must be created.

In Hungary a considerable number of the active managers are trainable for new skills and there is also enough talent available to challenge them from outside the companies. It is certainly more difficult for Czechoslovak company directors to adapt to market circumstances, and there is also less possibility for replacing them by already educated managers. In Romania the corporatization of state-owned enterprises had to rely on rather uncooperative directors. They expressed their wish for further state support, and the government was only too happy to keep the economy under control via new institutions (e.g. by nominating members of management councils from the ranks of the ministry bureaucrats). This suggests that privatization cannot, in fact, be faster than the development of a new managerial class. But it should certainly not be too slow as personal, social, and economic adaptation cannot take place without experiencing pressure.

There is also some possibility of importing skills. Western consulting firms play a major role in advising Hungarian companies and the State Property Agency. The mutual funds proposed for a wholesale privatization in Poland would also employ experienced foreign managers.

In Romania the whole concept and legislation of privatization was worked out by foreign consultants.

The development of a local managerial staff can actually be rather rapid. Domestic people are trained by foreign investors and consulting firms for the jobs they provide, and management courses are financed by a number of organizations. The emergence of private business paves the way not only for capital accumulation but also to developing managerial skills. Practice shows that people in private business are reluctant to transfer their skills to state companies unless these companies are offered them for sale.

In countries less prepared for privatization because of a massive lack of management skills and social acceptance, the temptation to impose privatization by force of law is big for the government, if it wants to (and with an eye on international creditors certainly has to) speed up the transformation process. To be sure, law may remain on paper, if the content of new legislation is alien to general social behavior. In the extreme case of Romania[10], the privatization law is not accepted by the public, ill prepared economically – a legal act understood and initiated only by top level technocrats eager to prove their determination to advance privatization. Considering its practical content, the Romanian law is one on property management funds and does not provide a practical strategy of privatization. Company managements' freedom to take the initiative is extremely restricted.

Too high a level of managers' autonomy can at a certain point block privatization, as managers would fear that powerful owners would introduce a controlling mechanism over management. In Hungary, managers were skillful enough to increase their autonomy versus state organs, and to use company councils having got some of the ownership rights in 1985 to support their power. It has turned out that corporatization and cross-ownership can be understood as a further step to get the companies away from state and under managerial control. A next logical step along this line was the attempt to transfer the company under full private control of the managers.[11] Several such instances were recorded in Poland, Hungary, and Yugoslavia, as the extreme cases of spontaneous or "nomenklatura" type of privatization. As a reaction, post-communist political leaders introduced more state control, that has unnecessarily slowed down privatization. Policy-makers should neither serve nor block management initiatives in the course of privatization. Well established and feasible rules of privatization should direct managers' initiative towards accepting private owners' control over their activities.

In 1990 there was a tendency to stress the negative effects of managerial privatization ("nomenklatura privatization"). The most simple way of control was the increased role of state supervision. The Polish law on privatization (July 1990) basically blocked privatization initiated from below. In Hungary, the law on the State Property Agency (March 1990) had the task of putting managerial privatization under close control and establish a state organ to initiate privatization. This legislation has slowed down privatization in both countries.

As a reaction to bad experience with both the former nomenklatura and state agencies, the idea of wholesale privatization became popular in 1990. As a result, all state property would get non-state owners within a short time. Mistrust against managerial privatization seems to be the major driving force for developing a privatization strategy like that of Lipton and Sachs (1991). We think that much of the criticism was directed against the wrong target. Managers do not initiate privatization for selfish reasons mainly. Their dominant driving force in Hungary was the needed access to outside capital, vital for technical reconstruction and market adaptation. Obvious misuse of power occurred only in the case of retail companies. In industry, corporatized firms did increase their chances of survival.

Finding the most efficient proportions of initiative and control as well as the best controlling institution is certainly a difficult task. As Borensztein and Kumar notes, no ideal solution exists in the West either. In the East, identifying the owner, and surface privatization would certainly make the position of managers more clear. But until deep privatization is achieved, legal and political balancing actions must be found so that managers can be subject to control and yet can be initiators of the privatization of their firms.

1.6 Public Shares (Vouchers)

Political efforts must be made to overcome public indifference, at worst hostility towards privatization, and to win the cooperation of the employees of specific companies to be privatized. Free distribution of shares appears as the extreme case among such efforts, because it abandons any state revenue usual in case of a sale. To be sure, dispersed ownership of free or almost free shares will not create active owners nor change employees' traditional interest as wage earners.

Free distribution can have various weights in privatization programs. Those that provide an initial solution for de-etatization without taking an interest in active owners include some part (e.g. 20%) of the stocks into a distribution scheme. The Czechoslovak plan of Triska differs in this respect, that individual citizens are placed in an active position of turning their vouchers into shares.[12] Their public bidding and later stock market operations would fix the actual value of their investment points. Polish and especially Romanian plans place the individual in a rather passive position as shareholders of investment funds.

The idea of total distribution of all the stocks among the population or the employees (except for the sophisticated employee share ownership program (ESOP)) is basically alien to privatization connected with a transition to market economy. No risk-taking owners emerge in this process. The idea comes from a collectivist attitude and is maintained in countries where the advantage of real privatization is not understood by the population. Jassin writes[13] that the idea of total "privatization" to the employees of enterprises dominates thinking in the Soviet Union. The transfer of "public" property to the "working people" is demanded by the democratic opposition, whereas selling such assets is associated with the selfish interest of the party-state bureaucracy. Jassin cannot, for the moment, see any politically feasible alternative to "people's enterprises". In Romania the debate was more complex, but the idea of free distribution of property to the whole population was most popular.[14] Trade unions were in favor of it, and opposition parties use it to maintain popularity. The government's privatization law suggested free distribution of vouchers in the value of 30% of the companies' assets. The opposition would have favored at least 50%, for other than economic reasons. Public shares will be managed by administratively created mutual funds, and sell real company shares to citizens within five years.

In Poland the massive privatization program taking shape in mid-1991 will introduce public shares managed by property managing funds, a kind of institutional investors advocated by Lipton and Sachs. Citizens will get the shares of these funds and not of the companies themselves. As the initiators of this program were rather concerned about the negative effects of dispersed, passive ownership, these funds would be run on a totally commercial basis, preferably led by experienced foreign managers.

The idea of free distribution appeared in the Polish debate not as a value in itself (equal distribution of wealth), but as a necessary complementary way to other methods, when total surface privatization of property became the aim. Another 10% of the assets will be given to the employees, again free of charge. This gesture can be understood as a compensation for disbanding the rather powerful workers' councils. Social peace, acceptance of privatization, is to be bought through gifts from the state. The positive social effect depends in the Polish case on the level of gratefulness of the population and employees for these gifts, and not on the future return on the distributed shares, nor on any personal skills. As there is a high possibility of no return on many of the shares, free distribution has its good logic.

Foreign consulting firms active in Central and Eastern Europe[15] believe that the voucher and ESOP methods would not hinder the privatization of the remaining part of the assets, if they are kept within minority limits. They find that investors are much more concerned with the supply than with the demand side of the privatization deal. Unclear property rights, government strategies, poor performance of governments in their primary tasks, unstable financial situation of firms are their major concern. Considerable risk is attached to these issues, making calculation of the return rather difficult for external investors. All these problems appear more strikingly in practice than in theoretical debates.

1.7 Debate on Privatization Escalates

In the middle of 1991, Czechoslovakia, Poland, Romania, and Croatia have a comprehensive law on privatization. Hungary has a set of earlier legislation allowing privatization. With most of the legislative work done in Eastern Europe, programs and methods of privatization do not seem to be consolidated. As practical implementation draws near, problems accumulate. There is also a growing fight for decision-making rights between government organs involved.

The idea of almost free distribution through privatization by vouchers (coupons) has been disputed in Czechoslovakia even after the law on big privatization was passed (February 1991). The voucher scheme appeared in earlier solutions as a key instrument for privatizing large state enterprises. The public bidding for equities on vouchers would have had a central role in establishing the market value of a firm – a rather funny method in a country eager to introduce market economy. The method was criticized both by researchers and government officials. An advisor to the Czech Ministry of Privatization told the Euromoney conference in June that coupons will be used to sell the rest of equities having remained with the state after a core investor has bought the majority of a firm.[16] The Czech Minister of Industry declared, that of the 859 firms to be privatized in the first wave of the large privatization only 290 will use the coupon method, and the majority of firms will be offered to real investors.[17] It is Minister of Finance, Václav Klaus, who insists on the key role of privatization by vouchers.[18] It remains to be seen, what weight the 1000 companies will give to vouchers in their privatization projects to be worked out by the end of October. (The deadline seems to be most unrealistic for serious work.) Anyway, the Ministry of Finance is the final instance if disputes emerge. Practice up to now also contradicts the preference for coupons. All the privatization cases up to now have been in form of foreign takeover, as in the case of the Volkswagen-Skoda deal. A role for coupons in these cases is excluded. In future the partial privatization by coupons will rule out 100% direct sale to an outside investor. Initially, part of the shares will be rather dispersed. For some firms even the majority of the shares will be distributed. One can expect a rapid concentration process of shares when the stock market will begin to function. One may find in a few years, that egalitarianism in ownership will give way to concentration.

In Poland, most of the privatization cases up to mid-1991 were privatization by liquidation. The official name is rather misleading, as it is a kind of leasing. Usually small and medium size firms are taken over by their management and workforce, who have to make a 30% down payment, and the rest of the value of the firm is paid by instalments in five years. The new owners will assume full rights over the property only after the price has been fully paid. Some 600 firms were sold in this way until September 1991.

The economic restructuring program of the government adopted in May 1991 will give more scope for takeover (called the "capital path of privatization"). Mass-scale corporatization and privatization should take place rather fast. The first 400 enterprises have already been selected. Mass privatization will aim at finding intermediary owners, and distribute part of the property between workers and mutual funds with public shares. Individual company strategies will certainly conflict with generally set rules. Already at the start of the program, the number of the companies involved was reduced to 240 because the others were found to be economically weak. Another restriction of the program was provided by the oncoming elections. It seems that only the setting up of the funds will take place this year. The method of shares distribution will depend on the future parliament.

Both Czech and Polish recent developments show a more complex approach than earlier programs. Recent debates in Hungary are worth analyzing at greater length, as they deal with practical details not yet faced by other countries. This country is also unique in the sense that no privatization law proper exists. A set of other laws accepted at different stages of the transformation process governs privatization.

2. Hungary: A New Privatization Strategy Emerging

2.1 Historical Background of the Hungarian Debate

It is a Hungarian specificity that there has been no corporatization campaign like in Czechoslovakia and Romania. Already under the former regime companies gained considerable independence from the founding and owning state agencies in running their business. Corporatization emerged as a necessity only in connection with privatization. In most other Central and East European countries where formerly the state organs had close control over enterprises, a level of enterprise autonomy already enjoyed in Hungary was introduced by corporatization on a mass-scale. The first version of the Hungarian transformation act valid in 1989-90 made corporatization only possible if external resources were attracted into the company. This could be the case only with prosperous companies. In the typical case, parts of companies were corporatized, where the mother company became one of the shareholders together with other domestic state-owned companies and/or foreign participants. In our framework this was a kind of surface privatization.

Beginning March 1990 all property related operations were put under the control of the State Property Agency (SPA). This certainly led to more bureaucracy, but also to a higher professional level of transformations and more state revenue. In August 1990 the government published its program on "Ownership and Privatization."[19] Small privatization and privatization initiated by the SPA were started in the following months.

Two basic forms of privatization existed. One was initiated by companies and since spring 1990 had to be piloted through a lengthy approval process at the SPA. During this process alternative solutions were tested, which necessarily took a long time. The other form was privatization from above, meaning that the SPA has selected a number of companies to be privatized. Privatization from above started late in 1990 with first letting consulting firms compete for the concession of privatization. This is also no fast procedure. Twenty companies, with assets worth Ft 70 bn (US$ 920 mn) and aggregate turnover of Ft 100 bn (US$ 1.3 bn) a year were selected for the first privatization package in September 1990. Consultants were selected through December, but until the end of May only half the companies agreed with its privatizer upon the method and schedule of privatization. None of the companies have been sold yet.[20]

Foreign consulting firms and investment banks play a crucial role in the privatization procedures. The SPA hires them as privatizing agents, for 3-5% of the revenues for their services. They not only make an assets evaluation and provide a strategy, but use their world-wide networks in finding foreign investors. Their credibility makes up for the low possible quality of assets evaluation based on socialist book-keeping. Until the end of May 1991, Ft 153 mn in hard currency was paid to consultants. The revenues of privatization were actually achieved also in hard currency, to about 90%.

The year-end plan of the SPA for privatization revenues 1991 is Ft 40 bn sales receipts minus Ft 2 bn spent on fees.[21] Until end of August Ft 16 bn were obtained, suggesting that it will be impossible to meet the target in the remaining four months.[22] It is most likely that the government will have to be satisfied with less income from privatization than originally estimated. Hungary is the only country in Eastern Europe where state revenues from privatization play a crucial role in the privatization strategy. The effort of raising revenues is certainly justified in a country with high government indebtedness, but maximizing income could slow down privatization.

2.2 Political Background of the Hungarian Debate

Substantial political compromise was necessary to win the coalition partners forming the government for speeding up privatization in 1991. Concessions had to be made to the Independent Smallholders' Party with a controversial law on re-privatization through compensation bonds. Bonds will increase purchasing power, especially for land and for items in small privatization. It is an achievement mainly of the opposition, and of the government specialists, against most leaders of the coalition parties, that no restitution in kind will take place, and compensation will be only partial in order to reduce the possible inflationary impact. A concession to the Christian Democratic Party is a law on partial, physical restitution of property of the churches. Only buildings where charitable or educational activities are to be conducted can be returned.

Workers' participation in big privatization was another disputed issue. Preferential sale of 10% of the shares to the employees is now promised as a concession to the national-populist wing of the strongest party of the governing coalition, the Hungarian Democratic Forum. The legalization of ESOP with the possibility of total takeover by employees has been a major demand of the Trades Union Confederation and will also be accepted.[23] The earlier aim of privatization specialists in Hungary to privatize nearly exclusively by direct sale or stock market has been modified in the political discussion. It remains to be seen if achieved compromises will satisfy the most active political forces, and if this will lead to more popularity of the privatization process. The compromises are not too high a price for a more conciliatory environment, where mainstream forms of privatization can function more efficiently. It can also lead to the opposite situation, if it turns out that popular expectations of some redistribution of wealth in favor of losers at nationalization and workers were raised in vain.

There was one compromise that could not be achieved: differences between the Government Commission on Privatization, the SPA and the Ministry of Finance over matters concerning competence could not be eliminated. A privatization strategy was worked out by a special government commission in May this year, but before the matter had been discussed, the Ministry of Finance prepared its alternative strategy.[24] The government commission had initially adopted a standpoint similar to the Ministry of Finance, wanting to cut back the licences of SPA.[25] Later the chairman of the commission changed his mind.[26] The committee's program now tends to maintain the SPA with its basically contradictory mandates of owner, property manager and privatizer, but to separate the activities under the supervision of SPA. While the government was unable to come to terms over the privatization program until mid-September, SPA has since May been working according to principles set by the government commission's program. The finally accepted government program was largely in line with the commission's text, but left some of the disputed questions open.[27]

2.3 The Government Commission's Privatization Program

The new privatization program gives a full account of different types of property and their possible future owners. As for the companies under big privatization, majority state and majority nationally owned companies are listed, all others not named can be fully privatized to anyone. The list of enterprises to remain in majority state hands has been reduced during the debates of the program to some twenty state agricultural farms and a dozen industrial and trade companies of "national importance". The category where majority Hungarian national participation is required is of similar size. (How the nationality of capital can be secured in a rather interwoven partnership is not clear.) There are altogether 8 enterprises on the list where 100% state ownership should be maintained (they are in the field of arms trade, forestry, and publishing.) Railroads, mail services, telecommunications are in the category of state ownership to at least 51%. It is a positive feature of the Hungarian program, opposed to other countries, that the exceptions are listed, not the preferential cases. This means that all companies not on the list can start working on their privatization. If they fail to come up with an acceptable strategy by the end of 1993, they will be put under direct state control. The list of companies is still under debate, but the majority of the cases is not disputed. According to the final government program, those properties that will not be subject to privatization in the near future will be managed by a state institution separated from the SPA. The latter will be manager and privatizer of property subject to privatization within two to three years. These units will be worth up to half the economically utilized property of the state.

The aim of the present program is to make company initiated privatization more simple, to determine which companies should not, or only partially be privatized and, third, to determine tasks and time horizons. In the future, corporatization should gather momentum, and by the end of 1993 all enterprises should be in corporate form. This means that the task of property management will increase in the coming years. No holdings established by the state, like in some other counties, but management concessions will be used for the interim management of non-privatized property. For the part of property, where only partial privatization is foreseen, ownership rights should be left with a new State Participation Institute, separated from the SPA.

The law on the Privatization Agency (No. 6, 1990) foresaw the separation of privatization and assets management. It took over a year until the SPA began looking for asset managers. These organizations should get a certain part of the profit of the state shares if they work according to established conditions. They would be authorized to look for new owners of the property but not to sell it without the agreement of the SPA. Assets management will be necessary in the cases where in the transformation and privatization process the SPA was not able or did not want to get rid of a certain portion of the stocks. At the beginning, as only a small part of the about Ft 2000 bn state-owned assets has been corporatized, the value of assets having remained with the SPA is moderate, Ft 95 bn at the end of May 1991.[28] There will be several portfolios offered for future assets managers. The first portfolio offered was not taken, because future managers found the conditions too tough, and risks too high.

Privatization would be accelerated by the following new forms:

- Outside investors' proposals to buy companies against their own wish (unfriendly takeover) can be addressed to the SPA.
- Companies can initiate their own privatization by approved consultants. Only firms up to 500 employees can manage their privatization in this way. SPA intervenes only if laws are disobeyed in the final agreement.
- Initiatives of other companies shall go through a more rapid procedure of approval, so the SPA promises.
- Employee participation and management buy-out becomes possible.

When any of the forms of privatization is applied for, 10% of the shares would be transferred to the employees under preferential conditions. ESOP would make it possible for employees to become majority shareholders of their firms. A basic principle for ESOP will be, that only if the majority of the work-force wants to participate can the project start.[29] There is no discount on the price of the share, but a ten-year credit is provided. The larger the credit needed by a person, the higher a share of own capital is required from the participant (up to a credit of Ft 5 mn, 2%, between 5-10 mn, 15%, between 10-50 mn, 25%). This means that for shares worth Ft 5 mn, Ft 100,000, or about 8 months' average wages is required, rather a high sum at a time when half the families use up their salaries by the end of each month. The interest rate on the credits will be preferential, 3/4 of the prime rate plus the bank's margin of 3-5%. Even under such conditions, banks will find these operations highly risky. The expected return is not high enough in case of a standard firm in manufacturing. There are two possible categories where ESOP could work: in very good firms, where recovery of the investment has a good chance, and in very bad firms, where the purchase price is low and the employees have no other choice in their desperate position, facing a close-down. Further discussions with the trade unions are going on to introduce more attractive terms.

2.4 Companies Entangled in Conflicts

In the course of privatization there is a tense relationship between participants because of conflicting interests.[30] The state wants to sell assets and maximize income, whereas the company wants additional capital and know-how. The companies themselves want to sell assets which have become redundant, thus finding additional resources. The company is interested in renewing the management, if need be, but not in politically motivated personal changes initiated by the political leaders. Further conflict arises in the field of environmental protection.

The state is interested in closing down the most polluting activities, or it may force the companies to finance protection arrangements. The latter on the other hand want to maintain profitable production also to the detriment of the environment, and ask for public money to finance environmental protection. A main question is the employees' attitude to privatization. They are usually not involved and lack information about the future of their work-place. A further collision of interests arises between the company's central management and individual outlets. Privatization as a whole or in parts both lead to a selection of the subsidiaries by their present and future efficiency, whereas their past contribution to the company's results can be very different. The company's management has constant conflicts within itself (between interests of subsidiaries, advocates of alternative partners and reorganization programs), and with the workers, as well as with local authorities.

Despite all the tensions, there is a growing interest of the companies to be privatized. Restrictive monetary, budget and fiscal policies, and the contraction of East European markets, are the main driving force. Both the financing of production and the sale of products have been put under most serious monetary restrictions. Attraction of additional capital has become the main objective of short-term strategy, a matter of survival. This is now possible only by undergoing privatization and the related reorganization.

The low level of efficiency of Hungarian companies hinders investment. The yield on invested capital is on the average 5-8% per year, about one quarter of the level a foreign investor wants to achieve.[31] Hungarian firms must therefore promise a higher share in the return than in the invested capital. In such case the SPA does usually not accept the companies' plans for privatization and wants a higher income for itself. The outside investor is thus put into an uneasy position in the conflict between his future partner and the SPA.

2.5 Some Lessons from the Hungarian Case

Summing up the Hungarian case, one can state that the existing legal framework still does not provide a blueprint for civilized conflict management. The interests of companies and SPA have come closer to each other, but still differ considerably. State level commitment to accelerated privatization is insufficiently supported by procedural possibilities. Different government bodies have not been able to come to terms on scopes of decision-making. In spite of this, domestic and foreign interest in buying state assets does not decrease. The demand is bigger than supply, therefore free or almost free distribution of property or re-privatization are out of place.

As for the privatization strategy pursued in Hungary, a return to privatization initiated from below can be observed. If the self-privatization program of smaller firms is successful, the method will be extended to larger ones. A case-by-case privatization would certainly be rather slow if initiated from above, but relying on the initiative of the companies affected, the process can be speeded up considerably. Asset managers working on a competitive basis and interested in privatizing the property they were entrusted with seems to be a possible solution for managing the non-privatized part of state assets. It would seem desirable that state authorities confine their activities to legal supervision and policy matters, and leave practical privatization to private institutions.

3. General Conclusions

(1) Strategies of privatization differ in the depth of privatization they can achieve. Surface privatization makes sense only if concurrent efforts are made for finding final owners for deep privatization. The emergence of concentrated and active owners must be a goal of the transformation process. General surface privatization is not a compulsory intermediate stage in privatization. A case-by-case approach is unavoidable if deep privatization is to be achieved. Managing state assets by specialized firms can take forms similar to surface privatization, but would not hinder the appearance of concentrated investors.

(2) Countries at different stages of transformation to market economy can have different privatization paths. Practical considerations and political debate lead to a more complex strategy of privatization than foreseen. Strong political groups try to influence privatization to their benefit, satisfying some of their demands seems to be unavoidable. Property rights must be clear before transfer of property to other owners can begin. Therefore restitution demands, landownership, and the property of communities must be settled. Social peace usually demands the inclusion of employees among the possible new owners of state-owned enterprises, even if they are not in a position to buy shares at public offerings.

(3) Privatization strategies must take into account to what extent state economic agents are ready to be privatized. Enterprise autonomy must be ensured even for non-privatized firms, e.g. by corporatization. Cooperation of the state privatizing agency or ministry with the management of corporatized enterprises is unavoidable. Privatization can be accelerated only if companies have a direct interest in undergoing this process. Shrinking East European markets and tight mone-

tary and fiscal policies have increased the pressure on enterprises to restructure and also to get privatized.

Notes

1. See e.g.: Stark, D. (1991), Institut für Angewandte Wirtschaftsforschung; Shearman & Sterling 1991; Grossfeld, I., Hare P.

2. *Magyar Hírlap*, July 29, 1991, p. 9.

3. *Magyar Hírlap*, September 7, 1991, p. 1.

4. The difference between public companies in East and West is discussed by Ellermann, D.P., et al., (1991).

5. Case-by-case privatization was defended by Kornai (1990). Wholesale privatization was strongly advocated by Lipton and Sachs (1991), and also Sachs in *IMF Survey*, May 27, 1991. A comparative analysis is provided by Bornsztein and Kumar (1991).

6. As an example of the magnitude of the debate, the resignation of the Slovenian Vice-Prime Minister Mencinger can be noted. He had a case-by-case privatization program, opposed by the new advisor to the government, Jeffrey Sachs, who advocated a wholesale solution. *Neue Zürcher Zeitung*, April 24, 1991.

7. For a recent analysis see: Gabrisch, H., et al. (1991).

8. Lipton-Sachs (1991), p. 35.

9. *Euromoney conference* (1991).

10. National Agency for Privatization (1991).

11. Móra, M. (1991) calls this process pseudo-privatization, we think it is a kind of surface privatization.

12. Stark, D. (1991) duly stresses the importance of this aspect.

13. Jassin (1991).

14. For a description of the debate see Hunya (1990), and Apáthy et al. (1991).

15. The opinion of this rather influential group could be tested at the Euromoney conference on privatization in Budapest. (*Euromoney conference* (1991)).

16. Francis (1991).

17. Quoted in *Der Standard*, August 10/11, 1991, p. 19.

18. *Hospodarské Noviny*, September 2, 1991, p. 4.

19. See the draft in *Figyelö*, Nos. 34 and 35, 1990.

20. *Stockmarket Kurír*, August 15, 1991.

21. *Magyar Hírlap*, June 24, 1991, p. 1.

22. *Magyar Hírlap*, September 13, 1991.

23. *Figyelö*, No. 21, 1991, p. 3.

24. *Figyelö*, No. 28, 1991, p. 1.

25. *Figyelö*, No. 8, 1991.

26. *Figyelö*, No. 21, 1991, p. 3.

27. *Napi Világgazdaság*, October 1, 1990.

28. *Figyelö*, No. 26, 1991, p. 1.

29. *Magyar Hírlap*, July 5, 1991, p. 8.

30. Csillag, I., in *Magyar Hírlap*, July 1/2, 1991, p. 8.

31. *Magyar Hírlap*, July 1-2, 1991, p. 8.

References

Apáthy, E., Csillag, I., Hunya, G., Mizsei, K., Pataki, I., Réti, T. (1991), *Privatizáció Kelet-Európában* (Privatization in Eastern Europe), Atlantisz, Budapest.

Borensztein, E., Kumar, M.S. (1991), "Proposals for Privatization in Eastern Europe," *IMF Working Paper* No. 36.

Ellermann, D.P., Vahcic, A., Petrin, T. (1991), "Privatisation Controversies in the East and West," *Slovenska ekonomska revija*, No. 1-2.

Euromoney Conference (1991), *Privatization and Corporate Finance in Eastern Europe*, Budapest, June 19-21, Proceedings.

Francis, C.J. (1991), "The Role of the "Privatisation Voucher" in the Creation of a Czechoslovakian Capital Market," paper presented at the Euromoney Conference *Privatisation & Corporate Finance in Eastern Europe*, Budapest, June 19-21.

Gabrisch, H., et al. (1991), "System Transformation Under Severe External and Internal Shocks. The Economic Situation in Early 1991 and Outlook 1991," *WIIW-Forschungsberichte*, No. 173, June.

Grossfeld, I., Hare, P. (1991), "Privatization in Hungary, Poland and Czechoslovakia," Centre for Economic Performance, *Discussion Paper* No. 1, May.

Hunya, G. (1990), "Privatisierung und Privatwirtschaft in Rumänien," *Südosteuropa*, 11-12.

Institut für Angewandte Wirtschaftsforschung, Berlin (1991), *Mittel- und Osteuropa, Beiträge zu den Wirtschaftsreformen* No. 3.

Jassin, E. (1991), *"Zum heutigen Stand des Entstaatlichungs- und Privatisierungsprogramms in der UdSSR,"* (About the Present State of De-etatization and Privatization Programmes in the Soviet Union), unpublished manuscript, Moscow.

Kornai, J. (1990), *The Road to a Free Economy Shifting from a Socialist System: The example of Hungary*, W.W. Norton and Company, New York.

Kozusnik, C. (1991), "The strategy of privatization," in: *Prognosticky Ustav CSAV: Prognosticke reflexe problemu prechodu k demokracii a k trzni ekonomice* (Future oriented thoughts about the problem of transition to democracy and market economy), Prague, May.

Lewandowski, J., Szomburg, J. (1990), *The Strategy of Privatization, Economic Transformation*, No. 7, Gdansk, October.

Lipton, D., Sachs, J. (1991), "Privatization in Eastern Europe: The Case of Poland," in: *Slovenska ekonomska revija*, No. 1-2.

Móra, M. (1991), "Az állami vállalatok (ál)privatizációja," ((Pseudo-) Privatization of state enterprises), in: *Közgazdasági Szemle*, No. 6, pp. 565-584.

National Agency for Privatization (1991), *Commercial Companies Privatization Law No. 58*, August 14, Bucharest.

Shearman & Sterling (1991), *Central European Privatization: Legislation and Experience*, paper presented at the Euromoney Conference "Privatization & Corporate Finance in Eastern Europe", Budapest, June 19-21.

Schmieding, H., Koop, M.J. (1991), "Privatisierung in Mittel- und Osteuropa: Konzepte für den Hindernislauf zur Marktwirtschaft," *Kieler Diskussionsbeiträge*, No. 165, Institut für Weltwirtschaft Kiel, February.

Stark, D. (1991), "Privatization Strategies in East Central Europe," *Working Papers on Transition from State Socialism*, Cornel Project on Comparative Institutional Analysis No. 6.

Triska, D. (1990), *Privatization in post-communist Czechoslovakia*, unpublished manuscript, Prague.

6

CZECHOSLOVAKIA'S AGRICULTURE AT THE CROSSROADS

Zdenek Lukas

1. Introduction

Following the Communist takeover in Czechoslovakia the agrarian economy had virtually been entirely collectivized on a compulsory basis by the beginning of the 1960s. Around the end of the 1970s/beginning of the 1980s the gigantomania in Czechoslovakia's agricultural sector had reached a climax when the average size of a state farm constituted around 7,000 hectares and the estate of an Agricultural Production Cooperative (APC)[1] measured around 2,600 hectares. The enormous size of the individual enterprises, whose internal units (processing plants) were intended to cooperate closely, brought about an extreme escalation in transport costs. These cost increases were further aggravated by the second oil crisis (in 1979). As a result, even the operative running of the various agrarian enterprises became increasingly cumbersome.

In the 1980s, the average size of the APCs remained more or less constant: in 1989 this was about 2,630 hectares. In the case of the state farms the size decreased slightly, down to 5,922 hectares in 1989. Of the total agriculturally productive land in Czechoslovakia, 64% is owned by the APCs, 31% by the State and only 5% by private landowners. At the end of the 1980s the agricultural share of the net material product constituted around 7%. At about 10% the farmers, too, represented a relatively small portion of the total of economically active persons, compared with other East European countries. On the other hand, the share of investments in agriculture, at 14%, represented a rather high level compared with total investments in the CSFR. Agriculture, as well as the whole of the Czechoslovak economy, faces a period of fundamental change.

2. Agricultural Policy

The apparently visible successes of Czechoslovak agriculture in the 1970s, which precipitated an improved food supply for the population, can in essence be traced back to the following causes: on the one hand, a few regulations were retained which had been introduced in 1966 in the course of the economic reform (fewer directive production targets); on the other hand, livestock production increased due to fodder imports and high investments in the agricultural sector, as well as various agricultural subsidies (for inputs, buying prices for agricultural products, tax concessions, negative taxes for retail trade); whereby, however, the costs per production unit rose sharply.

This thoroughly positive development, as seen by outsiders, led the government to start up a few "experiments" in the farming sector in order to "perfect the industrialization of agriculture." The degree of concentration of the agrarian concerns increased further, due to the amalgamation of the APCs and state farms; the already small private sector (small-scale and part-time farming) was considered superfluous by the authorities, and was thus allowed even less room to maneuver.

Thus, the self-suffiency of the farms decreased and the scarcity of basic fodder for the necessary additional manufacture of animal products in socialized farming increased. Due to the rapidly escalating fodder imports, these factors placed a considerable strain on the nation's balance of trade. This was a signal for the communist government to start thinking less ideologically and more pragmatically.

The average size of the socialized farms decreased moderately and in particular the private livestock breeders gained more freedom of movement. The retail price increase for meat in 1982 not only lowered both demand and meat production, but it also brought about a drop in fodder imports.

Nevertheless, in the 1980s the agricultural lobbies in Czechoslovakia proved their strength: all agrarian subsidies and the wages of the farmers increased. Thus for example, in 1986, a farmer in the socialized farms earned on average 2,986 Crowns (Kcs), whereas the total average monthly wage in Czechoslovakia came to Kcs 2,927. By 1989 this difference had increased to Kcs 135 in favor of the farmers, who were now earning Kcs 3,258 per month.

The "velvet" revolution (November 17, 1989) however, brought no immediate soft alternative to the further development of farming in Czechoslovakia. Although it is essential that costs and labor be reduced in the future, agricultural subsidies are at present decreasing too rapidly and too greatly to allow farming a chance to adapt to the new economic conditions.

3. Agrarian Trade

Czechoslovakia is traditionally a net agricultural importer; the proportional significance of agrarian trade decreased during the course of the 1980s. Whereas the share of agricultural exports in total Czechoslovak exports came to 8.6% in 1980, this share had fallen to only 6.1% in 1988. The share of agricultural imports fell from 16.1% in 1980 to 11.5% in 1988.

During the so-called "normalization process" in the 1970s, when the directive planning system was reintroduced, the Communist government attempted to pacify the population with adequate food supplies. Thus, by the beginning of the 1980s, the production and consumption – particularly of meat – had increased significantly.

Meat production rose in the socialized farms, mainly due to imported fodder (especially grain feed); simultaneously, in the suppressed private sector (e.g. small and part-time farmers, hobby breeders) meat production decreased, particularly in the mid-1970s. This led to a significant decline in consumption of self-produced agrarian goods in rural areas, and additional meat production requirements for the rural population, which was again realized through further fodder imports.

This spiral culminated in a significant escalation of grain fodder imports up to 1-2 million tonnes (net) and eventually also – as a result of the rise in the grain price on the world markets – in a rising trade deficit, which at the turn of the 1980s came to US $ 1.5 bn per annum in the agrarian sector.

In 1982 the government found a way out of this precarious predicament: retail meat prices were increased by up to 50%, depending on the type of meat. This brought about a drop in the demand for meat which in turn facilitated a cutdown of internal meat production, and at the same time allowed a reduction in grain imports. In 1985 the CSFR was currently importing only 0.25 million tonnes of grain. On the other hand, (net) sugar exports fell and (net) potato imports rose, reducing the agricultural deficit only moderately compared to 1980, i.e. to US$ 1.2 billion. In 1986, 1987, and 1989 it also remained basically unchanged. A moderate rise in the 1988 deficit (to US$ 1.5 billion) can be traced back to the increased grain imports (0.75 mn t).

4. Subsidy Policy

Due to the lack of transparency in a planned economy, it is much more difficult to conduct an examination of agricultural subsidization than in a market ecomomy. When price formation is determined by costs, the prices are essentially fixed by a markup on costs. In theory, this makes all branches of the economy equally profitable.

Before 1989, farming in particular (and to some extent, other areas of the economy as well), profited from the various tax concessions, (e.g. lower social security payments, lower taxation on earnings), as well as from various kinds of direct subsidy (such as for inputs and buying prices for farmland), and from the fact that a ground rent in its classic form did not exist.

By roughly converting to the Producer Subsidy Equivalent(PSE) common in the West, which compensates the farmers for the differences between the lower world market prices and the higher domestic prices for agricultural goods, the agrarian subsidies in Czechoslovakia in the 1980s increased to around 135% in 1986. As a comparison, agrarian subsidies (PSE) in 1986 amounted to 76% in Japan, 52% in the EC, and 50% in Austria. This peak in Czechoslovakia was followed by a moderate decline in agrarian subsidies, which accelerated perceptibly after 1989. In 1990 total agrarian subsidies had dropped to 35%.

On July 9, 1990, the deciding factor regarding food subsidies (the so-called negative turnover tax) was abolished. This led to a price rise of 25%, for which, however, the Czechoslovak population was fully compensated by a monthly sum of Kcs 140 per head. In spite of this price compensation, the price rise is expected to cause a drop in the excessive consumption of certain foodstuffs. Currently, foodstuffs are on the one hand very expensive for the Czechoslovak population, but on the other hand extremely cheap for – generally German and Austrian – tourists in consequence of the very favorable exchange rate for these tourists.

According to the principles of subsidy policy, the reform of the agrarian market in 1991 should in particular serve to moderate the fluctuations between supply and demand in both domestic and foreign trade. This was supposed to be achieved by support buying, processing, storing, export and import of agricultural goods, as well as by other measures. The main instrument of this reform was meant to consist in guaranteed minimum buying prices for selected agricultural goods through the Market Reform Fund. However, as all subsidies were halved in 1991 (down to approx. 16%), the new Market Reform Fund has only partly fulfilled its task.

This applies also to further subsidies, intended to promote and foster the following areas within agriculture:
- establishment and development of private farms,
- schooling, science, research, information, and counseling,
- temporary subsidies for the privatization of agricultural concerns,
- structural changes and social policy,
- protection and/or improvement of farmland funds,
- environmental protection programs.

Thus it can be observed that agricultural subsidies are being too rashly and too greatly reduced, thus failing to give farming a chance to adapt to the new economic conditions. A shrinkage process in both agrarian production and labor areas is certainly necessary; however, it should be a lengthy process, as may be learnt from experience in the West, where agricultural subsidies and various protective measures even today play a certain role in guaranteeing the continuity of agricultural production. A sudden cutting of subsidies could lead to over-indebtedness of most farms and to a collapse of the agrarian economy.

The rapid phasing out of subsidies has pushed the Czechoslovak agricultural sector into a crisis. Besides this, the decline in real income of the Czechoslovak population has led to a drop in the demand for food, which in turn resulted in the sales crisis for the agrarian enterprises. Furthermore, agriculture suffers from the government's lack of clear concepts concerning an agricultural policy. Interest in establishing private farms was only modest in Czechoslovakia in 1990 and 1991: here, lack of capital, knowhow and willingness to take risks, as well as the uncertainty concerning ownerships structures, and the current market crisis played an important role.

5. The New Land Act

The Land Act, which was passed, with some months' delay, on May 21, 1991, and became effective on June 24, 1991, concerns about 4 million citizens (almost 25% of the whole population). It has continuously been dealt with in the media, and was most extensively discussed in parliament. Originally, this Act was intended to regulate both the restitution to the original landowners, and also the transformation of the communist-type Agricultural Production Cooperatives (APCs) into market-conforming economic units.

However, the main point in dispute between the government draft bill and a draft by a group of three members of parliament causing the mentioned delay was the problem of how to assess the contribution to the enterprise assets made by the landless laborers who had been long-term members of the APCs. Also the question of how to transform these farms into market-conforming economic units remained a bone of contention between the two sides of the dispute.

In order to reduce the contentious issues to a minimuum, the questions of transformation and of church property were left out. Thus the Land Act exclusively governs the restitution to original landowners. The problems of transformation of agricultural production cooperatives are to be solved by a second law, to be finalized during the fall of 1991. The Land Act lays down the rights and obligations of the (original) owners, usufructuaries, and tenants of real estate. Persons other than owners are only conceded the right to make use of the land if they have concluded a contract to that effect with the owner.

February 25th, 1948 was taken as the key date for restitutions.[2] Landowners who had been expropriated before that date will hardly be allowed to benefit from this law: and that applies to roughly one quarter of all agricultural land confiscated from Germans, Hungarians, and "collaborators" in 1945, immediately after World War II. This is a problem that puts some strain on the relations with Germany, and has led to delays in concluding a German-Czechoslovak State Treaty. In July 1947, in a "second stage of land reform", the expropriation of large estate landowners was started. After the communist take-over of power (February 25, 1948) the land was at first distributed to individual peasants, but already in 1949 the first round of coercive collectivization had set in. By the early 1960s more than 90% of the land was already in state or quasi-cooperative possession. This means that the restitution now in the offing will bring benefits mainly to the individual peasants whose fields and forests – up to 50 ha – were forcibly absorbed into communist-type cooperative ownership in the latter period.

However, the Land Act allows for exceptions from the February 25, 1948 deadline. Indeed, one paragraph (9, section 1b) concedes restitution also to some large landowners who, after revision of the first land reform (Law no. 142/1947), had been expropriated without compensation. But in such cases, the upper limit of restitution is 150 ha of agricultral land or 250 ha of total area. These will apparently be subject to the jurisdiction of the two federal republics.

Restitution in the agrarian sphere will benefit only Czechoslovak residents. However, the law concedes to the parliaments of the Czech and the Slovak republic the prerogative to make separate decisions concerning restitution for some CSFR citizens of German or Hungarian nationality.[3] Claims for restitution must be entered by or before the end of 1992. The property affected comprises more than half of all agricultural land and forests, as well as other means of production (buildings, machinery, animals), farmyards, and dwellings.

If restitution of land and property to the original owner is impossible (e.g., because the property disappeared in the course of urbanization), he must be compensated by receiving other land or must be otherwise indemnified. Many of the former owners will be forced to become lessors: for instance, in the case of objects housing health installations, schools, sports grounds or diplomatic missions, the owner will be constrained to enter into a lease contract of 10 years' duration with the present user.

In the new Land Act no answer is given concerning the future organizational and ownership structure in Czechoslovak agriculture (e.g. share of state farms, church farms, APCs, and private farms). Therefore the agrarian enterprises will have to live with the uncertainty of their future form until the passing of the new Agricultural Transformation Bill.

6. In Search of a New Agrarian Policy

During all of the time following the "velvet" revolution, agriculture in Czechoslovakia has been suffering from a lack of clear concepts. This applies especially to the two most important aspects of agrarian policy: the degree of subsidization, and the degree of self-sufficiency of the agrarian sector. The first ever comprehensive plans concerning future agrarian policy drawn up under the new political and economic conditions were presented by the Ministries of Agriculture of the Czech and Slovak republics in October 1991.[4]

The intended agrarian policy assumes a decline in food consumption between 1990 and 1992, which over the whole of Czechoslovakia could average as much as a quarter as compared with the end of the 1980s. Because the degree of self-sufficiency with regard to food production is to be reduced in the long term to approximately 85-90%[5], an even greater reduction in domestic agricultural production than in food consumption (approx. 25%) must be assumed during the transitional period towards this limit. Indeed, if this plan is carried through, a severe shrinking process or the closing down of numerous farms must be reckoned with.

Similarly to other aspects of Czechoslovak economic policy, the suggested agricultural programs of the Czech and Slovak federal republics differ from one another. The main differences concern the agrarian subsidies, which are to be more generous in Slovakia than in the Czech republic. At a first glance, the Slovak demands seem justified on account of the fact that climate, weather and soil conditions are on average worse. It is nevertheless uncertain whether the Slovak republic's budget would be capable of financing this generous agricultural program.

7. Prospects

Like the entire economy of the CSFR, agriculture faces fundamental changes. The speed with which appropriate measures are taken up, and the extent to which they are realized, depends also on the ex tent of political changes, on the present state of farming, as well as on the availability of financial means. Thus it can be expected that the currently oversize farms in Czechoslovakia will be subdivided into smaller units (which would still be large farms); a splitting up into family farms (under 100 ha) would nevertheless be unlikely to take place.

With the formation of a new agrarian system in the CSFR it should be taken into account that a free agricultural commodities market does not exist in West European countries either, but rather that there is a considerable amount of state intervention into agriculture and marketing by various means (agricultural subsidies, protectionism, etc.). However, judging by first experiences in Czechoslovakia, liberalization of the agricultural commodities market in the transitional phase will probably be considerably greater there than in Western Europe. Thus there is a danger that even agrarian enterprises that would be perfectly capable of transformation will be unable to survive, and that there will be no appropriate financial means (earned in other sectors of the economy) available for importing agricultural products.

Obviously a step-by-step reduction of labor in the Czechoslovak agricultural sector (a significant proportion of its employees are of retirement age) is urgently required in order to raise productivity and profitability to a Western level. The main point, though, is that the tempo of the transformation in the agricultural sector should be secondary to the maxim that the costs to the whole economy should be as far as possible kept at a minimum. The danger that many of the redundant farm workers will be unable to find employment in other sectors of the economy is equally great. Unemployment in Czechoslovakia is already significantly on the increase as a result of the laying off of industrial workers.

During this imminent transition to a new agricultural system, it must also be taken into consideration that Czechoslovakia is presently starting out from a situation completely different from the situation before the compulsory collectivization. It is now starting out from an artificially created system in which not only gigantic agrarian enterprises have developed, but also huge corporations in both the upstream and downstream spheres of agriculture.

It would therefore be a mistake, after the compulsory collectivization up to the 1960s, to now introduce compulsory (re)privatization. Obviously privatization is necessary in Czechoslovakia's agricultural sector, or at least in the upstream and downstream areas of farming; whereby, however, various forms of ownership are conceivable. In this way, the costs of the transition to a new agrarian system could be kept within limits.

It is to be expected that after the disintegration, or rather transformation of the current socialized enterprises, various new economic units such as commercial companies, stock corporations, and private farms will emerge. A special role will be played here by the agricultural cooperatives, who will have to make the transition from a state-directed form to a Raiffieisen-type form[6]. Nevertheless, they would have to undergo a "slimming diet" as far as their size is concerned. Besides this, a great amount of diversification can be expected within the cooperatives, stretching from classical cooperatives through various transitional forms to lessors' cooperatives.

The future path of agrarian policy will largely depend on the intensity and speed of the transformation process in the upstream and downstream fields of agrarian economy. Judging from first experiences, privatization in the upstream spheres of agriculture in particular will proceed fairly slowly. In order to become competitive, these spheres (which produce inputs for the agricultural sector) would need a great deal of capital – which the domestic economy does not have. Other countries, however, remain hesitant in this particular area.

For agriculture to function properly, market institutions must be established parallel to an agricultural commodities market, in order promptly to provide the agricultural enterprises with the latest information about changes on the market. A great deal needs to be done in this field in Czechoslovakia, where there was no agricultural commodities market in the past. In addition, the farmers' cooperatives must be newly organized. In any case, the fate of Czechoslovak agriculture will be primarily shaped by the country's subsidization policy.

It is known that Czechoslovakia is taking steps towards a rapid incorporation into the EC. It is therefore to be expected that the future agrarian policy of the CSFR will also be influenced by the agrarian system of the European Community. Even so, an attempt to copy the agricultural model of the EC would be both wrong and unrealistic.

Direct imitation could be considered wrong because the current starting conditions for the transformation in the Czechoslovak agricultural sector itself, as well as in the upstream and downstream areas of its economy, are completely different from the conditions which existed in the past during the formation and development of the agrarian system in Europe. On the other hand, to follow the example of generous financial support of West European agriculture would be totally unrealistic, because, as mentioned, financial means are scarce in the CSFR. In the case of a future EC membership however, the other EC countries would be obliged to provide financial aid.

Assuming that the subsidization of farming is slightly raised from the current low level, a few comparative advantages of Czechoslovak agriculture (such as cheap labor and good conditions for the production of a few traditional agricultural specialties) could be retained or otherwise utilized. In this way, unemployment in the agricultural sector and the drift from the country to the cities could be kept under control, and the increasing social tension in rural areas as well as the dangers faced by this young democracy could be lessened. Furthermore, Czechoslovakia could thus continue to be a self-sufficient producer of basic foodstuffs and a moderate exporter of a few agricultural specialties.

When approaching the EC, however, a basis of mutual concessions would also be necessary. Up to now, Czechoslovakia has largely liberalized its agrarian trade, although access of Czechoslovak agricultural goods to the EC market remains extremely difficult. The concept of a completely liberal agrarian market in Europe is at present unrealistic, nevertheless the raising of import quotas or more relaxed customs regulations for East European agricultural products into the EC countries could speed up the reform process in Eastern Europe.

Notes

1. The communist-type Agricultural Production Cooperatives could scarcely be distinguished from state farms. The State also limited them considerably, by means of plan targets and various prescribed norms, in their decisions concerning production structure and quantities. The theoretically existing property rights of the original landowners, who had brought their land and other business assets into the APCs, could not be made effective.

2. *Zemedelské Noviny*, May 23, 1991, p. 4.

3. *Der Standard*, May 22, 1991, p. 19.

4. *Hospodarske Noviny*, October 22, 1991, pp. 1-2.

5. *Zemedelske Noviny*, October 29, 1991, p. 4.

6. These are cooperatives which concentrate on buying, selling and other services and/or on financing within the agricultural area.

7

ECONOMIC TRANSITION IN BULGARIA *

Ilse Grosser

1. Introduction

The following analysis of economic transition to a market economy in Bulgaria is based on a breakdown into the mutually interconnected aspects of systemic transformation and macro-economic stabilization. The systemic transformation embraces the creation of legal foundations for a market economy and the putting them into practice, the establishment of market structures and institutions, among them privatization of the economy, and steps of liberalization in the sense of replacing direct (vertical) control mechanisms by market (horizontal) coordination mechanisms. Stabilization policy is targeted on eliminating macro-economic imbalances by fiscal, monetary and wage policy measures. The behavior of the economic agents is in interaction with both these realms of transformation policy: while, on the one hand, their behavior is influenced by systemic transformation and stabilization policies, it is, in turn, a factor in shaping their course and results.

In early 1991 Bulgaria joined the group of countries embarking on the road of so called shock therapy (cf. Section 2), though setting out from far more unfavorable starting conditions (cf. Section 3). In accordance with the priorities of actual transition policy we shall first summarize liberalization measures (as part of systemic transformation) and stabilization policy (cf. Section 4), then separately treat systemic

---

* The present article, completed in September 1991, is a translation of the paper "Bulgariens Wirtschaft im Übergang", contributed originally to the volume *Bulgariens Weg zur Demokratie*, edited by Wolfgang Höpken (Südost-Institut), Munich (in print).

transformation in the institutional sense (cf. Section 5). Finally we shall summarily evaluate the transformation processes according to their first results (cf. Section 6).

2. Outline of the Current Economic Program

At the beginning of 1991, the first multi-party government, constituted at the end of 1990, backed by agreements arrived at between the country's dependable political and social groupings and the International Monetary Fund (IMF), embarked on an Economic Program characterized by the features of a so called shock therapy, comparable to programs initiated in Czechoslovakia (also in early 1991) and Poland (beginning 1990). In the case of Bulgaria these were the steps that – at a relatively late stage – brought a clear decision to proceed with transition to a market economy.

The overriding aims of the monetaristically oriented Economic Program are the elimination of chronic excess demand, and first steps in the direction of market mechanisms, in other words, transformation from a supply constrained to a demand constrained economy. Accordingly, measures of liberalization and stabilization take precedence over institutional reforms in both program and practice of transition policy. In February 1991, far-reaching price and foreign trade liberalization measures were simultaneously put into effect, and (limited) internal convertibility was introduced in conjunction with a drastic depreciation of the lev. To combat the inflationary pressure set free by these measures, the country's monetary, credit, fiscal, and wage policies were realigned onto an extremely restrictive course (cf. 4.1 and 4.2).[1]

The Program was based on the expectation that following the unavoidable inflationary shock and drop in output, induced by austerity policy, stabilization would set in very quickly. It anticipated already for the second half of 1991 a monthly rate of inflation of only 1-2%, and the onset of recovery in some sectors of the economy. Also for the second half of the year, following the hoped-for macro-economic financial stabilization, cautious supportive measures for supply side reactions (such as a judicious relaxation of credit- and employment policy measures), and an acceleration of institutional reforms were envisaged to ensure the productive utilization of idle resources.

In the course of the following months it became clear that these first programmatic assumptions had been over-optimistic – quite in keeping with what had been experienced in connection with Poland's stabilization program.[2] The economic forecasts for 1991 had to be revised accordingly (cf. Section 6).

3. Economic Starting Conditions

After the downfall of the Zhivkov regime in November 1989 the Communist Party, having changed its name in April 1990 to Socialist Party (BSP), was able to retain its hold on power for much longer than in most other East European countries. To wit, having been returned to parliament with an absolute majority in the country's first free elections (June 1990), it formed another one-party government – the third in that year. But the opposition, largely united in the "Union of Democratic Forces" (UDF), gained much strength. The BSP's declared intention to lead the country towards a market economy, was considered inadequate by the opposition, and the West, too, reacted skeptically. The internal power impasse and political disputes led to deep-going incapacitation and loss of control over the economy: with the old command economy rapidly collapsing, there was hardly a sign of the vaunted transition to a market economy.

Added to this, there was a cumulation of unfavorable external developments, hitting Bulgaria harder than most other Central- and East European countries. In trade with the CMEA countries, which in recent years had accounted for about 80% of Bulgaria's foreign trade (uncorrected for the transfer ruble's overvaluation vis-à-vis the US$), there was a sharp decline of Soviet deliveries of crude oil and other primary industrial inputs, and the decline to near vanishing point of the GDR market. Losses due to the gulf crisis, estimated at US $ 1.4 billion, included the loss of the relatively important Iraqi export market, and suspended Iraqi debt repayments, shortfalls of oil deliveries in the context of trilateral deals comprising the Soviet Union, and of hard currency receipts from international freight carrying trade. In March 1990 Bulgaria unilaterally declared a moratorium on repayments on loans granted by Western commercial banks, encompassing more than 80% of Bulgaria's debts (totaling US$ 10.3 bn gross at end of 1990). In July the moratorium was extended to interest payments, and in the course of the year debt service vis-à-vis official Western sources fell into arrears, too. Bulgaria's hard currency reserves exhausted and access even to trade credits barred because of the moratorium, the country was forced to curtail its imports from the West drastically.

In 1990 the economic frame conditions for transition to a market economy have deteriorated considerably. A supply constrained 11.8% contraction of gross domestic product (GDP) was accompanied by growing imbalances: the budget deficit and monetary overhang increased substantially; accelerating open and hidden inflation went hand in hand with spreading supply bottlenecks (some consumer essentials, and motor fuel were rationed); a rapid "dollarization" of the economy set in, and the balance of payments deteriorated.

The situation was aggravated at the beginning of 1991 by more external shocks: the burdens resulting from the switch to world market prices and settlement in hard currency in trade with the (former) CMEA countries, as well as the continuing repercussions of the gulf crisis were estimated in early 1991 to amount to US$ 3.5 bn, or 17%, of the then forecast GDP. Even assuming more than two thirds of the burden to be absorbed by internal adjustments, external finance requirements to cover the deficit on the current account obligations abroad, and an increase in foreign exchange reserves was estimated to amount to US$ 3.8 bn. Although a continued suspension of debt servicing was anticipated, the financing of these requirements was rather uncertain.

4. Liberalization Measures and Stabilization Policy

The implementation of liberalization measures (cf. 4.1) presupposed the abandonment of command economy type coordinating instruments, especially of plan directives and State orders, of central allocation of resources, and of arbitrary administrative price fixing. While the anchoring of market prices (representing relative scarcities) is the aim of domestic liberalizations, the concomitant foreign trade liberalizations, together with the reform of the exchange rate system and introduction of internal convertibility, are to achieve an adjustment of domestic price and production structures to the conditions of the world market.

To achieve internal equilibrium, aggregate demand must, in view of the inherited excess demand, in the short term be cut down (at least) to the level of potential output. Thus the concomitant stabilization policy is concentrating on limiting the components of domestic demand by restrictive monetary, fiscal, and wage policy. If resources thus set free can be directed towards increasing exports, (which presupposes, int. al., a minimal degree of competitiveness), this would contribute to enhancing net exports, as would a devaluation of the currency. In the event, first results of stabilization policy in Bulgaria largely fell short of expectations and objectives (cf. 4.2).

4.1 Liberalization Measures

In early February 1991, producer- and retail prices of 92% of goods and services were liberalized. Retail prices of a sub-group of 13 items of essential foods, and the public transportation tariff (totaling 18% of retail trade turnover) remained subject to government control, as is price formation for 117 national and some local monopoly enterprises.

Price controls are based on ceilings on the rate of profit for producers (20%), and trade margins, but are effective only to a limited extent. The price liberalizations were coupled with the abolition of the respective subsidies, a streamlining of the turnover tax system meant to link the various levels of pricing under more uniform conditions.

Solely energy prices initially remained officially fixed – but were then increased to the three- to fourteen-fold. Beginning June 1991, price ceilings for liquid fuels were introduced, equivalent to 46% to 141% increases over former fixed prices, and have since been subject to monthly adjustment to the development of international prices and exchange rates. At the same time the fixed prices of electrical and thermal energy and coal were raised by a further 70%. These measures were considered necessary, because the unexpectedly severe depreciation of the exchange rate had sent energy subsidies soaring, thus distorting price signals and putting the budget under pressure.

The first price shock turned out much more severe than anticipated in the Program (consumer prices, on a month-to-month basis: February, +123%; March, +51%), whereafter inflationary pressure abated distinctly (April, +2.5%; May, +0.8%). Energy price rises and their spill-overs, though, set off a new inflationary push around the middle of the year (June, +5.9%). In August, food prices were up substantially: the prices offered by the government grain procurement monopoly, intact until August 1991, were considered too low by the producers; reduced sales led to shortages in the processing industries and in retail trade. In consequence, price controls, which had since early June been based on official price forecasts, were extended to procurement and producer prices for nine agricultural products.

The formation of interest rates (being the price for use of capital) was also liberalized. While the National Bank, according to monetary policy criteria, sets the re-financing interest rate for commercial banks (basic interest rate) regulating the interest level, the individual rates are freely negotiated between the banks and their clients. With a basic interest rate of 45% per annum (February to early June 1991), the interest rate charged by the banks for enterprise loans lay between 52 and 56%, while interest paid on time deposits was 36-40% and more.[3]

The formation of wages (price for labor) is to be decisively liberalized in the second half of 1991.[4] Collective wage bargaining is anticipated on national (Government, national trade unions' and employers' organizations) and enterprise levels (employers, trade union representatives), and, if desired by one party, also on the level of sectors, branches, communities, and regions. Topics of national agreements are the determination of a nation-wide minimal wage (presently 620 leva per month, also basis for minimal social benefits), recommendations about differentiations of starting wage by education and training (at present 652 leva plus coefficients up to 1.35), as well as issues of wage bill regulation (cf. 4.2) and wage system in organizations funded from the budget. The issues to be negotiated on the enterprise level are, respectively, minimal and starting wages, job evaluation, wage formation, possibly inflation indexing, as well as other internal matters. On this basis individual wages are agreed on in the personal employment contracts.

In February 1991 most current account transactions were liberalized, in particular exports and imports of commodities; quantitative export restrictions and licensing requirements were minimized (cf. 4.2). If these measures were among the prerequisites for (limited) internal convertibility, the reform of the foreign exchange regulations and exchange rate system entailed the establishment of a uniform exchange rate (price for currency unity) on the basis of supply and demand on the so called interbank market, and of the lev as the sole means of payment in the country. Presently the intended introduction of a fixed rate is preceded by a phase of floating exchange rates – a decisive argument for this departure from what is done in Poland and Czechoslovakia was the lack of foreign exchange reserves and of a stabilization fund for supporting a fixed rate. Banks, and other institutions and private persons[5] licensed by the National Bank may deal at the interbank foreign exchange market at freely negotiable exchange rates. Based on these transactions, the Bulgarian National Bank fixes a daily "central" exchange rate, which is applied in statistics, accounting and in the calculation of customs values.[6]

The enterprises may purchase foreign exchange for imports and appurtenant transportation costs on presentation of documents; proceeds from exports must, within a month, either be sold to a bank, or – a specific Bulgarian regulation – be paid into a foreign exchange account, freely disposable within the general conditions. Bulgarian private individuals may also hold foreign exchange accounts, but are allowed to buy US$ 50 only annually for traveling purposes: this being the most conspicuous remaining restriction on internal convertibility.

At the beginning of February 1991 the commercial exchange rate was around 7 leva to the US dollar, on the black market the US$ fetched around 25 to 30 leva. The first fixing of the "central" rate at 28.25 leva to the US dollar implied a depreciation to one quarter for commercial transactions. Later on, the exchange rate recovered to a level of 17-18.5 leva (monthly averages March to June), yet it remained depreciated to a much lower level than anticipated in the Economic Program (about 10 leva), with the market volume relatively small.

4.2 Stabilization Policy

Restrictive monetary and credit policy is a central element of the stabilization program agreed upon with the IMF. Credit restriction is to be attained by a drastic increase of the interest level (a positive real interest rate being aimed at even in the event of high rates of inflation), but also by continued credit limits.

The basic interest rate, having been increased to 15% p.a. already shortly before the price reform, was further raised in February to 45%. As a reaction to renewed acceleration of inflation in June due to the increase of energy prices, there was another hike, to 52%. A short-lived reduction of the basic interest rate to 47% was followed already in August by a climb to 54%, in reaction to the upsurge of food prices, whereas the stabilization program had anticipated a loosening of monetary policy (for the sake of supply-side stimulation to economic recovery). Yet even so, the real interest rate remained negative.

The first price shock entailed a substantial absorption of the money overhang, at least in the household sector, and nominal growth of the money supply was kept below the rate of inflation in the first half of 1991. Massive advance repayments of private credits – which benefited, until the end of April, from very low interest – were a contributory factor. With the exception of the credits extended to the State budget (cf. below), the volume of credits did in fact remain even below the restrictive targets set by the program. The main reason why this should be so may be found in the behavior of the commercial banks: In view of the strain exerted on their portfolios by non-performing enterprise loans, the banks have become very cagey in granting fresh credit, and reacted in a monopolistic manner by raising "prices" (interest margins) and cutting (loan) volumes. The enterprises in turn, in view of spreading illiquidity and of the high interest rates, often side-step into barter arrangements; the sharp increase of forced inter-enterprise credits (non-settlement of due accounts) constituted another evasion of the desired financial discipline; and all this can hardly be brought under control by restrictive monetary policy alone. The same applies to inflationary developments caused, not by excess demand, but by institutional factors (market deficiencies), as happened in summer in the food sector. Efforts are under way to settle these problems.

The basic objectives of fiscal policy are a decrease of the government share (a cutback of redistribution by a drastic contraction of budget expenditure, especially of subsidies, and of budget revenue, relative to GDP); cuts in the budget deficit as a demand component; and creation of a market conforming (neutral) tax system.

The first version of the 1991 budget had envisaged a decrease of the budget deficit in relation to GDP, to about 3.5%. The relevant share having risen to 13% in 1990, this target appears moderate only at first sight, when compared with the budget surpluses envisaged by Poland and Czechoslovakia. The revised budget passed rather belatedly in July did indeed provide for a slight relaxation of the nominal deficit target; but its realization – which is in doubt – would nevertheless mark an ambitious fiscal adjustment.

By the unforeseen depth of the recession, reduced tax burden of the enterprises, and declining tax discipline the budget revenues came under pressure in the first half of 1991, while expenditures – despite the cuts in subsidies – were higher than budgeted for. The latter was mainly caused by higher expenditures for social purposes, energy price subsidies (until early June), and payments on settlements under old CMEA contracts. In the first quarter of 1991 bank credits to the government exceeded the stabilization program's target, and a waiver of IMF authorized the continuance of the stand-by credit. The National Bank granted two bridging loans to the budget in the first half of the year for financing social security benefits; in the meantime limits have been imposed for such loans by the new National Bank law (open claims on bridging loans to the budget may at no time exceed 5% of annual budget revenues). The financing by issue of bonds and treasury bills, which had been subject to considerable delays and difficulties so far, is in its beginnings.

While a comprehensive tax reform is still pending, the general profits tax rate was reduced from 50% to 40% (the profits tax base is to be formed according to the new accounting law), turnover tax tariffs were streamlined, (some goods are subject to excise duty beside turnover tax) and a uniform progressive income tax tariff was introduced, with a 40% marginal tax rate (exemptions and preferences are granted in the agricultural and consumer goods sectors respectively).

The overriding aim under the stabilization program of wage policy is the limitation of nominal wage increases (a nominal anchor of the program), amounting to a reduction of real wages and of domestic demand.

In the first half of 1991, so called incomes compensations were in force, i.e., supplementary payments on wages and social benefits, intended to compensate for a part of the first price shock effect on real incomes (the basic features of incomes policy, especially with respect to real income cutbacks, had been agreed on with the trade unions). The incomes indexation introduced in the fall of 1990 was abolished early in February 1991; the current wage bill increase in enterprises with State majority participation is subject to steep progressive taxation (payroll regulation). The latter will be retained after the changeover to wage bargaining, whereas income compensations are to expire.

Nominal wage increases (including income compensations) in the first quarter of 1991 even undershot the restrictive targets (as did nominal money and credit expansion) of the stabilization program, since enterprises often lacked the means for paying the compensations in full (whereas the increases of civil servants' salaries, pensions and social transfers were borne by the budget). At the same time the first price shock has substantially exceeded expectations, which had been the basis for computing the income compensations package. As a result, the decline in real wages was much more pronounced than expected (-55%). This gap, and the expected acceleration of inflation due to the increase of energy prices, led to further rounds of compensations. In June 1991, compensations – unrelated to performance – already made up one half of the employed persons' incomes; which, on average, lay 14% below the social minimum.[7]

In view of the restrictive fiscal policy it is intended that the development of a social safety net also encompassing a social assistance system on the communal level, should be streamlined to secure the subsistence minimum for the poorest social groupings. Yet in view of spreading poverty, such a policy, too, requires increasing expenditure.

In foreign trade policy, export control measures were taken primarily with an eye on domestic supply (the quantitative restrictions corresponding to the EC's import quotas are the exception). In February, export bans were imposed on 16 groups of agricultural and chemical products, and 30% and 20% supplementary export duties respectively were temporarily imposed on two further groups of six agricultural and twenty-seven industrial products. Export bans and export duties were successively cut in the following months. Since June 1991 minimum prices are applied for exports of live animals, meat, milk products, and lumber. Export licenses are needed int.al. for goods listed in a negative roster (e.g. tobacco, alcoholic beverages, antiques, military equipment), for exemptions from goods on the negative list, and for exports pertaining to external import quotas (concerning EC: meat, steel, textiles).

Due to the liberalization measures, the import customs tariff has gained in importance. Customs duties imposed on imports from developing countries amount to 6%, on imports under the most favored nation status 8.7% (un-weighted averages), and the tariff allows for differentiation by commodity groups (in ascending sequence: primary products, investment goods, consumer goods). The exemption from customs in the third quarter 1991 of 21 positions of the groups foods, consumer goods, agricultural inputs, and medicines were also granted with an eye to safeguarding domestic supply. A comprehensive reform of the customs tariff is planned. In February, a flat-rate 15% temporary (sur)charge on imports had been imposed (calculated on the basis of the much depreciated exchange rate), but by the middle of the year lists of 200 and 240 commodity positions were freed from the surcharge.

5. Institutional System Transformation

Beside the liberalizations dealt with above, the creation of functioning markets (of goods, labor and capital) characterized by competitive structures requires the establishment of a legal basis that lays down market conforming, consistent and stable rules of the game, as well as the development of institutions, structures and instruments for the putting of these rules into practice. An appropriate institutional framework, transmitted by way of the economic agents' behavior, is an essential prerequisite of the efficacy of the economic policy instruments applied.

Rather sluggishly, not least because of political disputes, were the institutional reforms getting under way – this holds good in particular for the most sensitive realms, privatization and commercialization of state enterprises. Not until July 1991 did the National Assembly pass the new constitution[8] and several important bills affecting the economy, the latter partly borrowed from analogous regulations in developed market economies. These are – in chronological sequence of their being passed – the accountancy bill, Land Act, bills on statistics and foreign investment, competition, Trade Act, National Bank-, and co-operatives bill. At the same time many legal foundations inherited from the past and only partly revised, in particular Decree No. 56 of early 1989 [9], as well as old and recent administrative acts remained in force. Pending a consolidation, the legal basis will remain tainted by disorder, inconsistencies and lacunae.

5.1 Privatization

Already the constitutional amendment of April 1990 had placed private ownership on an equal footing with other forms of ownership.[10] The new constitution of 1991 declares private property inviolate, and provides for the legal foundations and guarantees for uniform conditions and constitutional safeguards of the economic activities of Bulgarian and foreign citizens and legal persons. But in actual fact, privatization of the economy is yet at a very early stage.

Relatively most advanced, so far, are preparations for (re)privatization in agriculture. A relevant bill was passed in February 1991, the implementation regulations followed in April.[11] Qualifying date is April 9, 1946, and claims must be registered by September 1991. Upper limits per household of 20 ha of flat land and 30 ha of hilly ground are set by the law. Restituted land may not be sold for 3 years, but it may be leased immediately; foreigners cannot buy but may only acquire the right-of-use in land.

The Land Act has, however, remained hotly disputed; restitution of land in agricultural use is not only resisted by the established bureaucracy, but there are other difficulties, too. Among these are, in particular, the reduction since key-date of the agricultural land, and depreciated soil quality, as well as the erstwhile excessively small-scale farm structure, and fragmentation of allotments in (pre-communist) agriculture. To achieve profitable and efficient enterprise sizes, hopes are placed in lease agreements and in the establishment of new – voluntary – cooperatives under the new cooperatives law.[12] Until restitution of farm land is actually implemented, agricultural production, which was expected to yield quick and positive response to reform, will continue to be affected by unclarified ownership rights.

In the realm of small privatization, the establishment of new private enterprises was the most dynamic component. By mid-1991 more than 140,000 private enterprises had been registered, the majority of them one-person firms. Since the bulk of them are mini-enterprises, and many actually not operative, their overall economic significance is still marginal. Although most restrictions and discriminations were formally lifted, these enterprises are in fact hampered by the vagaries of bureaucratism (such as over-long registration procedures), and by problems in securing premises, raw materials, equipment and bank loans; and they complain of the heavy tax burden.

Small privatization in the sense of disposal of small facilities out of State property had been blocked from August 1990 till early 1991 by a politically caused "moratorium". It was a condition for the lifting of the moratorium that leading State officials and (where the immediately involved or an associated enterprise object was concerned) top managers in the State sector were debarred from participating in such privatization. In the absence of a privatization law, such small privatizations are based on the amended stipulations of Decree No.56. This lays down that state enterprises may sell or lease movable or – with the consent of the competent State authority – immovable property (except if acquired by expropriation), and single objects (shops, restaurants, workshops, gas stations, storage facilities, and offices). Such sales/leasings must invariably be carried out by way of auction, in which (also) foreign natural or legal persons are admitted.[13] Of the proceeds, 40% must be used for investments in the disposing enterprise, 30% each must go to the state investment fund and towards liquidating public debt. The scope of privatization actually carried out under these provisions so far was very limited.

While the establishment of a privatization agency, constituted as a body responsible to the Council of Ministers, had been decided on as early as February 1991[14], no decision exists as yet on procedure in big privatization. In particular the issues of restitution of ownership and the so called voucher method are in dispute. It will be one of the first tasks of the newly elected parliament to pass a privatization bill; it might provide for the issue to the population of shares in investment funds to be constituted.

5.2 Restructuring the State Sector

As privatization will be a time consuming process, restructuring the state enterprise sector, in the sense of commercialization and de-monopolization, is of great significance.

Commercialization of state enterprises (enterprises owned by central and local authorities) comprises the hardening of the budget constraints and establishment of conditions equal to those applying to private enterprises; the clarification and protection of the state's ownership rights; and the enterprises' autonomy from the state bureaucracy. An essential institutional measure in that direction is the transformation of enterprises into corporations – which in August 1990, after allegations of manipulations in favor of the old nomenclature had also been blocked by a "moratorium". This having now been lifted, state enterprises can, by Council of Ministers' or Municipal Peoples' Council's resolution, be transformed into joint stock companies or limited liability companies in terms of the new commercial code, with the state remaining sole owner for the time being.[15] Such transformations may go hand in hand with the restructuring of the enterprises, but pending a privatization bill, state enterprises may not transfer stocks among themselves.

The delimitation of property rights was not clearly defined under the Bulgarian model of self-management socialism, and in fact enterprise managements were often dominated by the labor force. In future, the state's ownership rights are to be secured by application of corporation law. Special rules apply with respect to managers of state enterprises: they must be appointed by way of public invitation of applications, and foreign natural and legal persons, too, are eligible.[16]. It is an open question whether the terms, among them a 3 year limit on contracts, are sufficiently attractive to induce qualified applicants.

The economic sectors where state monopolies are admissible in principle are enumerated in the new constitution.[17] Independently of the transformation into corporations, the administrative de-monopolization and decentralization of state-owned units was begun in late 1990 in the fields of supplies, procurement and distribution (particularly in parts of the agricultural sector), in domestic trade, construction, transportation and tourism. A further wave, since spring 1991, is also extending to industry. De-monopolization consists often in the disbanding of the associations, "Kombinate", and other structures of the intermediate level, with their former departments or plants turned into independent enterprises. As a result, regional monopolies have often survived, and such mechanical break-ups do not necessarily result in economically viable size- and production structures of enterprises most suitable for future privatization.

By the end of the year, restructuring and liquidation concepts of state enterprises are to be completed in cooperation with the World Bank. The bankruptcy provisions of Decree No.56 have never yet been applied; a new bankruptcy and insolvency code is still to come.

5.3 Competition Law and Forms of Enterprises

The principle of "free economic initiative", as laid down in the Constitution as the basic principle of the economy is supplemented by regulations to guarantee (fair) competition. The new Competition Law[18] defines and forbids the abuse of monopoly power (defined as a market share of above 35%), unfair competition, and other acts capable of putting restraint on competition. The institutional instrument to put this into effect is an independent commission to be appointed by parliament. Acts listed as capable of threatening and/or restricting fair competition are subject to notification and authorization. The commission is also entitled to submit proposals and file applications to government authorities and to the courts of law, who may take appropriate measures or apply sanctions.

The new commercial code[19], taking its cue from Western patterns, envisages the following legal forms of enterprises: sole traders (natural persons domiciled in Bulgaria), general partnerships ("'open' trading company"), limited partnerships, limited liability companies (minimum capital: 50,000 leva), joint stock corporations (minimum: 5 or 1 mn leva at founding, with or w/o subscriptions), and partnerships limited by shares. Cooperatives, too (excepting cooperative building societies), are subject to the commercial code.

5.4 Banking System and Capital Market

Resulting from the reforms of the banking system, initiated in 1987, there are more than 70 commercial banks, organized as joint stock corporations; among them the First Private Bank, a US-Bulgarian bank, and a joint Bulgarian-American bank, as well at the State Savings Bank, this latter being until recently the only bank for private households. However, this commercial banking sector suffers from grave structural problems: most of the banks have a weak capital basis, and in fact they enjoy a regional monopoly position; the links with other enterprises within and outside the financial sector are extensive; portfolios are insufficiently spread regionally and by branches; and they are increasingly burdened by non-performing enterprise loans. Though it is generally accepted that there are too many banks with respect to the country's size, they actually hardly compete with each other. A reform, preceding the banks' privatization, is to be carried out by a new state bank holding corporation, which is to restructure and consolidate (including merge) the banks. Non-performing enterprise credits are to be cleared up by government guarantees, and if need be by write-downs and/or write-offs. A new banking and credit system bill has not yet been passed.

The new National Bank Bill[20] provides a stronger underpinning for the creation of a two-tier banking system. In its activities the Bulgarian National Bank (BNB) is independent of the government; it is responsible to parliament, and has the classic functions of a central bank. Its main objectives are the establishment and maintenance of the currency's internal and external stability; it is to facilitate payment transactions, and supervise and control the commercial banks. The BNB is the only currency issuing bank, and the State's bank; it may hold deposits, conduct discount-, open-market- and lombard (lending on collateral) business, deal in precious metals and foreign exchange, etc. As an instrument of money supply regulation it also has at its disposal minimum reserve requirements (limited to 15% of total assets); and it fixes the re-financing interest rate and, if need be, credit limits for the commercial banks. In the field of foreign exchange, the BNB is responsible for drawing up the balance of payments, fixing the central exchange rate, and regulating banking activities (limits on holdings of gold and foreign exchange assets by institutions entitled to conduct such operations, and on their open foreign exchange positions; as well as laying down appropriate minimum reserves).

The creation of a capital market in the narrow sense presupposes the existence of negotiable instruments (stocks, bonds, etc.). The commercial code does contain provisions concerning enterprise bonds and stocks, but a securities law is yet to come. Whereas enterprise bonds have not yet been issued, a few (private) stocks have already come into existence; and stocks of the First Private Bank are already traded. As mentioned, the issue of government securities has already begun. But a secondary capital market of appreciable volume can only come into being once a perceptible degree of privatization has been reached. The establishment of a stock exchange is visualized for 1992.

5.5 Labor Market

The new constitution lays down every citizen's right to work, the state to create the necessary conditions; further, free choice of occupation and job are laid down, as is the formation of bodies representing workers' and employers' interests. Most of the administrative restrictions on labor mobility, especially concerning the place of residence (removal of restrictions on the establishment of residence); and limits on employment for private enterprises having already been lifted. A new labor code is yet to provide the legal prerequisites for full mobility.

The new labor offices were established on the basis of the 120 former labor bureaux. After their poor placement record had come under fire, private placement agencies have been admitted since July; they must register (yearly) with the Ministry for Work and Social Affairs.[21]

A system of unemployment benefits was established as early as the beginning of 1990, and has since been repeatedly modified. The regulation of June 1991 makes entitlement as a rule dependent on an employment record of at least 6 months within the last year; it ties the amount of benefit to the country-wide minimum wage and last wage earned, and the claim's term (6-12 months) to duration of employment and claimant's age.[22] The scheme is financed primarily from enterprises' contributions. By the middle of 1991 the number of registered persons out of work had already risen to 233,000 (end of 1990: 68,000), of whom only 56% received unemployment benefit. These figures do not include short-time work nor unpaid forced leave, accounting for 4% and 1% respectively of persons employed in the first quarter of 1991.

In view of drastically rising unemployment, first measures of an active employment policy were decided on in June; among them are: support for enterprises established by unemployed persons, interest and tax benefits for enterprises creating new jobs or abstaining from dismissals, etc. At the same time emphasis is placed on the possibility of introducing, in consultation with the trade unions' representatives, various forms of short work-time [23]. Vocational training and retraining programs are as yet in an initial stage.

5.6 Foreign Capital

In the course of the transition policy, the general setting of systemic and economic conditions has undergone considerable changes also for foreign investors, and changes also in the legal framework were recently introduced by the new law on foreign investments.[24] The principle of equal treatment is now accepted in principle, ownership guarantee and transfer possibilities were significantly improved. Now, that profits, labor remunerations, and liquidation dividends can be exchanged at a bank at market rate and transferred to foreign countries, the Bulgarian lev has practically become convertible (at the same time, as pointed out, to do business within the country in currencies other than leva was prohibited).

There are no ceilings on foreign participations; but a minimum of US$ 50,000 for foreign investments has been newly introduced: a measure meant to prevent speculative small-scale capital movements. Restrictions are in force in respect of land (real estate), mineral resources, etc.: foreigners and joint ventures may not acquire ownership rights, but right to use for up to 70 years. Whereas, in principle, foreign investments do not need authorization but must only be registered in terms of commercial code, a number of exceptions are stipulated, in respect of economic sectors, of regions and of type of assets (right to use). The true extent of authorizations needed will largely depend on the Council of Ministers' – not yet promulgated – implementing regulations. The administrations' decision-making margin regarding licensing, not bound by any clear criteria, has, at any rate, been increased. In view of massive criticisms of the restrictive elements of the law, amendments cannot be ruled out.

Even now, with the new law having come into force, some general conditions for foreign investments are still subject to Decree Nr. 56 (e.g. tax provisions) and other legal norms. The possibilities for foreign capital to participate in "big privatization" are still uncertain, in the absence of pertinent legislation. A special law is to cover the special economic zones, now regulated by Directive Nr. 2242 of 1987. Since then the establishment of six such special economic zones had been decided on – though by and large they remained on paper.

6. Summary Assessment

In Bulgaria, transition to a market economy began rather late: At the beginning of 1991, following a year of political confrontation and economic decline, an economic program bearing some typical features of a so called shock therapy was introduced by the country's first multiparty government. This step went hand in hand with the conclusion of a stand-by agreement with the International Monetary Fund, which Bulgaria had joined in September 1990.

This agreement was an important step to breaking free from the practically complete financial isolation that Bulgaria had faced since it had unilaterally suspended its debt service payments. It was an essential prerequisite for the transition to a market economy and foreign trade opening, inasmuch as neither of these is to be thought of without Western support and finance. Apart from giving access to funds under the Fund's standby credit and Compensatory and Contingency Financing Facility, the agreement paved the way to a rescheduling agreement with the Paris Club (April 1991), and financial means were now forthcoming, too, though hesitantly, from other official sources. Credit programs are in operation with the World Bank in the fields of technical assistance and structural adjustment. G-24 balance of payments support got under way, though by the fall of 1991 only about three quarters of the needed volume was secured. However, the country's debts to the most important group of creditors, that is, the Western commercial banks (London Club), is still an unsolved problem. Since March 1990 one made do with recurrent three-monthly roll-over arrangements; but a longer-term solution, especially a rescheduling agreement or partial remission of debt is required for normalization in the sphere of commercial credits, and for the urgently needed capital inflow of appreciable volume from the West, also in the form of foreign direct investments.

The switch, in trade with the former CMEA countries, and with the Soviet Union in particular, to world market prices in hard currency settlement causes Bulgaria not only a drastic deterioration of her terms of trade, but it also led to a trade volume decline, to an extent exceeding the economic program's expectations by far. This holds also for the foreign trade total; though, after the collapse in the first months of the year, there were signs of a – relative – recovery in the second quarter.

While developments in foreign trade were even more unfavorable than anticipated in the program, the assumptions regarding the effects of the shock therapy on the domestic economy, too, were (as in other countries), over-optimistic. Following the unexpectedly harsh inflationary shock released by the liberalization measures, restrictive monetary and wage policies contributed to combat inflation. Later, however, inflationary developments set in again without the austerity policy having been relaxed. Restrictions of credits (excepting those to the government) and wages were even harsher than had been anticipated or considered necessary in the stabilization program. The curb on absorption beyond the program formula contributed to the unexpected depth of the recession, as did shortfalls in export demand. The introduction of (limited) internal convertibility (based on foreign trade liberalization), alongside a floating exchange rate, resulted in a notably bigger depreciation than assumed in the program. Nevertheless, exports to the West declined by more than half at current US$ in the first half of the year. Although the remaining export restrictions and possibly further reduced re-exports of oil products may well have contributed, that export decline is also a signal of the failure, so far, of tangible adjustment processes.

Although the recession, in the course of the reforms, is increasingly demand caused, yet some supply-side constraints from import shortfalls remained effective, too. Alongside declining production, unemployment increased rapidly. The budget targets are threatened by shortfalls in revenues and additional expenditure for social purposes in view of the drastic decline of real incomes.

First results in 1991 disclose problems similar to those in other countries embarking on transition to market economy by shock therapies under agreements with the IMF.[25] Central to their programs are liberalization measures and the short-term objective of a radical macro-economic stabilization. In the case of Bulgaria the internal and external imbalances at the point of departure were exceedingly severe,[26] while the institutional and systemic transformation, forming the backdrop of the current program, dragged on at excessively slow pace. The almost complete absence of market compatible structures and institutions as well as specific behavioral patterns seem to be essential factors for the failure to achieve the program's targets. Thus inflationary pressure reappearing around mid-year was due primarily to exchange rate developments (energy prices), and monopolistic behavior (grain procurement), rather than to excess demand, which might be controlled by orthodox stabilization policy instruments. Contributory factors to the unexpectedly severe credit squeeze were the unresolved problem of the non-performing enterprise credits and the banks' monopolistic behavior. The enterprises' dodging into forced inter-firm credits can hardly be controlled by a restrictive monetary policy alone. Economic policy reactions to such frictions are ad-hoc measures, and a groping for solutions – which, in turn, needs time.

Institutional and systemic transformation was delayed mainly by continuing political disputes. In the legislative field, the new constitution, as well as a number of economic laws were passed during the first seven months of the year, but further steps may only be expected when the new parliament assembles and after a new government is installed. So far, for instance, there are as yet no implementing regulations for the new laws, nor market compatible laws covering the banking and credit system, securities, taxes, and social security, nor a comprehensive renewal of labor code, nor, last not least, a privatization bill. The legal framework of economic activities will for some time still be determined by a mix of new laws (along the lines of comparable norms in developed market economies), partly corrected inherited laws, and old and new administrative acts.

Privatization of the economy is still at a very early stage. Big privatization of the state enterprises has not even started, a relevant legal basis lacking, in view of continuing political disagreement on procedure. Small privatization of state-owned facilities only got under way again (following a "moratorium") until the middle of 1991, though very slowly. The expanding private sector, comprising in the main a multitude of small newly started enterprises, is of little weight. Preparations for land restitution in agriculture are well advanced, though not implemented, as restitution remains very controversial.

Under these conditions the reconstruction of the state enterprise sector is of especial significance. As far as commercialization is concerned, their transformation into corporation (now under the new commercial code) had also been subject to a moratorium. The administrative de-monopolizations that were carried out left regional monopolies largely untouched, while the resulting enterprise structure is not necessarily commensurate with economic criteria. In order to create effective competitive structures, on top of restructuring the state sector and implementing protection of competition, an expansion of the private sector, and import competition are essential. A reform of the banking sector is in the offing.

At the middle of the year, the short-term forecasts for the whole year 1991 has already anticipated a 20% drop in GDP (having anticipated a decline of 11% at the beginning of the year) and a more than 50% slump of average real wages. Inflation was expected do reach an annual average rate of 470% (retail trade prices), and an unemployment rate of 12% already for the fall. The target area for the exchange rate has been revised from originally 10 to 15-18 leva per US$. Further corrections of the economic forecasts cannot be ruled out: the recession may turn out even more severe than the variant reported here.

In a longer perspective the transition policy currently pursued – radical stabilization and opening up to the world market, under deficient market structures and low competitiveness – carries the risk of narrowing the scope for the necessary adjustments by a deep and prolonged depression (e.g. by liquidation of basically viable enterprises) without achieving the striven-for price stability. In attempting to reduce the role of the state to a minimum, extreme restraint is exercised in the fields of growth-, structural, and industrial policy. This constellation may delay the restoration the economy's growth potential and bring increasing social tensions: Up till now the population still accepted the massive real income losses with comparative patience. Social (and political) stability are essential determinants for availability of Western finance (critically important for the transition), of which Bulgaria has a relatively high need in the longer term, too.

The process of economic transition is in an early phase at present; the political and social background is characterized by specific imponderables, including national tensions with the ethnic Turkish minority. While it may be assumed that the Union of Democratic Forces will emerge from the elections in October 1991 with improved positions in parliament and in government, the establishment of stable majorities might yet be difficult. The outcome will shape the course of transition policies, once the stagnation of reforms caused by the election campaign will have been overcome. In any case Bulgaria is likely to stand by its commitment to transition to a market economy and an IMF supported stabilization policy.

Notes

1. Cf., e.g., Hughes, G.,: "Foreign Exchange, Prices and Economic Activity in Bulgaria," in: *European Economy, The Path of Reform in Central and Eastern Europe*, Special edition No. 2/1991, Commission of European Communities, p. 157 ff.

2. Cf., e.g., Gabrisch, H: "Restoring the Growth Potential of Formerly Centrally Planned Economies," in: *Intereconomics* 2/1991, p. 88 ff.

3. Cf: *Summary on the Present State of the Economic Reform in Bulgaria*, Bulgarian Chamber of Commerce and Industry, Sofia, p. 4.

4. Cf. *Dŭrzhaven vestnik* (further on: DV) 55/1991.

5. Up to the middle of 1991, licenses had been issued to 12 banks, 8 state enterprises, and 18 private individuals (Semi-annual Report January-June 1991, *News Bulletin* 5/1991, Bulgarian National Bank, Sofia, p. 11).

6. Cf., e.g., Parwanowa, R., Petkowa, I.: "Die Wirtschaft Bulgariens – der Öffnung zugewandt?" (Bulgaria's economy - facing the opening?)", in *Südosteuropa* 5/1991, p. 201 ff.

7. Cf. Semi-annual Report January-June 1991, *News Bulletin* 5/1991, Bulgarian National Bank, Sofia, p. 4.

8. Cf. DV 56/1991.

9. Cf. Grosser, I.: "Bulgarien", in: *Die Wirtschaft der osteuropäischen Länder an der Wende der 90er Jahre*, (the economy of the East European countries at the turn of the 1990s), HWWA-Institut für Wirtschaftsforschung, Hamburg 1990, p. 23 ff.

10. Cf. DV 29/1990.

11. Cf. DV 17/1991 and 34/1991.

12. Cf. DV 63/1991.

13. Cf. DV 23/1991.

14. Cf. DV 12/1991.

15. Cf. DV 55/1991.

16. Cf. DV 67/1991.

17. Beside exclusive state ownership in mineral resources, federal highways, nationally important waters, forests etc., state monopolies may be instituted by law for railroad transportation, national mail and telecommunications networks, utilization of

nuclear energy and the production of radioactive materials, arms, explosives and biologically highly active substances.

18. Cf. DV 39/1991.

19. Cf. DV 48/1991.

20. Ibid.

21. Cf. DV 67/1991.

22. Cf. DV 49/1991.

23. ibid.

24. Cf. DV 47/1991.

25. Cf., e.g., Laski, K.: "Transition from Command to Market Economies in Central and Eastern Europe: First Experiences and Questions," contribution presented at the "Conference on Medium Term Economic Assessment ", Vienna, October 14-16 1991, and Levcik, F., *Zentral- und Osteuropa auf dem Wege zur Marktwirtschaft – Bisherige Ergebnisse und kritische Bemerkungen zur eingeschlagenen Strategie* (Central and East Europe on the road to market economy – hitherto observed results and critical comments on the strategy adopted), lecture at the International Symposium of the Austro-French Center on 21-22 May 1991 in Paris.

26. Cf., e.g., Hishow, O.: "Struktur und Konjunktur der bulgarischen Volkswirtschaft, Vorhaben der Wirtschaftsreform" (Structure and economic conditions in Bulgaria, targets of economic reform), in *Südosteuropa* 2/1991, p. 81ff.

Part Three
Internal and External Environment of Transition

8

THE SOVIET ECONOMY ON THE BRINK OF CONFRONTATION

Peter Havlik

1. Disputes About Reform Programs

With the economy declining at accelerating speed, the search for new reform concepts intensified again at the beginning of 1991. First, the Prime Minister Mr. V. Pavlov announced a program for the stabilization of the economy, endorsed together with a joint "9+1 Statement" agreed on between Mr. Gorbachev and the leaders of nine Union republics in April 1991.[1] This program rested heavily on an early signing of a new Union Treaty as well as on various emergency measures for key industries. Besides, the central government demanded unspecified extraordinary powers as well. Early hopes that the new Union Treaty could be signed in late summer 1991 have soon vanished because of disagreements over details.

As in the last two years, there have been parallel efforts to elaborate an alternative, more radical program for transition to a market economy. A group of Soviet economists jointly with a US team worked out a program which would support Soviet political and economic reforms with Western assistance.[2] As the G-7 London Summit in July 1991 was approaching, this reform plan became famous in the West as "Grand Bargain" – a plan in which the Soviet Union would "trade market-oriented reforms for massive Western financial assistance" of at least US$ 100 bn over five years.[3] This reform program was to facilitate the Soviet Union's transition to a market economy. The strategy for cooperation with the West had to be gradual, based on mutual confidence. Western financial assistance should have to support the balance of payments deficit, the stabilization of the ruble exchange rate, as well as the modernization of key consumer goods industries. The economic reforms were to be linked to political reforms as well. The plan assumed the signature of a new Union Treaty in late summer 1991 and the conclusion of an "Economic Treaty" in autumn 1991. The latter should clarify also economic relations with those republics which do not wish to join the new Union. The adoption of a new constitution was envisaged for spring 1992, and in summer 1992 democratic multi-party elections were to be held.

According to the Yavlinski plan, the economic reform should have to proceed in two stages. During 1991-1993, the basic legal and economic institutions for a market economy were to be created and (small) privatization should have to be started. In the second stage (1994-1997), structural changes of the economy and (small and big) privatization was to be fostered. By the end of 1997, the Soviet economy should be open and integrated into the world economy and trade. But many Soviet government officials have rejected this plan outright, including the later coup leaders, among others Soviet Prime Minister V. Pavlov, not to mention KGB Chief Kryuchkov and Defence Minister Yasov, either because of suspicion that conditional Western assistance would be more advantageous to the West, or because of their aversion to privatization.[4] Outside the Soviet Union, there were reservations regarding the feasibility of this plan, too.

As a result, a similar situation as in summer 1990 was emerging again: at that time, the Soviet government of Mr. Ryzhkov successfully opposed the adoption of the more radical Shatalin reform plan. Mr. Gorbachev's attempt at a compromise failed completely, and the economy deteriorated rapidly. The worsening economic situation combined with political developments in 1991 (e.g. the election of Mr. Yeltsin as President of Russia in June, the establishment of the Movement for Democratic Reforms in July, and Mr. Yeltsin's ban of Party cells in enterprises in August) was bound soon to provoke a confrontation with the conservatives.

2. Rapidly Deteriorating Economy

In the first half of the year, the GNP fell by 10%, national income produced by 12%, and gross industrial production by 6.2%, against the same period of 1990. The rate of decline accelerated till April, but it might have stabilized in May and June 1991.[5] Despite reduced gross investments (-6%), the volume of completed construction projects (including housing construction) fell by about 20%. The deficit of the Union budget reached Rbl 39 bn in Jan.-May (revenues: Rbl 45.5 bn, outlays Rbl 84.8 bn) as individual republics failed to remit earlier agreed proceeds from taxes (especially from turnover and profits taxes) to the center. As a result of shifts in budgetary expenditures (and despite reduction in real terms), 46% of the Union's budget (Rbl 38.6 bn) were used to finance defense outlays. The Government's internal debt reached Rbl 800 bn as of July 1, 1991. With declining national income and total employment in the productive sphere almost unchanged (-1% as compared with the first half of 1990), labor productivity dropped by 11%. However, employment in the state sector declined by 2.2% (-2.6 mn persons), but it increased in cooperatives (+34%) and private activities (+7%). During the first half of 1991, the state sector (including kolkhozes) employed 91% of the working population (first half 1990: 92%). More than 250.000 cooperatives (employing 6.5 mn persons) produced goods and services for about Rbl 42 bn during Jan.-June

Table 1

USSR: Selected Indicators of Economic Development

	1989 act.	1990 Jan-June	1990 Jan-Sept	1990 Jan-Dec	1991 Jan-March	1991 Jan-June
National income						
produced	2.4	-2.0	-2.5	-4.0	-10.0	-12
distributed	3.2	.	.	0.0[a)]	.	.
Industry						
gross production	1.7	-0.7	-0.9	-1.2	-5.0	-6.2
employment	-1.4	-2.0	-2.2	-2.0	.	.
labour productivity	3.1	2.7	1.3	0.8	.	.
Agriculture						
gross production	1.3	.	.	-2.3	-13.0	-11
Gross investments	4.7	-7.0	-3.0	-8.7	-16.0	-6.0
Retail trade turnover[b)]	8.4	12.3	10.7	10.4	25.3	33.7
Public consumption[b)]	6.6	8.6	8.4	10.4	.	.
Average nominal wages	9.5	8.9	8.4	12.3	10.0	30.0[e)]
Per capita real incomes	1.0[a)]	1[a)]	-1[a)]	-2[a)]	-2[a)]	-8[a)]
Retail prices	7.5	5[a)]	7[a)]	10[a)]	23.8	55.8
Housing construction, mill. sq. m	128.1	43.8	92.0	115.0	8.4	34.6
Exports[c)]						
total	2.4	-9.3	-12.1	-11.9	-18.4	-23.4
to the West	11.8	-8.2	1.2	6.0	-10.7[d)]	-15.3[d)]
Imports[c)]						
total	10.9	2.2	0.2	-2.2	-45.1	-47.7
from the West	25.6	13.3	2.1	-1.5	-45.2[d)]	-47.0[d)]

a) Estimated. – b) Current prices. – c) Ruble basis. – d) Including LDCs. – e) Including compensation payments.

Source: WIIW data based on Soviet national statistics.

1991 (+40% at current prices; in real terms much less than during the comparable period of 1990).[6]

There were several jumps in the price level in the first months of 1991. First, wholesale prices were raised in January by more than 80%, in April retail prices followed suit. The level of wholesale prices in industry doubled during the first half of 1991, the GNP price deflator increased by 80%, and retail prices increased by almost 60%. In the second quarter of the year, retail prices jumped by 90% (first quarter 1991: 23.8%) and in June 1991, wholesale prices for industry were higher by 122%, and retail prices by 95% as compared with June 1990. About 40% of wholesale prices in industry and 60% of consumer goods prices were freely set by producers. Since the production of consumer goods has been declining (by 4.5% in the first half of 1991, of which foodstuffs: -8.5%), and imports were drastically curtailed, it is no wonder that prices at black markets have at least doubled even after the April price reform. The gap between supply and demand further fueled inflationary pressures: the annual rate of open inflation might reach 100% for 1991 as a whole.

Money incomes of the population amounted to Rbl 434 bn, nominally increasing by +44%, but taking into account the official consumer price index (+55.5%), they declined in real terms by at least 8%. Average monthly wages (remuneration for work, including compensation payments) amounted to Rbl 353 (+37%; first half 1990: Rbl 257) – this again would imply a decrease in real wages by about 12%. Monthly remunerations of kolkhoz farmers increased to 233 Rbl (+25%), i.e. decreased in real terms by about 20%. Private savings increased nominally by 10% between end December 1990 and end June 1991, and reached Rbl 421 bn as of July 1, 1991. Besides, private savings deposits were nominally increased by additional Rbl 160 bn as a compensation for the April price reform. About Rbl 35-40 bn of this compensation can be withdrawn after July 1 1991 (the rest was frozen). Cash holdings of the population amounted to about Rbl 150 bn in mid-1991, money supply expansion grew slower (+13%) than inflation. Retail trade turnover declined by at least 12% in real terms (of which in the second quarter of the year: -25%) – partly due to a drop in real disposable incomes, but also because of limited supplies. The price reform has thus eliminated only part of the monetary overhang (stock) while income compensations combined with declining production still result in an excess flow of money which is not backed by goods.

One of the most disturbing developments has been the accelerating decline of gross industrial production (-6.2%; first half of 1990: -0.7%). It must be pointed out that this has been happening virtually in the absence of any structural change: the exception is the (perhaps only reported) increase of civilian output at defense enterprises (equipment for food-, light and pharmaceutical industries). Energy production has been declining (oil: -9%, coal: -11%, gas: +0.2%, electricity: -0.9%) as well as the output of the machine building industry (machine tools: -5%, electromotors: -15%, trucks: -14%, tractors: -12%, passenger cars: -5%, combines: -18%, etc.), chemicals (fertilizers: -8%, sulfuric acid: -7%, artificial fibers: -16%, etc.), and construction materials (cement: -6% sawn wood: -14%). The situation in agriculture was no better: output of meat (-12%), milk (-10%), and eggs (-6%) drops, animal stocks are being depleted (cattle: -4%, swine: -10%, sheep: -9%). State purchases of animal products have declined by 13% (meat and milk) and 11% (eggs) during first half of the year; the expected poor grain harvest (about 160 mn tons, 1990: 218 mn tons) would indicate a more tense food supply situation in the coming months. The above quoted reduction of investment did not give much hope for economic recovery even in a medium-term perspective.[7] Not surprisingly, the new "Foreign Investments Law" has left many essential issues in doubt until the final adoption of a new Union Treaty. In June 1991 about 3,500 joint ventures were registered, but only about one third have already become operational.

3. Collapsing Foreign Trade

The critical state of the Soviet economy is best illustrated by foreign trade developments. In the first half of 1991, Soviet exports declined by 23.4% and imports were almost halved (-47.7%). As a result, a small trade balance surplus – Rbl 4.9 bn – has been reported (about US$ 2,850 mn at the commercial exchange rate). Major reductions in foreign trade occurred in trade with former CMEA countries (especially with Bulgaria, Cuba, Mongolia and Vietnam) after the abolition of traditional clearing arrangements and the switch to hard currency accounting at world market prices after January 1, 1991. Soviet exports to capitalist countries (i.e. the West, including former GDR, plus LDCs) dropped by 15.3%, and imports by 47%. Exports to the rest of the world (i.e. former CMEA countries without East Germany, plus China, Yugoslavia, etc.) dropped by almost 30%, and imports by more than 48%.[8] Soviet exports of crude oil were reduced by 50% (oil products: -52%), the import cuts affected mainly deliveries for light and chemical industries as well as consumer goods: e.g. imports of rubber were reduced by 67%, cellulose: -71%, newsprint: -75%, grain: -27%, textiles: -28%, leather shoes: -77%, pharmaceuticals: -34%. As of July 1, 1991, foreign trade rights (issuing of export and import licenses and quotas) were formally transferred to individual republics, and foreign trade operations will be coordinated by the Union's Foreign Exchange Committee.[9]

As far as indebtedness is concerned (estimated by the WIIW at US$ 56 bn gross as of end 1990), a drastic curtailment of Soviet imports during the first half of 1991 has so far prevented any larger deterioration of the current account. But still, the estimated short term credits due (US$ 14 bn in 1991), and the principal repayment (US$ 8 bn) and interest payments (more than US$ 4 bn) would add up to an estimated debt service of more than US$ 26 bn during 1991. Recently, one Soviet source provided an estimate of the gross debt at the end of 1991 at US$ 70.2 bn.[10] One of the urgent problems of the New Union (or any future agreement among individual republics) is how to share the accumulated foreign debt. The same source has also mentioned that an agreement in principle about this has been achieved and a general formula for splitting the debt among republics will be based on four indicators: the republican share in exports and imports, the share in the Union's national income produced, and the number of inhabitants. However, no agreement on the exact weights of individual indicators in the formula has been achieved yet. How this can matter, is illustrated by the data in Table 2. The share of Russia ranges from 51.2% to 76.5%, that of the Ukraine between 12.6 and 17.9%, of Kazachstan between 1.5 and 5.8%, of Uzbekistan between 1.3 and 7.1%. Based on a simple average of four indicators, Russia should take over 64.1% of the Union's debt (US$ 45.0 bn), the Ukraine 14.9% (US$ 10.5 bn), Kazachstan 3.4% (USS$ 2.4 bn) and Uzbekistan 3.3% (US$ 2.3 bn). The three Baltic republics would jointly account for about 2.5% of Soviet debt (US$ 1.7 bn). There is no doubt that Russia (accounting for more than 76% of the Union's export earnings) would have the least problems in servicing her share of the debt; she could take over an even greater share of the Union's debt – either in exchange for the republics' concessions in other areas, or in order to maintain credibility in the West. It can be expected that the respective negotiations will be extremely complicated.

4. The Failed Coup Opened the Way for Reforms

The attempted coup on August 19th, 1991 represented the latest massive escalation of the struggle for power. The coup failed because of apparently dilettant planning, disobedience within the army and the decisive resistance of Russian President B.N. Yeltsin and parts of the population. A return to the totalitarian old regime, with negative consequences for the economy and worsened prospects for trade and Western investments, has thus been prevented.

Table 2

How to Distribute Soviet Gross Debt of US$ 70 bn Among the Republics?

	Population 1991 (mn)	in % of total	Net Output 1988 (%)	Imports 1989 Rbl bn	in %	Exports 1989 Rbl bn	In %	Average of 4 indicators	Gross Debt US$ bn
Soviet Union	290.077	100.00	100.00	72.14	100.00	68.74	100.00	100.00	70.20
Russia	148.543	51.21	61.10	48.72	67.54	52.57	76.48	64.08	44.98
Ukraine	51.944	17.91	16.20	9.24	12.81	8.69	12.64	14.89	10.45
Belorussia	10.26	3.54	4.20	2.87	3.98	2.2	3.20	3.73	2.62
Estonia	1.582	0.55	0.60	0.29	0.40	0.12	0.17	0.43	0.30
Latvia	2.681	0.92	1.10	0.89	1.23	0.26	0.38	0.91	0.64
Lithuania	3.728	1.29	1.40	0.92	1.28	0.5	0.73	1.17	0.82
Moldavia	4.367	1.51	1.20	0.8	1.11	0.23	0.33	1.04	0.73
Georgia	5.464	1.88	1.60	0.68	0.94	0.36	0.52	1.24	0.87
Armenia	3.376	1.16	0.90	0.48	0.67	0.07	0.10	0.71	0.50
Azerbaidzhan	7.137	2.46	1.70	0.69	0.96	0.4	0.58	1.42	1.00
Kazakhstan	16.793	5.79	4.30	1.56	2.16	1	1.45	3.43	2.41
Turkmenistan	3.714	1.28	0.80	0.27	0.37	0.12	0.17	0.66	0.46
Uzbekistan	20.708	7.14	3.30	0.94	1.30	0.93	1.35	3.27	2.30
Tadzikistan	5.358	1.85	0.80	0.33	0.46	0.32	0.47	0.89	0.63
Kirgizia	4.422	1.52	0.80	0.61	0.85	0.04	0.06	0.81	0.57
Unallocated	.	.	.	2.85	3.95	0.93	1.35	.	0.93

Sources: Vestnik statistiki, No. 7/1991, p. 69, A Study of the Soviet Economy, IMF, The World Bank, OECD and EBRD, Vol. 1, 1991, p. 214, A. Lushin (mimeo).

Communism in the Soviet Union, as well as the zigzag course of Mr. Gorbachev, were discredited. Now – after the defeat of the conservative opposition – steps towards a market economy can be finally implemented. Also the climate for political reforms (signature of the Union Treaty, devolution of powers from the center, free elections, privatization, etc.) has greatly improved. However, a period of instability including possible conflicts between different parts of deeply split Soviet society is likely. The disintegration of the (former) Soviet Union is rapidly progressing. Existing economic problems will soon overshadow the current revolutionary euphoria. Experience of reforming countries in Eastern Europe shows that the problems of transition are enormous; they are even more complicated in Soviet conditions. Rapidly growing unemployment, further real income losses and even supply shortages in the short term seem unavoidable.

Not only the central bureaucracy, but also parts of the population supported the coup, since they either hoped for improvements in daily life or because they profited in various degree from the old system. The potential for future conflicts has by far not been completely eliminated. Nor will it suffice to implement the standard reform prescriptions, such as privatization, price liberalization, and foreign exchange convertibility. The existing privileges of the military-industrial complex must be systematically eliminated, the conversion of military enterprises must be speeded up, and clear relations between the center and individual republics must be established: thus the signing of a new Union Treaty, which takes into account new realities, will be the key factor in future economic development. The tug-of-war about a new Union Treaty could lead to instability and to further economic decline, including the danger of political and social unrest.

In order to implement rigorous reforms (differing in depth and speed in individual republics), large-scale assistance from the West – linked to appropriate conditions – will be required. In the short term, the economic situation will most likely worsen, but in the medium and long term the economic prospects would be definitely better. After a (hopefully) short interruption caused by the current events the conditions for Western investors would generally be much better than up till now – though it is likely that the economic and legal framework may differ in individual parts of today's Soviet Union, due to the expected progress in decentralization and even break-up into new entities. The establishment of special economic zones and the granting of concessions to Western firms for exploiting the raw materials and other resources can be expected.

Notes

1. See *Izvestiya*, April 23, 1991, pp. 2-3, and April 24, 1991, p. 1.

2. The main author, Mr. Yavlinski, one of the authors of Shatalin's 500 days plan of September 1990, served as Deputy Prime Minister of Russia, but has quit this position after Shatalin's plan had been rejected, and worked then inter alia as an advisor to the government of Kazakhstan.

3. See *International Herald Tribune*, June 15-16, 1991, p. 12.

4. The basic principles for privatization were adopted after heated discussions by the Soviet parliament on July 1 1991 – see *Izvestiya*, July 1, 1991, p. 1.

5. See supplement to *Ekonomika i Zhizn*, No. 30, 1991.

6. During the first half of 1990 the cooperatives produced goods and services for about Rbl 30 bn (for illustration: 6.6% of gross industrial production; in Jan.-June 1991 only 4.8%).

7. The slight reduction of investment decline over the previous period (see Table 1) results from the newly established "Central Stabilization Fund" (Rbl 38 bn for 1991 as a whole), and does not signal any improvement of investment activity. The volume of unfinished construction continues to grow.

8. The analysis is hampered by incomplete data, exchange rate changes (foreign trade figures are now converted by commercial exchange rates) as well as by unclear treatment of trade with former East Germany.

9. These regulations will probably change: import restrictions might be eased and, moreover, a partial return to bilateral clearing and barter trade with former CMEA countries and a certain recovery of imports might be expected in the second half of the year.

10. See *Izvestiya*, Sept. 2, 1991, p. 3.

9

EXTERNAL INDEBTEDNESS OF YUGOSLAVIA AND ITS FEDERAL UNITS

Franjo Štiblar

A lot has already been spoken and written about the Yugoslav debt crisis, its causes and consequences. It is the purpose of this paper to emphasize some of the less known specific aspects of that crisis. It deals with the evolution and current status of Yugoslav debt relations with foreign creditors and especially with the indebtedness of each of the country's constitutional federal units.

The basic findings can be summarized in the following way: firstly, without changes of the exchange rate the Yugoslav external debt would show an increase continuously up to 1984 and after that it would decrease continuously. Secondly, the external factors had a more important impact on the Yugoslav debt than domestic activity. Thirdly, according to the newest criteria of the World Bank, and contrary to popular belief, Yugoslavia cannot be listed as seriously indebted at all: it appears to have been moderately indebted only in 1984, and to a lesser extent in the period 1982-1983 and 1985-1987, while in other years it was only lightly indebted. Fourthly, in 1990, among the federal units only Kosovo was seriously indebted, the indebtedness of Montenegro, Macedonia, Serbia, and Bosnia and Hercegovina was moderate, while Voivodina, Croatia, and especially Slovenia were only lightly indebted. And finally, according to repayment projections made by Yugoslav and international financial authorities, the Yugoslav external debt should decrease considerably in subsequent years, although the reliability of these projections is questionable. Inability to service external debt is actually appearing again in 1991.

To evaluate the historical development of the Yugoslav external debt and present degree of indebtedness of Yugoslavia and its federal units, first the World Bank criteria for evaluation of a country's indebtedness are presented, and next they are applied in the evaluation of the level of indebtedness of Yugoslavia and each of its federal units. In this framework the indicators of indebtedness are constructed for the federal units without and with federal debt allocated to the individual federal units. Different criteria are proposed and applied to this allocation.

1. The World Bank Indebtedness Criteria

Different indicators of external indebtedness or repayment burden are known (proposed) in theory. The World Bank has applied some of them to evaluate a country's indebtedness with them. Thus, at the beginning of the 1980s as a threshold of critical indebtedness the 25% value of debt service ratio (the relation between principal and interest due for repayment, and hard currency earnings from export of goods and services in a given year) was used. At the end of the 1980s, the World Bank developed a more complex scheme of four indicators of indebtedness with their marginal values, which, when exceeded in at least three indicators, shift a country from the light to the moderately or severely indebted category.[1]

These criteria will be applied for evaluation of indebtedness of Yugoslavia and its federal units, depending on data availability.

Table 1

World Bank Indebtedness Criteria Limits

(in %)

External Indebtedness Indicator	Light (L)	Moderate (M)	Serious (S)
Debt/GNP = D/P	up to 30	30- 50	over 50
Debt/Export of goods and services = D/E	up to 165	165-275	over 275
Debt services[a)]/Export of goods and services = A/E	up to 18	18- 30	over 30
Interest/Export of goods and services = I/E	up to 12	12- 20	over 20

a) actually paid principal and interest on external debt.

Source: World Debt Tables, 1990-1991, vol. 1, The World Bank, Washington D.C., December 1990.

2. Evolution of Yugoslav Debt and Indebtedness

2.1 History of Yugoslav Debt

In 1964 the Yugoslav external debt was US$ 1000 million only. In Table 2 the evolution of aggregate debt (short, medium, and long-term, convertible and nonconvertible) as well as the amount of credits extended by Yugoslavia to other countries, and net debt as difference between the two is given for the period 1965-1990. The series are given, first, in current US$ (mostly according to the exchange rate set by the Central Bank).

Table 2

Debtor-Creditor Position of Yugoslavia

(in US$ millions)

	Current Dollars			Fixed Relation DM/US$		
Year	Debts (A)	Out-standings (B)	Net Debt (C)	Debts (A)	Out-standings (B)	Net Debt (C)
1965	1243	198	1045			
1966	1418	237	1181			
1967	1620	271	1349			
1968	1840	312	1528			
1969	2115	407	1708			
1970	2350	492	1858			
1971	3177	479	2699			
1972	3933	506	3427			
1973	4663	683	3980			
1974	5360	708	4652			
1975	6584	786	5798	7703	920	6783
1976	7934	916	7018	8886	1026	7860
1977	9540	1116	8424	10065	1177	8888
1978	11832	1107	10725	11666	1092	10574
1979	15232	1220	14012	14348	1149	13199
1980	18873	1526	17347	18873	1526	17347
1981	21096	1585	19511	22931	1723	21208
1982	20265	1718	18547	22575	1914	20661
1983	20577	1848	19792	24857	2232	22625
1984	20200	1917	18283	26381	2504	23877
1985	19837	1902	17935	22376	2145	20231
1986	20590	2162	18428	20652	2168	18490
1987	21961	2412	19549	20050	2202	17848
1988	20220	3391	16829	19573	3282	16291
1989	18569	3355	15214	17343	3134	14209
1990	17791	3052	14739	15834	2716	13118

Sources: Biltens NBJ, Belgrade; Yugoslalvia 1981-1988 (SZS, Belgrade); Yugoslavia – Statistical Survey, 5, 6, NBJ, Belgrade, 1991; Bremec (1988).

To some extent the evolution of Yugoslav debt followed a similar path as some other LDCs on the one hand, and other East European Countries on the other hand. The first oil crisis in 1973/1974 aggravated the Yugoslav balance on current account. The internal adjustment efforts to equilibrate it again were not strong enough (otherwise than, for instance, in some developed, net oil importing countries), and at the same time the supply of cheap "petro-dollars" appeared attractive to the LDCs, already over the threshold of development. Yugoslavia was one of them and, like most of them, quickly increased the volume of its debts in the second half of the 1970s. The underlying document for this was a decision of the Federal Government in 1976 to catch up on technological development in the world by intensive borrowing of foreign capital. But before a detailed agreement could be reached on how much each federal unit (or its commercial banks) can borrow within the planned total sum of borrowing, and for what purpose exactly, Yugoslavia's external debt increased to US$ 12 billion until 1978, and at the beginning of the 1980s, after the second oil shock (in the past Yugoslavia imported 10-12 million tons of crude oil yearly), the country became incapable of servicing its debts.

Under pressure of an IMF stand-by arrangement the new government of Milka Planinc started an austerity program in 1982. External pressure of creditors as an excuse helped the federal government to execute this program successfully until the end of 1984. The indications of success were, among other things, the regulation of debt relations with creditors (reprograming), and an equilibrated balance of payments in 1984. But, immediately after the external pressure had decreased a little (the reason being a well executed program and regular debt service), the "counter-attack" of the opponents of the economic program occurred at the end of 1984. The external equilibrium and overall economic situation worsened quickly under the new government of Branko Mikulic until 1987 (with substantial "help" by his government's economic policy, known as "programed inflation"), when Yugoslavia for the second time proclaimed its inability to service its debts, which meanwhile at the end of 1987 had reached its absolute maximum in current US$. In an arrangement with creditors (a new stand-by arrangement) a new stabilization program ("three anchors") was started in May 1988, but because of its harsh effects, and lost credibility, the government had to resign at the end of 1988.

A new government, under Ante Markovic, started its mandate without any stabilization program, which brought the country into enormous internal disequilibrium (hyperinflation) at the end of 1989, and that was the signal to start a "shock therapy" in December 1989. In the first half of 1990 inflation was checked, external reserves increased considerably, and external debts decreased continuously. But success in external relations was only transitory. Mistakes in the choice of program (a gradual approach would have been better, because the government lacked the know-how for executing such a complex stabilization program, and above all because of the lack of either social consensus or the necessary power to execute such a program regardless of its, at least temporary, negative social and thus political consequences), and also in its execution caused a substantial reduction of hard currency reserves and the second largest current account deficit in Yugoslav modern history at the end of 1990. In the middle of 1991 hard currency reserves are already at minimum level (below two months' expenses for import of goods and services), the current balance of payments is bound to be more negative than in 1990, and for the third time after the war the country is unable to service its debts, which will start to increase again.

2.2 The Impact of Exchange Rate Changes on the Volume of the Yugoslav Debt

Next, during the debt crisis (1975-1990), the three series (Table 2) were converted by fixed exchange rates under the following assumptions:

- fixed relation DM/US$ = 1.9378 from the year 1980,
- DM represents all non-dollar convertible currencies,
- about half of the debt is denominated in dollars (according to available information for 1987 and 1990).

It is the purpose of this calculation to eliminate the impact of the fluctuations of the exchange rate on the volume of debts and credits, because they are given exogenously to domestic policy. When the dollar becomes stronger, the value of debts and credits which are subject to exchange rate changes decreases, because the amounts of debts and credits, denominated in non-dollar currencies, when transformed into dollars, become smaller. As a result, the debt, expressed in current dollars, is de facto smaller, not as a result of successful domestic policy of the debtor country, but due to exchange rate changes in the world financial markets.

Thus, without the increasing value of the dollar in the first half of the 1980s, the Yugoslav external debt as well as net indebtedness would have continuously grown. Their actual stagnation during that time was therefore a result of exchange rate changes. In the second half of the 1980s, however, because of the decreasing value of the dollar, the external debt, expressed in current dollars, was falling slower than would have been the case, if the exchange rate changes, given from outside, would not have occurred. The estimate of the volume of debt on the basis of assumed fixed currency relations thus gives new information about the success of the economic authorities in their debt repayment efforts. Due to substantially improved external conditions (decreasing oil prices, interest rates, and dollar) the debt repayment policy was in fact much more successful in the second part than in the first part of the 1980s, but it was hidden because of the exchange rate changes (Štiblar, 1988). The data for the last few years in Table 2 differ slightly from the data in the World Debt Tables.

2.3 The Degree of Yugoslavia's Indebtedness in the 1980s

Different calculations exist about the indebtedness of Yugoslavia from domestic and foreign, individual and institutional sources, after it became a member of the "club" of Highly Indebted Countries in the early 1980s. The reasons for the differences lie in different definitions used for debt aggregates and indicators of indebtedness (Babic, 1989, for instance, defines more than 10 such indicators). But to show the official international evaluations of Yugoslav indebtedness that are the most relevant for its creditors, and at the same time to apply the newest World Bank criteria for Yugoslav indebtedness in the critical 1980s, we give the values of the four indicators mentioned before, as presented for Yugoslavia in the World Debt Tables, 1990-1991 (Table 3).

Table 3

Degree of Yugoslav Indebtedness in the 1980s

(in %)

Year Indicator	1982	1983	1984	1985	1986	1987	1988	1989
D/P	31.5	43.8	44.4	48.2	33.3	34.6	42.2	33.5
D/E	101.8	123.0	118.2	129.6	112.5	112.7	94.3	84.3
A/E	20.9	21.9	27.0	19.4	21.0	19.4	16.8	16.0
i/E	9.9	10.9	15.9	10.7	10.7	9.9	8.5	6.4

Symbols are explained in Table 1.

Source: World Debt Tables, 1990-1991.

It is clear from Table 3 that according to the World Bank criteria Yugoslavia never belonged to the severely indebted countries during the 1980s. The country was in the worst position in 1984 (as moderate debtor according to three out of four indicators); in the periods 1982-1983 and 1985-1987 Yugoslavia was a moderate debtor only by two out of four indicators, while before 1982 and after 1987 it was moderately indebted only by one out of four indicators.

2.4 Determination of Yugoslav Indebtedness – A Preliminary Analysis

The correlation analysis showed that the external factors (LIBOR, exchange rate changes, price of oil) are more relevant for growth of debts, indebtedness and repayment burden of Yugoslavia than internal factors (the economic activity indicators were the best available observables for "subjective" decisions made by the economic authorities in the country with respect to external debt growth and its repayment).

Next, some empirical results are presented, which indicate the impact of external factors and domestic activity on Yugoslav indebtedness and debt repayment burden as well as the dynamics between domestic economic activity and indebtedness (debt repayment burden) in the 1970s and 1980s.

D/P(%) = 39.198	– 2.057*LIBOR	– 6.551*DEM/US$	+ 1.069*OILP	R(2)	= .826	(1)
(5.529)	(-2.724)	(-3.530)	(6.181)	SE	= 4.591	
A/P = .067	– .0076*DEM/US$	– .0003*OILP		R(2)	= .873	(2)
(16.207)	(-3.530)	(-2.716)		SE	= .002	

Legend:
D/P(%) = debt/social product, in %, period 1970-1989
A/P = annuity/social product, period 1981-1989
LIBOR = London interbank offered rate, in %
DEM/US$ = ratio of two currencies
OILP = spot price of crude oil, in US$ per barrel
R(2) = coefficient of determination
SE = standard error of regression
(in parentheses are values of t-statistics).

The Role of External Factors. The following hypotheses have been followed:

a) the growth of LIBOR positively affects the repayment burden (increases interest to be paid, if a variable interest rate, related to LIBOR, was negotiated for external credits), and negatively affects the country's indebtedness (diverts the debtor from taking new credits if the interest rate, as its price, increases), if the country is free to decide about financial relations with foreign countries.

b) an increase in the DM/US$ relation means a stronger dollar with respect to other convertible currencies, which would (ceteris paribus) automatically decrease the value of the external debt, denominated in current dollars;

c) an increase of the price of oil would negatively affect the balance of payments (Yugoslavia is a net importer of 10-12 million tons of oil per year, at a cost of around 2 billion US$ in 1990, for instance), and thus could indirectly increase the country's external debt.

The estimated regression equations (yearly data, period 1970-1989 for indebtedness indicator D/P, 1981-1989 for indicator of debt repayment burden A/P) mainly support the above stated hypotheses. All explanatory variables are statistically significant and with plausible sign.

Thus, an increase in LIBOR by 1 percentage point decreased the D/P ratio by 2 percentage points; an analogous increase in DM/US$ decreased D/P by 6.5 percentage points (about 50% of Yugoslav convertible debt is denominated in US$); an increase in the price of oil by 1 US$ per barrel increased the D/P ratio in the same year by 1.069 percentage points (see equation (1)).

From equation (2), in the 1980s an increase of DM/US$ by 1 decreased debt repayment burden by 0.0076, or 0.76%, while the immediate effect of changes in the oil prices is smaller, because it is more indirect: an increase of the spot price of crude oil by 1 US$ per barrel decreased (not increased as expected) the debt repayment burden A/P, but only by 0.03%. In general, changes in external factors affect indebtedness more intensively than the debt repayment burden of Yugoslavia.

The Effect of Domestic Activity on the Debt Repayment Burden. There was a dispute in the literature whether positive domestic results increase or decrease the debt repayment burden of the debtor country. The first answer could hold only for critically indebted countries, whose debt repayment burden is so large that they cannot repay it, if domestic economic results are not good. For Yugoslavia in the 1980s empirical evidence shows exactly that. This result should be taken with certain reservations, because of the shortness of the observation period (yearly data, 1981-1989), although the estimated regression coefficient is moderately statistically significant (equation (3)).

$$A/XC\,(\%) = \underset{(30.199)}{28.427} + \underset{(2.074)}{1.103} * rP(\%) \qquad R(2) = .292 \quad SE = 2.68 \qquad (3)$$

Legend:

A/XC (%) = annuity/convertible exports, in %
rP (%) = yearly rate of growth of social product, in %
R(2) = determination coefficient
SE = standard error of regression
(in parentheses are values of t-statistics).

The estimated regression indicates that during the 1980s an increase of the social product growth rate by 1 percentage point increased Yugoslavia's debt service ratio by 1.1 percentage point in that year.

2.5 Yugoslavia as a Debtor Compared with the LDCs and East European Debtors

Yugoslavia belonged to the group of 17 Highly Indebted Countries (by World Bank classification) among Less Developed Countries (LDCs) as critical debtors in the past, and at the same time it belongs also to the East European Countries (in trasition) as potential critical debtors in the future. It is interesting to analyze similarities and differences of Yugoslavia and the two groups of countries with respect to the debt problem.

The Highly Indebted Countries (HICs) and Yugoslavia. The basic result arising from the empirical analysis (Štiblar, 1988) is that in the first subperiod 1980-1985 the HICs as a group followed more restrictive economic policies, but because of the unfavorable external economic conditions their economic results were highly negative. In the second subperiod, 1986-1987, however, more favorable external conditions, despite a less restrictive economic policy, led to better economic results. Within the group, Yugoslavia's economic performance worsened in the second period (because of a more expansive economic policy, inappropriate changes in the economic system, and an unfavorable political climate), despite a significant improvement of its external conditions and decrease in the external burden. The calculated loss was 7.5% of GNP yearly. Contrary to predictions for 1988, based on average economic behavior of the HICs as a reference criterion, Yugoslavia experienced a negative economic result in 1988 (equivalent to -6.6% of GNP).

The East European Countries (EECs) and Yugoslavia. The seven EECs handled the debt crisis emerging at the beginning of the 1980s better than the HICs among the LDCs, but not permanently, because after 1985 (contrary to the LDCs) their indebtedness started to increase quickly, and will probably achieve a new absolute maximum in 1991. Besides Poland, Yugoslavia was the most indebted among all EECs, but from 1988 on, its position among the EECs improved (Fink, Mauler, 1989). Currently, according to indicators of indebtedness, Poland, Hungary, and Bulgaria seem to be in a worse position, while Yugoslavia's is not above average indebtedness of the EECs. The empirical analysis (see Štiblar, 1990) shows that the Yugoslav debt burden seems to be below the average of EECs, taking into account average values of external factors (LIBOR, DM/US$) and economic performance (growth rate of social product). Apparently the special role of Yugoslavia as a member of the group of HICs, its stand-by arrangements with IMF, special political position, and its severe indebtedness at the beginning of the 1980s helped the country to achieve better repayment conditions than the EECs on average.

Comparative Characteristics. For both groups of countries, the HICs and the EECs, in which Yugoslavia is included, it is clear that the external determinants (LIBOR, exchange rate changes, price of oil) have been more relevant than internal ones (growth of economic activity in the country). The relation of economic activity to indebtedness is positive for the EECs as currently less indebted (and thus able to service their debt regularly), and negative for the HICs as more severely indebted. The implication for Yugoslavia is, that the deteriorating external conditions (increase of prices of oil, LIBOR and dollar) together with negative domestic economic performance would increase its indebtedness and debt repayment burden in the future. But as the country improved its position to become moderately indebted (disregarding current political problems), additional foreign capital could help to improve Yugoslavia's economic performance. That is more likely to happen under three conditions: that foreign investments are direct (bringing technology and management improvements additional to the fresh money); that a well prepared domestic stabilization program is executed, and political and social stability achieved; and that the external conditions are stabilized (continuous growth of the world economy and world trade, stabilized prices in world markets, and easier entry into the developed economies).

3. Repayment of Existing Yugoslav Debt

3.1 The Maturity of Yugoslav Debts

For its future economic performance the country's repayment burden has an important role. At least two independent sources of data on the time structure of Yugoslav debt repayment exist for the 1990s: a domestic source for maturity of convertible medium and long-term debts (Yugoslavia – Statistical Survey, BNY, Belgrade, No. 5 and 6, 1991), and a maturity schedule of the World Bank (World Debt Tables, 1990-1991; Washington, D.C., December 1990).

The schemes of debt repayment for Yugoslavia presented in Table 4 anticipate a significant decrease of debt in the 1990s, a prediction which should be taken into account with scepticism, firstly, because total debt repayment and debt extinction was never proclaimed as an official Yugoslav government strategy, and secondly, because such strategy cannot presently be realized, even if it were intended.

Table 4

Time Structure of Maturity of Yugoslav Debts, 1991-2000

(in US$ millions)

	NBY – Convertible Debt					World Bank – Total Debt		
Year	Multi	Govt.	Banks	Other	Total	Principal	Interest	Total
1991	571	1534	–	520	2625	1624	1285	2909
1992	563	748	–	272	1583	1425	1163	2588
1993	461	685	320	189	1655	1544	1057	2601
1994	332	631	374	111	1448	1597	914	2511
1995	270	619	374	76	1339	1647	799	2446
1996	228	472	374	31	1105	1422	682	2104
1997	173	365	374	24	936	1244	581	1825
1998	153	348	378	15	894	1071	478	1549
1999	100	38	382	17	537	655	394	1049
2000	70	45	382	8	505			
After 2000	635	248	2302	205	3390			

Sources: Yugoslavia, Statistical Survey, 1991, NBY, Belgrade; World Debt Tables 1990-1991, Volume 2, The World Bank, 1990.

3.2 Debt Repayment as an Element of Current Critical External Liquidity

Already in 1990 Yugoslavia's arrears in debt repayment amounted to US$ 640 million, and some additional rescheduling of debt repayments of above US$ 800 million due in 1991 are proposed by the Yugoslav government. Taking into account already reached refinancing of US$ 1.6 billion per year until 1995 (agreement with commercial banks in 1989), it still remains for Yugoslavia to repay around US$ 4.5 billion of principal and interest due in 1991.

But in mid-1991 Yugoslav external liquidity again became critical (previous examples had been 1981, 1982 and 1987).

In the face of collapsing external liquidity the federal government is proposing a new shock program (the fourth attempt since December 1989) which includes:

(1) A reduction of the federal budget by 40% (from US$ 6.5 billion to 4 billion). It will cover only expenses for army and administration, while all the subsidies are eliminated.

(2) An attempt to acquire at least US$ 3 billion to repay principal due and interest in 1991 and to keep financing minimal imports of goods and services to prevent domestic production from collapse. Hard currency reserves fell from over US$ 10 billion nine months ago to US$ 4,550 million at the end of June 1991, and are scheduled to decrease further, to US$ 3.6 billion by September 1991. They will not suffice to meet the country's external debt obligations and definitely indicate that the official time tables of debt repayment will not be

realized. Rather than decrease, an increase of Yugoslavia's external debt can be expected in the near future.

(3) Other measures, mentioned as elements of the Federal Government's "shock therapy" in its fourth version (July 1991), are some long run oriented changes in the economic system. They include privatization in the sphere of social ownership, development of a free capital market, and the development of the private sector. In principle there is nothing wrong with them, except that they do not belong to the economic policy measures which could prevent the collapse of the country's economy in the second half of 1991. And further, they show that the Federal Government is much more successful in proposing future visions of changes in the economic system than in the identification, quantification and sequencing of short run economic policy measures needed to bring the economy into a normal state first, or even to keep it alive, so that system changes can take place.

(4) No explicit announcement of monetary policy was included except for a general proposition that it should be restrictive. However, in view of the shortage of budget revenues (only about two thirds of expected revenues accrued in the first half of 1991, the rest was financed by central bank credits), the demand for further selective credits for agriculture and the constant danger of illegal credit demands and money emissions of individual federal units threaten to frustrate the maintenance of such restrictiveness. This will lead to increasing inflation, indicating growing internal disequilibrium in the economy.

At the same time, it is obvious to the Federal Government that the needed fresh money to close the external disequilibrium will not come from abroad, because a new standby arrangement with IMF (as a precondition for foreign governments and banks to negotiate new credits for Yugoslavia) will very probably not be concluded this year. Even financial assistance already promised by EC is not disbursed in the light of the present situation in the country.

Hard currency earnings from current international relations are diminishing, so that they cannot be a source of financing debt repayments. Thus, in the first four months of 1991 the country's current balance of payments deficit amounted to US$ 1,369 million. Because of the political crisis, export in the summer months of 1991 is at least 30% below last year's value, earnings from tourism are expected to be only US$ 250 million instead US$ 1,750 million, and net remittances from workers abroad are negative.

According to the attempt to save the country from external liquidity collapse (not to mention the hoped-for relief of the debt repayment burden), the Federal Government is therefore counting on the only remaining source of hard currency: the savings of the population held at home (not in banks, because their approximate volume of US$ 12 billion is already used) or abroad. The goverment is preparing to sell state owned apartments for hard currency or to permit private business investments in hard currency. However, this is apparently not a measure of short run effect, needed to acquire hard currency by the autumn of 1991.

The pessimistic scenario for the Yugoslav economy in the fall of 1991 is: hard currency reserves will diminish further, to US$ 3 billion, which will put a brake on imports, therefore production (falling already by a more than 20% yearly rate), will decrease further, and it can even happen that lack of hard currency will not enable the import of crude oil (at least US$ 2 billion yearly are needed for that purpose), leading to a "cold winter".

4. External Debt and Indebtedness of Yugoslav Federal Units

According to available data (Yugoslavia, Statistical Survey, No. 5, NBJ, Belgrade, March 1991) convertible medium- and long-term debt, pertinent to the Federation as such (and not assignable to any of its individual units, republics or autonomous provinces), in December 1990 was US$ 3,609 million out of the sum of US$ 16,017 million of this kind of total Yugoslav debt. At the end of 1989 the debt of the federation was US$ 3,917 million. The relevant question appears: according to what criteria should the federal debt by assigned to the individual federal units. Because the federation as such has no original assets or sources of income to repay her debt, its reallocation to federal units will thus give a more realistic picture of their indebtedness and the debt repayment burden. The federation, namely, neither produces a product nor earns hard currency income (Yugoslav National Army armaments production is an exception). Therefore, how can the federation repay its debts, if not by taking money from the federal units?

4.1 Criteria for Allocation of Federal Debt to Federal Units

First ideas about criteria for distributing the federal debt to the federal units have already appeared in public discussion. Thus, for instance, as one of the general principles it was suggested that debts and other obligations of the federation should be distributed among the federal units according to their shares in the already attributed (non-federal) debts. On the other hand, the claims and assets of the federation (for instance, hard currency reserves and credits given to foreigners) should be attributed by the share of federal units in the hard currency inflow of the country.

Obviously, a clear-cut and entirely just solution does not exist, because of, among other things, lack of statistical information and financial interrelations. It is not clear, for instance, who had the final benefit from credits taken by the federation abroad, the federal unit which actually received hard currency from these credits as a loan from the federation, or the federal unit, to which these credits were given in domestic currency (for use to finance the building of a road by domestic constructors, for instance) with favorable repayment conditions (sometimes they were never paid back at all). Therefore, some kind of compromise solution is necessary.

A whole spectrum of possible criteria for allocation of federal debts to federal units is presented next. These criteria could be classified as technical or functional. The first are based primarily on available economic aggregates today, the second on the economic aggregates that were relevant at the time of the maximum external debt burden during the second half of 1970s, more exactly in the period 1975-1981.

According to the first four criteria the apportionment is made according to the present economic power of federal units (except for the first criterion) and, therefore, according to the ability (possibility) to repay debts. These criteria are:

- the share in the debt, ascribed to the federal units, on September 30, 1989,
- the share in the Yugoslav social product in 1989,
- the share in total Yugoslav export of goods and services in 1989,
- the share in Yugoslav convertible export of goods and services in 1990.

The last three criteria would suggest that the shares of federal units are quite similar, but the shares in debt differ substantially from the actual share in debts: they are smaller in more developed and larger in less developed federal units.

Below, the five functional criteria intend to take into account the federal unit which actually used foreign credits. Therefore, it was taken into account that in the period of fastest growth of the Yugoslav debt (from 1974, when the debt was only US$ 5.3 billion, to 1981, when debt increased to US$ 21.1 billion), the new credits were almost exclusively used to import consumer goods, machinery and equipment, and for investment in fixed assets. In detail, the following criteria were formulated:

- share of federal unit in Yugoslav investment in fixed funds in the period 1975-1981,
- share in total Yugoslav import in the period 1978-1981,
- share in Yugoslav import of capital equipment, 1978-1981,
- share in Yugoslav imports of consumer goods, 1978-1981,

- share in Yugoslav imports of goods of a higher degree of processing 1978-1981.

Table 5

Criteria for Attribution of Federal Debt to Federal Units

(shares in %, Yugoslavia = 100%)

Criterium	Bosnia	Monten.	Croatia	Maced.	Sloven.	Serbia	Kosovo	Voivod.
Share in debt Sept. 1989	13.8	5.2	24.3	6.1	12.9	25.6	6.4	5.6
Share in product 1989	12.1	1.9	25.6	5.4	19.5	22.5	2.1	11.0
Share in exports total, 1989	15.2	2.0	21.0	4.9	35.5	21.5	1.7	8.2
Share in exports convert., 1990	13.0	1.4	20.9	3.9	30.8	20.6	1.1	8.3
Share in invest. fixed, 75-81	15.0	3.1	24.5	6.2	15.2	21.8	3.8	10.3
Share in imports total, 78-81	12.4	2.1	28.4	5.8	17.6	21.4	2.4	9.9
Share in imports equipment, 78-81	13.2	3.9	24.1	7.2	11.8	26.0	4.7	9.2
Share in imports consum., 78-81	7.3	1.5	23.5	6.2	20.0	33.3	1.9	6.3
Share in imports processed, 78-81	10.2	2.4	24.3	6.1	21.9	24.7	3.1	7.4
Average share	12.5	2.6	24.1	5.8	19.5	24.2	3.0	8.5

Source: author's own calculations.

The variability of shares for individual federal units is higher for functional than for technical criteria. Only the difference in the share of imports of consumer goods is more significant (with relatively higher share of Serbia on account of Bosnia and Hercegovina, Montenegro and Voivodina). The average shares calculated in Table 5 from all nine criteria respresent a rather mechanical operation.

4.2 External Debt of the Federal Units

According to available data the size of debt, credits and net debt as difference between the two on September 30, 1990 is given in the following Table 6 (no big changes could be expected to occur in the period thereafter):

Table 6

Debts, Credits Given and Net Debts of Federal Units, September 1990

(in current US$ millions)

	Convertible Area			Clearing Area			Net Debt
	Debt	Credit	Net	Debt	Credit	Net	Total
Bosnia and Herc.	1677	533	1144	456	43	413	1557
Montenegro	597	8	589	67	–	67	656
Croatia	2994	757	2237	34	117	-83	2154
Macedonia	761	20	741	75	1	74	815
Slovenia	1788	379	1409	10	4	6	1415
Serbia	3302	652	2650	522	28	494	3144
Kosovo	726	–	726	75	–	75	801
Voivodina	841	78	763	57	3	54	817
Federation	3609	–	3609	–	555	-555	3054
Yugoslavia	16295	2427	13868	1296	751	545	14413

Source: WIIW Forschungsberichte No. 175.

From Table 6 it is clear that the volume of debt varies a lot among republics and autonomous provinces, but that the largest convertible currency debtor is in fact the federation. As mentioned, the debt of the federation should be attributed to the federal units, because the federation as such has no material sources to service it.

The volume of debt to the countries under clearing arrangement with Yugoslavia (until 1991 the Soviet Union is the strongest partner, the others are Czechoslovakia, Mongolia, Vietnam, and North Korea) was considerably reduced recently, only slightly exceeding 1 billion dollars at present. If one takes into account a positive balance on Yugoslav clearing accounts from current transactions with these countries (around US$ 2.3 billion), it is clear that the Yugoslav net position with these countries is positive. In connection with this, the problem arises for Yugoslavia, not how to repay, but how to get paid back. According to the goals of economic policy for 1991 it was expected that one part of the positive balance on current clearing accounts will be used to repay some debts with these countries in advance, while the other part (US$ 550 million) should be used for additional imports of goods from this area.

Thus, from the perspective of debt repayment the problem of convertible debt of the federation (US$ 3,609 million) is crucial. To get a more realistic picture of indebtedness of the federal units, the federal debt should be allocated also to them. To do that, the following four of the previously proposed eight criteria are taken into account:

a) The share of federal unit in total debt, already apportioned to the federal units (Da),

b) the average share of the federal unit by three "technical criteria" of economic power of the federal unit (Db),

c) the average share of the five "functional" criteria of the share of the federal unit in investments, or imports during the period of fastest growth of Yugoslav debts in 1978-1981 (Dc),

d) the simple average of the shares for each federal unit according to all nine proposed criteria (Dd).

The share of federation debt added to each federal unit increases its own debt, given in Table 6, and their sum is given in Table 7.

Table 7

Medium- and Long-term Convertible Debt of Federal Units, September 1990

(in US$ millions)
with the part of Federal debt added

FEDERAL UNIT / DEBT	Original	Da	Db	Dc	Dd
Bosnia and Hercegovina	1677	2153	2161	2096	2125
Montenegro	597	767	662	691	687
Croatia	2994	3845	3806	3896	3860
Macedonia	761	978	931	988	970
Slovenia	1788	2297	2701	2412	2495
Serbia	3302	4240	4078	4219	4183
Kosovo	726	932	784	841	831
Voivodina	841	1079	1173	1151	1151
Federation	3609				
Yugoslavia	16295				

Note: Da, Db, Dc, Dd are estimated aggregate debts of federal units according to criteria presented above under these letters.

Sources: as in previous tables.

4.3 The Degree of External Indebtedness of the Federal Units

To calculate the first indicator of indebtedness, viz external debt/social product (D/P), the social product for individual federal units should be estimated for 1990 first, because official statistical information is not yet available. The known social product in 1989 is taken as basis in the process of its estimation together with known information about the fall of total Yugoslav social product in 1990 by 7.5% (source: Documentation Annex to the Federal Government Resolution on Economic Policy in 1991), and at the same time the industrial production (comprising half of social product) fell by 10.8%. Thus, the relation of the fall in the industrial production for each republic to its fall on the federal level is taken as a coefficient (proxy) for adjustment in the estimation of the 1990 social product on the basis of known 1989 social product for each individual federal unit. The fall, thus estimated, of the social product for individual federal units in 1990 with respect to 1989 would be within the limits of 5.5% for Bosnia and Hercegovina and 6.7% (Voivodina) on one hand, and 11.5% (Montenegro) to 18.8% (Kosovo) on the other.

Table 8

Convertible Debt/Social Product, (D/P), in the Federal Units in 1990

(Social Product in US$ millions, D/P in %)

	P	Do/P	Da/P	Db/P	Dc/P	Dd/P	Do/P 89
Bosnia and Hercegovina	6612	25.4	32.6	32.7	31.7	32.1	21.0
Montenegro	958	62.3	80.1	69.1	72.1	71.7	61.6
Croatia	13591	22.0	28.3	28.0	28.7	28.4	21.0
Macedonia	2862	26.6	34.2	32.5	34.5	33.9	25.3
Slovenia	10407	17.2	22.1	26.0	23.2	24.0	14.7
Serbia	11954	27.6	35.5	34.1	35.3	35.0	25.3
Kosovo	998	72.7	93.4	78.6	84.3	83.3	58.9
Voivodina	5779	14.6	18.7	20.3	19.9	19.9	13.4
Yugoslavia	53161		30.1				28.7

Sources: Indeks SZS, Saopstenje SZS and sources as in previous tables. (Do – original debt; Da, Db, Dc, Dd are calculated from Table 7).

Estimated coefficients of indebtedness (indicating a long-run solvency) D/P show:

- indebtedness of the federal units and Yugoslavia increased in 1990, above all because of the fall in social product. Thus Yugoslavia is returning from the lightly to the moderately indebted countries;
- if the adequate shares of federal debt are added to the federal units according to the previously presented criteria of the World Bank (limits are 30% for moderately, 50% for severely indebted), Voivodina, Slovenia, and Croatia still belong to the light debtors, Macedonia, Serbia, and Bosnia and Hercegovina are moderate debtors, while Kosovo and Montenegro appear to be severely indebted.

To calculate the indebtedness indicator (convertible debt/ convertible export of goods and services) D/E, which expresses the degree of urgency of indebtedness in the short run (thus in the sense of liquidity), it was necessary to estimate hard currency earnings from convertible exports of goods and services for the individual federal units, since neither official nor inofficial data exist about hard currency earnings from the export of services by individual federal units. For now, only certain internal estimations exist for some republics, like Slovenia and Croatia.

In this situation we made our own estimation for 1990 of hard currency earnings from nonmaterial convertible exports.

Calculated nonmaterial hard currency earnings represent 41.5% of total Yugoslav hard currency earnings from export of goods and services in 1990.

Slovenia is far ahead of other federal units with regard to convertible earnings from export of goods (the closest, Croatia and Serbia, lag by almost 1/3). In the earnings from nonmaterial exports, Croatia, with a 48% share in Yugoslavia, is far ahead, while the next to follow (Serbia and Slovenia), realize only 1/3 of Croatian hard currency earnings from nonmaterial exports. Addition of nonmaterial to the material exports greatly improves the position of Montenegro (as expected, because of its tourism and transportation), while the share of earnings from nonmaterial exports for the remaining federal units (Bosnia and Hercegovina, Macedonia, Kosovo, and Voivodina) in total Yugoslav nonmaterial exports are smaller by more than half than the share of their earnings from material convertible exports. If earnings from material and estimated nonmaterial exports are added together for federal units in 1990, Croatia's share in Yugoslavia is almost 1/3, Slovenia's almost 1/4, Serbia's almost 1/5, the share of Bosnia and Hercegovina is 1/10, while, on the other hand the share of Kosovo for instance is only 1% (Table 9).

Table 9

Shares of Federal Units in Hard Currency Earnings of Yugoslavia in 1990 and Their Openness to the World

(in %)

Indicator/Federal Unit	Bosnia Herc.	Monte.	Croa.	Mac.	Slov.	Serb.	Kos.	Voi.	Yu.
Share in Hard Currency Earnings of Yugoslavia	10.7	3.2	32.2	3.2	24.2	19.1	1.1	6.2	100
Openness to World (Hard Currency Earnings/ Social Product)	33	67	48	23	47	32	22	22	38

Source: own estimations on the basis of NBY and SZS data.

It is interesting to estimate the "openness" of federal units to the World in 1990 as ratio of estimated total hard currency earnings to their social product. For Yugoslavia as a whole the coefficient is 38% (which is not a very large openness, and the goal of the present federal government is to achieve 50% by 1995, but in any case, it increased considerably in recent years). However, somewhat surprisingly (taking into account the lower level of economic development), by far the largest openness to the convertible world is shown by Montenegro (tourism, transportation), followed in the second group by Croatia and Slovenia. Below average, in the third group, are Serbia and Bosnia and Hercegovina, while the least open federal units are Macedonia, Kosovo, and Voivodina.

Now we turn to the estimated indicators of indebtedness D/E in Table 10. Apparently, Yugoslavia and its individual federal units are less indebted from the liquidity than from the solvency point of view, according to the criteria proposed by the World Bank.

Table 10

Convertible Debt/Export of Goods and Services, for Yugoslav Federal Units in 1990

(Export in US$ millions, D/E in %)

	Export Total	Do/E	Da/E	Db/E	Dc/E	Dd/E	Export Services
Bosnia and Herc.	2157	77.7	99.8	100.2	97.2	98.5	622
Montenegro	640	93.3	119.8	103.4	108.0	107.3	461
Croatia	6533	45.8	58.9	58.3	59.6	59.1	4065
Macedonia	652	116.7	150.0	142.8	151.5	148.8	185
Slovenia	4904	36.5	46.8	55.1	49.2	50.9	1281
Serbia	3864	85.5	109.7	105.5	109.2	108.3	1430
Kosovo	220	330.0	423.6	356.4	382.2	377.7	75
Voivodina	1260	66.7	85.6	93.1	91.3	91.3	274
Yugoslavia	20230		80.5				8394

Source: WIIW Forschungsberichte No. 175.

As a criterion to treat a country as moderately indebted, the value of coefficient D/E over 165% is proposed by the World Bank, and for severe indebtedness its value must be over 275%. Yugoslavia with its value of 80.5% in 1990 remains among lightly indebted countries. Without federal debts added to their individual debts (Do/E), Kosovo only among all federal units is severely indebted. If addition of adequate shares of federal debt to each federal unit is taken into account (indicators Da/E, Db/E, Dc/E, Dd/E), only Macedonia, besides severely indebted Kosovo, is approaching the limit of moderately indebted countries. Among other federal units the situation of Croatia, Montenegro, and Voivodina is considerably improved with indicator D/E compared to the indicator D/P.

To complete the picture of indebtedness of individual federal units in 1990, the remaining two indicators proposed by the World Bank are presented next: the ratio of debt service annuity to exports of goods and services, A/E, and the ratio of interest to exports of goods and services, i/E. However, in view of the lack of data on principal and interest repayments by each federal unit in 1990, they are estimated from the values for Yugoslavia as a whole, and ascribed to individual federal units. The share of a federal unit in total convertible debt of Yugoslavia (Dd) is taken as criterion of distribution. The reliability of this procedure was partially tested by comparison of estimated and actual data available only for Slovenia. Obviously, such an estimation rests on a large number of more or less unrealistic assumptions (equal interest rates, margins, maturity and other conditions for debts of individual republics), but they are necessary, if we want any kind of estimation at all of these indicators.

In interpreting the relatively favorable values of estimated indicators A/E and i/E in Table 11, it should be taken into account that the realized repayments of principal and interest are included and not the debt service annuities due, which, in fact, were much larger. The difference consist of two parts: the refinancing part of debt, and arrears in principal repayments in 1990, amounting to US$ 640 million. Thus the annuity due is approximately twice the annuity actually paid in 1990, and, with the first included in the calculation of both indicators, the picture of Yugoslav (and its federal units') debt burden would be much darker.

The coefficients in Table 11 indicate that according to the A/E, Kosovo and Macedonia (value of coefficient above 30%) are severely indebted, Bosnia and Hercegovina, Voivodina, Serbia, and Montenegro are moderately indebted (values above 18%), and Croatia and Slovenia are lightly indebted. At the same time, according to indicator i/E Kosovo was severely indebted in 1990 (its value was above 20%), Macedonia was moderately indebted (value above 12%), while all other federal units appear to be only lightly indebted.

In the calculation the four indicators of indebtedness together, the sum of them should not exceed 6 for light indebtedness, for moderate indebtedness it should be between 6 and 10, and for severe indebtedness above 10. The federal units are ranked by the level of indebtedness from the most severe (rank 1.) to the least severe (rank 8.).

Table 11

Debt Repayment Burden of Federal Units in 1990 and Their Classification by Level of Indebtedness

	A/E(%)	i/E(%)	Sum of 4 Indicators D/P	D/E	A/E	i/E	Rank
Bosnia and Hercegovina	21.0	9.7	L/M,	L,	M,	L = 5(6)	4-5. (L/M)
Montenegro	22.8	10.6	S,	L,	M,	L = 7	3. (M)
Croatia	12.6	5.8	L,	L,	L,	L = 4	7-8. (L)
Macedonia	32.1	14.9	L/M,	L,	S,	M = 7(8)	2. (M)
Slovenia	10.9	5.0	L,	L,	L,	L = 4	7-8. (L)
Serbia	23.1	10.7	L/M,	L,	M,	L = 5(6)	4-5. (L/M)
Kosovo	80.4	37.3	S,	S,	S,	S = 12	1. (S)
Voivodina	19.6	9.0	L,	L,	M,	L = 5	6. (L)
Yugoslavia	17.2	8.0	M,	L,	L,	L = 5	... (L)

Sources: WIIW Forschungsberichte No. 175, Federal Government resolution documents and previously mentioned statistical sources.

Legend:
A = annuity = actually paid principal and interest of convertible debt in 1990,
i = actually paid interest on convertible debt in 1990,
D = Debt
P = estimated social products in 1990,
E = estimated convertible export of goods and services in 1990,
L = light indebtedness (value 1 is given in the process of summing up),
M = moderate indebtedness (value 2),
S = severe indebtedness (value 3).

The way the variables of debts, their repayment, social product, and hard currency earnings were calculated (estimated), has a decisive impact on the picture of Yugoslavia's and its federal units' indebtedness in 1990, which is too favorable. But all these approximations do not considerably modify the relative position between individual federal units. Their ranking with respect to the degree of indebtedness is more credible, especially if the mistakes made in the process of estimation of the values of variables are of systematic nature. Therefore the evaluation of aggregate indebtedness of federal units is ultimately made by addition of the four indicators used as criteria of indebtedness by the World Bank; as figures in the second part of Table 10 show:

- Slovenia, Croatia, and to lesser extent Voivodina can be classified as lightly indebted (Slovenia's indebtedness is the smallest);
- Bosnia and Hercegovina, Serbia, Montenegro, and Macedonia belong to the group of moderately indebted countries (Bosnia and Hercegovina is the least, Macedonia the most indebted among them);

- Kosovo can be treated by all indicators and with all extenuating circumstances mentioned (decrease in the value of debt and annuity of its repayment, increase of hard currency earnings (from convertible exports of goods and services)) as severely indebted.

4.4 The Prospect of Debt Repayment by Federal Units

If Yugoslavia continues to disintegrate, the question arises whether its federal units will be able to service their debt. As movements for independence are strongest in Slovenia and Croatia, the above question is most relevant for each of them and then, maybe, for the remaining units of Yugoslavia together. Among them, however, Macedonia could also try to separate from the rest of Yugoslavia. Until now, only Yugoslavia as a whole was promised financial assistance from creditors, if and after political disputes are settled. Ability to service their debts can therefore be treated as one element of economic ability of federal units to become independent states.

The fact is, in that regard, that 85% of the current Yugoslav US$ 4.6 billion hard currency reserves is with the central bank (NBY). The remaining 15% (less than US$ 700 million) are on accounts of commercial banks belonging to individual federal units. Thus, according to inofficial estimates, Ljubljanska Banka of Slovenia has about US$ 125 million on its accounts. However, information on maturity of debts by federal units is not available; without additional foreign financial assistance (in Slovenia they reckon that up to US$ 1 billion would be necessary for a 6-12 month period after total economic independence), Slovenia will be unable to service its debts. The critical situation with respect to hard currency liquidity in Slovenia is stressed by three facts: first, in the final instance, not only direct credits (up to US$ 2 billion) should be serviced by Slovenia but, it could be, also credits taken by Ljubljanska Banka for debtors in other republics, and guarantees given for other credits (in which case the extent of Slovenia's financial obligations to foreigners almost doubles from US$ 2 billion); secondly, the principle of solidarity of responsibility for repayments of Yugoslav debts between all its federal units could be applied from the outside world in case of total economic disintegration of Yugoslavia; and third, besides foreign creditors, the domestic population is also a creditor to the state with its convertible currency accounts (around US$ 12 billion for Yugoslavia, US$ 2.7 billion in Slovenia) and they should be paid. As far as the latter is concerned, not only is that republic unable to pay out these convertible currency accounts to the public, but in Slovenia, for instance, the proposal came from banking circles that each citizen should pay (sell) additional

DM 100 from domestic savings to the state as a form of "tax for independence".

With regard to debt service, the situation is even worse in Croatia as second federal unit with strong independence intentions. Its current inflow of convertible currency is the most imperiled (tourism and transportation badly damaged, export greathly decreased), its own reserves of convertible currency can not be larger than Slovenia's, while its debt (and thus debt service) is substantially larger than Slovenia's.

To settle its economic situation, Croatia must count, with the recognition of its independence, on even much larger short-run foreign financial assistance (at least double of Slovenia's, it is estimated).

Notes

1. More about that can be found in the World Debt Tables, 1990-1991, Volume 1, The World Bank, Washington D.C., December 1990, page 121.

References

Analiza razvojnih moznosti Republike Slovenije, Zavod za plan Republike Slovenije, (1990), Ljubljana, April.

Babic M. (1989), "Medjunarodna ekonomija," *Privredni Vjesnik*, Zagreb.

Bilten NBJ, different issues, NBY, Belgrade.

Bremec, N. (1988), *Jugoslavanski dolg v luci svetovne dolzniske krize*, Pravna fakulteta, Ljubljana, January.

Bouchet, M.H. (1987), *The Political Economy of International Debt*, Westport, USA.

Cuddington, J.T., Smith W. (ed.) (1985), *International Debt and the Developed Countries*, A World Bank Symposium. Washington, D.C.

Economic Survey of Europe in 1988/1989, in 1989/1990, (1989), (1990), UN ECE, Geneve.

External Debt, Definition, Statistical Coverage and Methodology (1988), OECD, Paris.

Financial Market Trends, Special Feature on East-West Relations, OECD, Paris, different issues.

Fink, G., Mauler, K. (1989), *Hard Currency Position of CMEA Countries and Yugoslavia*, Reprint 115, WIIW, Vienna, January.

Fisher, S. (1989), "Public and Academic Debate in the Debt Crisis", *The World Bank Research News*, Washington, D.C., September.

Fried, E.R., Trezine, P.H. (1990), "Third World Debt: Phase Three Begins, Economic Impact", *US Information Agency*, Washington, D.C.

Indeks SZS, different issues, SZS, Belgrade.

Kobal, S. (1986), *Principi razdolzevanja Jugoslavije*, mimeograph, Ljubljana.

Miklic, A. (1990), *Polozaj Slovenije v ekonomskih odnosih s tujino*, DDG, ARC NB Slovenije, November.

Milkovic, N. (1991), *Strategija razdolzevanja Jugoslavije*, Pravna fakulteta, Ljubljana, April.

Predlog skupine zveznih zakonov ob stabilizacijskem paketu, Skupscina SFRJ Beograd, April 1991.

Rogoff, K. (1990), Symposium on New Institutions for Developing Country Debt, *Journal of Economic Perspectives*, IV/1, Winter.

Smerom reforme, Sekretariat za informisanje SIV, Beograd, April 1991.

Štiblar, F. (1990), "Comparative Empirical Analysis of the Performance of Yugoslavia and other Highly Indebted Countries," in Mrak, M. (ed), *Financial System and Policies in Yugoslavia*, Report for UNCTAD, Ljubljana, July.

Štiblar, F. (1990), "Spoljna zaduzenost zemalja istocne Evrope," PKJ, 1990/6, *EIPF* Ljubljana, June.

Štiblar, F. (1991/2), Znacaj resavanja duznicke krize Zemalja u razvoju za resavanje problema dugova Zemalja istocne Evrope, PKJ, *EIPF*, Ljubljana.

Vacic, A. (1989), Jugoslavija i Evropa, *Ekonomika*, Belgrade.

Winiecki, J. (1988), *East European Economies: Forced Adjustment Forever?* mimeograph, Institute for International Economic Studies, University of Stockholm, August.

World Debt Tables, 1990-1991 (1990), The World Bank, Washington, D.C., December.

Yugoslavia, *Statistical Survey* (1991), No. 5, No. 6, March, June, NBJ Beograd.

10

EAST-WEST GDP COMPARISONS: PROBLEMS, METHODS AND RESULTS*

Peter Havlik

1. Introduction

International comparisons of the level of real products (resp. incomes and productivity) have gained an importance which goes far beyond academic interest in knowing what the world does look like. Financial contributions to international organizations, preferential customs duties, access to soft term credits, and other preferential conditions in international relations (e.g. foreign aid) have traditionally been made dependent upon the economic strength of nations. An evaluation of the economic development level of the former Eastern Bloc countries is required also for the appropriate assessment of the need for potential Western assistance (e.g. relative to developing countries), for estimating the time period required by these countries for closing the generally acknowledged gap behind the West, for decisions pertaining to Western investments, and for other issues related to the ongoing transition to market economies.

Recalling that a pioneering study in this field, comparing GDP levels in Western Europe and the USA, was inspired by needs of international organizations (OECD, at that time OEEC, coordinating the Marshall Plan – see Gilbert and Kravis (1954)), and by practical problems in assessing contributions of member and associated states, we

---

* Research on this project was supported by a grant from the Austrian Forschungsförderungsfonds der gewerblichen Wirtschaft. The author is grateful to F. Levcik and K. Laski for useful comments, and to H. Rusek for the data processing. Needless to say, all remaining errors are the sole responsibility of the author.

can understand that today – when the idea of Western assistence is being discussed in relation to the reconstruction of Eastern Europe – an assessment of the comparative levels of these countries' economic development is extremely important. It can also be imagined that conflicting interests, controversies, and theoretical disputes arise because not only mere theory, but also substantial sums of money may be involved. Given this variety of economic and political interests (in addition to methodological and conceptual problems), it is no big surprise that a uniformly accepted comparison approach has not yet been either developed or applied in East-West comparative economic studies. This study reviews the appropriateness of individual estimation methods for comparative per capita GDP levels, discusses the available results and, last but not least, presents indigenous estimates of comparative East-West development levels.

For international comparisons of incomes there is a quasi standard point of reference in the form of the methodology elaborated within the UN sponsored International Comparison Project (ICP). Nevertheless, the unequivocally accepted data on comparative economic levels between market economies of the West (MEs) and the formerly centrally planned economies (CPEs) of Eastern Europe and the USSR are still lacking, inter alia, since the majority of former CPEs did not until very recently participate in ICP.

Comparative development levels can always be characterized only with the help of various statistical proxies which approximate, to a more or less acceptable degree, what is intended to be measured (we refer in this context also to the well-known index number problem). The lack of reliable information relating to East-West GDP comparisons in particular results from a mix of additional factors such as political differences in the past, purely methodological variations, and differences in the coverage between statistical systems. The problems have been further aggravated by the differences in socio-economic systems and in understanding what is considered as output: in MEs everything that finds a price on markets, as well as various non-market services (e.g. government), is treated as output; in the CPEs' methodology only the production of tangible goods (and services related to the production of such goods) enters the national income.

The switch from the traditional CPEs' accounting system (Material Product System – MPS) to the Western SNA standards forms one of the statistical priorities for countries in transition, but has not been completed yet. Moreover, the prices in CPEs were mostly artificially fixed and bore little relation to costs and scarcities. Even now, the statistical information generally published by the former CPEs leaves much to be desired as far as quantity and reliability of available data is concerned, and because of other problems related to revamping the traditional statistical systems to the needs of market economy.

Usually, the reporting bias by measurement of output may result both from national interests and from specific interests of the statistical reporting units. On the national level, on the one hand, most former CPEs presented their incomes until very recently rather on the high side (mainly for reasons of ideology and national pride). On the other hand, a desire to obtain favorable credit conditions from international financial institutions has led some CPEs to present their real incomes as low as possible. The discussions connected with Hungary's, Poland's, and Romania's applications for membership in the World Bank and IMF at the beginning of 1980s may serve as an example for the latter (see below). On the level of statistical reporting units (enterprises) we can observe that in CPEs, these often tended to overreport the main plan target (e.g. gross output, or net output) in order to reap premiums for planfulfilment, whereas in MEs there is a tendency to underreport profits in order to avoid taxation. Although the so called "shadow economy" has always been present to various degrees in both East and West, the statistical coverage of the newly emerging private sector in the East forms an especially acute and controversial problem today.

2. Available GDP Data for Eastern Countries in National Currencies

As mentioned above, the commonly used statistical measures of the level of economic activity differ in East and West. The Gross Domestic Product (GDP) and Gross National Product (GNP) measures respectively (the value of final goods and services produced in a country in a certain period)[1] had not been published until very recently by most CPEs, who used an indicator of Net Material Product (NMP) and National Income respectively for similar purposes. The NMP concept is based on a simplified Marxian perception of value and productivity and as such is narrowly defined since it includes the value of goods and services turned out by the so-called "productive sectors" only, i.e. most of the output of services is excluded from NMP. Moreover, NMP is net of depreciations. Since parts of the GDP and NMP (e.g. some "material consumption of the non-productive sectors") are overlapping, the conversion of GDP into NMP and vice versa is not straightforward.[2] Experience shows that the GDP may be 10-50% higher than the corresponding NMP – the difference being greater in countries with higher incomes (and with a more developed service sector)[3], and also growing over time, and may vary, depending on the rules for establishing depreciation charges. The diverging coverage of both indicators has, of course, an impact not only on absolute levels, but on growth rates of both indicators as well.

Hungary, Poland, and Romania (all members of the World Bank and IMF since the first half of 1980s) publish both indicators (though for Romania there have been reporting gaps during the last years of Ceausescu's rule). Recently, the Soviet Union introduced the GNP into its statistical accounting practice (see Vestnik statistiki (1988)), and started – since 1989 – to publish GNP estimates in rubles in official statistics. Czechoslovakia, too, presented first official GDP figures in late 1990 to IMF and World Bank during negotiations about its re-admission to both institutions, and started to publish the data on GDP in the 1990 statistical yearbook.

All countries of the former Eastern Bloc – now on the path of transition from the command to a market economy – plan to switch gradually to the system of statistical reporting which would correspond to the internationally standardized System of National Accounting (SNA). Eastern participants at the recent conference on Statistics of Central and Eastern European Countries (see Blades (1991)), organized jointly by OECD and the UN Economic Commision for Europe, declared the switch to the SNA system one of their statistical priorities. Naturally, the technical prerequisities for such a switch differ in each country of the region. On the one hand, Hungary may already have achieved the statistical standard of OECD countries; on the other hand Bulgaria, Romania, and the Soviet Union have yet to solve numerous conceptual and technical problems. The introduction of SNA in the CSFR and Poland could proceed without greater problems, given the substantial amount of conceptual work already done. But the problems of transition even in the field of statistical reporting must not be underestimated: even in Germany it will take at least two years before the statistical systems of its Eastern and Western parts will be united and comparable.[4]

The available GDP/GNP data for East European countries (in national currencies) are listed in Table 1 below. Obviously, these figures have little meaning for the purpose of international comparisons, and are presented here only for illustration.

3. Search for a Proper Convertor: Official Exchange Rates Versus PPPs

Unfortunately, the simple conversion of NMP into GDP in the national currency of an individual country does not solve the problem of international comparisons of real income levels, since the conversion of GDP (in national currency) into some common unit (e.g. US dollars)

Table 1

Gross Domestic Product

(billions of national currency, current prices)

	1985	1986	1987	1988	1989	1990
Bulgaria	32.6	34.4	36.5	38.3	39.5	44.5
CSFR	677.0	694.7	711.1	740.0	759.5	798.1
GDR	311.8	321.9	332.8	346.1	353.3	230.8
Hungary	1033.7	1088.8	1226.4	1409.5	1706.0	2106.9
Poland	10444.8	12953.0	16939.9	29628.7	119107.4	628887
Romania (GNP)	.	.	823.2	854.3	793.7	800
USSR (GNP)	777	799	825	875	924	960
Yugoslavia	11951.3	23399.8	52339.7	158328.3	.	.

Gross Domestic Product Per Capita

(thousands of national currency, current prices)

	1985	1986	1987	1988	1989	1990
Bulgaria	3.642	3.836	4.066	4.262	4.392	4.944
CSFR	43.624	44.667	45.621	47.360	48.530	50.834
GDR	18.721	19.345	19.975	20.756	21.498	14.247
Hungary	97.152	102.514	115.654	133.110	161.431	199.706
Poland	279.714	344.751	448.573	784.347	3140.107	16506.220
Romania (GNP)	.	.	35.885	36.963	34.282	34.483
USSR (GNP)	2.787	2.836	2.900	3.052	3.199	3.310
Yugoslavia	516.835	1005.405	2235.116	6718.505	.	.

Sources: National statistical yearbooks, IMF, DIW and own estimates (Year 1990).

is a far more difficult task. The very problem of international GDP and related (e.g. productivity, income, wages, etc.) comparisons consists in the search for the proper convertor from national currency. We take it for granted that ordinary exchange rates (ERs) do not serve well for such purposes even in MEs, since they do not reflect real purchasing power parities (PPPs) of national currencies and are subject to great fluctuations. This, of course, applies even more to deliberately set exchange rates of countries with non-convertible currencies (i.e. all CPEs) and, respectively, to countries with a multiple exchange rate system (till 1990 all former socialist countries except Hungary and Poland).[5] Research into the problems of PPPs shows that, apart from perhaps speculative reasons, which may have played a role in recent sharp fluctuations of the dollar exchange rate with respect to other major Western currencies, other "purely economic" factors may have come into play as well. Differences in productivity between high- and low-income countries in tradable and non-tradable goods as well as economic policy reasons (e.g. interest and budgetary policies, efforts to promote tourism, or exports, etc.) may be just as important. Naturally, in the case of the former CPEs market criteria used to play a much smaller role in establishing their official exchange rates, and such exchange rates were suited neither to secure a balanced current account nor did they reflect purchasing power parities: this found its ultimate appropriate reflection in the non-convertibility of the CPEs' currencies (Havlik (1990)). The establishment of proxy exchange rates for CPEs' currencies which could be used as convertors of national GDP data into common units thus forms the most serious bottleneck in East-West GDP comparisons.

But it must be stressed that even in the case of MEs the use of market exchange rates for purposes of international GDP comparisons is highly inappropriate. An illustration of the impact of different convertors on GDP per capita levels (converted with current exchange rates and/or PPPs respectively) for the OECD countries are provided by the data in Table 2 below. Experience of the EC countries shows that differences between market exchange rates and PPPs are considerable, especially for lower-income EC countries (in 1989 up to 76% in the case of Portugal, 45% in Greece, 16% in Spain – relative to PPP, in terms of ECU); the relation between the exchange rate of US$ and its domestic PPP in terms of ECU increased by more than 30 percentage points during 1985-1989.[6] Differences between exchange rates and PPPs (so called "exchange rate deviation indexes" – ERDI – defined as ratio of exchange rates and PPPs, both in terms of national currencies per US$) for the OECD countries are presented in Table 3. In 1980, the US$ was undervalued (e.g. DM 1.818 per US$) and its real PPP was much higher (DM 2.72 per US$; ERDI=0.669). In 1985, the opposite situation emerged: the US$ was grossly overvalued (DM 2.944 per US$) as compared with ist real PPP (DM 2.48 per US$; ERDI=1.188). Towards 1990, a situation similar to that in 1980 reappeared as the US$ exchange rate (DM 1.62 per US$) was again much below the PPP (DM 2.388 per US$; ERDI=0.678). Deviations of exchange rates from PPPs are even greater in lower income OECD countries (with a per capita GDP less than US$ 10,000 at PPPs) like Greece, Portugal and, especially, Turkey. There is a strong correlation between ERDI and the relative level of per capita GDP: PPPs are generally above exchange rates in the higher income countries, and below in the countries with lower incomes.[7] In sum, fluctuations of market exchange rates thus affect international comparisons of real GDPs in both space and time, and there is general agreement that for such comparisons the use of PPPs is much more appropriate.

Table 2

GDP per Capita in Selected OECD Countries

(in US dollars)

	1980	1985	1986	1987	1988	1989
	at current prices and exchange rates					
Austria	10184	8624	12258	15389	16683	16590
Belgium	11986	8095	11314	14153	15267	15393
FRG	13216	10189	14565	18253	19557	19182
Denmark	12941	11350	16086	19841	20967	20401
Finland	10802	11026	14342	18063	21342	23268
France	12335	9482	13213	15913	17101	17061
United Kingdom	9522	8047	9863	12055	14612	14642
Italy	8023	7451	10518	13174	14484	15051
Netherlands	11970	8688	12005	14475	15399	15063
Norway	14121	14009	16664	19919	21242	21498
Sweden	15028	12051	15869	19173	21551	22303
Switzerland	15920	14201	20581	25803	27492	26350
Japan	9069	10981	16120	19447	23235	22896
USA	11804	16559	17283	18254	19523	20629
Greece	4164	3366	3941	4606	5283	5399
Ireland	5656	5285	7120	8408	9250	9644
Portugal	2701	2144	3041	3765	4265	4629
Spain	5737	4307	5967	7542	8834	9703
Turkey	1272	1042	1126	1289	1313	1432
OECD Europe	9124	7317	9954	12247	13510	13623
OECD Total	9966	10852	13185	15216	16937	17375
	at current prices and PPPs					
Austria	7866	10748	11096	11640	12457	13407
Belgium	8099	10770	11156	11742	12668	13587
FRG	8840	12105	12646	13242	14100	14985
Denmark	8391	12279	12981	13277	13686	14392
Finland	7939	11447	11899	12708	13803	15022
France	8687	11720	12210	12769	13603	14565
United Kingdom	7873	11048	11693	12571	13555	14345
Italy	7974	10927	11426	12103	12999	13902
Netherlands	8626	11339	11749	12113	12768	13709
Norway	9392	13963	14801	15493	15920	16663
Sweden	9117	12727	13264	14015	14751	15533
Switzerland	10760	14437	15077	15734	16594	17696
Japan	7861	11805	12279	13140	14289	15501
USA	11804	16559	17283	18254	19523	20629
Greece	4522	6010	6204	6349	6808	7253
Ireland	4978	6911	7032	7557	8118	8984
Portugal	4278	5516	5826	6290	6739	7360
Spain	5767	7682	8070	8744	9466	10263
Turkey	2483	3547	3844	4170	4374	4484
OECD Europe	8817	12349	12900	13658	14624	15563
OECD Total	7277	9869	10327	10907	11632	12378

Source: National Accounts. Main Aggregates, Vol. 1. OECD, Paris, 1991.

Table 3

Differences Between Exchange Rates and PPPs

(ERDI = ER/PPP, in terms of NCU per US$)

	1980	1985	1986	1987	1988	1989	1990
Austria	0.772	1.246	0.905	0.756	0.747	0.808	0.700
Belgium	0.676	1.330	0.986	0.830	0.830	0.883	0.749
FRG	0.669	1.188	0.868	0.725	0.721	0.781	0.678
Denmark	0.648	1.082	0.807	0.669	0.653	0.705	0.595
Finland	0.735	1.038	0.830	0.704	0.647	0.646	0.564
France	0.704	1.236	0.924	0.802	0.795	0.854	0.734
United Kingdom	0.827	1.373	1.186	1.043	0.928	0.980	0.899
Italy	0.994	1.467	1.086	0.919	0.897	0.924	0.787
Netherlands	0.721	1.305	0.979	0.837	0.829	0.910	0.788
Norway	0.665	0.997	0.888	0.778	0.749	0.775	0.701
Sweden	0.607	1.056	0.836	0.731	0.684	0.696	0.604
Switzerland	0.676	1.017	0.733	0.610	0.604	0.672	0.573
Japan	0.867	1.075	0.762	0.676	0.615	0.677	0.734
USA	1.000	1.000	1.000	1.000	1.000	1.000	1.000
Greece	1.086	1.786	1.574	1.378	1.289	1.343	1.126
Ireland	0.880	1.308	0.988	0.899	0.878	0.932	0.810
Portugal	1.584	2.573	1.916	1.671	1.580	1.590	1.321
Spain	1.005	1.784	1.352	1.159	1.072	1.058	0.884
Turkey	1.952	3.404	3.414	3.235	3.331	3.131	2.554
OECD Europe	0.966	1.688	1.296	1.115	1.082	1.142	.
OECD Total	0.730	0.909	0.783	0.717	0.687	0.712	.

Source: Table 2, Energy, Prices and Taxes. Fourth Quarter 1990. OECD, Paris 1991, and own calculations.

Similar (and very likely even greater) fluctuations and differences between ERs and PPPs may be expected in former CPEs as well, although only scattered statistical evidence is available. The PPP data available for Hungary, Poland, and Yugoslavia (year 1985, with respect to Austrian Schillings) suggest very high ERDI figures (especially for Hungary: 2.329 in terms of Austrian Schillings) and undervalued currencies by official exchange rates (see Table 4).[8] Differences between ER and PPP were of a magnitude similar to the lower income OECD countries (e.g. in Turkey, Portugal, and Greece) already before the series of recent devaluations which attempted to fix the exchange rate at a "competitive level" (e.g. in Poland and Yugoslavia at the beginning of 1990, in the CSFR during 1990).

If we use the available PPPs as an approximation, we obtain (year 1985) for Hungary a per capita GDP of 5,625 international dollars (I$), for Poland I$ 4,018, and for Yugoslavia I$ 4,594 – figures which are roughly comparable with PPP-based values for the OECD countries in Table 2 above. Unfortunately, only for three former CPEs (which have been regularly participating in the ICP) are there more recent data on per capita GDP converted with PPPs. In 1989, PPP-converted (extrapolated from 1985 benchmark – see below) per capita GDP for Hungary amounted to I$ 6,200, for Poland to I$ 4,980, and for Yugoslavia to I$ 5,320. Comparable figures for Austria were I$ 13,710, for FRG I$ 15,220, and for the United States I$ 20,690.[9] The implicit ERDIs in 1989 would be 2.27 for Hungarian Forint and 2.28 for Polish Zloty.

Table 4

CPE's ERDIs Compared with Lower Income OECD Countries

(year 1985, ERDI with respect to US$ estimated)

	PPP (NCU per AS)	ER	ERDI	PPP (NCU per US$)	ER	ERDI
Austria	1.000	1.000	1.000	16.600	20.690	1.246
Spain	5.742	8.257	1.438	95.340	170.060	1.792
Ireland	0.0436	0.0457	1.050	0.723	0.950	1.308
Greece	4.658	6.760	1.451	77.340	138.060	1.808
Portugal	3.989	8.327	2.088	66.220	169.930	2.602
Turkey	9.786	25.463	2.607	153.300	519.517	3.248
Hungary	1.040	2.422	2.329	17.271	50.119	2.902
Poland	4.193	7.114	1.697	69.603	147.140	2.114
Yugoslavia	6.890	13.284	1.928	112.490	270.200	2.402

Note: ERDIs in terms of US$ were estimated with the help of results from the European comparison project (ERDI with respect to international Austrian Schillings (AS)). Moreover, US$ PPPs for Hungary, Poland and Yugoslavia were calculated from estimated ERDIs and official US$ exchange rates.

Source: International Comparisons of Gross Domestic Product in Europe 1985, op. cit., p. 24; Energy, Prices and Taxes, op. cit., p. 296; WIIW Database, and own calculations.

A rush introduction of so-called "internal convertibility" (for most current account transactions) forms an inherent part of the standard program for a rapid transition to a market economy in most former CPEs.[10] However, in the situation of great external and internal disequilibria, large pent-up demand for convertible currency and, last but not least, because a major part of trade was conducted in non-convertible currencies in the past, the concerns, to prevent large current account deficits, depend on the exchange rate being fixed far above real PPPs. The latter – implicitly – results in fixing the US$ GDP per capita at the level of developing countries. The questionable value of official ERs for purposes of international GDP comparisons – acknowledged in the case of OECD countries as well – for Central and Eastern European countries may be illustrated by the fact that e.g. the Hungarian per capita GNP (put officially at US$ 2,733 in 1989, i.e. about at par with Algeria and Uruguay) may fluctuate from 15 to 60 and more percent of the Austrian level, depending on the type of convertor used. Czechoslovakia, too, appears to be an extremely low-income country in its data officially submitted in 1990 to the World Bank: GDP per capita of US$ 3,200 in 1989 (about 20% of the Austrian level, and less than in Portugal and South Korea).[11] Similar problems in the selection of a proper convertor for the comparative assessment of real output levels are being faced in other former CPEs as well.

Just for illustrative purposes, we have converted the available GDP(GNP) per capita data in national currencies with current official exchange rates to US$ (Table 5). Apart from large jumps in levels of GDP over time (caused not primarily by fluctuations in output, but rather by changes in exchange rate systems, devaluations, etc.), it is mainly the extremely low GDP per capita level which arrests our attention. The per capita GDP level of US$ 2,200-3,200 in 1989 (curiously, Bulgaria, at US$ 5,210, would appear as the most developed country in Central and Eastern Europe) is on par with such countries as Argentina (US$ 2,160), Mexico (US$ 2,010), Malaysia (US$ 2,160), Algeria (US$ 2,230), Iran (US$ 3,200), and Venezuela (US$ 2,100), and foms only a fraction of the neighboring Western countries' (Austria: 17,300, FRG: 20,440, Italy: 15,120).[12] On the other hand, the level of Soviet per capita GNP is unrealistically high – again due to the artificial official exchange rate. Such an assessment is clearly inappropriate, especially when compared with results for other East European countries (though perhaps plausible when compared with figures for the OECD countries in Table 2). But in order to get consistent data for a comparison both in time (note the fluctuations caused by jumps in official exchange rates) and space, we have to look for more plausible (preferably PPP-like) convertors.

4. Overview of Benchmark GDP Estimates

After highlighting the key issues in East-West GDP comparisons and the inappropriateness of official exchange rates as convertors for East European GDPs, we now look in more detail into methods that have been used to deal with these problems. Basically we can distinguish between methods which require a convertor for GDP data expressed in national currencies, and those which try to estimate comparable GDPs directly. Methods relying on a convertor either use purchasing power parities (e.g. ICP) or exchange rates (e.g. the World Bank); direct GDP

Table 5

Gross Domestic Product per Capita

(in current US$ and official exchange rates)

	1985	1986	1987	1988	1989	1990 (est.)
Bulgaria	3530	4064	4685	5110	5210	6291
CSFR	6368	7444	8340	8902	3224	2832
GDR	5060	5862	7134	7413	2641	8816
Hungary	1938	2237	2462	2640	2733	3160
Poland	1901	1967	1692	1822	2182	1737
Romania (GNP)	.	.	2465	2589	2297	1537
USSR (GNP)	3330	4023	4581	5019	5078	5659
Yugoslavia	1913	2651	3033	2663	.	.

Sources: National statistics yearbooks, IMF, WIIW Database and own calculations.

estimates are mostly based on quantitative indicators for which a correlation with GDP levels can be established (PIG method). It must be stressed from the outset that each approach has its own merits and disadvantages (neither is free of a certain bias); the application of a particular method depends largely on the availability of the necessary input data. Results of each of the available methods require adequate interpretation.

4.1 Repricing Method – ICP

Largely along the lines set by Gilbert and Kravis (1954), the Statistical Commission of the United Nations launched a special International Comparison Project (ICP) in 1968 in order to obtain more reliable data on per capita real products of different (not only Eastern) countries through an assessment of PPPs. The first three phases of the ICP project were mainly devoted to establishing an appropriate methodology. The latest phase for which preliminary data are available (phase V with data for the year 1985) covers about 60 countries; so far only part of the results from the European Comparison Program (ECP) have been published – though currently phase VI (data for 1990) has already been in progress. Unfortunately, Hungary was the only CMEA country participating in all previous phases of ICP (Poland and Romania participated in Phases III and IV, Romania decided against publication of her data for Phase IV and did not participate in Phase V). Yugoslavia (not a CMEA member) has been participating in all phases of the ICP. After recent political changes there are good prospects that more former CPEs will take part in the ICP in future: Czechoslovakia has joined the ICP for 1990 (Phase VI – and will perhaps even resupply data for the 1985 ICP comparison as well). The Soviet Union, too, will join ICP in Phase VI (the Soviet Central Statistical Office also cooperates in bilateral comparisons with the Statistical Offices of Austria, FRG and Hungary).[13] Some of the coordinating tasks related to the ICP could perhaps be delegated to the reformed CMEA Secretariat in Moscow, which worked on similar comparisons in the past (see below). The participation of Bulgaria and Romania is unclear. Unfortunately – as the number of participating countries overall has been increasing – the time span between the year of comparison and availability of results has been partly growing.[14]

The basic ICP approach is as follows (Kravis et al (1982)): As a first step, the GDP of each participating country is broken down into a number (about 300 in Phase V) of homogeneous commodity groups ("basic headings") according to GDP final use components. Prices are then recorded within each basic heading for selected commodities, and the average ratio between prices in different countries is calculated for each commodity group. The national expenditures are then converted to internationally comparable (real) values with the help of these price ratios. The real value of total GDP is obtained by summing up the real values over the individual commodity groups. The resulting GDP is expressed in "international" currency (e.g. international dollars, Schillings) of the benchmark year. Thus, the international dollar (I$), for instance, has the same purchasing power as the US$ over the whole US GDP, but differing purchasing powers – depending on the price structure of all countries compared – in individual GDP components. ICP comparisons (benchmark estimates) have been conducted in five-year intervals. The most important results for the two latest benchmark years are presented in Table 6 below.

It is broadly recognized that the ICP methodology doubtlessly could give the best possible basis as far as international comparability of all participating countries is concerned, not only at the global GDP level but also in GDP final use components. It is a standard point of reference already for the EUROSTAT and OECD countries (PPPs are being extensively used in OECD National Accounts and Main Economic Indicators – see Part 3 above) which currently plan to shorten the time span for benchmark PPPs to three years, and eventually to calculate PPPs annually (in the meantime, the PPPs in non-benchmark years are being interpolated – see below). The ICP method, however, can be applied only in close cooperation with the statistical authorities of the countries involved, and requires substantial efforts and financial resources. Until very recently the willingness to cooperate was missing in a majority of CPEs, and the method, unfortunately, could not help in solving the problem of comparing real GDP levels between MEs and all

European CPEs. Moreover, there are still serious problems in comparisons of countries from different regions, in quality adjustments and in the selection of commodity baskets for countries with widely different consumption patterns etc., inter alia because of limited resources and therefore fewer exchanges of experts among regional groups (World Comparisons (1986)).

Table 6

GDP per Capita for Selected Countries at PPPs

(years 1980 and 1985, in international $ (I$))

	1980			1985		
Country	GDP per cap.	USA = 100	Austria = 100	GDP per cap.	USA = 100	Austria = 100
Austria	8 625	75.3	100.0	10 903	66.1	100.0
Belgium	9 436	82.4	109.4	10 672	64.7	97.9
Denmark	9 831	85.9	114.0	12 239	74.2	112.2
Finland	8 641	75.5	100.2	11 463	69.5	105.1
France	9 780	85.4	113.4	11 430	69.3	104.8
FRG	10 200	89.1	118.3	12 173	73.8	111.6
Greece	5 097	44.5	59.1	5 855	35.5	53.7
Hungary	4 632	40.5	53.7	5 146	31.2	47.2
Ireland	5 480	47.9	63.5	6 746	40.9	61.8
Italy	7 788	68.0	90.3	10 820	65.6	99.2
Luxembourg	10 626	92.8	123.2	.	.	.
Netherlands	9 316	81.4	108.0	11 249	68.2	103.2
Norway	11 325	98.9	131.3	13 921	84.4	127.7
Poland	4 322	37.8	50.1	4 041	24.5	37.1
Portugal	3 832	33.5	44.4	5 575	33.8	51.1
Spain	6 353	55.5	73.7	7 587	46.0	69.6
United Kingdom	8 253	72.1	95.7	10 903	66.1	100.0
Yugoslavia	4 042	35.3	46.9	4 816	29.2	44.2
USA	11 447	100.0	132.7	16 494	100.0	151.2

Sources: World Comparison of Purchasing Power and Real Product for 1980, UN/ Eurostat, New York, 1986.

4.2 Intra-CMEA (ICP-like) NMP Comparisons

The CMEA Secretariat in Moscow has been making intra-CMEA NMP comparisons since 1973 (the methodology is similar to that of ICP); thanks to "glasnost" the first figures (data for 1983 and 1988) were published in late 1990 (Martynov (1990), Georgieva and Ivanov (1990)). The main results of this comparison (for the year 1988) are presented in Tables 7 and 8 below. Disregarding the GDP/NMP and other methodological differences, the intra-CMEA ranking of individual Central and East European countries (data for Romania and Hungary in 1988 are not available) corresponds closely to analogous independent Western

Table 7

Results of Intra-CMEA ICP-like NMP Comparison for 1988 (USSR = 100)

(geometric averages of bilateral comparisons with the Soviet Union)

Per capita levels	NMP produced	NMP used	of which consum.	accum.	Labor product.	Industrial output
Bulgaria	106	113	123	88	92	108
Czechoslovakia	132	127	151	67	137	123
GDR	143	147	174	92	132	133
Hungary	.	.	.	.	.	.
Romania	.	.	.	.	.	.
Poland	101	99	105	85	92	.
Soviet Union	100	100	100	100	100	100

(in Rubles)

Per capita levels	NMP produced	NMP used	of which consum.	accum.	Labor product.	Industrial output
Bulgaria	2332	2440	1998	471	4570	3409
Czechoslovakia	2904	2742	2453	360	6805	3883
GDR	3146	3174	2826	492	6556	4198
Hungary	.	.	.	.	.	.
Romania	.	.	.	.	.	.
Poland	2222	2138	1706	455	4570	.
Soviet Union	2200	2159	1624	535	4967	3157

Note: The figure for per capita accumulation in Czechoslovakia (167% of Soviet level) must be a misprint in the original source. I have corrected the Rouble figure to 67% of the Soviet level.

Source: Georgieva and Ivanov (1990), p. 107, Narkhoz (1989), and own calculations.

estimates as far as the global level of output is concerned:[15] the former GDR was the highest per capita income country within the CMEA, followed by Czechoslovakia and then (with a considerable gap) by Bulgaria, Poland, and the Soviet Union. Interesting insights are provided by the analysis of NMP components. The Central and East European countries have enjoyed much greater per capita consumption levels relative to the Soviet Union (East Germany by more than 70%, Czechoslovakia by more than 50% in 1988), whereas the level of net investments (on a per capita basis) was much lower than in the Soviet Union. It is difficult to say whether these figures reflect actual disparities in consumption and investment levels respectively, or rather differences in relative prices and/or in defence expenditures. In any case, the great disparities between the CMEA countries, and the relative backwardness of the Soviet economy (even when compared with its former CMEA allies) is clearly apparent. The purchasing power parities of national currencies with respect to the Soviet Ruble (Table 8) reveal interesting differences between relative prices (mainly considerably lower PPPs of Czechoslovak Kcs, GDR Mark and Polish Zloty for the non-food components of national income used (i.e. relatively expensive industrial consumer goods and investments as compared with the Soviet Union)), but they are of little value for a linkage with income levels in the West.

Table 8

Purchasing Power Parities over NMP in 1988

(NCU per Ruble, Soviet weights)

	NMP used	Consumption of food and beverages							
		Food total	Meat prod.	Fats	Cereals prod.	Fruits	Vege- tables	Soft drinks	Tobacco
Bulgarian Lev	1.42	1.47	1.66	1.29	1.32	0.88	1.21	0.87	1.62
Czechoslovak Kcs	13.67	12.19	11.74	12.27	12.34	11.46	13.55	8.43	20.03
GDR Mark	5.12	3.62	3.95	2.71	3.16	2.65	3.73	2.84	8.00
Hungar. Forint	.	.	.	.	.	.	.	.	.
Romanian Lei	.	.	.	.	.	.	.	.	.
Polish Zloty	325.50	286.37	226.67	209.38	277.43	433.51	469.56	396.92	234.71
Soviet Ruble	1.00	1.00	1.00	1.00	1.00	1.00	1.00	1.00	1.00

Source: Georgieva and Ivanov (1990), p. 110.

If we attempt a crude approximation, using the above intra-CMEA relative NMP positions and various available Western benchmark GDP estimates based on PPP comparisons, we arrive at the following tentative figures for a linkage of the CPEs' comparative development levels with the West.[16]

First, the East German GDP per capita in 1989 was recently estimated at 48% of the West German level.[17] Taking the PPP-based estimate for the FRG as a yardstick (US$ 14,985 in 1989 – see Table 2), we get a level of about US$ 7,200 for the GDR (Soviet Union about US$ 5,000 as compared with US$ 20,629 for the USA). Next, taking as a yardstick the bilateral Soviet-US comparison for 1985 (Soviet GNP per capita estimated at 37% of the US level of US$ 16,559 in 1985)[18] shows a Soviet GNP per capita of US$ 6,130 in 1985, and the East German level would be about US$ 8,760 (using intra-CMEA NMP relations for 1988). Further, using the preliminary ICP Phase V result for Poland (24.5% of the US GDP per capita level in 1985 – see Table 6 above), and the same intra-CMEA relations, we get for Poland and the Soviet Union GDP per capita levels of about US$ 4,060 and US$ 4,020 resp., for the GDR about US$ 5,800 (i.e. 35% of the US and 48% of the West German level). Finally, taking the CIA estimate of Soviet per capita GNP (US$ 8,824 in 1988), the above intra-CMEA relation would imply that the East German GDP per capita level exceeded US$ 12,600 in 1988 (i.e. about 89% of the FRG's). The results are summarized in Table 9 below.

Clearly, the above results, too, provide no unequivocal answer either for relative GDP per capita positions of East European countries in comparison with the West. The assessment of East German GDP per capita in 1988-1989 varies between 35 and 65% of the US level, Soviet GDP per capita in 1985 ranges from 24% to 45% of the US level, depending on the estimate used as benchmark, etc.

Table 9

Linkage of Intra-CMEA NMP Ranking with Alternative Western Benchmark Estimates

(GDP/GNP per capita in US$ at PPPs)

Benchmark source	DIW	USA= 100	ICP USSR-US	USA= 100	ICP Pol-US	USA= 100	CIA USSR-US	USA= 100
Benchmark year	1989		1985		1985		1988	
Bulgaria	5330	26	6495	39	4258	26	9353	48
Czechoslovakia	6640	32	8088	49	5302	32	11648	60
GDR	7200	35	8762	53	5744	35	12618	65
Poland	5080	25	6188	37	4057	25	8912	46
Soviet Union	5030	24	6127	37	4017	24	8824	45
Reference items:								
USA	20629	100	16559	100	16559	100	19523	100
FRG	14985	73	12105	73	12105	73	14100	72
Austria	13407	65	10748	65	10748	65	12457	64
OECD Europe	15563	75	12349	75	12349	75	14624	75

Sources: Tables 2 and 7, Institut für Weltwirtschaft Kiel, op. cit., p. 26, Martynov (1990), Ekonomika i zhizn, No. 6, 1991, p. 20, Handbook of Economic Statistics (1989), own calculations.

4.3 Mixed Approaches to GDP Estimates

The foregoing section has again illustrated problems with mixing data derived from different sources and obtained by various estimation methods, and relating to different time periods. Below we briefly discuss various other mixed approaches which are – unfortunately – frequently used not only in economic literature but in practice as well.

A more or less complete set of national accounts may be reconstructed from desegregated data by computing GDP as a sum of value added in individual sectors using the CPEs' statistics (see e.g. Alton (1990)). This was important in the past, when most CPEs did not publish their own GDP figures in national currency (meanwhile, GDP and GNP figures respectively have become available for practically all former East European CPEs). The method ends up with GDP values in national currency; and the most crucial problem of international comparisons, namely the meaningful conversion into dollars or other comparable units, remains. Another method had been used by the World Bank in its Atlas between 1977 and 1980. Here the scaling up from NMP to GDP was made on the basis of an average regression relationship found for a benchmark year in a group of Western countries. The conversion of estimated GDPs to US dollars was made with official ERs. The method was highly unsatisfactory and was finally abandoned by the World Bank.

The criticism of the original Atlas method inspired the World Bank to launch the research project on national income statistics in CPEs, and subsequently, to stop the publication of GDP data for the non-member CPEs in the following issues of the Atlas. But for the member countries (including former CPEs) the World Bank now uses official exchange rates as convertors for national GDP data, and it may be expected – since all former CPEs (except the Soviet Union) have already become World Bank members by the end of 1990 – that the above discussed extremely low dollar GDP estimates (resulting from inflated official exchange rates) will appear in the forthcoming issues of the World Bank Atlas and will be used in economic and political decision-making.

At the beginning of the 1980s the World Bank launched a research project (studies on individual countries and problems, e.g. exchange rates, price formation, etc. as well as the final report (Marer (1985)) which has greatly facilitated the understanding of the main problems related to East-West GDP comparisons. Unfortunately, the project has not produced uniformly acceptable dollar estimates of comparable GDP levels for all CPEs. The exercise was largely successful in calculating (at that time not available) GDP estimates in individual CPEs' national currencies. There was also broad agreement among experts that PPP-like convertors would be preferable to other convertors (e.g. official, commercial or black market exchange rates) to obtain internationally comparable GDP values for CPEs. However, the available PPP information was (and still is) rather inconsistent and incomplete: for Hungary, Poland, and Romania the ICP results for 1975, for Czechoslovakia the results of bilateral comparisons with Austria and FRG for 1980, for GDR a bilateral comparison with FRG for 1980, and for the Soviet Union a bilateral comparison with the USA for 1976, were used. No PPP-like information was available for Bulgaria, therefore no GDP in dollars could be estimated.

In order to get the required "Atlas-type" GDP estimates comparable with MEs (i.e. converted with market exchange rates), a further crude adjustment of estimated PPPs to proxy exchange rates, using the estimated exchange rate deviation index (ERDI) was performed. These adjusted PPPs were finally used for the conversion of estimated GDP from national currencies to US dollars. The main results of the study (Marer (1985)) are summarized in Table 10 below.

Table 10

Dollar per Capita GNP Range of the European CMEA Countries in 1980

(convertors based on PPPs and estimated alternative ERDIs)

	Estimated PPP (NCU/$)	GNP Convertor (NCU/US$)			Per capita GNP in US$			PPP-based estimate
		Low	Best	High	Low	Best	High	
GDR	1.96	1.67	2.20	3.27	4000	5910	7800	6630
Czechoslovakia	6.38	5.87	7.78	11.80	3100	4740	6300	5790
Hungary	13.55	11.21	15.22	23.60	2830	4390	5960	4632
Poland	16.14	13.87	18.73	29.03	2400	3730	5040	4322
Romania	.	7.37	10.40	17.77	1570	2680	3800	.
Soviet Union	0.40	0.39	0.53	0.82	2700	4190	5700	5550
Bulgaria	.	.	.	.	.	.	.	.

Source: Marer (1985), pp. 86-88, World Comparison (1986).

The "best" estimates compare fairly well with ICP Phase IV results for Hungary (I$ 4,632), but much worse with the ICP result for Poland (I$ 4,322) – see World Comparisons (1986). Unfortunately, there are not more ICP results for CPEs which could be used as a reference (PPP estimates for other countries are rough approximations based on different bilateral comparisons). A separate problem is posed by the rather broad interval of possible estimates (resulting form uncertainties in estimated ERDIs).

Besides the adjustment of estimated PPPs to what might be a proxy exchange rate (an implicit quasi-devaluation), a certain element of "justice" came into the exercise, turning the CPEs into newly underdeveloped countries (NUCs). The logic of the argument was as follows: since the World Bank has been using official exchange rates for conversion of national GDP data for market economies, and there is a systematic discrepancy between PPP and exchange rate (observed for a variety of countries, the order of magnitude in the difference increasing with lower GDP levels – see above), a proxy exchange rate has to be used for CPEs as well. In order to assign to the CPEs what can be considered an appropriate place in the per capita GDP ranking between market economies (measured in current US$), such adjustment[19] has been made.[20]

The variety of meaningful economic arguments, used to explain the then (during 1975-1980) observed gaps between exchange rates and PPPs (poor export performance, weak marketing capabilities, etc.), and largely still valid today, needs only to be supplemented by one more argument: the national interest in remaining eligible for the main lending program of the World Bank. Nowadays the East European countries resort to a similar strategy when fixing their exchange rates much higher (in terms of NCU per US$) than real PPPs (ERDIs presumably between 2-3). However, the East European exchange rates are mostly still fixed rather arbitrarily – nowadays near levels prevailing at semi-legal parallel markets (e.g. in Poland and Czechoslovakia). Under these circumstances the use of official exchange rates (and/or ERDIs) for GDP conversions and international comparisons is still rather problematic.[21]

As far as can be concluded from the available publications, the CIA has also been using heterogeneous methods in determining the Soviet and East European GDP/GNP levels (Handbook of Economic Statistics (1989), (1990)). CIA's dollar GNP benchmark estimates for Hungary, Poland, Romania, and Yugoslavia are even now still taken from ICP-Phase III (data for 1975). Adjusted ECE benchmark PIG estimates for 1970 (see below) are used for Bulgaria, Czechoslovakia and the GDR. Separately estimated growth rates are then used for obtaining the time series in 1975 dollars (estimated GNP growth indexes in constant domestic currencies, derived from official national statistics, are applied to 1975 benchmarks);[22] the values in current dollars are obtained by applying the US GNP deflator. A separate estimation procedure is used for the Soviet Union: the quantity output data (mostly from Soviet sources) and value-added weights are used for the compilation of Soviet GNP. The resulting ruble estimates are then converted with a separately constructed PPP-like convertor for 1982 (for details see Handbook of Economic Statistics (1989), and specifically Edwards et al. (1979)). As a result, CIA's benchmark dollar GNP estimates for Eastern countries as a group also stem from three different sources (are obtained by different methods).

Moreover, in the last issue of CIA's Handbook of Economic Statistics (1990), the GDP estimates for East European countries were scaled down (without any explanation regarding the new estimation method), but those for the Soviet Union remained unchanged.[23] We suspect that the CIA made a crude downward adjustment of its previous estimates along the lines performed by Planecon already in late 1989.[24] However, it is not clear why the CIA estimate for the Soviet Union was not adjusted as well. As a result, even the comparison between individual CPEs has been hampered.

4.4 Physical Indicators Global (PIG) Method

The PIG approach, originally devised by Hungarian scholars (see, for instance, Ehrlich (1966), Janossy and Ehrlich (1969)), has been based on an intuitive notion of a relationship between various physical indicators and the level of per capita GDP observed in MEs. The logic of the method is as follows (Fink and Havlik (1989)): Assuming for the moment that the level of income is sufficiently represented by the GDP per capita in US dollars, the relationships between GDP and selected physical indicators can be established for countries for which both sets of data are available. Let us say we have n such countries (core sample) and k physical (non-monetary) indicators. In some way (we return to this problem later) we establish individual relationships, thus obtaining k partial estimates (each corresponding to a particular physical indicator):

$$GDP_{ij} = f_i(x_{ij}) \qquad (1)$$

where x_{ij} denotes the individual physical indicator i for a country j

$$i = 1,2, \dots k$$

$$j = 1,2, \dots n$$

Having convinced ourselves that the estimated functions f_i adequately model the actual relationships between GDP_j and the individual physical indicators x_{ij} within the core sample, we can aggregate the partial GDP_{ij}s (for each indicator a separate GDP estimate is obtained) in order to obtain global GDP_j estimates for each of the core sample countries:

$$GDP_j = g_j(GDP_{ij}), \text{ so that} \qquad (2)$$

$$GDP_j = g_j(f_i(x_{ij})), \text{ and finally} \qquad (3)$$

$$GDP_j = G_j(x_{ij}). \qquad (4)$$

The PIG method can be interpreted in a different and less intuitive manner, too. Let us assume we know the GDP of country j in national currency ($GDP^n{}_j$) and we have to look for an adequate convertor (e_j) into the internationally comparable GDP_j, so that

$$GDP_j = e_j(GDP^n{}_j). \qquad (5)$$

The convertor e_j can be expressed as a function F of a representative sample of goods x_{ij}:

$$e_j = F^e{}_j(x_{ij}). \qquad (6)$$

Usually, this function is based on ratios of foreign to domestic prices expressed in foreign and domestic currencies weighted by the basket of goods x_{ij}.[25] If the basket is representative for the GDP convertor e_j, we are justified in assuming that this basket is representative of GDP^n, too:

$$GDP^n{}_j = g^n{}_j(x_{ij}). \qquad (7)$$

So we receive the functional relationship (substituting (6) and (7) in (5)):

$$GDP_j = F^e{}_j(g^n{}_j(x_{ij})), \qquad (8)$$

which permits us to establish a direct functional relationship, identical with (4), between the representative basket and the internationally comparable GDP:

$$GDP_j = H_j(x_{ij}). \qquad (9)$$

The functions G from (4) and F(g) from (8) can thus be treated as two alternative expressions for a GDP convertor H, which may be based alternatively either on relative prices and quantities (F – ICP approach) or on physical indicators (G – PIG approach). The only requirement in both cases is the adequate typicality of the respective samples (baskets of commodities, physical indicators), and the correct input data.

At this point numerous problems with the selection of appropriate non-monetary indicators, estimation of adequate model relationships, and, if estimated for each indicator separately, with the aggregation of partial GDP estimates arise. Nevertheless, the critical point of the method will be reached as we move on to the actual purpose of the whole exercise, namely to the extrapolation of GDPs for countries outside the core sample (which either do not release any or release only unreliable GDP data). Here we need to adopt the crucial assumption that the estimated core sample relationships are valid outside the core as well, and therefore may be used for meaningful extrapolations. The problem is essentially similar to any projection in general: are we entitled to broaden the validity of an estimated model beyond the core sample boundaries? If we are ready to accept this assumption, we can easily estimate missing desired GDPs on the basis of estimated model relationships and respective non-monetary indicators (which still are relatively easier available, especially for CPEs, than proper convertors).[26]

Let us comment a little on the validity of the "projection possibility" assumption, since it is indeed critical for the acceptance of the whole PIG method. The core sample usually consists of data from market economies (mainly OECD countries and some third world countries for which appropriate data are available), and we make "projections" for the CPEs. First of all, estimating GDPs for these additional countries is not an extrapolation in the normal sense of the word, since the "extrapolated" GDPs of the CPEs will probably not fall completely outside the core sample boundaries as far as their numerical values are concerned, at least if a sufficiently large number of developing countries is included in the core.

A great number of various non-monetary (physical) indicators correlate in some way with GDP. However, the indicators selected for partial GDP estimates should serve as a good sample representation for the characterization of global income. The sample should be large enough to represent each of the structural elements of GDP, such as outputs, inputs, consumption, investment etc. In theory, one should select a random sample from all possible non-monetary indicators related to GDP, but in practice we are limited by the availability of international statistics. The number of selected indicators should be sufficiently large, since the larger the sample the less important – for purely mathematical reasons – is the problem of weighting, when partial estimates have to be aggregated. The market economies in the sample should include developing countries in order to catch some quality variations by the estimated parameters and, finally, in order to avoid the exchange rate bias in the valuation of individual GDPs, the GDPs of countries in the core sample should be converted into dollars with purchasing power parities (results from ICP) rather than with market exchange rates.

Even if above conditions are fulfilled, at least one important additional argument against the PIG method – namely that the method was "transplanting" patterns valid for the core sample countries (largely market economies) to the different socio-economic conditions of the CPEs – cannot be easily dismissed (though this relates to any international comparison in general – we refer again to the well-known index number problem). Of course these conditions were different in CPEs (alas, otherwise we would not estimate their GDPs in such a roundabout way), but in this case such "transplantation" should not necessarily be viewed as an obstacle to the method, but rather as a tool providing additional analytic insights into varying structural patterns of both economic systems. In other words, the global level of economic development should be treated independently of both socio-economic and structural conditions of its origin for purposes of international

(GDP, development level, etc.) comparisons. Such differences are of secondary importance since the main interest in this case is the absolute level of the country's income and/or its ranking within a family of countries. Doubtlessly, varying production, consumption and other patterns do matter, but only at a more detailed stage of investigation. On the other hand, it could be argued that a high consumption or production of many available physical indicators (e.g. of cement, electricity, steel, etc.) does not necessarily increase the welfare level of a country, and could indicate high material intensity and the waste of resources instead. However, the production of certain inputs (provided the output figures were not deliberately distorted) has generated a certain income and is being treated as a contribution to GDP.

Given the above described problems with various methods for comparable GDP estimates, the PIG method was particularly suited for estimation of internationally comparable income (or development) levels in (both from a socio-political and economic point of view) different countries, since it produces reasonable results at relatively modest cost and does not require intensive cooperation with national statistical offices. Moreover, the PIG method avoids some of the most important obstacles to international comparability, like for instance the different scope of traditional GDP/NMP measures, lack of reliable PPP estimates, unrealistic or completely inadequate exchange rates of national currencies with respect to the US dollar, and so on. No less advantageous is the fact that by this method uniform criteria are applied to the whole sample of countries compared – no other method could so far claim the same. Even though it cannot be used for the estimation of individual GDP components, other important analytical insights into the structure of compared economies may be obtained by studying the relationships between the various physical indicators and GDPs.

For countries in transition from the command to a market economy – since only historical data reflecting old production and consumption patterns can be used – the systemic weaknesses (only partly reflected in the PIG results) of former CPEs may rapidly come into the open, especially when the policy of shock therapy is adopted for transition. Curiously, the sudden opening of the economy to foreign competition (foreign trade liberalization, accompanied by the introduction of internal currency convertibility, usually at an exchange rate far above purchasing power parity) leads to a drastic depreciation in the value of domestic assets, output, and incomes (in terms of foreign currency). This is numerically similar to using inflated exchange rates as GDP convertors instead of PPPs (recent examples of Poland, CSFR, and East Germany show that this can happen irrespective of whether domestic currency has been devalued or revaluated). As the adjustment of real output follows only gradually (and finds its expression in the change of physical indicators only ex post), the PIG-based per capita GDP estimates obtained by the method described in this section (see Table 11) appear unrealistically high for the transforming CPEs.

5. Assessment of Alternative GDP Estimates

Wide divergences in data availability and reliability mostly prohibit the use of more sophisticated estimation methods which could be uniformly applied for comparisons both within the group of former CPEs and for comparison with the West. All former East European CPEs (except the Soviet Union) are now members of the World Bank and the IMF; Hungary, Poland, and Yugoslavia have also been participating regularly in the ICP. For some CPEs various bilateral comparisons with comparable MEs were undertaken (e.g. Poland – Austria, Czechoslovakia – Austria, GDR – FRG, USSR – USA). Apart from the conversion of national data with current official exchange rates, almost no suitable data are available for Bulgaria and Romania. This situation makes it extremely difficult to get comparable results both for CPEs within their group and relative to MEs. Since none of the existing methods for international East-West GDP comparisons is free from bias, mixed procedures (like those used, for instance, by the CIA) most likely contain distortions which are inherent not only in every single method, but they may, in their combination, impede comparability even within the group of CPEs. Whereas at least the direction of likely bias inherent in each particular method can be more or less clearly identified, the same task is much more difficult when countries compared are treated differently. The estimation of benchmark GDP levels is a crucial case in point, and it is especially here that the mixing of various methods in estimating comparable GDP levels cannot be recommended.[27]

5.1 The ICP Methodology

As already mentioned above, the ICP method theoretically produces the best internationally comparable GDP values. Of course, this does not mean that existing (and future) estimates are free from any bias. ICP quantity and price comparisons have been criticized particularly as far as the treatment of non-tradable products and services is concerned (e.g. assumptions about equal productivity in the government sector, education, health) and we shall not repeat this criticism here (Marris (1984), Kravis et al. (1982)). Rather, we mention possible sources of bias that may directly affect the results of ICP (and other PPP-based) comparisons as far as the comparability between CPEs and MEs is

Table 11

Relative Ranking by PPP-based GDP per Capita

(in current international dollars, geometric averages)[a)]

Country	GDP in 1975	USA =100	Austria =100	GDP in 1975	USA =100	Austria =100	GDP in 1975	USA =100	Austria =100
Argentina	3200	50.6	68.0	5142	51.3	65.5	6170	47.9	57.8
Brazil	2034	32.2	43.2	3554	35.5	45.3	4398	34.2	41.2
Chile	2320	36.7	49.3	4027	40.2	51.3	5105	39.7	47.8
Mexico	2198	34.8	46.7	3591	35.8	45.7	3401	26.4	31.8
Egypt	1343	21.2	28.5	2266	22.6	28.9	2852	22.2	26.7
Philippines	1423	22.5	30.3	2281	22.8	29.0	2486	19.3	23.3
South Korea	1710	27.0	36.3	3429	34.2	43.7	4919	38.2	46.0
India	709	11.2	15.1	1140	11.4	14.5	860	6.7	8.1
Israel	3973	62.8	84.4	6369	63.6	81.1	8256	64.2	77.3
Austria	4705	74.4	100.0	7853	78.4	100.0	10682	83.0	100.0
Belgium	5262	83.2	111.8	8576	85.6	109.2	10422	81.0	97.6
Denmark	5054	79.9	107.4	8244	82.3	105.0	10585	82.2	99.1
Finland	5085	80.4	108.1	8289	82.7	105.6	11226	87.2	105.1
France	4732	74.8	100.6	8065	80.5	102.7	10552	82.0	98.8
F.R.G.	4875	77.1	103.6	8137	81.2	103.6	10411	80.9	97.5
Greece	3167	50.1	67.3	5496	54.9	70.0	7332	57.0	68.6
Ireland	4100	64.8	87.1	6830	68.2	87.0	8403	65.3	78.7
Italy	3953	62.5	84.0	6604	65.9	84.1	8822	68.5	82.6
Netherlands	5066	80.1	107.7	8196	81.8	104.4	10443	81.1	97.8
Norway	5021	79.4	106.7	8346	83.3	106.3	11144	86.6	104.3
Portugal	2889	45.7	61.4	4910	49.0	62.5	6247	48.5	58.5
Spain	3783	59.8	80.4	6418	64.1	81.7	8082	62.8	75.7
Sweden	5448	86.1	115.8	8705	86.9	110.8	11602	90.2	108.6
Switzerland	4768	75.4	101.3	7880	78.7	100.3	10641	82.7	99.6
Turkey	1684	26.6	35.8	2693	26.9	34.3	3151	24.5	29.5
United Kingdom	5026	79.5	106.8	8060	80.5	102.6	10312	80.1	96.5
Japan	4290	67.8	91.2	7369	73.6	93.8	9767	75.9	91.4
Canada	5882	93.0	125.0	9437	94.2	120.2	12006	93.3	112.4
U.S.A.	6324	100.0	134.4	10018	100.0	127.6	12870	100.0	120.5
Australia	5552	87.8	118.0	8990	89.7	114.5	11245	87.4	105.3
New Zealand	5423	85.7	115.2	8161	81.5	103.9	10405	80.8	97.4
Bulgaria	3167	50.1	67.3	5535	55.3	70.5	7474	58.1	70.0
Czechoslovakia	4048	64.0	86.0	6588	65.8	83.9	8153	63.4	76.3
G.D.R.	4258	67.3	90.5	7050	70.4	89.8	8993	69.9	84.2
Hungary	3610	57.1	76.7	5881	58.7	74.9	7431	57.7	69.6
Poland	3233	51.1	68.7	5241	52.3	66.7	6441	50.0	60.3
Romania	2739	43.3	58.2	4623	46.1	58.9	5852	45.5	54.8
Soviet Union	3485	55.1	74.1	5847	58.4	74.5	7328	56.9	68.6
Yugoslavia	2675	42.3	56.8	4555	45.5	58.0	6022	46.8	56.4

a) Calculated as simple geometric averages from partial PIG estimates (27 indicators in 1975, 30 in 1980, and 27 in 1985).

concerned. Here the accounting of (sometimes substantial, but often also exaggerated) quality differences probably plays the foremost role, and its effects on estimates of real output levels might be similar to undervaluated exchange rates. Secondly, much higher prices at various grey and black markets cannot, as a rule, be sufficiently taken into account. Such markets were extremely important in most former CPEs, since a number of goods was only in limited supply at official retail outlets (various forms of formal and informal rationing had been frequently applied) before the recent price and import liberalization. Relying mostly on information provided by individual governments, some price inputs to ICP may also have been deliberately distorted in the past (Marer (1985)). Detailed and reliable quality comparisons represent a serious problem per se and have proved increasingly difficult because of the lack of resources needed for on-site inspections and the necessity to rely on raw data supplied by national statistical offices (World Comparisons (1986)). Apart from these and other conceptual problems, the most serious drawback is that ICP estimates are currently available only for three former CPEs (year 1985: Hungary, Poland, and Yugoslavia).

Whereas participation of more former CPEs seems to be secured for the current ICP Phase VI (data for 1990) (at least as far as the Soviet Union and Czechoslovakia are concerned), new problems related to radical economic changes in the region will arise. In the past, when CPEs were essentially closed economies characterized by distorted prices and autarktic production structures, it has been virtually impossible to find proper representative commodities, and/or to make appropriate quality comparisons (the share of tradables destined for Western markets has been extremely low). Nowadays, part of the past invisible transaction costs (e.g. bribes, queuing, etc.) is already reflected in (higher) liberalized prices. On the other hand, previously overpriced manufactures (produced for heavily protected domestic and intra-Bloc markets) will either cease to be produced after the collapse of the protected intra-CMEA markets, or else offered at supported prices against foreign competition in the open markets. As a result, overproportional price fluctuations during the first stages of price and foreign trade liberalization can be expected.[28] From this point of view, the latest benchmark year for ICP (1990) will be especially problematic, as this was the year of the beginning of transition, though prices were still mostly administratively controlled (except in Poland and Hungary).

Though the ICP methodology is designed to prevent many sources of price and quality distortion and has been perfected over time, the limited possibility of direct independent checks of price/quality data supplied by individual CPEs' governments left the possibility open of a quality bias in any direction. In addition, all quality adjustments raise numerous unresolved problems with the selection of the appropriate relationship between price and quality. More often than not the relatively "minor" differences in design, fashion, etc. may lead to "overproportional" reductions in prices, especially on saturated markets. Some products may have still served well for certain purposes in supply-constrained CPEs or in developing countries, even if they would be hardly marketable (at any price) in advanced market economies. In addition, it has to be taken into account that the production of such goods, even if inferior to products of highly sophisticated markets, has generated income in the respective country and was usually consumed as well.[29] Finally, the quality of goods consumed (or durables in use) by the lower income groups in richer economies might also deviate significantly from the quality otherwise accessible to the average consumer. All these questions would suggest rather to treat with due care any large quality adjustments.

5.2 The PIG Methodology

As far as the PIG method is concerned, a number of serious objections have been raised to the reliability of its results as well. Apart from conceptual problems as regards questions of what is being measured, critics of this method mainly raise the following points: difficulties with weighting, poor comparability of physical indicators from the qualitative point of view, and the system-immanent inefficiencies as possible sources of bias in PIG-based international comparisons of real products (Marer (1985). The CPEs' inefficient use of resources (including labor) which contributes to relatively high PIG estimates of GDP may indeed be seen as an inherent feature of centrally planned systems, which – in contrast to MEs – have been to a much lesser degree guided by criteria of economic efficiency. The partial PIG-based estimates show quite clearly such inefficient use of CPE's resources (see below). Different systems of weights – a problem which is, by the way, related to the analysis of "systemic deficiencies" – may also result in slightly different global GDP estimates. While the exact impact of different weighting on final GDP estimates cannot be easily foreseen (especially as far as changes in inter-country GDP ranking are concerned), the inclusion of indicators related to production inputs into the sample doubtlessly leads to higher global GDP estimates not only for CPEs but for some less developed market economies as well. The greater the number of such indicators in the sample, the greater also the resulting bias for CPEs.

Although an ex post check of partial GDP estimates (i.e. GDP estimates resulting from individual physical indicators) revealed that, despite the relatively large spread of such estimates, essentially no bias in any direction existed,[30] many indicators which refer to more complex products and services and have – as may be argued – increasing importance with the rising level of development, indicate the backwardness of the infrastructure in all former CPEs (especially in the transportation and telecommunications sectors). The representativeness of the sample of physical indicators is thus extremely important.

Generally, two types of physical indicators can be linked to the level of GDP: flows and stocks. Flows are typical output figures: production of a sufficiently well defined product. Stocks are indirectly related to the level of GDP or income: e.g., provision of the population with cars, telephones, etc. It is assumed that with a given level of income (GDP, development, etc.) the population can afford to maintain a certain level of stocks. The flow based indicators deliver systematically higher partial GDP estimates for CPEs, thus a greater weight of flow-type indicators in the sample of physical indicators may push the global GDP levels for CPEs up, relative to the generally more balanced MEs of higher development level, and vice versa. It is another fact that all CPEs need significantly more production inputs in order to generate the same GDP as MEs at comparable levels of development: the average input-type GDP estimates for CPEs are usually larger than the estimated global GDP, despite the fact that the classification of physical indicators is sometimes rather arbitrary (Havlik (1986)).

Partial GDP estimates based on any particular physical indicator differ widely. A complete set of partial GDP per capita estimates for 1980 and 1985 has been reproduced elsewhere[31], and we shall here review only the most striking features. First, an ex post check of partial GDP estimates revealed that, despite relatively large spread of individual estimates, essentially no bias in any direction existed.[32] In all CPEs, the level of GDP per capita estimated from such indicators, like share of employment in services, number of telephones per head, or the consumption of paper, are substantially lower than average estimated per capita GDP. In the extreme case of service employment, the respective partial GDP per capita estimate amounts to only 40-60% of average estimated per capita GDP – clearly indicating a major systemic weakness of all CPEs in this area (note that the same partial estimate for most less developed countries (e.g. in Latin America) is higher than average). On the other hand, other physical indicators deliver systematically higher partial per capita GDPs for CPEs: stocks of hospital beds, consumption of non-vegetable calories, or dwelling construction. Partial GDP per capita estimates thus fluctuate between I$ 3,800 and I$ 11,500 per capita for Czechoslovakia (year 1985), I$ 3,100-9,900 for Poland, I$ 3,700-11,600 for Hungary, I$ 4,200-13,700 for the Soviet Union, etc. – see Graph 1.[31] Selection of "appropriate" physical indicators, and

Graph 1

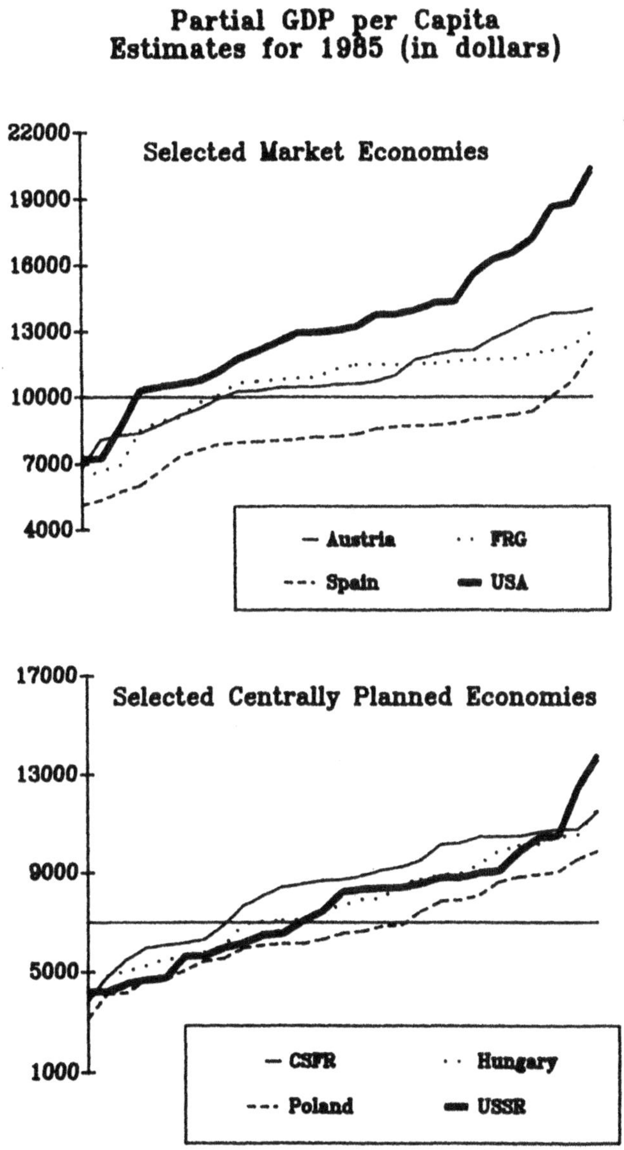

Distribution of partial GDP estimates (N = 27)

Source: WIIW

the use of a specifically constructed system of weights, could thus produce "desired" (i.e lower or higher) GDP per capita levels for CPEs. The large spread of partial GDP estimates illustrates the dilemma of evaluating the development level by any single number.

One of the pioneers of the PIG approach, E. Ehrlich, raised objections relating to the above discussion and pointed out that the per capita GDP PIG estimates obtained by a "more sophisticated" regression variant of the method endorsed by the present author (Havlik (1986), Fink and Havlik (1989)) contains a systematic bias: underestimating GDP per capita level for the more developed countries and, vice versa, overestimating the levels for less developed countries (including former CPEs). According to Ehrlich, none of the more sophisticated mathematical methods is "flexible" enough correctly to reproduce the original (e.g. PPP) scale for per capita GDP estimates. In order to avoid such a bias, a more "flexible graphical method" should be prefered.[33] There are two points in Ehrlich's argument which have to be addressed. The first one is whether the PIG method can and should exactly reproduce the original (either PPP or ER-based) scale. The second relates to the existence of any systematic bias regardless of the fact whether the original scale is exactly reproduced or not.

As concerns the first point, there is no question that results of any regressional analysis certainly cannot exactly reproduce the original data. On the contrary: it has been pointed out earlier that the PIG scale differs from the original scale (either PPP-based or exchange rate-based), depending inter alia on the aggregation method of partial PPP estimates (arithmetic and/or geometric averages, selection of physical indicators, etc. – see Havlik (1986)). An attempt at the exact matching of both scales, i.e., a deliberate adjustment of the PIG results to the anticipated GDP level, for instance by the graphical method used by Ehrlich, can lead to distortions as well (similar to a deliberate selection of physical indicators, quality adjustments, etc.). The PIG scale is simply different – just as the PPPs differ from ERs (see the above discussion of ERDIs). Therefore the PIG results (absolute levels of per capita GDP) cannot be directly compared with either PPP- or ER-converted GDP estimates. Basically, only the ranking of individual countries on the PIG scale may be taken for granted, since the absolute values of PIG estimates differ from original GDP per capita values expressed in PPPs. The plot of original GDP per capita data (ICP results) and PIG estimates illustrates how both sets of data are scattered around the "ideal" regression line (see Graph 2). Indeed, the PIG estimates for many lower income countries (according to ICP) and for all three Central and East European countries for which ICP results are available lay below the "ideal" line. Similarly, the per capita GDP for a

Graph 2

Relation Between Alternative GDP per Capita Estimates for 1985 (in 1000$)

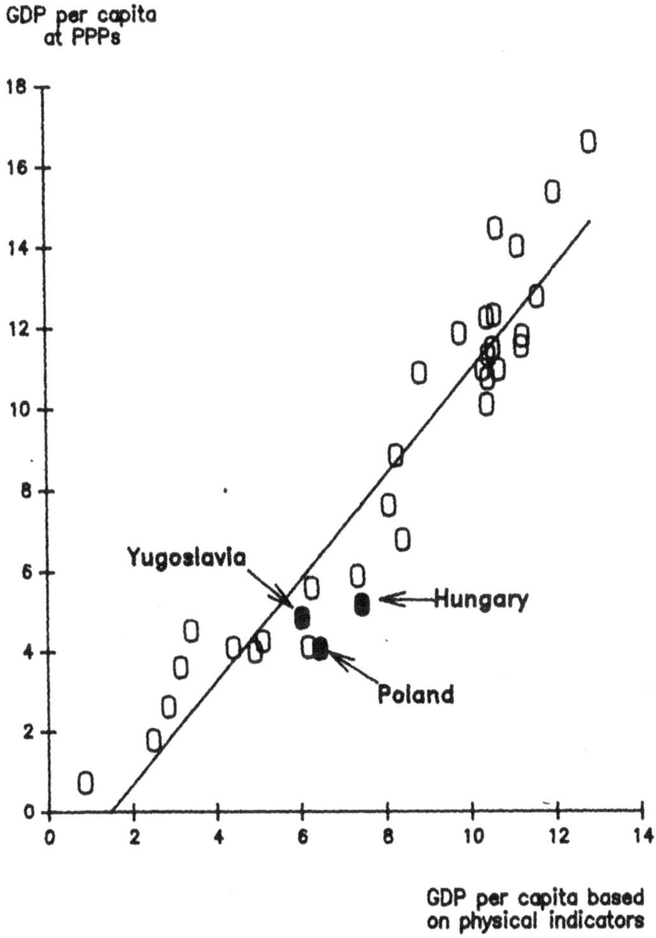

$$GDP(ppp) = 1.278 * GDP(pig) - 1.8593$$
$$\ln GDP(ppp) = 1.141 * \ln GDP(pig) - 0.2886$$

Source: WIIW

number of higher income countries is underestimated by the PIG method because of differences in both scales. An attempt at exact matching of both scales leaves room for various adjustments.

6. Real Growth Rates and Extrapolation of Benchmark GDP Estimates

Real growth rates for CPEs, comparable to those for Western countries, are not available either. There is wide agreement that official growth indexes published by CPEs used to be upward biased, mainly because the price increases were not sufficiently reflected in deflating current price series. Evidence that official data contained a considerable amount of hidden inflation is numerous. Not only Western experts and Eastern dissident economists provided alternative growth rates which were substantially lower than official ones, but the outright falsification of statistics has now been even officially admitted (e.g. in Bulgaria, the former GDR, Romania, and the Soviet Union).[34] The degree of bias in official growth indexes has been different in individual CPEs. Hungary probably has the most reliable statistics, whereas Romania, the GDR, Bulgaria, and the Soviet Union used to be at the opposite end of the spectrum as far as the quality of statistical reporting is concerned.

Recently, with the beginning of transformation of CPEs into market economies, an opposite problem appeared. Statistical systems of former CPEs, designed for the needs of a command economy – mainly to help check the fulfillment of the plan – are not able to measure the advances of the rapidly expanding private sector. Even in Hungary (which is probably most advanced in this area) the statistical organs have considerable difficulties in providing data for small economic units (with less than 50 employees), most of which belong to the private sector. Similar problems now face the statistical authorities in Poland, Czechoslovakia, and in other East European countries as well. As a result, it has often been claimed that nowadays the official growth rates are biased downwards, i.e. that the current decline of output (e.g. in Poland, Czechoslovakia, and Hungary) is exaggerated, as it largely excludes the activities of the private sector gradually emerging from the underground (shadow) economy. Again, it will take some time before the statistical systems of the countries concerned will be adjusted to the needs of a market economy.[35]

The methods used for the establishment of benchmark comparative GDP levels are laborious, and the estimates are available only for selected benchmark years. In order to obtain GDP time series, missing values between the benchmark years have to be estimated. Again, there are several possibilities how to extrapolate the benchmark estimates. One can take the latest equations obtained by the PIG method, plug in the physical indicators for the desired extrapolation period, and simply compute resulting GDPs. It has been shown earlier that, when using "old equations" with more recent physical indicators, the actual GDP levels are underestimated because of insufficiently reflected structural change (Havlik (1986)). Alternatively, one can take the last benchmark GDP estimates (PIG or ICP), and with available growth rates move the benchmarks to the future (the latter approach is more commonly used, inter alia by CIA as well as by OECD, in extrapolating PPPs for member countries – see, e.g., Blades (1991)). In the former case one has to assume the stability of GDP/non-monetary indicators relationships during the period in question (which is problematic in view of the above mentioned structural changes – see Appendix[31]), the second method requires plausible information on (or estimates of) real growth rates.

Assuming that baskets of goods used for both PPP and national inflation measurement were identical (or equally representative), the relative change of PPP for two countries' currencies in a certain period should be equivalent to the ratio of their respective rates of inflation:[36]

$$ {}_{i}PPP(A/B) \;/\; {}_{j}PPP(A/B) = {}_{(i/j)}I(A) \;/\; {}_{(i/j)}I(B) \qquad (10) $$

where:

$.PPP(A/B)$ is the purchasing power parity of currency A in terms of currency B (e.g. US or international dollars) in year i resp. j,

${}_{(i/j)}I.$ is the price index for the period (i/j) in country A and B respectively.

Obviously, if rates of inflation in two countries are the same, the PPP relation of their currencies remains unchanged. The higher the inflation in country A, the lower will be the purchasing power of its currency in terms of currency B in the subsequent period. A similar argument is valid also for relative GDP levels, and an analogous relationship may be used for updating real (PPP-based) GDPs. GDP values at international dollars of year i (${}_{i}GDP^{n}/{}_{i}PPP$) may thus be obtained from values expressed in dollars of year j with appropriate growth rates of countries compared, after adjustment for the rate of inflation measured in international dollars. Since the purchasing power of the international dollar is the same as that of the US dollar over the whole GDP, the internal rate of inflation of the USA (GNP deflator) is usually used as an approximative deflator.[37] A similar procedure can be used for updating other benchmark GDP estimates as well.

Estimates of growth rates for six East European countries are regularly computed by T. Alton and his group (see, e.g., Alton (1990)), analogous estimates (including estimates for the Soviet Union) are being performed by the CIA (Handbook of Economic Statistics (1990)). Here, more or less independent estimates of sectoral indexes of output growth for the various production and service sectors are derived from national statistics and then aggregated into an index of GDP with weights reflecting estimated sectoral contributions to GDP in terms of so-called "adjusted factor costs" of a particular base year. These estimates depend (as any other method) also on data provided by CPEs. For those countries, which report a sufficiently large and reliable sample of quantitative data (e.g. Hungary and Poland), a tendency of underestimating growth creeps in as the sample becomes less representative over time. For other countries (e.g. Bulgaria, the GDR, Romania, and the Soviet Union), where the lack of quantitative data has to be compensated by the officially reported (usually upward biased) growth indexes, an overestimation of real growth rates may occur. Besides, the contribution of an emerging private sector is insufficiently reflected anyway. Although the bias in estimated annual growth rates may not be too large, a more distorted picture of the relative GDP levels emerges as the bias is cumulated over longer periods of time.[38]

The ICP-like comparisons at various points of time have been problematic, as the conditions of a supply-constrained economy in former CPEs differed markedly from demand-constraint market economies in the past, and were different from conditions for economies in transition (former CPEs) today. There has been a striking difference between official and estimated implicit growth rates when data for longer periods of time were compared. The widening gap between ICP estimates for Hungary and Poland and the results of other methods in the three consecutive benchmark years 1975, 1980, and 1985 raises some concern about the consistency of past quality adjustments in ICP: the implicit ICP-based growth rates for Hungary, Poland, and Yugoslavia seemed to underestimate real developments. During 1975-1985 the ICP results suggest that Hungary's and Poland's per capita GDP dropped by 24.6% and 40.8% respectively, that of Yugoslavia stagnated. Official (NMP) figures report a growth by 23.8% (Hungary), a drop by 6.6% (Poland), and a growth by 28.4% (Yugoslavia) (Fink and Havlik (1989)). Although it is widely believed that official growth rates overestimated real growth at that time, such great differences can hardly be explained only by the bias in reporting official growth rates (especially as far as Hungary is concerned).

Taking into account the above reservations, an extrapolation of benchmark GDP estimates for East European countries must be treated with extreme caution. Table 12 below shows the 1985 benchmark PIG estimates (from Table 11), extrapolated with estimated GDP(GNP) per capita growth rates (CIA), and moved to current prices with US GNP price deflator (moreover, data for 1990 and 1991 are preliminary).

Table 12

Extrapolation of Benchmark (1985) GDP per Capita PIG Estimates

(at current international dollars)

Year	1985	1986	1987	1988	1989	1990	1991
Bulgaria	7474	8021	8165	8495	8871	8384	6976
CSFR	8153	8516	8844	9275	9752	9832	8589
GDR	8993	9365	9813	0250	0896	9383	6765
Hungary	7431	7800	8100	8570	8815	8887	8503
Poland	6441	6740	6771	7080	7268	6640	6215
Romania	5852	6184	6283	6570	6716	6066	5236
USSR	7328	7744	8002	8368	8781	8945	7908
Yugoslavia	6022	6370	6478	6653	6829	6455	5035
USA	12870	13482	14223	15196	16137	16947	17448
Austria	10682	11080	11633	12476	13535	14641	15683
				USA = 100			
Bulgaria	58.1	59.5	57.4	55.9	55.0	49.5	40.0
CSFR	63.3	63.2	62.2	61.0	60.4	58.0	49.2
GDR	69.9	69.5	69.0	67.5	67.5	55.4	38.7
Hungary	57.7	57.9	56.9	56.4	54.6	52.4	48.7
Poland	50.0	50.0	47.6	46.6	45.0	39.2	35.6
Romania	45.5	45.9	44.2	43.2	41.6	35.8	30.0
USSR	56.9	57.4	56.3	55.1	54.4	52.8	45.3
Yugoslavia	46.8	47.2	45.5	43.8	42.3	38.1	28.9
USA	100.0	100.0	100.0	100.0	100.0	100.0	100.0
Austria	83.0	82.2	81.8	82.1	83.9	86.4	89.9
				Austria= 100			
Bulgaria	70.0	72.4	70.2	68.1	65.5	57.3	44.5
CSFR	76.3	76.9	76.0	74.3	72.1	67.2	54.8
GDR	84.2	84.5	84.4	82.2	80.5	64.1	43.1
Hungary	69.6	70.4	69.6	68.7	65.1	60.7	54.2
Poland	60.3	60.8	58.2	56.8	53.7	45.4	39.6
Romania	54.8	55.8	54.0	52.7	49.6	41.4	33.4
USSR	68.6	69.9	68.8	67.1	64.9	61.1	50.4
Yugoslavia	56.4	57.5	55.7	53.3	50.5	44.1	32.1
USA	120.5	121.7	122.3	121.8	119.2	115.8	111.3
Austria	100.0	100.0	100.0	100.0	100.0	100.0	100.0

Sources: Table 11, Handbook of Economic Statistics (1990), own calculations and projections. Data for 1990 and 1991 are own preliminary estimates.

Disregarding for a moment the absolute GDP per capita figures, the moststriking feature is that all East European countries have lost, during the second half of the 1980s, their relative development positions as compared with both USA and Austria. This retardation of economic development has been most pronounced in the former GDR, which worsened her position by more than 14 points with respect to USA and even by 20 percentage points as compared with Austria during 1985-1990.[39] Other "big losers" were Poland (11 and 15 percentage points respectively) and Romania (10 and 13 percentage points), too. On the other hand, Czechoslovakia, Hungary, and the USSR have performed relatively better – although they too have worsened their relative positions by about 9 percentage points between 1985-1990. Preliminary results for 1991 indicate a further substantial drop in East European relative per capita GDP levels.

7. Conclusions and Final Assessment

Like in MEs, there is no unequivocal answer as far as the level of per capita GDP in former CPEs is concerned. But for the latter countries, too, the use of current exchange rates is inappropriate in most international comparisons, especially when the real levels of real output, consumption or living standards are to be compared. The reliable and up-to-date information on purchasing power parities – which are preferable as convertors of national GDP data for purposes of international comparisons – is still lacking. This, however, does not mean that current official exchange rates should be used as convertors instead. Owing to the exchange rate deviation bias, great fluctuations in current exchange rates over time and, last but not least, different exchange rate policies (mainly grossly undervalued currencies in most countries in transition from the command to a market economy) the use of current exchange rates as convertors for (now mostly readily available) national GDP/GNP data leads to substantial underestimation of their respective real development levels.

If we take into account that every comparison of this kind is prone to a certain amount of uncertainty, the relatively modest costs of the PIG method, the possibility of applying this method without close co-operation with CPE statistical offices, and of applying it to all countries compared (including all former CPEs) uniformly, makes it clearly an attractive approach for obtaining internationally comparable data on economic development levels. But again, we must warn against comparisons with data obtained with other methods, since the above discussion showed that ER, PPP, and PIG scales differ. The PPP-based comparisons are clearly preferable for assessing real GDP levels, but they are, unfortunately, not available for all former CPEs. The per capita GDPs converted with current exchange rates may serve as a proxy for assessing the size of a market for Western exports, but do not correctly reflect either the real strength of Eastern economies or their real development levels. The PIG estimates form an approximation for the assessment of real output levels, but disregard important systemic differences between market and command economies. Now, when most political obstacles have largely fallen, it would be highly desirable that all Central and East European countries participate in future in ICP-type comparisons. Given the limited resources in most former CPEs, this is an important field where Western financial and expert assistance would be required.

The crucial question is, which of the available alternative estimates (i.e. ER-based, PPP-based, or PIG) should be recommended? As elsewhere, the purpose of a comparison partly determines the results applied. Not the strength of an economy in producing exports competitive on Western markets (implied by results obtained with traditional exchange rate conversions), is compared by the PIG- and PPP-based measures of economic development, but rather the ability of an economy to turn out goods for largely domestic use. Moreover, the PIG estimates, more than other methods (PPPs), often disregarded substantial quality differences; on the other hand, they might more properly reflect the real economic potential of a country. Until reliable PPP estimates for all former CPEs become available, the PIG estimates provide a more complete and realistic picture for a ranking of relative economic development level in individual countries, though not for comparing absolute levels of per capita GDPs.

An overview of alternative GDP per capita estimates is summarized in Table 13. The today readily available ER-converted GDP data for all former CPEs, which put these countries in transition to a market economy (especially Hungary, Poland, and Czechoslovakia) basically at par with many African and Latin American developing countries, are hardly acceptable as a reliable yardstick for assessment of either the real economic strength and development level or even of development ranking of these countries. At the same time, they indicate how deeply domestic economic activities have been recently undervalued to enable them to compete with market economies. The two sets of PPP-based estimates (ICP-extrapolated results for 1989 and Planecon data for 1990 – the latter are similar to the CIA estimates, except for the Soviet Union) provide a much more realistic picture. Finally, the PIG estimates (extrapolated with estimated growth rates from the author's 1985 benchmarks) represent the ranking of individual countries fairly well, but probably constitute an upper boundary as far as absolute development levels of individual former CPEs are concerned.

Table 13

Alternative Estimates of per Capita GDP (GNP)

(in current dollars and percent)

Method/Source Year	ICP 1989			CIA 1989			Physical indicators 1990			PPP 1990			Exchange rates 1990		
	$	USA =100%	Austria =100%	$	USA =100%	Austria =100%	$	USA =100%	Austria =100%	$	USA =100%	Austria =100%	$	USA =100%	Austria =100%
Bulgaria	.	.	.	5690	27.2	.	8380	49.5	57.3	5430	25.0	37.7	6290	28.9	30.5
Czechoslovakia	.	.	.	7900	37.8	.	9830	58.0	67.2	7940	36.5	55.1	2810	12.9	13.6
GDR	.	.	.	9670	46.3	.	9380	55.4	64.1	8500	39.1	59.0	8820	40.6	42.8
Hungary	6200	30.0	45.2	6090	29.2	.	8890	52.4	60.7	5920	27.2	41.1	3160	14.5	15.3
Poland	4980	24.1	36.3	4560	21.8	.	6640	39.2	45.4	3910	18.0	27.2	1740	8.0	8.4
Romania	.	.	.	3440	16.5	.	6070	35.8	41.4	2950	13.6	20.5	1540	7.1	7.5
USSR	.	.	.	9230	44.2	.	8490	52.8	61.1	5060	23.3	35.1	5660	26.0	27.4
Yugoslavia	5320	25.7	38.8	5460	26.1	.	6455	38.1	44.1	5140	23.6	35.7	.	.	.
USA	20690	100.0	150.9	20890	100.0	.	16950	100.0	115.8	21730	100.0	150.9	21730	100.0	105.4
Austria	13710	66.3	100.0	.	.	.	14640	86.4	100.0	14400	66.3	100.0	20620	94.9	100.0

Source: Havlik, Peter, "East-West GDP Comparisons: Problems, Methods and Results", WIIW-Forschungsberichte, No. 174, Vienna, September 1991, p. 37.

For the time being we have to accept the fact that there is reliable evidence only as far as the ranking of GDP per capita in Central and East European countries is concerned. In the mid-1980s (and immediately before the political changes in 1989/1990), the former East Germany has been a leader, followed by Czechoslovakia, then by a group formed by Hungary, Poland, Bulgaria, and the Soviet Union, trailed by Yugoslavia and Romania. In 1990, the GDR might have been temporarily surpassed by the CSFR, largely as a consequence of the shock imposed on the East German economy by German unification. A relative improvement in Bulgarian and Soviet standing suggested by the extrapolated PIG estimates results most likely from overstated growth rates. Unfortunately, there are no uniformly accepted data regarding comparable GDP levels with respect to Western countries. A crucial, not yet adequately solved problem is whether for example the Polish GDP per capita level amounted either to 8%, 27%, or 45% of the Austrian level in 1990. As with many similar questions, the truth may be somewhere in between, and a more detailed explanation rather than a single figure must be required. But even if we take the higher end estimates as a crude approximation, the deterioration of East European levels of per capita GDPs is extremely disturbing.

Notes

1. Here we disregard the differences between GDP and GNP (basically the balance of factor incomes with abroad), which is very small for the CPEs.

2. Such methodological differences between the GDP and NMP are well documented (e.g. *Comparisons of the System* (1981)) and individual attempts to recalculate GDP into NMP and vice versa were done (*Comparisons of the System* (1981), Havlik and Levcik (1985)), but the conversion from NMP to GDP has not been easy, since necessary input data were not generally available.

3. For example, East German GDP amounted to 353.3 bn Mark in 1989 (see *Statistisches Jahrbuch der DDR 1990*, Berlin, 1990, p. 107), i.e., it exceeded the corresponding NMP by 35.7%. The official Soviet data put the Soviet GNP in 1989 at Rbl 924 bn, i.e. 40.7% higher than the corresponding NMP. This figure is suspiciously high, given the underdeveloped Soviet service sector (in Hungary, the corresponding GDP/NMP ratio was 121%, in Czechoslovakia 122%).

4. See *Süddeutsche Zeitung*, No. 229, 1990, p. 32.

5. The recent introduction of so called "internal convertibility" (for most current account transactions) in Poland and Yugoslavia (since Jan. 1, 1990), and in Czechoslovakia (since Jan. 1, 1991), makes hardly any difference, since the new official exchange rates of the respective currencies were artificially fixed much below actual purchasing power (except for the Yugoslav Dinar), in order to protect the current account balance.

6. In 1985, the US$ exchange rate (US$/ECU) valued US Dollar by about 25% less than its real purchasing power; in 1989 the US$ was overvalued by about 8%, the German Mark and Japanese Yen by 13% and 26% respectively – see *EUROSTAT*, No. 3, 1990, p. 48.

7. In terms of foreign currency per national currency unit – see *International comparison of gross domestic product in Europe 1985, United Nations*, New York, 1988, p. 24.

8. See *International Comparison of Gross Domestic Product in Europe 1985, op. cit.*, p. 24.

9. See *World Development Report 1991*, The World Bank, Oxford University Press, 1991, p. 263.

10. See, for instance, Lipton, D., Sachs, J., "Creating a Market Economy in Eastern Europe – the Case of Poland". *Brookings Papers on Economic Activity*, No. 1, 1990, pp. 75-133.

11. After abolishing the internal rates and further subsequent devaluations of the Kcs during 1989-1990 (from Kcs 5.3 per US$ in 1988 to Kcs 15.1 per US$ in 1989, Kcs 17.9 per US$ in 1990 and Kcs 28 per US$ at the beginning of 1991), the Czechoslovak per capita GDP would drop below US$ 2,500 in 1991.

12. See *World Development Report 1991*, op. cit., p. 205. The World Bank gives different figures for Bulgaria (US$ 2,320) and provides no estimate for the Soviet Union.

13. A bilateral Soviet-Hungarian comparison for 1985 was already completed: Soviet per capita final consumption of the population amounted to 90.1% of Hungary's or, indirectly, about 25% of the USA. Detailed results are to be published soon – see Zarubin, G., Sergeyev, C., "Uchastiye SSSR v rabote nad proyektom mezhdunarodnykh sopostavlenyi OON," *Vestnik Statistiki*, No. 8, 1990, pp. 57-64.

14. The results for 1980 (Phase IV) were published in 1986 (see *World Comparisons* (1986). The preliminary results for 1985, however, were published for OECD countries already in mid-1987 (*OECD Observer*, No. 145, April/May 1987), for the European comparison at the end of 1987 (Auer (1987)) and in 1988 resp. (*International Comparison of Gross Domestic Product in Europe*, 1985 (1988)). The final 1985 data linkage between various regions of the world is not yet (August 1991) available.

15. The exception is the latest CIA assessment of the Soviet Union – see below.

16. These comparisons are very crude indeed. Apart from varying methods, we disregard differences between GDP/NMP, different benchmark years, and different price structures in non-benchmark countries.

17. East German GDP in 1989 was estimated at about DM 285 bn, i.e. about DM 17,340 per capita (US$ 7,200 at PPPs and US$ 9,200 resp. at exchange rates – see Table 2 and "Gesamtwirtschaftliche und unternehmerische Anpassungsprozesse in Ostdeutschland," Institut für Weltwirtschaft Kiel, *Discussion Paper No. 168*, March 1991, p. 26.

18. This result, obtained by the ICP methodology and using Hungary as a bridge, was recently published in the Soviet Union – see *Ekonomika i zhizn*, No. 6, 1991, p. 20.

19. I.e., the lowering of PPP-based per capita GDP estimates needed to arrive at the ER-based GDP estimate (resulting from an estimated ERDI ranging between 1.12 (GDR) and 1.32 (Soviet Union)).

20. Note that the average ERDI for European OECD countries in 1980 was 0.966, and only for Portugal (1.584) and Turkey (1.952) significantly greater than 1 – see Table 3 above. (However, these ERDIs were not available at that time, and ICP results for 1975 were extrapolated instead).

21. A recent report by Planecon shows that only 5 basic commodities (steel, grain, coal, gas, and oil) would account for 43% of Soviet GNP in 1989 (sic!) when evaluated at market exchange rate (commercial rate) – see *Planecon* (1990), p. 4.

22. The same approach to benchmark estimates is used by T. Alton and his group (see Alton (1990)). The Alton group does not compute GDP estimates for the USSR.

23. The CIA estimates for GDP per capita in 1988 and 1989 (in % of the US level) were the following: Bulgaria 38% and 27%, Czechoslovakia 51% and 38%, East Germany 63% and 46%, Hungary 44% and 29%, Poland 37% and 22%, Romania 28%

and 17%, Yugoslavia 33% and 26%. Curiously, the evaluation of the Soviet Union remained the same (about 44-45% of US level), thus raising the relative GDP level of the USSR with respect to Central and East European countries.

24. Here the original CIA estimates of 1988 GDP for the CEE countries were scaled down by a flat rate of 25% (and 37% for the Soviet Union) in order to reflect: (i) lack of availability of many goods and services at officially posted prices, (ii) differences in quality between East and West, (iii) differences in use value of durable products due to lack of spare parts, etc. – see *Planecon* (1989), p. 7.

25. Usually, both alternative baskets are used, and the geometric mean of both ratios (Fisher's index) is used as a meaningful compromise. In ICP, more elaborate price indexes with specifically designed weights, reflecting different baskets of all countries compared, are being applied – see Krijnse Locker and Faerber (1984)).

26. Note that analogous problems are basically faced by the ICP as well when representative commodities are being selected. Here the prices and quantities of goods established for largely saturated markets in MEs are being compared with similar data for CPEs where markets are plagued with shortages, and, apart from officially reported prices, a number of other factors (e.g. rationing) affect the general availability of goods and services.

27. It is certainly not very satisfactory when the current CIA GNP estimates for the smaller East European countries are based partly on benchmarks for 1970, and three different estimation methods are applied for the CPEs as a group (*Handbook of Economic Statistics* (1990)). The above mentioned recent adjustment for East European countries constitutes a separate problem.

28. Double-, sometimes even three-digit inflation has been characteristic for the initial period of price liberalization in Poland, Czechoslovakia, Bulgaria, and Romania.

29. An illustration is presented by former East Germany, where domestically produced consumer goods have virtually disappeared from the shops after unification with FRG in 1990. Such development, however, is exceptional in the East European context, since it was facilitated by massive income transfers from the FRG.

30. See Fink and Havlik (1989) for the analysis of 1980 data, and more details for 1985 partial GDP per capita estimates below.

31. Havlik (1991) – Appendix.

32. The distribution of partial GDP estimates in the majority of the sample countries (of the CPEs, only Bulgaria was the exception) matches the Gauss normal distribution fairly well. The Jarque-Bera test for normality (see Jarque and Bera (1980)) showed some departure from normality only for the distribution of partial GDP estimates for South Korea, Greece, Norway, Turkey, and Bulgaria (year 1980), and Egypt, Finland, FRG, Greece, Turkey, and Bulgaria (year 1985) – see[31]. This implies, inter alia, that the sample average may be used as an unbiased estimate of the average per capita GDP.

33. See Ehrlich (1991), p. 72.

34. The Soviet State Committee for Statistics (Goskomstat) noted in one of the last statistical yearbooks that "growth rate calculations for 1985-1987 ... were corrected in order to eliminate the impact of reduced production and sales of alcoholic beverages" - see *Narodnoye khozyaystvo SSSR v 1988 godu*, Moscow 1989, p. 7.

35. It could be argued that the PIG method (which measures the development level indirectly) can take better account of activities of the unofficial economy.

36. In reality this is, of course, never exactly the case (see Szilagyi (1984)), and we do not know exactly whether the ICP or national statistics are to be blamed. In practice, the two indexes usually do not deviate from each other too much. The indicated relationship has been used for both checking the officially reported inflation (see Havlik (1985)), and for extrapolating PPPs (see Kravis et al. (1982), Hill (1984)).

37. This is mostly approximated by the US implicit price deflator. More details on updating procedures in international comparisons may be found in Szilagyi (1984).

38. However, an internal CIA (1988) review suggested that its estimates of Soviet growth rates were essentially correct – see Pitzer, J.S., Bankol, A.P., "Recent GNP and Productivity Trends," *Soviet Economy*, Vol. 7, 1991, p. 50.

39. Note that Austria improved her position with respect to USA during the same period.

Selected References

Alton, T.P. et. al. (1990), "Economic Growth in Eastern Europe, 1975-1989." *Research Project on National Income in East Central Europe*, Occasional Paper No. 110, New York.

Ancyferova, L., Zarubin, G. (1984), "K provedeniyu mezhdunarodnykh sopostavlenyiy vazhneyshikh ekonomicheskykh pokazateleyi stran-chlenov SEV." *Vestnik statistiki*, No. 2, pp. 47-55.

Auer, J. (1987), "Ergebnisse bilateraler Wirtschaftsvergleiche mit Polen, Ungarn und Jugoslawien für das Jahr 1985." *Statistische Nachrichten*, No. 12, pp. 957-962.

Blades, D. (ed.) (1991), "Statistics for a Market Economy." *Centre for Co-operation with European Economies in Transition*, OECD, Paris.

"Comparisons of the System of National Accounts and the System of Balances of the National Economy," (Part Two: Conversion of Aggregates of SNA to MPS and Vice Versa for Selected Countries). New York, United Nations, *Document Series F*, No. 20 (Part II).

"Comparative GDP Levels" (1980), *Economic Bulletin for Europe* Vol. 31, No. 2, New York, United Nations, Economic Commission for Europe.

Edwards, I., Hughes, M. and Noren, J. (1979), "U.S. and U.S.S.R.: Comparisons of GNP." *Soviet Economy in a Time of Change*, Joint Economic Committee, Vol. 1, Oct., pp. 369-401.

Ehrlich, E. (1966), "An Examination of the Inter-relation Between Consumption Indicators Expressed in Physical Units and per Capita National Income." *Czechoslovak Economic Papers* 7, Academia, Prague, pp. 109-136.

Ehrlich, E. (1991), "The Competition Among Countries, 1937-1986." in *Eastern European Economics*, Winter 1990-91, Vol. 29, No. 2, pp. 67-100.

Fink, G., Havlik, P. (1989), "Problems of East-West GDP Comparisons". *WIIW-Forschungsberichte No. 152.*

Georgieva, D. Ivanov, Yu. (1990), "Makroekonomicheskiye pokazateli: ophyt mezhdunarodnogo sopostavleniya." *Ekonomicheskoye sotrudnichestvo stran-chlenov SEV*, No. 10, pp. 105-111.

Gilbert, M., Kravis, B. (1954), "An International Comparison of National Products and the Purchasing Power of Currencies," *OEEC*, Paris.

Handbook of Economic Statistics (1989), CIA, U.S. Government Printing Office, Washington D.C.

Handbook of Economic Statistics (1990), CIA, U.S. Government Printing Office, Washington D.C.

Havlik, P., Levcik, F. (1985), "GDP of Czechoslovakia, 1970-1980." *World Bank Staff Working Paper* No. 772, The World Bank, Washington, D.C.

Havlik, P. (1985), "A Comparison of Purchasing Power Parity and Consumption Levels in Austria and Czechoslovakia." *Journal of Comparative Economics*, 9, pp. 178-190.

Havlik, P. (1986), "Comparison of Real Products Between East and West, 1970-1983." *WIIW-Forschungsberichte* No. 115, April.

Havlik, P. (1990), "Die Wechselkurspolitik der RGW-Länder und Probleme der Konvertibilität". *WIIW-Forschungsberichte* No. 162, March.

Havlik, P. (1991), "East-West GDP Comparisons: Problems, Methods and Results." *WIIW-Forschungsberichte* No. 174.

Hill, P. (1984), "Real Gross Product in OECD Countries and Associated Purchasing Power Parities." OECD, Economics and Statistics Department, *Working paper No. 17*, Dec.

"International Comparison of Gross Domestic Product in Europe 1985." (1988), *United Nations*, N.Y.

Janossy, F., Ehrlich, E. (1969), "Structural Trends and Prospects in the European Economy." *Economic Survey of Europe in 1969*, UN, New York.

Kravis, Irving B., Heston, Alan, and Summers, Robert (1982), *World Product and Income: International Comparisons of Real Gross Product*. Baltimore and London, The John Hopkins University Press for the World Bank.

Krijnse Locker, H., Faerber, H.D. (1984), "Space and Time Comparisons of Purchasing Power Parities and Real Values." *The Review of Income and Wealth*, No. 1, March.

Marer, Paul (1985), *Dollar GNPs of the U.S.S.R. and Eastern Europe*, The John Hopkins University Press, Baltimore.

Marer, Paul (1985), "Alternative Estimates of the Dollar GNP and Growth Rates of the CMEA Countries," in Joint Economic Committee, US Congress, *East European Economics: Slow Growth in the 1980's*, Vol. 1, Oct. 28.

Marris, R. (1984), "Comparing the Incomes of Nations: A Critique of the ICP." *The Journal of Economic Literature*, Vol. XXII, No. 1, March, pp. 40-57.

Martynov, V. (1990), "SSSR i SShA po materiyalam mezhdunarodnykh sopostavlenyi OON i SEV" (The USSR and the USA According to International Comparisons in the Framework of UN and CMEA). *Vestnik statistiki*, No. 9, pp. 10-15.

Mikkelsen, J.G. (1989), *Long Run Purchasing Power Parity in Latin America*. Paper presented at the World Congress of Econometric Society, Barcelona, October.

PlanEcon Report (1989), Washington, D.C., November 3.

PlanEcon Report (1990), Washington, D.C., December 28.

Rajewski, Z. (1985), "Miedzynarodowe porownania wielostronne realizowane w ramach RWPG" (International Multilateral Comparisons Performed within the CMEA). *Wiadomosci statystyczne*, No. 6.

Summers, R., Heston, A. (1988), "A new set of international comparisons of real product and price levels estimates for 130 countries, 1950-1985." *The Review of Income and Wealth*, No. 1, March, pp. 1-26.

Szilagyi, G. (1984), "Updating Procedures of International Comparison Results". *The Review of Income and Wealth*, No. 2, June, pp. 153-165.

van Brabant, Jozef (1985), "Exchange Rates in Eastern Europe: Types, Derivation, Application." *World Bank Staff Working Paper* No. 778, The World Bank.

Valeshko, M., Dyakin, B., Perevertaylo, V. (1983), "Spetsiyalisatsiya narodnokhosyaystvennykh komplexov stran-chlenov SEV" (Specialization of CMEA Economies). *Ekonomicheskoye sotrudnichestvo stran-chlenov SEV*, No. 3, pp. 63-68.

Wolf, Thomas A. (1985), "Exchange Rates, Foreign Trade Accounting and Purchasing Power Parity for Centrally Planned Economies." *World Bank Staff Working Paper* No. 779, The World Bank, Washington D.C.

"World Comparisons of Purchasing Power and Real Product for 1980." *United Nations*, N.Y.

Zarubin, G., Sergeyev, C. (1990), Uchastiye SSSR v rabote nad proyektom mezhdunarodnykh sopostavlenyi OON. *Vestnik Statistiki*, No. 8, pp. 57-64.

11

INTERNATIONAL ASPECTS OF THE ECONOMIC TRANSFORMATION IN CENTRAL AND EASTERN EUROPE *

Hubert Gabrisch

1. The International Context of Systemic Transformation

In Central and Eastern Europe (CEE)[1] the past three years brought the collapse of the centrally planned economies and totalitarian systems that had been installed by the Soviet Union after 1945. This chapter deals with the challenges posed for the governments of East Europe and the international community by the transformation from the socialist command economy to a market economy. It will further survey the financial assistance granted to the countries concerned, and foreign direct investment, as well as examine the problems of fashioning the new economic order. Assembling these elements, this chapter is based on the author's conviction that in a modern world systemic changes may succeed only in a strong international context, or otherwise will fail. The systemic transformation we are witnessing takes place at the end of the 20th century, in a world characterized not only by highly integrated commodity and financial markets, but also by growing integration of information flows. Easily accessible information from other parts of the world makes people aware of their own living conditions, and also of the reasons why they are subject to these living conditions. There have always been rich and poor nations, but it is the information on the rich nations that causes emigration from the poor nations,

---

* This Paper was presented at the *Symposium on Eastcentral Europe and Germany*, at Ann Arbor, Michigan, November 15-16, 1991.

unless their systems are changed. And one of the main reasons for the breakdown of communist systems in East Central Europe was the manifest inability of these systems to keep up with the immediately neighboring West in economic, social and political terms.

2. The Way Back to Europe

The nations of the former CMEA countries – especially the Poles, Czechs, Slovaks and Hungarians, but also the Slovenes, Croats and the Baltic people – have always thought of themselves as belonging to the Western and Central European cultural milieu. Communist rule, lasting for 45 years, disrupted a centuries old common history of Europe. The planned economy destroyed some flourishing economic organisms, such as Czechoslovakia, which had been one of the main industrial regions before the Second World War. In 1948, Czechoslovakia had grossed an equivalent of 78% of the Dutch per capita national product, and exceeded the Finnish GNP by 13%; in 1985 the Czechoslovak GNP was only half the Netherland's or Finland's (Butschek, 1990, p. 556). Forty-five years of separation from the world economy resulted in a wide technological gap, in non-competitive economic structures, stagnating or even shrinking production, inflation, rising budget deficits and foreign indebtedness, and declining living standards.

Table 1

GDP of CEE Countries and the Soviet Union in 1990-1991

in %, as against the preceding year

	1990	1991 WIIW estimate
Czechoslovakia	-2.0	-15.0
Hungary	-4.0	-7.0
Poland	-12.0	-8 to -10
Bulgaria	-11.8	-20 to -25
Romania	-7.3	-17.0[a)]
Yugoslavia	-7.6	-25.0
Soviet Union	-2.0	-13.0

a) Official Romanian forecast: -5%.

Source: For 1990, national sources.

The CEE nations aim at catching up with economic and social developments in Western Europe as fast as possible. But one indicator for the difficulty of this task is provided by a comparison of per capita gross social products:[2] e.g., in Czechoslovakia the 1989 GDP was only 47% of that in the former Federal Republic of Germany. The corresponding figures for Hungary and Poland are 36% and 27% respectively. But while the economy in Western Europe is continuing to grow, it is declining dramatically in CEE countries in the course of their transition to market economies. The negative growth rates in CEE countries have reached levels unknown elsewhere since the great crisis of 1929-33 (Table 1). In Poland, the GDP fell by more than one fifth over the past two years, in Czechoslovakia by more than 10% in 1991, in Hungary by about 10% in 1990/91. The situation is even more critical in the poorer countries, Bulgaria and Romania, where declines of 20% are likely this year. Thus we need not be surprised at the growing disappointment and unrest of people who had been promised quick recovery by the former opposition parties who had taken power after the communist regimes' overthrow.

3. External Challenges

Simultaneously with the systemic change in the CEE countries, the Council for Mutual Economic Assistance (CMEA), and thus the network of economic relations, which had linked these countries and the Soviet

Table 2

CEEs' Exports to Western Industrialized Countries

(in US$ mn)

	1989	1990	1991 (1st half)
	in % as against the preceding period		
Poland	8.8	30.7	12.7
Czechoslovakia	10.8	13.0	4.9
Hungary	5.2	21.4	25.1
Bulgaria	17.9	-12.3	-49.7
Romania	-6.1	-30.2	-16.7
Yugoslavia	6.7	24.5	-0.4

Source: National statistics; WIIW estimate.

Union, has collapsed. The CMEA had been set up in 1949, after Stalin had prevented the East European countries' participation in the Marshall Plan, and when they had turned to the Soviet Union for resources to rebuild their war-destroyed economies, and for their industrialization. In the 1970s the CMEA claimed to represent a socialist alternative to EC integration. But in fact only the trade flows were adjusted, while all the countries concerned were developing their industries in a more or less autarkic manner. Direct investment, the most important factor of economic integration, was lacking completely. The fragility of this economic network was disclosed by the shift to world market prices and hard currency accounting in mutual trade at the beginning of 1991: the CEE countries' trade turnover with the Soviet Union fell by up to 60-70% in that year. Also trade turnover among the individual Central and East European countries was on a steep decline. In particular this affected countries such as Bulgaria and Romania, who could not find new markets in the West. Only Czechoslovakia, and especially Hungary and Poland could expand their exports to the West in the past two years, despite declining production (Table 2). The high Soviet share in these three countries' trade – which had been determined politically, not economically – has dropped significantly; this is generally regarded as an important structural improvement.

Table 3

Foreign Direct Investment in Czechoslovakia, Hungary and Poland

(number of authorized projects per end of period)

	1988	1989	1990	1991 (1st quarter)
Czechoslovakia	n.a.	60	1,600	2,850
Hungary	176	4,000	5,000	7,000
Poland	40	900	2,800	3,750
Total	216	4,960	9,400	13,600

Source: United Nations Economic Commission for Europe, East-West Joint Ventures News, No. 8, July 1991.

In the case of Western direct investment, too, a dynamic development has set in; up to the late 1980s Central and Eastern Europe had been completely insignificant as a target of foreign direct investment. While only slightly more than 200 foreign participations (Joint Ventures) were registered by the end of 1988 in Hungary, Poland, and Czechoslovakia, the figure was almost 15,000 by the end of March 1991 (Table 3). However, only a small fraction of enterprises registered has already started operations, and the overwhelming majority of enterprises is very small. The capital invested so far (end of March 1991) is estimated at about US$ 1.6-1.8 bn in Hungary, US$ 131 mn in Czechoslovakia, and some US$ 300-400 mn in Poland. At present considerable risks exist, which have rather increased due to the instability of the general economic, social, and political conditions in all countries of the East at the present stage of transition (Gabrisch, 1991).

All these developments show that, in the long run, the tightening of real and institutional links with Western industrial countries is a matter of life and death for Central and Eastern Europe. Without far more intensive commodity and capital ties, without the flow of services, the CEE countries will not be able to overcome the difficulties connected with their efforts to speed up economic growth (WERI, 1991, p. 159).

All this takes place on the eve of the Single European Market, feared as "Fortress Europe" by other countries, who are threatened not so much by new protectionist measures of the EC, but rather by raised barriers to market access by way of trade diversion, productivity effects and increased factor endowment within the EC (Jennewein, 1991, pp. 4ff, 8ff.).

This heightens the aspirations of Central and Eastern Europe to become associate members of the EC. EC association makes sense only if, in the long run, it leads to EC membership (but surely, any assumptions that this goal might be reached as early as by the year 2000 appear unrealistic). Association thus becomes a starting point for drawing up a timetable of adjustment activities to the rules under which the EC is functioning. Any other options – such as the revival of a market reformed CMEA, accession to EFTA, orientation of Poland and the new Baltic states towards the Scandinavian economic area, evolution of the so-called Hexagonale (Austria, Italy, Yugoslavia, Hungary, Poland, CSFR) into an economic community – appear to be either unrealistic or just steps on the way to full membership in EC (Paszynski, 1991, pp. 6ff).

The still substantial dependence on the Soviet Union, mainly of the three countries Poland, Hungary, and Czechoslovakia, who have gone furthest on the road of reform, but also of the new Baltic states, has induced these countries – even more so after the failed coup in the Soviet Union – to reinforce their wish for EC association, and to attempt to accelerate the association procedure.

4. Internal Challenges

However, the transformation of the economic order is of greater importance than the shaping of contractual relations between the EC and the Central and East European countries; which does not mean, though, that transformation could be carried through without regard for its international context. This context must be kept in mind when the central internal challenges facing the CEE countries are formulated.

4.1 Restoring the Growth Potential

The first challenge to be met is the danger of the CEE countries becoming the poorhouse of Europe: that would seriously hamper access to the EC. Let us briefly discuss the first actual experiences with transition programs:

A characteristic of most of the programs started in CEE countries (Poland: January 1990, Czechoslovakia: January 1991, Bulgaria: February 1991 and, originally, also the Yugoslav program of early 1990) is the freeing of prices, and price stabilization, as a first stage of transition. Their purpose is to remove economic distortions and to prepare the ground for the next and more difficult stage of institutional and other structural changes (Gomulka, 1991, p. 1). In addition, limited foreign exchange convertibility is established, and markets are opened with abroad. The exchange rate is to be set at a level well below purchasing power. Price stabilization is to be achieved by macroeconomic means: by curbing demand by a restrictive monetary, incomes and fiscal policy: interest rates are to be raised to a level above inflation, wage increases to be controlled by a prohibitive tax, and the state budget is to be balanced or turned into a surplus by expenditure cuts and tax increases.

Undoubtedly, achievements have resulted from these programs, popularly called "shock" or "big bang" approach: people do no longer waste time in queues as in the command economy, and the liberalization of foreign trade, internal convertibility of the zloty and its drastic devaluation led to a conspicuous increase of the surplus in trade with the Western industrial countries.

However, one should not close one's eyes to some dangerous and discouraging aspects of this approach. All countries that initiated this policy recorded a much deeper recession than anticipated, without definitive success in combating inflation. In Poland, over the year 1990 GDP fell by some 12-14%, as against the 5% the government had expected. For 1991 a 3-5% growth rate had been envisaged, but actually the GDP shrank by a further 7% in the first half of the year; for the whole year 1991 an 8-12% decline is to be expected. The monthly pace of price increases has slowed down, but in spite of a surprisingly large budget surplus the rate of inflation was higher than aimed at by the government. Annual inflation 1991 will still be about 75% as against 1990. The success in consolidating the state budget in 1990 turned out to be only temporary. Recession-caused income losses of households and additional expenditures, due partly to higher inflation, partly to growing unemployment, result in a renewed high deficit in the Polish state budget in 1991. Moreover, production structures did not change as intended. While large state owned enterprises could easily survive monetary and financial stringencies, smaller, relatively more efficient state and private units got into trouble (Winiecki, 1991, p. 16 and 17). A similar development seems to take place in Czechoslovakia in 1991.

We have dealt in somewhat greater detail with Poland's stabilization plan, not only because it has been trend-setting for other countries, but also because it was developed in close cooperation with the IMF and with Western experts, who had gathered experiences with stabilization programs in Latin America. These are sort of export-led growth programs, in which a competitive real exchange rate would promote the (small) export sector. To dampen domestic absorption and inflation, measures are confined to balancing the budget (sometimes even to budgeting for a surplus), to sustaining a restrictive monetary policy, and to achieving a positive real interest rate even in the face of very high rates of inflation. The Eastern countries are assured that these conditions would create a sound basis for future growth.[3]

There are some very weak points in this approach. The first is the assumption that foreign demand is perfectly elastic, meaning, a devaluation will increase foreign demand.

– First: a large part of exports in the command economy was highly subsidized. For many exporters, there is a shift only from subsidy revenues to devaluation profits, which does not hold good for a lower price. Of course, many other exporters, already in the profit zone before devaluation, may now lower prices.

– Second: From the point of view of Western industrial lobbies faced with cheap imports from formerly socialist countries, a drastic devaluation may have the same effect as subsidized, that is, dumping prices. Thus, the harsher the devaluation, the more will these industrial lobbies press their governments for protective measures.

Besides, there is another argument against a harsh devaluation: a devaluation making competitive all hitherto exported goods, including those subsidized, will not contribute to the structural changes that are urgently needed in Eastern economies.

Another assumption, namely, that realistic relative prices and macro-economic constraints on demand are sufficient to produce a prompt take-off, is mere wishful thinking. Of decisive importance is the reform of the micro-economic sphere: the birth of a competitive market structure, consisting of a multitude of autonomous enterprises on every level of size, operated by competent owners and managers imbued with a sense of responsibility, profit orientation and a readiness to take risks. The creation of this market structure is the actual task of transformation. In addition to a mere liberalization of prices, and a restrictive monetary and fiscal policy, it requires the privatization of state enterprises, a reform of the finance and banking system, the creation of functioning factor markets, i.e., in the first place, capital and labor markets, etc. etc. The less developed these market structures are, the less elastic is supply, and the stronger are the inflationary impulses in an environment of free prices. And the more one-sided the economic policy in its efforts to combat inflation, the greater are the risks of the price shock being accompanied by a severe demand shock leading to a deeper than necessary recession.

To give an example of the weaknesses of the one-sided macro-economic approach of stabilization: In Poland the restrictive monetary policies (a positive real interest rate, credit ceilings for commercial banks) had little impact on large state owned enterprises, which form the inefficient sector of the economy. These enterprises were anyway able to find financial sources to avoid bankrupcy (inter-enterprise-lending, withholding taxes, etc.). On the other side, the more efficient sector – smaller state owned enterprises in consumer and export market oriented sectors, and private firms – was very effectively hit by general financial restrictions, and is factually suffering a sharp deceleration of growth.

It seems a rather simple exercise to bring production down, but it is a very difficult undertaking to bring it up. This, obviously, is the basic dilemma of shock policies, experienced not only by economies in transition. Bolivia, for example, commonly considered a successful case of stabilization policies, is still waiting, five years after implementation of the program, for recovery.[4] IMF and other experts' advice to CEE countries is often characterized by the uncritical faith they put in the forces of the free market, while any kind of state intervention, any structural or industrial policy, any kind of incentives and discrimination for sectors are thought to be harmful. But the general conclusion from two years' practice are that price liberalization and macro-economics should be complemented by policies distinguishing between inefficient and efficient sectors in an economy in transition, and discriminating against the former. However, this implies a more active role of the state in the process of transition.

4.2 Fashioning a Market Economy

That brings us to the second challenge: the making of a market economy that will fit into the European framework. One would be mistaken to confine the systemic change to establishing private ownership, liberalizing commodity and factor prices, and exchange rate, as well as trade and commerce. These are microeconomic preconditions characterizing every market economy. But the economic system must be fashioned in a way to make possible its involvement in the European integration process. This requires an active role of the state, at least to protect and to shape competition, but also concerning, in the West European model, countercyclical policy, taxation policy, redistribution, active industrial policy, etc.

One does not always get the impression that this challenge is properly understood in Central and Eastern Europe. An example might illustrate this: Germany and Austria, in view of their remarkable economic and social achievements and success, exercise a strong fascination on the East European nations. That is convincingly demonstrated by the inflowing stream of immigrants. But as soon as the principles of the "social market economy" are brought up in discussion with younger economists and politicians, one will encounter a sudden cooling-off of that enthusiasm, because the economic systems of Germany, and also of Austria, conform in no way to the "pure" liberal model dreamt of by many in Eastern Europe. In this model, "market economy" seems to become an aim in itself. Václav Klaus, Czechoslovakia's Minister of Finance, in public lectures and discussions, has been consistently propagating a "market economy without adjectives". This happens mostly when he puts out the absurd argument against social market economy that he rejects any Third Way between market economy and planned economy, because this would lead straight to a descend into the Third World.

Another frequently encountered argument claims that only rich countries could afford a "social market economy". In Eastern Europe one would first of all have to liberalize prices, to privatize state enterprises, to liberalize trade, commerce, and external economic relations. Everything else would have to be postponed to a later date. This argument is not valid, as proved by the fact that West Germany, immediately after the Second World War, in spite of a wrecked industry, ruined currency, and impoverished population, steered clear of dismantling its social security system, which had been created a century ago, under Bismarck. What is important is not the absolute, but the relative level of social expenditures and their structure. The expenditures themselves may grow together with the social product.

4.3 Two Success Stories: Hungary and Eastern Germany

There are two success stories: Hungary and Eastern Germany – the former GDR. Both countries are far advanced in the transition process, for both countries a recovery of their economies is to be expected in 1992 (Eastern Germany) and 1993 (Hungary) respectively. Both countries, especially Eastern Germany, record a significant inflow of investment capital.

The government of Hungary, which came to power in 1990, was the only one among CEE countries to pursue, in continuation of its precedessor's year-long policy, a gradual reform path. Other than Poland and Czechoslovakia, Hungary does not aim at stabilizing the economy at all costs before introducing the most important institutional prerequisites for a functioning market economy: it aims to achieve this, in the framework of a four-year program, simultaneously with those other measures. What are the effects:

- The recession is not as deep as in other CEE countries,
- inflation remains more or less within the expected limits,
- exports to the West are remarkably increasing, and,
- similar to Eastern Germany, Western capital is coming in for investment: up to the middle of 1991, foreign capital of about US$ 1.6 bn to 1.8 bn has been invested, compared with a meagre US$ 130 mn in Czechoslovakia, and US$ 300 mn in Poland; and US$ 230 mn alone after the first quarter of this year.[5]

Eastern Germany is a special case. No country is experiencing such quick systemic transformation as the former GDR. The currency, economic, and social union of July 1990 set in motion a gigantic price and demand shock, nearly halving industrial production (Akerlof et al., 1991). But transfers from the federal and other public budgets cushion the social consequences of this real big bang, and massive injections of private capital fill the growing body of the market economy with life. This case clearly shows that a big bang or shock approach without massive capital transfer and other financial assistance making adjustments easier, and helpful in structural transformation, will be a very risky maneuver.

5. Financial Assistance

Thus, the wisdom of producing, in a dramatically recessive economy, a significant export surplus, and thereby pushing internal absorption even further below the strongly declining GDP, is doubtful. One would expect a capital starved country like Poland to receive means from abroad rather than exporting them.

All examples of successful transformation – the reconstruction of a free market economy in Western Germany and Austria after World War II, or the industrialization of South Korea and Taiwan in the 1950s and 1960s – took place with substantial credit support, granted mainly by the United States, and were accompanied by a considerable inflow of private investments. Very soon after the political changes in the Central and East European countries the hope was voiced that the West might instal a second Marshall Plan to cushion the transition to a market economy financially, and thus also socially. The Marshall Plan was indeed another important prerequisite for the reconstruction of Western Europe after the Second World War. Over four years the recipient countries received US$ 3.1 bn per year, in total US$ 12.4 bn, mostly in the form of grants. Though this amount represented only about 1% of the US social product, it constituted a substantial support for the recipient countries, in which the transfers amounted to between 2% (Great Britain) and 14% (Austria) of their social product. The Marshall Plan was motivated also by the then political situation, the beginnings of the Cold War, and helped establish democratic order and flourishing market economies in Western Europe. Today the East-West conflict belongs to the past, but the failed coup in the Soviet Union, border conflicts, and national unrest make it clear that a peaceful and democratic order in Europe has so far not been realized, and must still be considered an important objective, yet to be achieved. It would be reasonable to tie financial assistanced to certain conditions; essentially to the implementation of a radical and consistent reform program. That condition is being carried out by Poland, Hungary and Czechoslovakia.

In view of the enormous sums invested by Western Germany in the reconstruction of the East German economy[6], Western aid to the extent of the Marshall Plan appears rather modest: at prices of 1989 the Marshall Plan would make available only US$ 16.4 bn per year, and a total of US$ 65 bn;[7] meaning that it would absorb less than 1% of the Gross National Product of the 16 European countries involved in East European aid, and of the United States. A share of 1% of GNP would mean as much as US$ 56 bn annually, and US$ 224 bn over four years.

If the Gross National Products, calculated according to the official exchange rate, are taken as a rough indicator for estimating the capital needs of Poland, Hungary and Czechoslovakia[8], then financial assistance comparable to that granted to Austria by the Marshall Plan (14% of its GDP)[9] would amount to US$ 20 bn per year, and to a total of US$ 80 bn. A comparison with the support promises up to May 1991 by the most important western institutions, the G-24 and the Bretton Woods institutions (IMF and World Bank), amounting to about US$ 21 bn for Poland, Hungary and Czechoslovakia (and for all CEE countries to some US$ 40 bn, see Table 4), shows that the Western aid program is only a minimalist program. Moreover, so far only a part of these sums has been disbursed.

The need for capital and other financial support at present exceeds the ability of the Central and East European countries to put such vast sums to successful use, i.e. to establish internationally competitive production structures. But to conclude from this that international credit support should be adjusted solely according to the absorptive capacity of the recipient countries would go too far. Financial assistance might also serve the purpose of tempering social unrest caused by the growing costs of the transformation process, and thus contribute to alleviating social resistance to change. That also consumption spending of credits and grants may be justified, at least in the early stages of transformation, has been shown not only by the Marshall Plan for West Germany,[10] but also by the mainly US-source based financial assistance for South-Korea and Taiwan in the 1950s.[11]

Table 4

Financial Assistance to CEE Countries

Global cumulative pledges and commitments up to May 1991, US$ bn

	Total Assistance	of which Grants
Total	40.4	9.1
G-24	30.9	9.1
for Economic restructuring	9.6	4.4
Macro-financial assistance	6.9	1.4
Emergency assistance	1.0	0.9
Export credits and investment guarantees	11.4	0.6
Non-specified	2.1	2.1
Bretton Woods Institutions	9.4	–
IMF (net)	4.1	–
World Bank	5.3	–

Source: EC 1991, Table I.

The issue of absorptive capacity is of very great importance, but only in answering the question whether the capital invested will create sufficient income from which a backflow and, in addition, interest or profit payments can be financed. These are, in essence, criteria for structural adjustment programs, but also for export credits and investment guarantees – the latter make up 42% of the cumulative pledges and commitments for Poland, Hungary and Czechoslovakia (in total 36%; see Table 5). It may sound paradoxical, but although export credits and investment guarantees would benefit Western banks and institutions as indemnity bonds, they are, under the aspect of absorptive capacity, the most efficient instrument of support, as they presuppose corresponding private transactions and investments, and thus corresponding profit expectations of Western enterprises.

6. Relationship with EC

The transformation process in the East creates not only financial challenges to the Western community, but also challenges in terms of general and trade policy, and here first of all the EC is affected. The EC signed trade and cooperation agreements with Hungary (September 1988), Czechoslovakia (October 1988), and Poland (July 1989), including the removal of a series of existing import quotas and an offer of

Table 5

G-24, EC and German Assistance to CEE Countries

Cumulative pledges and commitments by May 1991
US$ bn

	G-24	of which EC			
		Total	Joint	Members	(Germany)
Total	30.9	24.1	10.0	14.1	9.9
of which grants	9.2	6.7	3.2	3.5	1.8
credits, guarantees	21.7	17.4	6.8	10.6	8.1
Economic restructuring	9.6	7.0	5.5	1.5	1.0
of which grants	4.4	2.6	1.3	1.3	0.9
credits, guarantees	5.2	4.4	4.2	0.2	0.1
Macro-financial assistance	6.9	5.6	3.0	2.6	2.6
of which grants	1.6	1.8	0.5	1.3	0.9
credits, guarantees	5.3	3.8	2.5	1.3	1.7
Export credits, investment guarantees	11.2	9.2	0.1	9.1	6.3

Source: as Table 4.

most favored nation treatment. But comparatively soon, namely in 1989, the wish to become full members of the EC emerged in the Central and East European countries (mainly in Poland and Hungary). This caught the EC completely unprepared, as the EC concept of relations to the then CMEA dated back to the early 1970s, while the EC Single Market concept came up in 1984 and has been developed since then, taking no account of the political and economic changes in Central and Eastern Europe. Therefore, the idea of these countries' membership was initially met with an overwhelmingly negative response by the EC, because it was feared that the enlargement of the Community would further complicate the decision-making process. The idea of association of these countries was officially raised in early 1990, but it was stressed that the implementation of the more pressing EG integration plans should receive absolute priority (internal market, monetary union, and political integration).

In the meantime the implementation of trade liberalization included in the trade and cooperation agreements has been speeded up, and Poland, Hungary, and Czechoslovakia were included in the General System of Preferences (GSP), normally restricted to developing countries, so that their trade conditions with the EC are now more favorable than trading conditions for, e.g., the USA and Japan.

In November 1991, agreements on association were signed by the representatives of EC, Poland, Hungary, and Czechoslovakia, and these shall become effective from March 1, 1992. The core of association, at the first stage, is the establishment of a free trade area between the EC and individual CEE countries by trade liberalization. According to the principle of asymmetry the EC will initially open its markets earlier to CEE countries than vice versa.

The negotiations turned out to be difficult. The CEE countries' present massive reorientation from intra-East-European trade towards the Community was perceived by some EC member countries (e.g. France) as a potential threat. The main difficulties emerging in the negotiations – apart from the question of services and transportation – were trade concessions of the EC in the case of sensitive goods, mainly textiles, steel, and agricultural products (of the latter, especially Poland is a strong exporter), whereby "sensitive" actually means "subsidized" EC products. Above all, as the effect of heavily depreciated currencies on trade is felt, the pressure from EC producer lobbies will grow.[12]

Table 6

Trade Between the EC and Czechoslovakia, Hungary and Poland in 1989 and 1990

shares in % of trade with the world

	1989	1990
1. EC Trade with Cz, H, P		
EC Exports	0.90	0.93
German Exports	1.70	1.74
EC Imports	0.87	0.98
German Imports	1.73	2.03
2. CEE(3) Trade with EC		
Czechoslovakia		
Exports	18.2	26.5
Imports	17.8	23.8
Hungary		
Exports	24.8	32.2
Imports	29.0	31.0
Poland		
Exports	32.1	47.2
Imports	33.8	45.6

Sources: WIIW databank.

However, limited access to EC markets in the case of sensitive products and sectors might stultify not only any advantages from the asymmetric approach, but also from the granting of credits, which, of course, are to be repaid out of appropriate export revenues. It should be kept in mind, that, realistically viewed, despite a considerable increase in 1990, the actual trade volume between CEE and EC is extremely low (Table 6). Only 0.9% of overall EC exports went to Hungary, Poland, and Czechoslovakia, and only close to 1% of imports came from these countries. The share of the three reforming countries in EC imports of the sensitive commodity group products textiles and steel is lower still. Moreover, Eastern economists point out that tardy structural adjustment, the sluggish process of devestiture in industry, and underdeveloped financial intermediation may slow industry's reactions to whatever opportunities the introduction of a free-trade area might create in the Community markets.[13] On the other hand, some 30% of the three countries' exports and imports were conducted with the EC in 1990.

7. The Role of Germany

The way back to Europe – a governing principle of Polish foreign policy – leads through Germany; this indicates the hopes attached to Germany concerning the economic recovery of Central and Eastern Europe. The important role of Germany has been recognized also by German foreign policy. Foreign Minister Genscher, during his visit to the Baltics in September, pleaded for an EC association of the three Baltic republics as soon as possible,[14] and this, in fact, implies an acceleration of the association procedures also for Poland, Hungary, and Czechoslovakia.

Germany's central importance, not only in political, but also in economic terms, for Central and Eastern Europe may be illustrated by statistical data.

In trade, the shares of EC exports and imports to/from the Central and East European economic area – i.e., apart from Poland, Hungary, and CSFR, also Bulgaria, Romania, and Yugoslavia, with a total population of 120 million people – in overall EC exports and imports are a meagre 2% (1990). These shares are not much higher in the case of EFTA (2% in imports, 2.7% in exports). Among EC countries, Germany holds good for about 3.5% of CEE countries in its exports as well as in imports. Austria has a similar position among EFTA countries: here the share of Central and Eastern Europe in its imports is some 5%, that in exports around 8%. From the viewpoint of the CEE countries the picture is of course quite different: the significance of EC and EFTA has been high traditionally, and has increased enormously over the past two years. Poland, Hungary, and Czechoslovakia are now conducting about one fifth to one quarter of their trade with unified Germany, whereas the Soviet Union, their most important trading partner until two years ago, fell far behind.

The role of Germany and Austria in trade corresponds to the part they are playing in financing. Germany is the biggest creditor of CEE countries, and also Austria's claims by far exceed the share that would fall to this country according, e.g., to its size among OECD countries.

Likewise, Germany and Austria dominate in direct investments (Table 7). In Poland, some 36% of all foreign investments come from Germany, in Czechoslovakia close to 30%, and in Hungary close to 20%. This has already created fears among the population of the three countries that the Germans might buy up the countries, especially after the strong devaluation of the Polish zloty and of the Czechoslovak crown.

Table 7

Foreign Direct Investment:
Shares of Germany, Austria, and Switzerland

in % of registered projects

	CSFR[a)]	Poland[b)]	Hungary[b)]
Germany	29.8	36.1	cca. 20
Austria	28.4	6.4	cca. 20
Switzerland	6.8	3.0	4.4
Total	65.0	45.5	44.4
Projects (absolute)	2,901	2,616	5,622

a) 29.5.1991. – b) End of 1990.

Source: Various WIIW publications.

Finally, financial aid: up till May 1991, 32% of G-24 aid for Central and Eastern Europe, and 41% of EC aid, were provided by Germany. In comparison, France ranks second, with 4.6% of EC aid. Austria grants just 2.6% of G-24 support, but 42% of EFTA aid. Besides, the individual countries in their national reports generally include additional support measures. According to Austrian statistics (Stankovsky, 1991, pp. 530ff), AS 15.1 bn (US$ 1.3 bn) were supplied, i.e. 56% more than according to G-24 data.

According to German data a sum of about DM 31 bn (see Table 8) was supplied – this exceeds the G-24 data (about DM 17 bn) by close to 70%, since it also includes the German shares in EC support (about DM 3.7 bn), as well as a transferable ruble balance of about DM 7.5 bn, accrued in 1990, stemming from East German trade with the Central and East European countries.

Table 8

Cumulative Pledges and Commitments of Germany to CEE Countries

(without Soviet Union) since 1989 in DM bn

	Total	Poland	Hungary	Czechoslovakia
Export credits and investment guarantees	10.1	2.9	2.9	1.5
Debt relief, interest subsidies	6.7	6.2	–	–
Emergency aid	0.3	0.03	0.05	–
Promotion of economic and social development int. al.	0.60	0.15	0.15	0.03
Assistance by German Federal States	0.59	0.02	0.51	0.003
German contribution to the Europ. Bank for Reconstruction and Development	1.74	–	–	–
Claims from transferable ruble accounting (end of 1990) of which				
balance from trading operations	7.31	2.02	1.30	1.60
interest costs	0.13	–	–	–
German contribution to EC assistance	3.67	0.36	0.83	0.23
Total	31.12	11.68	5.74	3.36

Source: WIIW documentation.

In both cases it is of course important to distinguish between genuine and only apparent assistance. Just as the extension of motorways in Austria leading to Hungary and Czechoslovakia can only with reservations be considered as support for the East, so can the transferable ruble balance in German trade with the CEE countries hardly be regarded as a present, but rather as an interest-free credit, the repayment modalities of which must still be negotiated.

The central role of Germany creates some serious political problems:

One is the acceptance on the part of the German population. The West German taxpayers have already been burdened by the assistance granted to the former GDR. Including the transfers to the former GDR, assistance to former CMEA countries except the Soviet Union amounts to 6% of GDP in 1990. Adding the aid grants to the Soviet Union cumulated between 1989 and May 1991, amounting to some DM 60 bn (Table 9), this share rises to about 8% of GDP. These facts raise the question to what extent the German economy can be burdened by supplying the overhelming share of financial aid for the transition from planned to market economy.

Table 9

Cumulative Pledges and Commitments of Germany to the Soviet Union (1989 – May 1991)

	DM bn
Grants, free-of-charge deliveries of goods	15.7
of which	
transitional agreement on the withdrawal of Soviet troops from Eastern Germany (housing program etc.)	13.5
Credit guarantees and Hermes export credit guarantees	27.7
of which	
guarantees for free financing credits	8.0
Hermes export credit	19.5
Claims from transferable ruble accounting	16.9
of which	
balance from trading operations	15.0
interest cost 1990/1991	1.4
Total	60.3

Source: Own computations.

The strong German involvement creates further problems, mainly concerning the economic and political integration process of the EC. Basically a Germany that is larger and reaches further to the East touches upon the old distribution of power in the EC, mainly the balance between France and Germany. In the economic sphere there are fears that the net payer Germany might reduce its alimentations mainly for the structurally weaker, and the poorer EC regions. A hasty association of additional poor states is therefore opposed, first of all by the southern EC countries (Portugal, Greece). Likewise it is feared that a weakening of the DM, as a result of Germany's involvement in the East, might cause delays in introducing the currency union – the second of three important cornerstones of EC integration. And finally there are fears, mainly on the part of France, the Benelux countries, and Great Britain, that Germany might dominate Central and Eastern Europe by its economic strength, and might therefore no longer be interested economically in the EC. From a political viewpoint these considerations lead to two options: The one recommends a speeding-up of the integration process among the present members, which would tie up Germany in a way that it won't attain a dominant role in Central and Eastern Europe. The second advocates an acceleration of Central and Eastern Europe's association and later membership with the EC, to counterweigh the strong German position. An example supporting the latter option is provided by Ireland, whose economy was dominated by Great Britain to an extent of 60% before EC; today this share is only 40%.

8. What Should Be Done?

It seems that the collapse of the CMEA and the Warsaw Pact has once more revived the shades of the old patterns of interests and conflicts that existed up to World War II. This might represent a threat to European integration, and expose the integration efforts to new challenges. These challenges become the greater, the more difficult the transition from plan to market economy in Central and Eastern Europe turns out to be, since the problems thereby created increase the expectations of the peoples concerned mainly towards Germany, an immediate neighbor, and the strongest and richest West European economy.

1990 and 1991 had already brought many disappointments for the populations in Eastern countries, and this constitutes a big danger for future attempts at promoting democracy and a healthy economy, but also for future integration processes in Western Europe. Today social tensions are increasing in all countries. They may force governments to adjust their policies, but they may also lead to a long lasting period of political, social and economic instability. Concepts which promise people a quick renewal of growth, if only deregulation, privatization and liberalization are carried through radically enough, are at best a pipe-dream, a pious hope – at worst, however, the source of social unrest and resignation.

Democracy is not yet fully established in the Central and East European countries. Europe's landscape shows strong tendencies to change, and national emotions, fed by the tristesse of a seemingly indefinite economic decline, might lead to conflicts between peoples and states, which in turn make an economic recovery impossible. This state of affairs may currently be observed in Yugoslavia, but national clashes as a reaction to economic problems are rife also between Czechs and Slovaks, and in the Soviet Union.

Let us revert to the author's initial contention, according to which a country's attempt to achieve an autonomous transformation in a modern world is likely to fail: in this context the growing disappointment in East Central Europe and the setbacks in establishing a stable democratic order, e.g. in Poland, can be seen as a consequence of the weak internationalization of the transformation.

What could or should be done?

1. In the absence of precedents to transition from command to market economy and of relevant theories, any ideological attitude is highly dangerous. What is needed in Central and Eastern Europe is a pragmatic approach, a well-considered economic policy, based on and making use of other countries' experience in transformation processes. Foremost among these are the West European countries. The reconstruction of a functioning market-economic structure, combined with high social standards, and the reconstruction and privatization of the nationalized industries, can provide some useful lessons for our neighboring countries. Only under such conditions can Western aid be expected to provide "help towards self-help" – not merely "emergency aid", meaning continuous transfers – to obviate a collapse, and, incidentally, increasing immigration from these countries.

2. Help towards social cushioning of the transformation process appears the primary objective in the present phase. It would obviate the East European countries being constrained to undervaluate their currencies in order to earn the financial means needed to pay their debts. It will also reduce the otherwise well founded fears in the EC of import pressure of sensible goods.

3. In addition, forms of assistance must be increased that improve the absorptive capacities of the countries in transition, and make them more attractive for direct investments. That does not only encompass investment- and other guarantees, but in the first place technical, legal, and institutional assistance. Thus, e.g., more than 7,000 legal acts of various sorts must be verified in Poland to make them legally compatible with EC law (WERI, 1991, p. 165). The difficulty of importing such kind of know-how is exemplified by the expieriences of East Germany!

4. Finally, there is the open task of promoting trade relations among and between the Central and East European countries, equally affected by the collapse of the CMEA trade system. Mainly relations between Poland, Hungary, and the CSFR are affected in that respect. A Central European Payments Union along the lines of the European Payments Union (EPU), as it existed after World War II and up till 1958, is often mooted in that context. But this would not be the best solution, in view of the progress achieved so far in the matter of convertibility. What would be more desirable would be the institution of a free trade zone between these three countries. Unfortunately, this does not seem to be a matter of interest in these countries. Therefore the emergence of the quite absurd situation cannot be excluded, that after association with EC there will be bilateral free trade relations of these countries with the EC, but not among these countries themselves.

Notes

1. CEE countries in this paper are Bulgaria, Czechoslovakia, Hungary, Poland, Romania and Yugoslavia.

2. These estimates are not based on current exchange rates, but on physical indicators. This method qualifies for international country ranking only, not for estimating the absolute amount of GDP in international currency (Havlik 1991).

3. This is more or less the economic strategy of the IMF as exemplified, e.g., in the paper of Khan and Knight (1985), cited after Laski (1991, p. 11).

4. Laski (1991, p. 12), extensively quotes Dornbush (1990, p. 4), who illustrates the Bolivian example. This example is interesting, since Jeffrey Sachs – the famous adviser to Poland and other CEE countries – earned his credentials as the author of the successful Bolivian stabilization. Dornbush writes that Bolivia "has tamed hyperinflation, stabilized public finance and administered a heavy dose of supply side economics. The easy work is done, and now the country waits for recovery and growth: Per capita income ... is no longer plummeting, but it has fallen desperately low and there is no assurance, four years after stabilization, of a major turn of events. (...) Bolivia's case is so important because there is consensus that the country implemented all required reforms, did so firmly and, by now, many years ago. The case confirms the suspicion that stabilization may not be enough."

5. See *Világgazdaság*, June 15, 1991.

6. In 1991 alone some US$ 91 bn, that is, 5.9% of the West German gross domestic product (Institut der Deutschen Wirtschaft: Der West-Ost-Transfer, Berichte No. 26, Bonn 1991), or 35-40% of the estimated East German GDP in 1991 (See R. Dietz, "The Impact of the Unification on the East German Economy," in: *WIIW-Forschungsberichte*, No. 172, Vienna, May 1991, pp. 15ff).

7. According to calculations of the Economic Commission for Europe, *Economic Survey of Europe in 1989-1990*, Geneva 1990, pp. 1-10ff.

8. Computed according to P. Havlik, "East-West-GDP Comparisons: Problems and Results," *WIIW-Forschungsberichte* No. 174, Vienna, September 1991, p. 37, Table 13.

9. We use the Austrian, not the German case, because the FRG's share of Marshall aid was relatively small, but it received considerable sums under the GARIOA (Government Aid and Relief in Occupied Areas) program.

10. See M. Knapp, "Reconstruction and West-Integration: The Impact of the Marshall Plan on Germany," in: *Zeitschrift für die gesamte Staatswissenschaft*, Vol. 137, Tübingen 1981, pp. 415-433, here p. 424.

11. See A. Amsden, "Stabilizacja nie moze byc obsesja," in: *Zycie gospodarcze*, Warsaw, April 28, 1991, pp. 1-4.

12. See J. Rollo, "EC trade policy and the reforming countries of Central and Eastern Europe," in: *Goodbye to Fortress Europe? The community's external trade relations*, Royston 1990, pp. 113-120, here: p. 115.

13. See M. Paszynski, "The Single Market and Commercial Relations for Non-Member Countries. Views from Central and Eastern Europe," *Discussion Papers of the Foreign Trade Research Institute*, No. 19, Warsaw, March 1991, pp. 13.

14. See *Süddeutsche Zeitung*, September 13, 1991, p. 2.

15. West German GDP stood at DM 2,415 bn in 1990.

References

Akerlof, George A., Rose, Andrew K., Yellen, Janet L. and Hessenius, Helga (1991), *East Germany In From the Cold: The Economic Aftermath of Currency Union*, presentation paper, Berkeley, March.

Amsden, Alice H. (1991), "Stabilizacja nie moze byc obsesja," in: *Zycie gospodarcze*, Warsaw, April 28, pp. 1/4.

Butschek, Felix (1990), "Wohlstand und Wirtschaftssystem," in: *Wirtschaft und Gesellschaft*, Vol. 16, No. 4, Vienna, pp. 551ff.

DIW (Deutsches Institut für Wirtschaftsforschung) (1991), *Wochenberichte*, 58 (23).

Dietz, Raimund (1991), "The Impact of the Unification on the East German Economy," in: *WIIW-Forschungsberichte*, No. 172, Vienna, May.

EC (Commission of the European Communities) (1991), *Scoreboard of G-24 Assistance*, Brussels, June 13.

Gomulka, Stanislaw (1991), "The causes of recession following stabilization," *working paper* no. 95, London School of Economics, Centre for Economic Performance, London, April.

Gabrisch, Hubert (1991), "Schwierigkeiten bei der Gründung von Joint Ventures in Osteuropa," *WIIW-Forschungsberichte*, No. 171, Vienna, March.

Havlik, Peter (1991), "East-West GDP Comparisons: Problems and Results," *WIIW-Forschungsberichte*, No. 174, Vienna, September.

Institut der Deutschen Wirtschaft (1991), "Der West-Ost-Transfer," *Berichte* No. 26, Bonn.

Jennewein, Marga(1991), "Implikationen des EG-Binnenmarktes für die Sowjetunion," in: *Osteuropa-Wirtschaft*, Vol. 36, No. 1, Munich, March, pp. 1ff.

Knapp, Manfred (1981), "Reconstruction and West-Integration: The Impact of the Marshall Plan on Germany," in: *Zeitschrift für die gesamte Staatswissenschaft* 137, Tübingen, pp. 415-433.

Laski, Kazimierz (1991), *Transition from Command to Market Economies in Central and Eastern Europe: First Experiences and Questions*, paper presented at the conference on Medium Term Economic Assessment in Vienna, October 14-16, first draft.

Palankai, Tibor (1991), *The European Community and Central European Integration: The Hungarian Case*, New York, Prague.

Paszynski, Marian (1991), "The Single Market and Commercial Relations for Non-Member Countries. Views from Central and Eastern Europe," *Discussion Papers of the Foreign Trade Research Institute*, No. 19, Warsaw, March, pp. 6ff.

Rollo, Jim (1990), "EC trade policy and the reforming countries of Central and Eastern Europe," in: *Goodbye to Fortress Europe? The community's external trade relations*, Royston, pp. 113-120.

Stankovsky, Jan (1991), "Ansätze zu einer Osteuropa-Hilfe," in: *Wifo-Monatshefte*, Vienna, No. 9, p. 528.

United Nations Economic Commission for Europe (1990), *Economic Survey of Europe in 1989-1990*, Geneva.

WERI (World Economy Research Institute) (1991), *Poland. International Economic Report*, Warsaw, p. 159.

Winiecki, Jan (1991), "The Polish Transition Program at Mid-1991: Stabilisation under Threat," *Kiel Discussion Papers* No. 174, Institut für Weltwirtschaft Kiel, September.

12

ECONOMIC LESSONS FROM TWO NEWLY INDUSTRIALIZING COUNTRIES IN THE FAR EAST?

Waltraut Urban

1. Introduction

1.1 Why Should the East European Countries Try to Learn from the Far Eastern NICs?

The "four little tigers": Hong Kong, Singapore, South Korea, and Taiwan are so far considered the most successful examples of economic development after World War Two.[1] With average annual growth rates of real GDP close to 10% over a period of now more than forty years they have within a few decades turned from poor underdeveloped countries into modern industrial states. It has already been suggested that these countries should become members of the OECD, thus officially joining the "club" of advanced industrialized nations.[2] As a case of successful upward mobility in the modern world system they have called in question dependency theories, according to which late development in a capitalist world is simply not possible, because of latecomers always remaining a kind of "periphery" to the economically advanced "centers". Furthermore, they seem to present "an enigma to prevailing theories that suggest that rapid growth and distributive equity are somewhat incompatible" (Chan et al. 1990, p. 113).

Thus at first sight the Far Eastern NICs seem to have brought into reality what is at present striven for by the former socialist countries in Eastern Europe, or rather what is expected by their peoples: a rapid process of catching up with the economically further advanced economies, largely independent development, and "growth with equity".

Moreover, the example of the Far Eastern NICs could render moral support to the East European countries, as in their days of economic struggle nobody was to predict such a success to them either.[3]

1.2 What Could the East European Countries Possibly Learn from the Successful Far Eastern NICs?

The transition from a command to a market economy now taking place in Eastern Europe is a process unique in history; there is neither a theoretical foundation nor sufficient practical experience concerning this kind of systemic and/or political change (cf. Gabrisch, Laski, 1990, p. 1).

It is largely agreed, however, that price liberalization, stabilization, privatization, integration into the world economy, and modernizing and restructuring the economy are the most important steps to be taken in the transformation process. But there is a great deal of uncertainty with regard to their implementation and how to provide for undesirable side effects, such as inflation, social hardships, etc. Lacking an adequate model, the East European countries therefore have to rely on "trial and error" to a very high degree (Gabrisch, Laski 1990, p. 2). While no proper substitute for a complete model, other countries' experience with similar problems made in a different context could be of some help: either in giving new ideas, or helping to prevent certain failures in advance. This is the reason why we are going to deal with the economic performance of Korea and Taiwan in this paper, as indeed many similarities can be found; besides, their special model of a "mixed economy" might be interesting. So far the new political leaders in Eastern Europe who stand up for the transformation process from the command into a market economy have not said much about what particular kind of market economy they envisage. Even in the case of the CSFR, where a clear stand for a "market economy without adjective" (Vaclav Klaus) is taken, the details are not yet clear. In any case, the process of transformation will take some time, in which a certain "cohabitation" of state and private business will be unavoidable (Gabrisch, Laski 1990, p. 4), but in which, nevertheless, the foundations for further economic development will be laid.

It cannot be denied that there exist some fundamental differences between the East European countries and the Far Eastern NICs with regard to the general background as well as to specific features, which have to be taken into account when trying to learn from their example: sometimes it will be a certain principle rather that should be followed, in other cases a concrete measure that could be taken over.

The first prominent objection is, that the East European countries in transition cannot be referred to as "developing countries", as their "take-off" from a traditional agricultural society to a modern industrial society[4] has decidedly taken place already before or shortly after the Second World War (as in Romania and Bulgaria). But due to the failure of their economic systems, they could not keep pace with the economic progress of the industrialized countries of the West and thus fell considerably behind. The ongoing process of transformation therefore takes place against the background of some kind of "late development", which has so far been characteristic for developing countries. Thus East European countries have in common with developing countries their main task, namely to grow faster than the further advanced industrialized countries in order to catch up with them in the forseeable future. But they also share other characteristic problems of late development, i.e., the urgent need for technology transfer, imbalanced trade relations, the debt problem, etc., which are superimposed on their problems of transition.

Looking at the development process of Korea and Taiwan, we find first of all that the numerous problems the East European countries are facing now in one sweep, have occurred, resp. have been tackled by those countries over quite a long period of time: Reprivatization and overcoming of shortages were the first tasks for Korea and Taiwan after decolonization from the Japanese empire in 1945. (Re)integration into the world economy and expanding exports have become a major goal during the sixties, and modernization and restructuring of the economy towards high-tech and high value added production began in the late seventies, while questions of social security, environmental protection, and reforms towards a more pluralistic political system gained importance in the 1980s.

Foreign aid has been substantial in Korea and Taiwan during the first period of economic development, while foreign loans and direct investment have played a significant role from the second phase onwards only.

The second, and indeed very serious argument against the East European countries following the example of Korea and Taiwan is, that their story of economic success is closely connected with authoritarian leadership, restriction of civil liberties, and political oppression. Jones, Sakong (1980), however, came to the conclusion, that a strong (hard) state in G. Myrdal's sense[5] was essential for the fast economic development in Korea, but that "it is not at all clear that political suppression is a necessary concomitant of hardness" (Jones, Sakong 1980, p. 140). The development process in Korea and Taiwan suggests further, that government compulsion will probably speed up the adjustment process striven for during a crisis or in a transition period, but as the economy grows increasingly complex, compulsory measures become proportionally more difficult to exercise intelligently. As market mechanisms develop, compulsion becomes less necessary because indicative measures work more appropriately. It is of utmost importance, therefore, to switch to a more liberal economic regime in time, which in turn will ask for a more liberal political system. Recent developments show, that Korea and Taiwan are going to approach liberal democracy in the reverse order to the East European countries rather, i.e.: economic liberalism first, political liberalism later.[6]

1.3 Korea and Taiwan: Unique Cases, or Models for Economic Development: Some Theoretical Aspects

In fact, there exists a vast literature on the subject, whether or not South Korea and/or Taiwan could serve as a model for developing countries. The answers cover a wide range indeed, depending on the kind of theory that is assumed to explain the respective developments. On the one extreme, Korea and Taiwan are considered a model case for neoclassical economics and cultural modernization theories. According to this "developmental" approach, Korea and Taiwan have succeeded because "they got prices right", and their example could be followed by any country that gets the prices right, too. "The almost irresistible conclusion from Korean development experience is, that with proper economic policies and a continuation of reasonable international aid levels most developing countries can achieve at least a 6 percent annual growth rate, and many countries could sustain growth rates as high as 10 percent (Brown 1973, p. 265, quoted after Jones, Sakong 1980, p. 2). Basically this is the recipe that is presently tried out in the former socialist countries. On the other extreme, the development of Korea and Taiwan is considered a prototype of state led development. According to the "statist" approach, development is led by the state, and highly depends on the very specific political and socio-cultural environment – therefore a given model cannot be copied easily – if at all – by other countries.

The development of Taiwan and Korea obviously contradicts another type of development theories, the so called "dependency theories". The dependency perspective views Third World countries as enmeshed in a global capitalist system that distorts their societies and economies, and gravely constrains their development potential. Initially, adherents to this perspective believed that foreign dependency precluded significant growth and industrialization in the "periphery" (see e.g. Galtung 1971). Subsequently, discussions of "dependent development" recognized that some upward mobility in the capitalist world system was possible based upon alliances among state, foreign and domestic capital. However, such Third World industrialization is

Table 1

Basic Economic Indicators for the Republic of Korea and Taiwan

	KOREA					TAIWAN			
Year	Population in mn[a)]	Real growth of GNP in %	GNP at current prices in US$ bn	GNP/ capita US$	Year	Population in mn	Real growth of GNP in %	GNP at current prices in US$ bn	GNP/ capita US$
1952	20.6	n.a.	n.a.	n.a.	1952	8,1	12.0	1.7[c)]	207[c)]
1953	20.8	n.a.	2.7	128.3	1953	8,4	9.3	2.2	264
1954	21.1	5.6	3.7	174.1	1954	8,7	9.6	2.5	280
1955	21.4	4.5	2.3	107.4	1955	9,1	8.1	1.9[d)]	212[d)]
1956	22.0	-1.3	3.0	137.9	1956	9,4	5.5	2.2	234
1957	22.7	7.6	3.9	173.7	1957	9,7	7.3	2.6	265
1958	23.3	5.5	4.1	175.7	1958	10,0	6.6	1.8[e)]	180[e)]
1959	24.0	3.8	4.4	181.7	1959	10,4	7.7	2.1	200
1960	24.7	1.2	3.9	157.1	1960	10,8	6.5	2.5	234
1961	25.4	5.6	2.4	92.7	1961	11,1	6.8	2.8	254
1962	26.1	2.2	2.7	104.7	1962	11,5	7.8	3.1	271
1963	26.9	9.1	3.9	143.8	1963	11,9	9.4	2.2[f)]	183[f)]
1964	27.7	9.6	3.3	121.0	1964	12,3	12.3	2.5	207
1965	28.3	5.8	3.0	106.8	1965	12,6	11.0	2.8	222
1966	29.0	12.7	3.8	132.0	1966	13,0	9.0	3.1	241
1967	30.1	6.6	4.7	157.2	1967	13,3	10.6	3.6	272
1968	30.8	11.3	6.0	193.8	1968	13,7	9.1	4.2	309
1969	31.5	13.8	7.5	237.1	1969	14,3[b)]	9.0	4.9	341

(continuing)

Table 1 (continued)

Basic Economic Indicators for the Republic of Korea and Taiwan

	KOREA					TAIWAN			
Year	Population in mn[a)]	Real growth of GNP in %	GNP at current prices in US$ bn	GNP/ capita US$	Year	Population in mn	Real growth of GNP in %	GNP at current prices in US$ bn	GNP/ capita US$
1970	32.2	7.6	8.8	273.3	1970	14,7	11.3	5.6	384
1971	32.9	9.4	9.7	295.7	1971	15,0	12.9	6.6	437
1972	33.5	5.8	10.6	315.5	1972	15,3	13.3	7.9	514
1973	34.1	14.9	13.5	396.0	1973	15,6	12.8	10.8[g)]	691[g)]
1974	34.7	8.0	18.6	534.7	1974	15,9	1.1	14.4	906
1975	35.3	7.1	20.8	589.4	1975	16,2	4.2	15.3	948
1976	35.8	15.1	28.5	796.4	1976	16,5	13.5	18.3	1,111
1977	36.4	10.3	36.8	1,010.5	1977	16,8	9.9	21.4	1,272
1978	37.0	11.6	49.6	1,341.4	1978	17,1	13.9	27.0[h)]	1,576[h)]
1979	37.5	6.4	63.6	1,695.7	1979	17,5	8.1	32.5	1,858
1980	38.1	-6.2	60.5	1,587.1	1980	17,8	6.6	40.2	2,257

a) End of fiscal year. – b) From 1969 onwards incl. military personnel. – c) 1 US$ = 10.25 NT$. – d) 1 US$ = 15.55 NT$. – e) 1 US$ = 24.58 NT$. – f) 1 US$ = 40.00 NT$. – g) 1 US$ = 38.16 NT$. – h) 1 US$ = 35.85 NT$.

Sources: Korea: IMF, International Financial Statistics, Yearbook 1989, p. 456-459; Taiwan: Menzel 1985, Table 36, p. 150.

distorted by the foreign-dominated enclaves, and most of the people remain excluded from the modern sector (Evans 1979; Wallerstein 1974 and 1979, quoted after Chan et al. 1990, p. 109). The failure of general applicability of this theory has caused rethinking, and two former "dependentistas", U. Menzel and O. Senghaas, have added a further model of development to the discussion, which claims to explain the development of Korea and Taiwan: Their model of "autocentric development" has been derived from European history, after investigating the economic developments of successful latecomers of European industrialization, as e.g. Switzerland, Denmark, Finland: by establishing adequate forwards and backwards linkages of the driving export sector with the rest of the economy they were able to build up a selfsupporting, "autocentric" economic structure, whereby government played a different role in different countries. In the case of Taiwan and Korea, a significant role is ascribed to government (Menzel 1985; Senghaas 1982).

Empirical evidence gives little support to the neoclassical theory of the "invisible hand", and thus the developmental approach – as some authors state, it was the "iron glove" rather that ruled. But there is no doubt about it, that the large driving and ever growing export sector, deliberately exposed to international price competition, promoted productivity and efficiency of the economy in a significant way; and although the state decidedly played a significant part in economic development, it was always a capitalist state, explicitly opposed to and in ideological and economic competition with the socialist regimes of North Korea and (mainland) China. Thus, the economic system in Korea and Taiwan is sometimes referred to as "state capitalist" and sometimes as "partriarchal" in analogy to the economic system of Japan. P. Jones and Il Sakong, who went into a very thorough empirical investigation of the interaction of government and business sector in Korea, refer to the system as a "mixed economy", and stress that pragmatism and flexibility of government action were the key factors to economic success. "The Korean miracle is not a triumph of laissez-faire, but of a pragmatic non-ideological mixture of market and non-market forces" (Jones, Sakong 1980, p. 3).

It has to be said, however, that the system of political economy of both Korea and Taiwan has changed over time in reaction to changing internal and external factors. In the beginning, when after decolonization both countries suffered from severe shortages, governments via land reform and reprivatization of former Japanese properties (which had been nationalized after the Japanese left the country in 1945), as well as the allocation of foreign aid, laid the foundations for the formation of a new entrepreneurial class. During the 1960s, in the face of persistent foreign trade deficits, these new forces were then channeled into export-oriented activities by direct and indirect government action. Another major change took place in the second half of the 1970s, when the state began to withdraw from the economy, but became more engaged in science and technology as well as stabilization policies. In this way, both countries were able to overcome the structural weaknesses which came to light only after the oil crises and the following world wide recession. They were thus well prepared to take part in the new international upswing in the 1980s, and continued their process of catching up with growth rates well above the industrialized nations' (the average real growth rates of Korea and Taiwan were about 10% between 1986 and 1989, compared with the average of OECD countries of 3.5%). To be mentioned further is the process of political liberalization that has been put in motion in Korea and to some extent in Taiwan in the 1980s, and the increased concern with social security and welfare problems.

2. Learning from Taiwan and Korea: Tackling Similar Problems in a Different Context

2.1 Historical and Ideological Background

For a long time both countries were part of the Japanese colonial empire (Taiwan 1895-1945, Korea 1910-1945).[7] The important consequences of Japanese colonial rule for the future development of Taiwan and Korea were:

- Modernization and opening up of the economy: Agriculture was transformed to a large extent from subsistence production into export production, though for the Japanese market mainly.
- First steps towards industrialization were taken: In Korea light industries (food and agricultural goods processing, clothing) were concentrated in the South, heavy industry (mineral extraction and processing) in the North. Industry and commerce were mainly in Japanese hands, nevertheless the local population got in touch with industrial techniques, and thus the nucleus of a skilled labor force was formed.[8]
- A modern and rather sophisticated bureaucracy replaced the old class structures. It implemented economic measures and large infrastructure projects, such as irrigation, improvement of transport facilities (roads, railroads, harbors), as well as education. The main purpose was, of course, to improve the supply of goods for the mother country.

After World War Two, both countries played an important role in the East-West conflict as "bulwarks" against communism:

As a result of the Japanese surrender in 1945, Taiwan became a province of China again. The National Government of China under Kuomintang (KMT) installed a provincial government, which consisted of "mainlanders" only. This, together with the bad economic performance, led to an upheaval of the local population of Taiwan in 1947,[9] which was brutally suppressed, and a considerable part of the local elite was exiled. As a communist victory in mainland China became more and more likely during 1948, more than one million mainlanders fled to Taiwan, and in 1949 the National Goverment itself was transferred, and Taipeh declared the "temporary" capital of China. But KMT rule in Taiwan was only consolidated when the Korean War began in 1950, and Taiwan became an integral part of the US defence line against communist advance in Asia.

Korea was divided into two zones of occupation. Due to the Kairo and Potsdam conferences of 1943 and 1945, the Russians came in from the North, the Americans from the South – the line of demarcation being the 38th parallel. After landing on September 17, 1945, US troops established a military government (AMG). Soon after, an interim government under Syngman Rhee, a Korean, who had returned from many years of exile in the USA, was installed. The new regime was backed by US military and economic aid: Rhe was expected to act as an effective counterpart to the left-leaning forces in the country, and he was indeed effective in gradually destroying the left opposition. As a result of the US-UN proposal of separate elections in South Korea in 1948, he became the first president of the "Republic of Korea", which was proclaimed on August 15, 1948.[10] Thereafter US troops left the country, but returned when North Korean forces crossed the South Korean border, and President Truman decided to go to war to stop the communist advance. When the Korean War was over in 1953, South Korea remained an important US base, and massive US aid and military and economic support was given furtheron.

Both in Korea and Taiwan society is based on Confucian tradition, but has been exposed, to a considerable extent, to Western thinking. Yet, the ideological background is somewhat different in the two countries.

In Taiwan, the ideas of Sun Yat-Sen (1866-1925), the founder of the Kuomintang, have become the leading principle in her constitution. Sun's main task was to built up "a new, free, modern and industrialized China" – consequently there is a strong will to economic development, combined with a certain kind of nationalism, geared to strengthen self-confidence, and thus efficiency of the Chinese people. (His party was therefore named "National Party"). The way this should happen is described by Sun's "Three Principles of the People" (the principle of nationalism, the principle of democracy, and the principle of livelihood), and should avoid the failures of capitalism as well as communism. In practice, this meant, that he was eager to encourage private initiative in economic affairs, but that he took a different stand with regard to "big capital". In this sector, the state was to play an important role: either in "regulating" big private firms (for reasons of income distribution mainly), in supplying infrastructure (traffic, communications, energy etc.) or in initiating industries important to industrial development.[11] He further stressed the importance of "foreign capital" and "foreign brains" (Sun Yat-Sen, translated by Price (1927), p. 183) for speeding up the process of economic development. Because he was concerned with "People's Livelihood" (= Min Sheng = the existence of society, the welfare of the nation, the life of the masses) social welfare and services have always played a bigger role in Taiwan than in Korea. Although Sun stressed industrialization as the key factor for an increase of welfare in the future, China beeing more or less a rural society, a land reform had first of all to be implemented. By giving the "land-to-the-tiller" and various methods of increasing production of food and clothing materials,[12] the basic needs ("necessities") of the people should first be adequately satisfied. The third principle, the principle of democracy, deals with the political power of the people – which was, however, dodged from the very beginning by the introduction of martial law in Taiwan in 1948 – and the administrative power of the government: in addition to the legislative, judiciary and executive power, "Civil Service Examinations" and censorship are considered separate important functions of the government. This reflects the Confucian tradition of a high quality standard of bureaucracy on the one hand, and an attempt to control corruption on the other. Both probably helped the Taiwanese government in dealing with economic affairs more efficiently than other countries.

In Korea the ideological background is less definite. In any case, a distinction has to be made between the rule of Syngman Rhee (1948-1960), and after. Rhee was preoccupied with political and integrative tasks (reunification!) and gave little thought to economic development; accordingly, economic performance in his times was rather poor. In brief his ideological background can be described as nationalist and anticommunist, which was reinforced by the Korean war 1950 to 1953. Under the Chang Myon Regime (1960-1961), economic affairs gained importance, and were in fact given priority over politics when Park Chung Hee took over the reins, and governed from 1961 until 1979;[13] accordingly, Park took a more pragmatic view on economic affairs. The change of attitudes is best illustrated by the example of public enterprises: The 1948 constitution in Article 87 and 88 is specifying public

Table 2

Plan Targets and Actual Performance in the Republic of Korea

	First Five-Year Plan (1962-1966)		Second Five-Year Plan (1967-1971)		Third Five-Year Plan (1972-1976)	
	Planned	Actual	Planned	Actual	Planned	Actual
GNP Growth Rate						
(annual average, in %)	7.1	8.3	7.0	11.4	8.6	11.2
Agriculture, forestry and fisheries	5.7	5.5	5.0	2.0	4.5	5.8
Mining and manufacturing	15.1	14.8	10.7	20.9	13.0	20.1
Social overhead capital and other services	5.4	8.9	6.6	13.2	8.5	8.5
Industrial Structure						
(terminal year, in %)						
Agriculture, forestry and fisheries	34.8	37.9	34.0	24.2	22.4	20.3
Mining and manufacturing	20.6	19.8	26.8	29.9	27.9	36.0
Social overhead capital and other services	44.5	42.3	39.2	45.9	49.7	43.7
Investment as Share of GNP						
(annual average, in %)	22.6	16.9	19.0	30.6	24.9	27.0
Domestic savings as share of GNP	9.3	6.7	11.6	15.5	19.5	17.0
Foreign savings as share of GNP	13.3	10.2	7.4	15.1	5.4	11.8

Sources: Kyongje Kihoegwon (Economic Planning Board), Kyognje paekso (Economic white paper), 1972, 1976, 1977. Kyongje Kihoegwon (Economic Planning Board), Che samch'a yondo ch'ogjawon yesan, 1977 (Overall resources budget for 1977). Bank of Korea, Monthly Economic Statistics, January 1977, from Jones, Sakong 1980, Table 8, p. 54.

ownership in a broad range of economic activity[14], and open-ended provisions allowing nationalization of any other industries "related to public welfare" or where "required for vital and urgend needs for national defense or the livelihood of the people". The 1954 constitution, in contrast, reserves no specific industries for public ownership and explicitly prohibits nationalization "except in cases specifically designed by law to meet urgent necessities of national life" (see Jones, Sakong 1980, pp. 144 and 145). In fact, by 1960 most of the former Japanese enterprises had been divested, with 36 entities left, producing about 5% of GDP.[15] Under Park, the 1954 constitution remained unchanged (until 1972), but was obviously interpreted in a different way, led by Park's strong commitment to economic development[16]: by 1972, the public enterprise sector consisted of 108 enterprises instead of 36, producing 9% of GDP and 13% of non-agricultural GDP (Table 3). This is rather a high level, being similar to that of India, and probably larger than that of Italy or the UK (in the late 1960s), despite substantial socialist advocacy in all three states (see Jones, Sakong 1980, p. 148).

Table 3

Republic of Korea:
Growth of Public Enterprise Sector, 1960-1972

		Sectoral Value Added (billions of Won)		Sectoral Share[a)]	
Year	Number of Enterprises	Current Prices	1970 Prices	GDP	Non-Agri-cultural GDP
1960	36	n.a.	n.a.	n.a.	n.a.
1963	52	31.8	80.4	6.98	12.70
1964	54	42.9	90.6	6.49	12.56
1971	119	262.1	246.7	9.17	13.46
1972	108	320.7	271.7	9.07	13.14

a) At current prices.

Source: Jones 1976, pp. 73-74, from Jones, Sakong 1980, Table 24, p. 149.

According to Jones and Sakong, Park's pragmatism, which "in the selection of instruments to deal with a particular problem is not constrained by any ideological predilections," was not confined to the enterprise sector, but a general principle of his rule.

Other authors maintain, however, that the Korean system was in fact based on the Japanese model of development, which had been adjusted to the special conditions in Korea (see Blumenthal, Lee 1985, Kim, Römer 1979, Kuznets 1980 and 1980a). This was to be done in an implicit rather than an explicit way, as, in spite of the Normalization Treaty between Korea and Japan in 1965, strong sentiments against the former colonial power prevailed. According to T. Blumenthal and H. Lee,

> the essence of the Japanese experience can be regarded as a case of a future-oriented development strategy .... A future-oriented strategy stands in contrast to the principle of static comparative advantage, which calls for a maximization of total output measured by international prices, at each point of time. Under a future-oriented strategy short term costs caused by e.g. inefficient allocation of resources are tolerated if needed for capturing long-term benefits (Blumenthal, Lee 1985, p. 222).

There are three ways in which government performs this task: planning, change in relative prices, and "administrative guidance".

- The Economic Planning Agency (EPA) in Japan, and the Economic Planning Board (EPB) in Korea both issue plans to put forward the priorities of the government, and to show private business the direction in which government wants the economy to move.
- Changing relative (factor) prices to influence the choice of products or processes was utilized frequently by both governments (the large devaluation of the Won in 1964 signified the transition from a policy of import substitution to one of export promotion in Korea, likewise a large increase in interest rates was taken as a means to increase private savings). Both countries used direct and indirect subsidies to promote industries favored by the government, particularly for export, and took protective measures to reduce foreign competition with newly founded industries.
- The technique of "administrative guidance", namely an informal way of persuasion by the government ministries, was also undertaken by both governments as a means to influence the economy (Blumenthal, Lee 1985, p. 227).

Western influence was introduced into both countries by foreign (US) experts and scholars studying abroad, but played a less important part in Taiwan than in Korea.

2.2 Laying the Foundations for Capitalist Development

Economic Planning and Implementation of Economic Policy. In both countries, economic (development) plans are an integral part of economic policy. Though planning is basically indicative, certain command elements cannot be denied. However, contrary to the planning experience in socialist countries, plan targets were rather surpassed by actual performance (see Table 2).

In Taiwan, the First Four-Year Plan was implemented in 1953. From 1965 onwards One-Year and Ten-Year Plans have been added. "An Economic Outlook Until the Year 2000" was published in 1986.[17] Planning methods were not very sophisticated in the beginning, and generally less complex than in Korea. Given a high commitment to modernization and industrialization, drawing up a plan was simply the attempt to put together in a consistent way, what could be done realistically in a given period of time, stressing long-term perspectives. As a matter of fact, from the beginning Taiwan had a quite specific and differentiated official system of statistics, which gave the authorities a rather objective picture of the status quo and thus helped to make meaningful projections for the future. Though there was a certain influence of foreign (US) advisers on the planning process, their general impact is considered not as great as in Korea.[18]

In Korea the First Five-Year Plan (1962-1966) was implemented by the Park regime (earlier planning attempts had failed),[19] but was not satisfactory at all: Statistical data were poor, planning techniques had been very simple and the plan had to be revised soon. As a consequence, a second plan (1967-1971) was prepared much more carefully and was drawn up with considerable help of foreign experts from the American Agency for International Development (AID; I. Adelman et al.),[20] the Robert Nathan Associates and the government of the FRG. Foreign experts were involved in the third plan, too (Menzel 1985, p. 89). In 1970 the Korea Development Institute was established with a large staff of experts, mainly educated in the US, to support the Economic Planning Board (EPB). The Forth Five-Year Plan (1977-1981), finally, was embedded in a longterm plan on perspectives until the year 1990, which was in essence prepared by the World Bank.[21] After Park's death in 1979 and the bad economic performance following the second oil crisis, the Fifth Five-Year Plan (1982-1986) dealt above all with the improvement of the external competitive position of Korea, and critized government intervention in the past as having led to a misallocation of resources: consequently, private business should be more involved in the planning process, direct government intervention in the business sector should be replaced by indicative measures, social policy and technology policy should be extended. Thus economic planning in Korea was brought nearer to the system of economic planning in Taiwan.

The debate on the impact of economic planning on real economic performance is controversial,[22] but at any rate plans have served as a framework for economic policy. In Taiwan, the relatively big public enterprise sector offered a good opportunity to put through government plans directly. It must be stated, however, that in general public enterprises were not subsidized in Taiwan, and made a positive contribution to the government budget. As for the rest, indicative measures were preferred, but, e.g., in the very important field of foreign trade policy highly selective measures were employed. In Korea the public enterprise sector, though important too, is smaller than in Taiwan. Instead, more direct pressure was put on the private business sector. Besides indicative measures, privileges on the one hand, compulsion on the other – ranging from "friendly persuasion" to explicit threats – were used to implement the will of the government.[23] There is an interesting debate on the efficiency of public enterprise in Korea: Jones and Sakong (1980), evaluating the different views, came to the conclusion, that public enterprises in Korea are less efficient than private enterprises, but that the public-private gap is much smaller than in other countries, the main reason being "generally intolerant government attitudes towards public enterprises" (Jones, Sakong 1980, p. 164).[24] Another explanation would be, that chief executives, basically drawn from the bureaucratic or military elite, were more qualified than elsewhere. This leads over to the role of the bureaucracy: The quality of economic planning as well as formulating and implementing economic policy is highly dependent on a competent and credible bureaucracy; Confucian traditions prevailing in both countries are conducive to both.

The Role of the Bureaucracy.

> The Confucian cultural heritage inculcates a value system based on "correct" superior-subordinate relationships of the sort conducive to a smoothly operating hierarchy. Further, the prestige attached to government work, the stress on education and the competitive merit-based selection procedure insure civil service quality (Jones, Sakong 1980, p. 48).[25]

However, as has been pointed out very clearly by T. Michell for the case of Korea, the term "hierarchy" has to be qualified: due to the traditionally great autonomy of the government official, important decisions will be left to lower officials and are not usually interferred with.[26]

> A more careful analysis of the bureaucratic traditions and the consequent patterns of decision-making within the Korean state shows, that the way in which government decisions were often, though not always, reached, involved a wide degree of opinion-taking and modifications, and even formulation of policy from the bottom rather than the top. While no system is fool proof, this potential for consultation and modification at lower levels of the administrative structure prevents the implementation of many potentially damaging policies. At the same time the strong drive from the top, especially in the 1960s, providing what Lewis calls "the will to economise" (Lewis 1966) injected a sense of urgency and national purpose into a system which would easily have become lethargic and corrupt (Michell 1984, p. 32).

This describes what other authors have characterized as "executive dominance, speed and flexibility, openess of the system". Corruption in fact has been relatively low[27] in both countries and cannot be solely attributed to the existing formal mechanism of control, as the "Board of Audit and Inspection" in Korea, which reports directly to the president, and the aforementioned Principle of Censorship (government auditing) laid down in the constitution of Taiwan.

Conclusions for Eastern Europe. Perhaps the East European countries have been too fast in opting for a pure market economy. Korea and Taiwan give examples of economic systems other than market socialism, yet quite different from a social market economy or a welfare state of the Western type, which, adjusted to the special conditions of a country, seem to be more efficient in catching up with the advanced market economies than a pure market economy.

(1) East European countries sometimes give the impression that marketization has become an end in itself. In Korea and Taiwan, eco-

nomic growth and development have been the primary target for most of the time, therefore economic policy was rather pragmatic. Because growth was a common target for both business and government, an alliance was easily formed between them; moreover, economic development became a "national goal" and a matter of pride of the bureaucracy as well as of a significant part of the population. As shown clearly by the transition from the Rhee to the Park regime in Korea, "leadership commitment to growth" might indeed change a lot. Most East European countries seem to be in the first phase of political consolidation and economic stabilization rather than in a phase of enforced economic growth; accordingly their economic performance is rather poor. In the light of modern experience and awareness of environmental problems, however, economic goals to be attractive will have to be put into new words, perhaps such as "modernization and sustainable development"[28] before being applied to the East European countries.

(2) Another important principle in Korea and Taiwan, so far missing in Eastern Europe, is future-orientation, which implies giving up present for future benefits. Among other things, it expresses itself in medium and long term economic programs, which serve as a framework for short term economic policy and show private business the direction in which the government wants the economy to move. It is not surprising, that in Eastern Europe after forty years of the statist regimes trying to convince the people that they have to sacrifice their present welfare to the future, a high preference for current as opposed to future consumption is the consequence. But "this utopia must not be replaced by vague promises contradicting equally to daily experience" (Simai 1991). Instead, an empirically founded economic program will reduce uncertainty about the future and help to decrease the rate of time preference, so important for capitalist development.[29]

(3) Besides an appropriate statistical data base, an efficient and well trained bureaucracy will be needed to draw up realistic plans or economic programs. In Korea and Taiwan, Confucian tradition combined with a merit based selection system obviously worked quite well. Basic values and traditions are not transferable, but one might well think of a system of examinations for the East European countries to select from their oversized bureaucracy those who qualify for the new tasks; and to attract new, competent staff at the same time. Only competent bureaucrats at all levels will allow an open and flexible planning process (from the bottom rather than from the top) which proved so much more efficient in Korea and Taiwan than in the socialist countries.

(4) Korea and Taiwan also give a good example of effective implementation of economic programs. Besides their prestigious and competent bureaucracy, this is largely attributed to both countries re-

presenting a "hard state" in G.Myrdal's sense. A hard state need not necessarily be connected with political suppression. It simply means "to place obligations on people and require enforcement of the obligations, in which compulsion plays a strategic role" (see endnote 5). It can be understood as a warning to the East European countries, strongly wishing to become liberal democracies, to avoid anarchic economic relations between the individuals and the state (e.g. with regard to tax paying, tariff declarations etc.).

(5) Finally, the examples of Korea and to a limited extent of Taiwan show, that foreign advisors can be very efficatious; but should be supplemented and increasingly substituted by local experts. In Eastern Europe too, foreign experts might be of great help in coping with the new tasks, as long as not enough local experts are available. But why should the East European countries not look for the expertise of Korea and Taiwan directly? Taiwan at least can refer to a long tradition of sending experts to developing countries, although in the field of agriculture mainly. In fact, Hungary has already started some kind of co-operation which, as stated after the Second Korean-Hungarian Round-Table Conference in Seoul 1989, "can rapidly reach beyond trade relations and be converted into a relationship based on a specific and comprehensive technical, structural and financial partnership and based on a common stance in third countries" (Kim et al. 1990, p. vii).[30]

(Re)privatization of Industrial Property and Land Reform. As mentioned above, under colonial rule, in both Korea and Taiwan, 80-90 percent of industrial property was owned by the Japanese, and was taken over by the new governments after independence. Though part of the land was state-owned, too, most of the arable land was private, belonging to (local) landlords but cultivated by tenants. In both countries reprivatization of industrial property and the land reform were interrelated by a system of exchanging assets in land for assets in Japanese built factories. Though under different conditions, certain similarities to the ongoing "voucher-experiments" in Eastern Europe can be found.

The land reform took place between 1949 and 1953 in Taiwan, and was promulgated in its final form in 1950 in Korea (after first attempts starting in 1948). In both cases the law set an upper limit of about three hectare per household, above which landlords had to sell their land to the government, which in turn sold it to the former tenants.[31] The price for land was defined in terms of the main crop, payable over several years. The landlords were to receive the sales price in government bonds, so called "land bonds" exchangeable for natural products as well as public industrial facilities (in Korea), or were given shares of government enterprises directly (in Taiwan). The purpose of this rigorous reform was, first of all, to increase agricultural production by giving the "land to the tiller", but also to deprive the landlords of their political power, and last but not least to shift the main field of capital accumulation from the agricultural to the industrial sector, thus laying the foundations for capitalist development.

In Korea the price of land was 1.5 times the annual output of the main crop, payable over five years. The landlords were to receive the equivalent in bonds, whose value was to be expressed in terms of rice, but which were also exchangeable for industrial facilities formerly owned by the Japanese. However, since the government often did not redeem the bonds on time, the bonds were sold on the secondary market well below their face value[32], and correspondingly the price for industrial facilities fell. Thus "the effort at converting landlords directly into capitalists by this method is generally held to have been a failure" (Jones, Sakong 1980, p. 35. Obviously it was by a "detour" rather that former landlords became industrial entrepreneurs, because according to a survey on industrial entrepreneurs' fathers in 1976, 47 percent were "large to medium" landowners).[33] Others – among them technical or managerial employees of former Japanese companies – took the opportunity to buy factories rather cheaply, often financed by low-interest government loans, and frequently in return for political favors. Several of today's large industrial concerns emerged in this way.[34] According to one survey of 11 plants, sales prices ran between 38% and 82% of the "government estimated price".[35] It must be said, however, that by the years of neglect under government rule, and the damages of the Korean War, factories were handed over in a very bad condition.

The process of reprivatization stretched over a considerable period of time. Starting in 1949, by 1953 only two thirds of the enterprises (in value) had been sold;[36] it was by 1960 only, that most of the former Japanese enterprises had been divested, with 36 entities left, comprising an estimated share of 10% in non-agricultural GDP and less than 15% of manufacturing. (Those figures had to be extrapolated from Table 3, and Jones, Sakong 1980, p. 151). Most of them had been public enterprises under the Japanese as well, as "natural" monopolies like electricity and railroads or profitable "state monopolies" like ginseng, salt, and tobacco. (Profits from public enterprises contributed almost 10 percent of government revenue in 1960. Menzel 1985, p. 93). Apart from the Korean War 1950-1953, the process of reprivatization of industrial property was certainly hampered by the greater opportunities for private entrepreneurs to make profits in commercial activities, connected with partly illicit foreign exchange allocations, as will be elaborated in more detail in the subsection 2.3 on "managing foreign aid". Foreign direct investment was of no importance for reprivatization, as it was allowed in Korea from 1965 onwards only. It should be noted, however, that under the Park regime the number of public enterprises was increased again by founding new enterprises, and until the early 1970s production of public enterprises increased faster than the economy as a whole, and kept pace with the rapidly expanding private manufacturing sector. (Between 1963 and 1972 the public enterprise sector's contribution to GDP increased from 7 to 9 percent, and remained approx. 13 percent of non-agricultural GDP). Public enterprises' share in manufacturing value added was 15 percent in both years (see Tables 3 and 4, and Jones, Sakong 1980, p. 151).

Table 4

Republic of Korea:
Sectoral Origin of Public-Enterprise Value Added, 1972

(in %)

	Share of Public Enterprise in Sector	Share of Sector in Public Enterprise Total
Agriculture, forestry, and fishing	0.20	0.68
Mining	31.01	3.63
Manufacturing	15.11	34.92
Construction	5.44	2.98
Electricity, water, and sanitation	66.19	13.66
Transportation and communication	30.51	18.95
Trade	2.35	4.10
Finance	86.95	19.28
Ownership of dwellings	0.40	0.09
Public administration	0.00	0.00
Services	1.70	1.72
TOTAL	9.09	100.0

Source: Jones 1976, p. 76, from Jones, Sakong, Table 25, p. 150.

In Taiwan, (re)privatization was less extensive, but the system was quite similar to that of Korea. Following the principles of Sun Yat-Sen, monopolies, enterprises important for national security and public welfare, as well as "big capital", remained state property, probably to be denationalized later on. Furthermore, the state should retain a certain share in private enterprises in case of market imperfections or for reasons of technical cooperation or financial support: 100 percent of electricity, gas, oil, fertilizers, sugar, salt, wine, and tobacco were further supplied by state enterprises, and the state retained a major share in the metal industry, the chemical industry, and the paper and pulp industry. The banking sector too, was dominated by the government (Gälli 1988).[37] It was the light industry mainly, that was rapidly sold off to dispossessed landlords and monied classes (Hamilton 1983, p. 47). Thus the important fields of clothing and textiles, plastics, and later on electronics, became entirely private. However, before selling them off to private interests, a certain number of smaller state enterprises was combined into four big enterprises: Taiwan Cement Co., Taiwan Paper and Pulp Co., Taiwan Agriculture and Forestry Co,. and Taiwan Industrial and Mining Co., which were forming the avantgarde of the new private enterprise sector. Out of 755 former Japanese enterprises, 376 had been divested (the remaining 399 government enterprises were reorganized and integrated into 22 units, the most prominent being China Petroleum Co., Taiwan Power Co. (incl. Aluminium), Taiwan Fertilizer Co., and Taiwan Sugar Co. (Chang 1984, pp. 123 and 124). By 1952, the share of government enterprises in industrial output had fallen to 56% (see Table 5).

Table 5

Public and Private Enterprise in Taiwan, 1952-1982

(percentage shares)

	Industry[a)]		Manufacturing	
	private	public	private	public
1952	43.4	56.6	43.8	56.2
1955	48.9	51.1	51.3	48.7
1958	50.0	50.0	52.8	47.2
1961	51.8	48.2	54.7	45.3
1964	56.3	43.7	61.1	38.9
1967	65.3	34.7	71.2	28.8
1970	72.7	27.7	79.4	20.6
1973	81.1	18.9	86.2	13.8
1976	77.9	22.1	83.4	16.6
1979	79.3	20.7	84.4	15.6
1982	80.3	19.7	85.5	14.5

a) Mining and manufacturing, gas, electricity and water supply.

Source: Taiwan Statistical Data Book 1983, p. 81 from Menzel 1985, Table 67, p. 216.

The land reform in Taiwan took place in three stages: rent reduction, public land sales, and a "land-to-the tiller" program. The price of land was 2.5 times the annual output of the main crop, and landlords were to receive 70% of the price for land in government bonds (land bonds), and 30% in shares of state enterprises; but as in Korea, a great part of them was sold off quickly at low prices. Among those who acquired government enterprises or bought shares on the secondary market were many mainland refugees, who had been able to save part of their wealth, and often had already some industrial experience.[38] Contrary to Korea, and again following the principles of Sun Yat-Sen, foreign direct investment was allowed from the very beginning; but coming from overseas Chinese mainly, the inflow of capital from this source was rather low during the 1950s, and did not contribute significantly to the (re)privatization process.

By 1963 the share of public enterprises in industrial production was slightly below 50%. The further significant decrease of this share during the 1960s until the early 1970s to somewhat less than 20% was not a consequence of further divestiture, but of the enormous dynamism of the expanding private sector; the public sector could not keep pace, though several new state enterprises were founded (Menzel 1985, p. 217). The public share in manufacturing industry stabilized at approx. 15%, quite similar to the figures given for Korea.

What Can Be Learned from This by the East European Countries? In both countries (re)privatization took 10-12 years to reach the desired levels. The process was fast in the beginning, but slowed down later on. The secondary market played an important role in allocating public enterprise shares to the final owners. Though the level of (re)privatization of industry aimed at was quite different in the beginning between Korea and Taiwan, a certain convergence can be found: while still somewhat higher in the industry as a whole in Taiwan, the public share in the manufacturing sector found its own level at 15% in both countries. While the Korean government was again actively bringing up the by then low share of public enterprises to foster industrial development, the dynamic private sector in Taiwan simply "outgrew" the public sector up to a certain level. This can be interpreted in two ways: First, both strategies seem viable for forced (accelerated) development: the one, bringing the public enterprise sector down to a minimum level and waiting for the private sector to take the initiative; where this is not the case, though desirable from a long term developmental aspect, government will step in anew. Or the other: retaining a relatively big public sector which is not in competition but rather in support of the private sector, and by boosting its expansion will automatically decrease in relative importance. However, the examples of Korea and Taiwan show, that the first strategy was connected with rather low growth rates in the initial phase, which of course cannot be solely attributed to privatization policies, but nevertheless gives the impression that from the point of view of political and social stability this strategy looks less favorable.

A second interpretation would be, that accelerated development was simply not possible, if the public enterprise sector fell below a certain level – because of lack of private capital and entrepreneurship. I personally would rather incline to the latter interpretation. However, one serious reason why East European governments should divest first as much as possible is: one might believe that the existing public enterprises cannot be (re)organized in a way to work efficiently under the competitive conditions envisaged for the future; but this argument will be viable to a different degree in different countries, and the appraisal should be made very carefully.

Though the conditions of the land reform in Korea and Taiwan were quite different from the conditions under which reprivatization of agriculture will take place in Europe now, three points seem to be relevant:

First, the awareness of a close relationship between the agricultural and the industrial sector: agriculture as a source of food for the industrial worker, agricultural surplus as a source of foreign currency for investment in agriculture as well as in industry, agricultural products as industrial inputs. Second, in both countries productivity in agriculture was made to rise considerably by giving "the land-to-the-tiller". But comparing Korea and Taiwan, agricultural development turned out more dynamic in Taiwan, where the land reform was embedded in an extensive modernization program, monitored by the "Joint Commission for Rural Reconstruction" (JCRR) composed of both Chinese and American experts. It comprised technical and financial assistance, practical and scientific advice, as well as training on the spot. Farmers' associations, whose membership was quasi compulsory, also played an important role in modernizing the agricultural sector. But this leads over to the third point: In connection with the land reform, state interference with the agricultural sector remained high for a long time; most important, prices for basic foodstuffs were kept low by different measures, therefore costs of living, and wage levels remained low too, which in turn was an important precondition for export oriented growth, based on labor intensive production. Nevertheless, growth of agricultural production was relatively high compared with other developing countries, and this fact certainly contributed to the relative equality of the income distribution.[39]

2.3 Managing Foreign Aid

Aid given to Taiwan and Korea came mainly from US sources. Beyond doubt, aid was substantial in terms of national product as well as compared with US aid given to other developing countries; but because of its complexity, quantification is not so easy. The purpose of

US aid was both to create self-supporting economies able to sustain large military forces, and to advance these countries as a show case of capitalist development (see Hamilton 1983, p. 43). Therefore a clear distinction between "military" and "economic" aid cannot be made. According to the literature on the subject, economic aid for Taiwan amounted to US$ 1.4 bn between 1951 and 1965, and approximately US$ 4.4 bn for South Korea, the bulk of which was pumped in between 1945 and 1963. Afterwards US aid to Korea declined rapidly, and except for a minor trickle came to an end in 1971 (see Table 6).

Table 6

Economic Aid to the Republic of Korea and Taiwan

(in US$ mn)

Year	US and UN economic aid to Korea[a)]	US economic aid to Taiwan[b)]	Year	US and UN economic aid to Korea[a)]	US economic aid to Taiwan[b)]
1945	4.9	n.a.	1963	216.4	84.6
1946	49.9	n.a.	1964	149.3	143.5
1947	175.4	n.a.	1965	131.4	42.7
1948	179.6	n.a.	1966	103.3	n.a.
1949	116.5	n.a.	1967	97.0	n.a.
1950	58.7	n.a.	1968	105.9	n.a.
1951	106.5	77.9	1969	107.3	n.a.
1952	161.3	65.5	1970	82.6	n.a.
1953	194.2	74.0	1971	51.2	n.a.
1954	153.9	81.8	1972	5.1	n.a.
1955	236.7	102.5	1973	2.1	n.a.
1956	326.7	91.6	1974	1.0	n.a.
1957	382.9	100.4	1975	1.2	n.a.
1958	321.3	80.1	1976	1.7	n.a.
1959	222.2	124.5	1977	0.9	n.a.
1960	245.4	108.1	1978	0.2	n.a.
1961	199.2	97.3	1979	0.2	n.a.
1962	232.3	67.3	1980	0.4	n.a.
			TOTAL	4,431.8	1,341.2

a) Including agricultral commodities imported under the US Public Law 480; The two UN-programs: CRIK (Civil Relief in Korea) and UNKRA (United Nations Korea Reconstruction Agency) played an important role between 1951 and 1956 only, and the major donor to the fund was the United States. – b) Excluding direct military support ("Direct forces").

Sources: Korea: Menzel 1985, Table 10, p. 74, using Korean Sources. Taiwan: Menzel 1985, Table 38, p. 166; calculated after Jacoby 1966, p. 40. There exist certain differences compared to Taiwanese sources.

Regarding the same period, namely 1951 to 1965, the annual average of economic aid was US$ 89 mn for Taiwan and US$ 219 mn for Korea in absolute terms, and 4.5% and 9% as a share of GDP respectively.[40] In addition, much higher amounts of military aid are reported: US$ 2.4 bn for Taiwan[41] and US$ 7 bn for Korea.[42] If these were included, average annual support for the period of 15 years indicated above would "leap" to US$ 248 mn for Taiwan, and US$ 564 mn to Korea, which was 12% and 23% respectively of their GDP. The reasons why at least a part of this military aid should be added to the figures for economic aid are the following: Modernization and training in the military sector has had positive side effects on the modernization of the economy as a whole; the local procurement program stimulated local industry (e.g. construction, plywood producers, tire industry);[43] a considerable part of the military equipment was later sold to the local civilian population; and finally, local governments could save on military expenditures, which anyhow put a great strain on the budget.

Economic Aid and Its Impact on Further Economic Development. US economic aid was in kind rather than money, and money was mainly given in form of grants; and financial aid was supplemented by technical and economic assistance. The main impact of economic aid was to reduce severe shortages, to supply the economy with the foreign currency necessary for imports, to finance large parts of government expenditures, e.g. for improving the infrastructure (including education); and to promote the process of capital accumulation in general.

In order to reduce shortages, large quantities of cotton and grain were shipped to Korea and Taiwan as well as other raw materials and intermediate goods, fertilizers, spare parts, tools, and machinery. This helped to instal new import substituting enterprises particularly in the so called "three white industries" (spinning and textiles, flower milling, sugar refining), partly based on former Japanese enterprises, in a rather short time.

In both countries aid constituted the largest portion of national budgets for several years (Hamilton 1983, p. 42f.)[44], and as already pointed out, economic advisors influenced economic strategies to a certain extent.

Technical assistance was mainly directed to the military and agricultural sector. In Taiwan, e.g., the aforementioned "Joint Commission for Rural Reconstruction" (JCRR) was fully financed by the US. The JCRR, with both Chinese and American members, played the leading part in modernizing the agricultural sector there. In Korea, US aid is considered essential to the rapid expansion of education.[45]

Until the early 1960s the proportion of foreign aid in total investment was nearly 70% in Korea. (From 1962 onwards aid was increasingly supplemented by foreign loans; Menzel 1985, p. 75, Table 11 and p. 76). In Taiwan the share of aid in investment was less than half, namely between 27% and 34% on the average during the period 1951 to 1965, depending on whether original aid only is considered or counterpart funds are included (aid to Taiwan was given along the lines of the Marshall Plan, largely in the form of goods deliveries; the proceeds realized were paid into so called Counterpart Funds, from which capital continued to become available to the economy; Menzel 1985, pp. 166 and 211).

As already mentioned, the way in which foreign aid was channeled into the accumulation process was quite different in the two countries, and apparently led to a different economic performance. In Taiwan, economic growth was remarkable from the very beginning of aid flowing into the country. Real GDP increased at an average rate of 10% from 1952 to 1954, and of 8% from 1955 to 1965. In Korea, growth only surged from 1962 onwards, when aid was already leveling off. It must be taken into consideration, however, that the initial level of economic development was much lower in South Korea than in Taiwan, and that the Korean War caused considerable damage to the economy. After the war, average growth rates of real GNP were 4% for the period 1954-1962, 8% for 1963 to 1965, and more than 10% for the rest of the decade (see Table 1).

In Korea the process of foreign exchange allocation to private businessmen played the crucial role in the transmission of US aid to the economy. Due to severe shortages, imported goods fetched very high prices, and foreign exchange was a precious commodity, the allocation of which became a privilege, tied to good relations with, and support of, the Rhee government. It was thus concentrated on the bigger companies, and in particular the emerging "chaebols" (family based industrial conglomerates). By importing goods or reselling the foreign currency at a high premium to other importers, US aid was turned to a large extent into commercial rather than productive capital[46], and the foreign exchange gap widened. By the end of the 1950s the value of imports was at least 10 times that of exports, and only US aid kept the economy afloat (see Hong 1979, p. 46, quoted after Hamilton 1984, p. 41). From the mid-1950s US aid officials and the State Department had been pressing hard for a more efficient and productive allocation of funds – and a large part of the explanation of the withdrawal of US support for Rhee lay in his unwillingness to embrace their view of Korean economic future development.

It must be stressed, however, as officially foreign exchange loans were preferably given to "exporters who used local raw materials, and domestic producers who relied on imports of capital goods", that the Special Foreign Exchange Loan nonetheless provided an impetus for the formation and development of new businesses, because new firms of the right sort could attract these loans. From South Korea's 50 most powerful industrial groups, 31 of which were established between 1945 and 1961, no fewer than 11 began business in foreign trade (Byun and Kim 1978, quoted after Hamilton 1984, p. 48).

To the East European countries, the foregoing discussion on aid for Taiwan and Korea will show clearly:

(1) that strategic interest of the donor is indeed a very good stimulus for granting aid, and

(2) that the way aid is managed, plays a crucial role: Korea, receiving a much higher amount of aid in absolute terms as well as in terms of share of GDP, was obviously less successful in using it. Besides political favoritism, the main reason was, that the donors' money was channeled into non-productive activities, such as commerce first, thus widening the foreign exchange gap further. This is a concrete danger for the East European countries, too.

(3) One has to take into consideration, however, that from the start, the level of economic development was less in Korea than in Taiwan, and other things equal one might therefore expect foreign aid to be less effective or at least working slower in Korea than in Taiwan. Applied to the East European countries, this would mean, that aid to the less developed East European countries has to be relatively higher.

(4) For political reasons, and given the low level of economic development, aid for Korea and Taiwan was given in form of grants mainly, and it was certainly part of their success, that future budgets and balances on foreign account were not burdened by repayments and interest. This should be taken into consideration as well when offering loans instead of grants to the East European countries.

(5) Taiwan can be considered another successful example of implementing aid according to the principles of the "Marshall Plan": by establishing counterpart funds, aid is multiplied, but can nevertheless be controlled to avoid surplus demand exerting inflationary pressure; this is of particular interest for the East European countries, all of which are confronted with an inflationary gap of some kind for the time being. Even bearing in mind that the example of Taiwan cannot holus-bolus be applied to the East European countries, the overall impact of aid on economic performance estimated by Jacoby (1966) remains impressive, and stresses the significance of a considerable amount of foreign aid

for accelerating the process of catching up with the advanced industrialized countries.

3. Reintegration into the World Economy

3.1 Export Orientation Versus Import Substitution

Before the 2nd world war, both Korea and Taiwan were relatively open economies, exporting agricultural and other primary products mainly to Japan.[47]

After the war, traditional trade links broke down (very similar to the situation of the East European countries today) and a huge overall demand surplus prevailed. Thus, exports were very low and imports were to a great part financed by foreign aid.

In the beginning, both countries followed a policy of import substitution with the support of their main donor, the USA. In those days, import substitution was considered the proper method of industrial development and was pursued by many third world countries.[48]

By 1957, however, reconstruction of the economy was considered complete and both countries appeared to have largely exhausted the possibility of growth through easy import substitution of nondurable consumer goods, and should thus enter the next stage of import-substitution of consumer durables, machinery and intermediate products.

But now the US began to put pressure on both countries to open up their economies and expand exports. Basically there were three reasons for that: first, the US wanted to reduce aid, so far needed to fill the ever increasing gap between imports and exports. Second, for geopolitical reasons the US wanted to withdraw from direct economic engagement in Korea and Taiwan and wanted the latter countries to re-establish their trade links with Japan. Finally, import substitution policy so far had fallen short of expectations in many developing countries, which set going a general process of rethinking in development policies. The principal argument against import substitution was, that the narrowness of domestic markets in poor, underdeveloped economies was a serious restraint for realizing the economies of scale necessary for efficient production, especially in the field of capital- and intermediate goods.[49]

While the Taiwanese government did not offer much resistance to US pressure for a more export oriented policy (initiated by a marked devaluation of the NT$ in 1958/59), it took until the fall of Syngman Rhee in 1960,[50] that Korea started to change its policy significantly, though the actual turning point in Korean economic policy is dated with 1965 only, when the Normalization Treaty with Japan was concluded and President Park's economic policy took full effect.

As pointed out before in more detail, Park explicitly gave economics priority over politics, and in brief his philosophy can be described as: "a strong commitment to economic growth;" "growth by industrialization," and "exports first." With respect to Taiwan, the first two postulates, too, were an integral part of the teachings of Sun Yat-Sen, which after all formed an important element of political thinking in Taiwan. Exports as a means to improve production and product quality were also mentioned by Sun Yat-Sen, but he had strongly favored infant industry protection. In fact, though implying an extensive export promotion scheme similar to Korea's, direct pressure for exports was less in Taiwan, which had, on the other hand, from the very beginning been more open to foreign capital.

Some remarks on the empirical and theoretical links between exports and growth are called for: Though it is difficult from the methodological standpoint to study the relationship between openness to trade with the outside world, and growth rate of an economy, "sufficient cumulative evidence exists to suggest that countries more open to world trade have higher GNP growth rates" (Corbo, Osso 1985, p. 11). Yet the theoretical causal mechanism linking exports and economic growth is less clear (Fransman 1984, p. 52).[51]

We hence will describe the concrete steps Korea and Taiwan have implemented as part of their trade policies, and then discuss how these relate to the existing explanatory hypothesis, which goes right to the heart of the matter whether these countries can be considered a model case for neoclassical theory or not. We will concentrate, however, on the aspects considered relevant for Eastern Europe.

3.2 Devaluation and Unification of Multiple Exchange Rates

In accord with import substitution policy, (official) exchange rates were heavily overvalued in the 1950s in Korea and Taiwan, and different exchange rates were applied to different transactions.

In Taiwan, e.g., the exchange rate was lower for exporters than for importers, as was that for public enterprises, compared with that for private business. In addition, a certain part of foreign exchange earnings from exports was turned into exchange settlement certificates, which could be sold on the free market at a higher price than the official rate. The demand for foreign exchange was, however, brought down by import quotas, import licenses, and high tariffs.[52]

In Korea, as described in the section on foreign aid, foreign exchange allocation at the very low (official) exchange rate for the US$ was a great privilege, and foreign currency was allocated by quotas and licenses to those, who were on good terms with the Rhee-government. By a complicated auction system as well as by selling foreign exchange on the free market a high distortion premium could be earned, which amounted to 100% and more of the official rate.[53] As a result of the significant devaluations after the fall of Rhee in 1960 (-30%), 1961 (-100%) and 1964 (-65%), the distortion premium was gradually reduced, but was abolished completely only after another devaluation in 1965 (-24%), see Table 7.[54] Thus, from 1965 onwards, there was no longer any multiple exchange rate system, and the uniform exchange rate was a kind of equilibrium exchange rate, balancing the supply and demand for foreign currency under the given system of import control. Taking into account adjustments for inflation

Table 7

Republic of Korea: Official Exchange Rate and Foreign Exchange Market Distortions, 1955-1975

(current Won per dollar)

Year	A Official Rate[a)]	B Distortion Premium[b)]
1955	31.3	48.1
1956	50.0	52.9
1957	50.0	58.9
1958	50.0	64.0
1959	50.0	84.7
1960	63.8	83.9
1961	127.5	N.T.
1962	130.0	N.T.
1963	130.0	39.8
1964	214.3	39.7
1965	266.5	0.0
1966	272.2	0.0
1967	272.5	0.0
1968	276.8	0.0
1969	286.8	0.0
1970	310.1	0.0
1971	346.1	0.0
1972	391.8	0.0
1973	398.4	0.0
1974	406.0	0.0
1975	484.0	0.0

Notes: a) Twelve month average from Wontack Hong, Factor Supply and Factor Intensity of Trade in Korea (Seoul, 1976), p. 140. – b) Estimate of windfall profit accruing to importers with privileged access to foreign exchange at official rate.

Source: Jones, Sakong 1980, Table 12, p. 88.

(see endnote 54), this kind of equilibrium rate was retained until the mid-1970s. As will be shown below, until the late 1970s import controls were by no means negligible. Thus, compared with a free trade regime, the Won was still overvalued to a certain extent!

In Taiwan the turning point came in 1958[55]. With the "Program for Improvement of Foreign Exchange and Trade Control", comprising stepwise devaluation of the Taiwan dollar and gradual abolition of the multiple exchange rate system. Under a system of multiple exchange rates it is difficult to quantify devaluations correctly. We refer to the figures given by Menzel (see Table 8), according to which a gradual devaluation of the NT$, beginning in 1958, up to 1963 was approximately 40%, with the bulk of the devaluation taking place in 1958 and 1959. (Overvaluation in Taiwan must therefore have been less than in Korea. One reason, presumably, was the much higher amount of aid in absolute and relative terms given to Korea than to Taiwan.)

With respect to the abolition of the multiple exchange rates, and in order to approach a kind of equilibrium exchange rate, exporters (except those of sugar, rice, and salt) from 1958 onwards were awarded exchange certificates representing the full amount of export proceeds they had surrendered to the Bank of Taiwan. At the same time, to make the market demand for exchange certificates reflect the market demand for imports more correctly, the quota restrictions on all types of permissible imports were relaxed, though luxury goods could still not be imported. (In general, the existing high tariffs on imports were maintained, see next subsection.). The resulting market or effective rate was gradually made applicable to all imports and exports, and to most remittances and transfers (Tsiang 1985, p. 35). By 1961 the unification of the exchange rate had progressed well and was completed on Sept. 30, 1963 (Menzel 1985, p. 225).[56] Henceforth the exchange rate of the NT$ was pegged to the US$ at a rate of 40 NT$ to one US$, until 1973, when the Bretton Woods system broke down. But as will be shown in the next paragraph, considerable quantitative restrictions and high tariffs prevailed throughout the 1960s until the beginning of the 1970s, holding the demand for foreign currency artificially low, and the exchange rate for the NT$ artificially high – thus, as in the case of Korea, the Taiwanese currency was overvalued to a certain extent, compared with a free trade regime.

Table 8
Official Exchange Rate and Financial Export Incentives in Taiwan, 1956-1978

	Official rate NT$ per US$ (1)	Export Incentives per One US$ of Exports in NT$: Interest-subsidy (2)	Tariff-reductions (3)	Tax reductions (4)	Total (5)	Effective nominal rate NT$ per US$ (6)
1956	24.71		0.21	0.01	0.220	24.93
1957	25.53	0.005	0.22	0.06	0.285	25.82
1958	34.14	0.017	0.50	0.15	0.667	34.81
1959	39.38	0.021	1.22	0.36	1.601	40.98
1960	39.73	0.031	1.69	0.68	2.401	42.13
1961	39.83	0.038	1.87	0.97	2.878	42.71
1962	39.83	0.086	2.23	1.00	3.316	43.15
1963	39.87	0.086	2.48	0.77	3.336	43.21
1964	40.00	0.060	2.69	0.92	3.670	43.67
1965	40.00	0.073	2.97	1.07	4.113	44.11
1966	40.00	0.083	3.24	1.07	4.393	44.39
1967	40.00	0.077	3.49	1.19	4.757	44.76
1968	40.00	0.096	3.37	1.23	4.696	44.70
1969	40.00	0.100	3.48	1.27	4.850	44.85
1970	40.00	0.093	4.06	1.36	5.513	45.51
1971	40.00	0.100	4.27	1.34	5.710	45.71
1972	40.00	0.095	3.68	1.24	5.015	45.02
1973	38.16	0.074	2.82	0.98	3.874	42.03
1974	37.90	0.083	2.47	0.87	3.423	41.23
1975	37.95	0.083	2.70	1.12	3.903	41.85
1976	37.95	0.076	2.14	0.89	3.106	41.06
1977	37.95	0.057	2.11	0.89	3.057	41.01
1978	35.95	0.050	1.65	0.77	2.490	38.44

Source: Liang, Liang 1981, pp. 158, 159, from Menzel 1985, p. 225, Table 72.

3.3 Concrete Measures of Export Promotion and Import Control

For exporters, the overvaluation of domestic currency as stated above was effectively counterbalanced by many direct measures to promote exports:[57]

(1) Largely unrestricted access to and tariff exemptions for imported intermediate and capital goods for export industries[58] ("export-import link system").

(2) Various tax incentives, e.g. exemption of export industries from payment of indirect taxes on major intermediate inputs, whether imported or purchased domestically.

(3) Substantial reductions of indirect taxes on income earned in exporting, along with accelerated depreciation allowances and generous tax assessments.

(4) Easy access to highly subsidized short- and medium-term credits to finance exports.

(5) Preferential railroad- and electricity rates.

In addition to these, less "tangible" measures have also helped to increase exports – though they are of less importance in Taiwan than in Korea:

(6) Increased information on export opportunities and procedures, export-marketing support.

(7) Non-pecuniary incentives.[59]

In Korea, e.g., the Monthly Export Promotion Meeting chaired by the President was a forum of multifaceted information exchange. In 1962, the Ministry of Commerce and Industry began, together with the industrialists concerned, setting annual targets classified by commodity and by region and country of destination. This had a signal effect in "suggesting profitable markets and implicitly promising non-quantifiable government support in pursuit of these targets" (Jones, Sakong 1980, p. 97).

In Taiwan, besides government plans, industrialists' associations were formed for each branch, representing some sort of "export promotion cartels", coordinating their demand prices for inputs, as well as production quotas. For each firm, a production quota was determined; underfulfillment was punished, overfulfillment was rewarded in pecuniary terms.

In the field of export marketing, the "Korean Trade Promotion Corporation" (KOTRA) played a significant role: KOTRA has established its offices all over the world. It provides information on trade opportunities, investment possibilities, and industrial cooperations abroad: it initiates business contacts and supports exporters in every respect. Taiwan, instead, spread a net of semi-official trade representatives around the world.[60]

Import Control. There are basically two ways to restrict imports and thus to give protection to local industries: tariffs, and quantitative restrictions. Both were used extensively during the first years of import substitution, and only reduced gradually when a policy of export promotion was adopted. It has been stated, however, that import substitution policy has never been given up completely, but was shifted to ever new sectors instead: protection was shifted from simple, non-durable goods to intermediates, and to durable consumer goods (household electronics), and then further to machinery, industrial electronics, and other high-tech products.

Empirical evidence for Taiwan indeed suggests, that there was little overall liberalization until 1972/73; for Korea this seems to hold even until 1979.

Quantitative Restrictions. In both countries imports were divided into three categories:

(1) permissible (automatically approved) items, which may be imported in any quantity,
(2) controlled (restricted) items, which may be imported in limited quantity,
(3) prohibited items, which may not be imported at all.

In 1953, 55% of Taiwan's imports were permissible, 36.5% were controlled, and 55% where prohibited items (on a four digit SITC level), the latter consisting mainly of luxury goods and dangerous items, while restricted imports helped mainly to protect the textile, wood, leather, paper, cement, and bicycle industry. In fact, this composition remained fairly constant until the 1970s, when permissible items held a proportion of 57%, the rest consisting of 41% controlled and 3% prohibited items. A big change came in 1972 only, 14 years after the beginning of export promotion policies, when the share of permissible items rose to 82% and reached nearly 100 percent in 1978.[61]

In Korea there was a "permit system" in the beginning, which simply distinguished between prohibited and permitted items. In 1949 a quota system was introduced, placing quantitative restrictions on categories of permitted items: thus a "restricted" category was added. In 1955 a "positive list" of items, whose import was unrestricted, was issued, and adjusted regularly with certain attempts to liberalize in 1962, 1963, and 1965 – but restrictions had to be extended for balance of payments reasons in 1964. A significant change took place in 1967 only, when a "negative list" system was introduced, i.e., items not otherwise specified were automatically unrestricted. Nonetheless, the restricted category remained substantial, comprising 30% out of 1312 SITC categories; 60% were unrestricted and 9% prohibited items. But in the following years, the share of unrestricted items decreased again to approximately 50%. A new, massive liberalization effort was started in 1978, bringing the proportion of unrestricted items significantly up by 1980 to 69%.[62] Again, a substantial overall reduction in quantitative restrictions only took place 15 years after the turning point in trade policy towards export promotion.

The Tariff System. Taiwan, as mentioned above, left GATT in 1950 and immediately afterwards tariffs were raised substantially: In September 1949, the average legal tariff was 27%, and in 1950 it was 44.7%, which, it must be said, was not particularly high compared to other developing countries. In Korea, by the Tariff Law of 1950, tariffs had been set at a similar level as in Taiwan, at a rate of 40%. In both countries, tariff rates varied widely from very low tariffs or no tariffs on raw materials and other inputs for import substituting industries, to tariffs of 100%, and more, on competitive imports and luxury goods.

In Taiwan, average legal tariffs were reduced only gradually to 38.8% in 1959 and 35.4% in 1965. While tariffs were reduced, special duties were levied on imports (e.g. a defense premium), so that by 1968 the total burden on imports was only 15% less than in 1960 (Sai Chang 1981, p. 186). But the structure of tariffs changed significantly, providing for the changing structure of industry: The basic criterion was, that local manufacturers who desired protection must show, that quantity and quality of their products were sufficient to satisfy domestic demand, and that the cost of the imported raw materials to manufacture such products locally did not exceed 70 percent of the total cost of production. The ex-works price for the products whose importation was restricted was not allowed to exceed the price of complementary imports by more than 25%. In 1964 this margin was reduced to 15%, in 1968 to 10%, and in 1973 to 5% (Fajnzylber 1981, p. 120).

In Korea, in 1957 and 1958, average tariffs were slightly increased and special tariffs were imposed temporarily after the devaluations in 1961 and 1964.[63] The tariff reforms of 1968 and 1973 mainly increased the flexibility of the system.[64] The average legal protection in 1968 still covered 54.3% (Westphal 1978, p. 357) but in 1972/73 tariffs were reduced substantially to an average rate of 31.3% (Frank, Kim, Westphal 1975 according to Serfas 1987, p. 129). At the same time protection was shifted from mature consumption goods to heavy industry, such as steel, (petro)chemicals, and vehicles. In the following years, the average legal protection decreased further, with 37.7% in 1978 (Fajnzylber 1981, p. 119) and 22.6% in 1983.

Legal vs. Nominal vs. Effective Rates of Protection. As Westphal 1978, p. 355, points out, with existing quantitative controls on the one hand, and tariff exemptions on the other, legal tariffs do not reflect actual protection. Therefore he suggests the advisability of considering rates of nominal protection[65]. Based on a sample of 365 items, he calculates a very low nominal protection for the Korean industry of 14%, compared with 54.3% of legal protection in 1968. However, recalculation of nominal rates for 1978, given by Fajnzylber 1981, shows an increase in nominal protection to 17.8%, in contrast to the above mentioned reduction in the level of legal protection from 54.3% to 37.7%.

Table 9

Exports and Imports of Taiwan, 1952-1980

Year	Exports US$ mn	Annual increase in %	Imports US$ mn	Annual increase in %	Exports in % of GNP	Imports in % of GNP
1952	116	n.a.	187	n.a.	8.6	14.8
1953	128	10.3	192	2.7	8.7	12.1
1954	93	-27.3	211	9.9	5.8	13.2
1955	123	32.3	201	-4.7	6.4	10.5
1956	118	-2.5	194	-3.5	8.6	14.0
1957	148	25.4	212	9.3	9.2	13.2
1958	156	5.4	226	6.6	8.7	12.6
1959	157	0.6	231	2.2	11.1	16.4
1960	164	4.5	297	28.6	9.6	17.4
1961	195	18.9	322	8.4	11.2	18.5
1962	218	11.8	304	-5.6	11.4	15.9
1963	332	52.3	362	19.1	15.3	16.7
1964	433	30.4	428	18.2	17.1	16.9
1965	450	3.9	556	29.9	16.1	19.9
1966	536	19.1	622	11.9	17.1	19.9
1967	641	19.6	806	29.6	17.7	22.3
1968	789	23.1	903	12.0	18.7	21.5
1969	1.049	33.0	1.213	34.3	21.5	24.9
1970	1.481	41.2	1.524	25.6	26.3	27.1
1971	2.060	39.1	1.844	21.0	31.4	28.2
1972	2.988	45.1	2.514	36.3	38.0	32.1
1973	4.483	50.0	3.792	50.8	41.9	35.6
1974	5.639	25.8	6.966	83.7	39.2	48.7
1975	5.309	-5.9	5.952	-14.6	34.7	39.0
1976	8.166	53.8	7.599	27.7	44.5	41.5
1977	9.369	14.7	8.511	12.0	36.7	39.9
1978	12.687	35.4	11.027	29.6	48.4	42.2
1979	16.103	26.9	14.774	34.0	49.8	45.8
1980	19.811	23.0	19.733	33.6	49.4	49.4

Source: Taiwan Statistical Data Book 1983, p. 23, 184, Menzel 1985, Table 57, p. 199.

Table 10

Exports and Imports of the Republic of Korea, 1952-1980

	Exports[a)] in US$ mn	Annual increase in %	Imports[a)] in US$ mn	Annual increase in %	Exports[b)] in % of GNP	Imports[b)] in % of GNP
1952	28	n.a.	213	n.a.	n.a.	n.a.
1953	40	42.9	347	62.9	1.5	12.9
1954	24	-40.0	241	-30.5	0.6	6.7
1955	18	-25.0	328	36.1	0.8	14.8
1956	25	38.9	340	3.7	0.8	12.7
1957	19	-24.0	390	14.7	0.6	11.2
1958	17	-10.5	344	-11.8	0.4	9.2
1959	20	17.6	274	-20.3	0.5	7.0
1960	33	65.0	306	11.7	0.9	8.9
1961	41	24.2	283	-7.5	1.7	13.4
1962	54	31.7	390	37.8	2.0	15.4
1963	87	61.1	497	27.4	2.2	14.5
1964	120	37.9	365	-26.6	3.5	12.1
1965	175	45.8	416	14.0	5.8	15.3
1966	250	42.9	680	63.5	6.5	18.7
1967	335	34.0	909	33.7	6.8	21.0
1968	486	45.1	1322	45.4	7.6	24.5
1969	658	35.4	1650	24.8	8.3	24.4
1970	882	34.0	1804	9.3	9.5	22.5
1971	1133	37.5	6454	67.7	24.0	36.9
1975	5003	28.6	10523	25.2	27.3	29.4
1978	12711	26.5	14491	37.7	25.6	30.2
1979	14705	15.7	19100	31.8	23.7	32.0
1980	17214	17.1	21598	13.1	28.9	36.8

a) Balance of payments figures. – b) National account figures.

Source: IMF, International Financial Statistics, Databank of The Vienna Institute for Comparative Economic Studies.

But, as Westphal 1978 argues, even the nominal rate does not include the effect of other incentive policies, e.g., subsidies for key import substituting industries. This is taken into account if an "effective rate of protection" is calculated (effective protection calculations express the impact of protection measures on value added per unit of production instead of gross price).

> The resulting effective protection rate of -0.9% for manufacturing output as a whole thus indicates that protection measures on balance provide no protection to value added in the manufacturing sectors, the protection on outputs being slightly more than offset by the cost-raising effects of protection on imports (Westphal 1978, p. 356).

This is most important, as it is the main basis for the assertion that the industry in Korea operated under world market conditions, and can thus be considered a model case for neoclassical theory. Though calculations of effective exchange rates are not incontestable, his results cannot be ignored. But calculations of the effective exchange rates show another interesting phenomenon: quite atypical for developing countries, effective protection in 1968 and 1978 was higher for primary, including agrarian, producers, than for manufacturing industry. Effective protection in agriculture of more than 70%, calculated by Hong, Krause 1981, would by itself be a sufficient reason not to describe Korea as a "free trade" country (see Fransman 1984, p. 53).

Tables 9 and 10 are showing the actual development of exports from Korea and Taiwan. The impressive average increase of exports (in terms of US$) of more than 25% over 20 years for both Korea and Taiwan strongly support the view of a combined effect of comparative advantage and export promotion, obviously in line with (dynamic) comparative advantage – the latter being due, most probably, to the very general approach to export promotion instead of promotion of special export items, and branches, as was the case for import control.

Imports, however, developed less satisfactorily in Korea than in Taiwan, which was obviously more successful in gradually substituting imported inputs needed for export production. Because of the expanding trade deficit, together with a persistent gap between savings and investments, Korea became one of the most highly indebted countries in the World. Because of her high exports, so far debt service and import payments have not been a serious problem, but are certainly a burden on the further economic development of Korea as compared with Taiwan, which owns one of the biggest foreign currency reserves in the World. The relatively higher share of foreign direct investment in Taiwan does not seem to play a very important role in this context, as it is relatively small in both Korea and Taiwan, as will be pointed out below.

4. Internal and External Sources of Capital

Though there exists no comprehensive and generally valid growth theory so far, the increase in productive capital per capita is commonly regarded as the most essential condition for real economic growth.[66] Investment, however, must be financed by domestic savings and/or foreign sources of capital, i.e., foreign direct investment (FDI) and foreign loans and/or transfers.

In the beginning, quite typical for any less developed, low income country, the formation of capital was low in both Korea and Taiwan. But after some time, investment increased rapidly, and the share of investment in GNP soon surpassed the levels reached by the further advanced developing countries of Latin America and even those characteristic for highly industrialized economies: In Korea, the share of investment in GNP was about 10% during the 1950s, rose to 20% during the 1960s, and stabilized at a level slightly above 25% during the 1970s. In Taiwan, where per capita income had been markedly higher, and economic growth started off earlier, the share of investment was already up to 15% during the 1950s, reached nearly 25% during the 1960s and oscillated between 25% and 30% in the years after – climbing up to an exceptional 39% in 1974 (see Table 11). In comparison, the share of investment in the OECD area as a whole was 20% on the average during the period 1960-1982.[67] Though initially they were heavily relying on foreign aid to finance investment, both countries did extremely well in mobilizing domestic savings, and subsequently substituting foreign sources of capital by domestic savings. This was even more true for Taiwan than for Korea.

In Korea, from the very low levels in the Rhee era, the share of savings in GNP increased rapidly after 1963, reaching a level of 25% in 1970, and increased further to an average level of 28% in the following years. In Taiwan, the saving rate was already about 10% in the 1950s, increased to 20% during the 1960s, and was even higher than 30% thereafter (Table 11). Both countries thus surpassed even Japan, which used to have the highest level of savings in the world. In both countries, however, the rapid increase of domestic savings cannot be solely attributed, to the rapid increase in personal incomes due to high rates of economic growth, but is also due to the financial policies applied to promote savings.

In both countries, the institutional interest rates were set by the government, as banks were either public or under government control. To promote savings as well as investment, a two-tier system of interest rates was applied: interest rates on savings and time deposits were kept high, while those for loans were kept low – the difference being covered by subsidies.

Taiwan was probably the first among the developing countries to abandon, as early as 1950, the traditional policy of low interests rates, by raising the interest rate on savings deposits to approximately the prevailing rate of inflation; and interest rates were further increased to 125% for so called "Preferential Interest Rate Deposits" (PIR). As a consequence, total time- and savings deposits quickly rose from a meager NT$ 6 million at the end of March to NT$ 28 million at end of June! Even more remarkably, inflation rapidly came to a halt.[68] Since then, real deposit rates of interest have been kept positive (except briefly

Table 11

External and Internal Sources of Capital in the Republic of Korea and Taiwan

	KOREA				TAIWAN			
	Investment as a share of GNP	Gross domestic savings as a share of of GNP	Gross domestic savings as a share of investment	External sources of capital as a share of investment[a)]	Investment as a share of GNP	Gross domestic savings as a share of of GNP	Gross domestic savings as a share of investment	External sources of capital as a share of investment
	in % (1)	in % (2)	in % (3)	in % (4)	in % (5)	in % (6)	in % (7)	in % (8)
1952	n.a.	n.a.	n.a.	n.a.	15.4	9.2	60.0	40.0
1953	16.0	n.a.	n.a.	41.6	14.1	8.9	63.1	36.9
1954	11.7	n.a.	n.a.	44.9	16.1	7.7	47.8	52.2
1955	11.9	n.a.	n.a.	58.7	13.4	9.0	67.5	32.5
1956	9.5	n.a.	n.a.	114.6	16.2	9.2	57.2	42.8
1957	15.3	n.a.	n.a.	63.7	15.9	10.6	66.8	33.2
1958	12.9	n.a.	n.a.	61.8	16.8	9.9	55.8	44.2
1959	10.7	n.a.	n.a.	63.7	19.0	10.3	54.2	45.8
1960	10.9	n.a.	n.a.	78.4	20.3	12.7	62.7	37.3
1961	13.1	n.a.	n.a.	65.2	20.1	12.8	64.3	35.7
1962	12.8	3.2	25.0	83.5	17.9	12.4	65.3	34.7
1963	18.1	8.7	48.0	57.5	18.4	17.1	96.0	4.0
1964	14.0	8.7	62.1	49.3	18.8	19.6	101.2	-1.2

(continuing)

Table 11 (continued)

External and Internal Sources of Capital in the Republic of Korea and Taiwan

	KOREA				TAIWAN			
	Investment as a share of GNP	Gross domestic savings as a share of of GNP	Gross domestic savings as a share of investment	External sources of capital as a share of investment[a)]	Investment as a share of GNP	Gross domestic savings as a share of of GNP	Gross domestic savings as a share of investment	External sources of capital as a share of investment
	in % (1)	in % (2)	in % (3)	in % (4)	in % (5)	in % (6)	in % (7)	in % (8)
1965	15.0	7.4	49.3	42.6	22.8	19.6	84.5	15.5
1966	21.6	11.8	54.6	39.4	21.3	21.5	95.4	4.6
1967	21.9	11.4	52.0	40.1	24.8	22.5	91.1	8.9
1968	25.9	15.1	58.3	43.2	25.3	22.1	87.6	12.4
1969	28.8	18.8	65.2	36.8	24.6	23.8	96.6	3.4
1970	25.3	15.7	62.0	36.0	25.7	25.5	99.1	0.9
1971	25.1	14.6	58.1	41.8	26.4	28.8	109.2	-9.2
1972	22.2	16.5	74.3	23.0	25.8	32.1	124.4	-24.4
1973	25.7	22.8	88.7	14.4	29.3	34.6	118.2	-18.2
1974	31.7	19.9	62.8	38.1	39.5	31.7	80.2	19.8
1975	30.0	19.1	63.7	33.7	30.8	26.9	87.3	12.7
1976	25.6	23.9	93.4	8.9	31.1	32.5	104.7	-4.7
1977	27.7	27.5	99.2	2.1	28.6	32.9	115.2	-15.2
1978	31.2	28.5	91.3	9.9	28.6	34.9	122.0	-22.0
1979	35.6	28.1	78.9	19.9	33.3	34.5	103.5	-3.5
1980	31.3	21.9	70.0	30.0	34.3	33.0	96.1	3.9

(continuing)

Table 11 (continued)

External and Internal Sources of Capital in the Republic of Korea and Taiwan

	KOREA				TAIWAN			
	Investment as a share of GNP	Gross domestic savings as a share of of GNP	Gross domestic savings as a share of investment	External sources of capital as a share of investment[a)]	Investment as a share of GNP	Gross domestic savings as a share of of GNP	Gross domestic savings as a share of investment	External sources of capital as a share of investment
	in % (1)	in % (2)	in % (3)	in % (4)	in % (5)	in % (6)	in % (7)	in % (8)
Ø1950	12.6	n.a.	n.a.	64.1	15.9	9.3	59.0	41.0
Ø1960	18.2	10.6	58.2	53.6	21.4	18.4	84.5	15.5
Ø1970	28.0	21.6	77.2	22.8	29.9	31.4	106.3	-6.3

a) Due to considerable statistical discrepancies of up to 8% of investment, the share of gross domestic savings as a share of investment and the share of external sources of capital will in general not add up to 100 percent. For that reason, no figures were given for the share of domestic savings before 1962.

Sources: Data from national sources, although in case of Korea from secondary sources only. (1) 1953-1962: Calculated from Menzel 1985, p. 75; 1963-1983: Serfas 1987, p. 180. – (2) 1962: Menzel 1985, p. 75, 1963-83: Serfas 1987, p. 190. – (3) 100 times (2)/(1). – (4) 1953-62: Menzel 1985, p. 75, 1963-83 calculated from Serfas 1987, p. 190. – (5) Taiwan Statistical Data Book 1988, p. 26 and 42. – (6) Taiwan Statistical Data Book 1988, p. 56. – (7) Taiwan Statistical Data Book 1988, p. 55. Differences to (6)/(5) are due to roundings. – (8) Taiwan Statistical Data Book 1988, p. 55.

1951, 1973-74 and 1978-80) and were relatively high in the 1960s.[69] The tax system, too, promoted savings[70]. To ease the collection of savings, a postal savings system with 1019 post offices and 505 postal agencies was installed.[71]

In Korea, the turning point came in 1965 only, when as a part of Park's financial reform the twelve-month deposit rate was increased from 15% to 30% in September 1965, and real interest rates on deposits were kept high for the following six years.[72] (Afterwards real interest fell and even became negative again). However, though relatively high, institutional interest rates were below the free market interest rates on the thriving non-institutional markets in both countries. There was therefore always an excess demand for institutional loans under the credit rationing schemes, with the well known danger of misallocation of resources on the one hand, but providing a powerful tool for economic policy, and structural policy in particular, on the other. It has been stated, therefore, that in neither Taiwan nor South Korea much attention has been paid to efficient resource allocation as opposed to resource mobilization.[73]

To make institutional loans even more attractive, an extensive system of loan subsidies was developed in both countries, e.g., priority sectors were getting cheaper loans in Taiwan, and heavily subsidized loans have been offered to exporters (Fry 1985, p. 289). In Korea, while the twelve months deposit rate was set at 30%, the general loan interest rate was set at 26% by the aforesaid financial reform of 1965. The negative spread was covered by subsidies to the commercial banks from the Bank of Korea. In Taiwan, too, loan rates have often been held below comparable deposit rates, the loss of commercial banks again being covered, though in a more indirect way, by the Central Bank.

If savings are set beside investment (see Table 11), it can be seen how both countries relied heavily on external sources of capital to finance investment in their initial stages of economic development; but in Taiwan, by rapidly increasing savings, the dependence on external sources of capital – mainly aid from the US – was reduced from an average of 40% during the 1950s to a mere 15% during the 1960s. From the 1970s onwards, savings on the average even surpassed investment, thus turning Taiwan into a net exporter of capital. (At the same time, Taiwan became holder of one of the biggest foreign currency reserves of the world.) There is no doubt, therefore, that Taiwan has become a self-supporting economy in less than twenty-five years.

In Korea, though impressive, the increase of savings could not keep pace with the even faster growth of investment, and the country thus remained dependent to a certain extent on external sources of capital for the financing of investment. Dependence, however, decreased considerably. Before 1963, when real growth was still very low, nearly 70% of investment was financed by external sources, mainly US aid. For the rest of the decade, the share of external sources fell continuously, and was below 40% in 1970. The dependence on foreign capital to finance investment continued to fall until a minimum of less than 5% was reached in 1977, but surged again afterwards as a consequence of the very ambitious investment program of the Fourth Five-Year Plan of the government and the following recession, enforced by the Second Oil Crisis (Menzel 1985, p. 142f).

The failure to match the increase in investments by an adequate increase in savings has in general been attributed to overambitious investment plans, and thus too much "forced" promotion of investment on the part of the government on the one hand, and on the other to a considerably lower rate of personal savings in Korea than in Taiwan, due to low or even negative real interest rates after 1972.[74]

Table 12

Net Direct Investment Flows 1977-1983

	As Shares of Gross Domestic Capital Formation in %	As Shares of Total Foreign Resource Inflows in %
Hong Kong	2.4	53.6
Singapore	8.1	67.1
Republic of Korea	0.2 (0.4)[a)]	3.2
Republic of Taiwan	0.7 (1.1)[a)]	28.4
Argentina	2.3	28.5
Brazil	2.5	23.1
Chile	2.6	15.4
Columbia	3.9	23.5
Mexico	1.6	13.5

a) As direct investment abroad is relatively important for Korea and Taiwan, the share of capital inflows in contrast to net flows is added in brackets. Figures were taken from Table 13.

Source: balance of payments figures, shares calculated from Göbel, Langhammer, Weiss 1988, Table 20 on p. 50.

The Role of Foreign Direct Investment. The importance of foreign direct investment flows can be measured in two ways: first, by examining such investment in relation to gross domestic capital formation, and second, in comparing these inflows with net total resource inflows from abroad (Table 12). On the average, the share of foreign direct investment in gross domestic capital formation was rather small in Korea and Taiwan, as for example compared with Singapore and

Table 13

Foreign Direct Investment (FDI) in the Republic of Korea and Taiwan

	KOREA				TAIWAN			
	FDI, realized, official figures	FDI, inflows, B.o.P. figures	FDI, realized, official figures as a share of investment	FDI, inflows, B.o.P. figures as a share of investment	FDI, approved by government a)	FDI, inflows, B.o.P. figures	FDI, approved by government as a share of investment[b)]	FDI, inflows, B.o.P. figures as a share of investment[b)]
	in US$ millions (1)	in US$ millions (2)	in % (3)	in % (4)	in US$ millions (5)	in US$ millions (6)	in % (7)	in % (8)
1952	n.a.	n.a.	n.a.	n.a.	1.1	n.a.	0.5	n.a.
1953	n.a.	n.a.	n.a.	n.a.	3.7	n.a.	1.6	n.a.
1954	n.a.	n.a.	n.a.	n.a.	2.2	n.a.	0.9	n.a.
1955	n.a.	n.a.	n.a.	n.a.	4.6	n.a.	1.8	n.a.
1956	n.a.	n.a.	n.a.	n.a.	3.5	4.6	1.6	2.1
1957	n.a.	n.a.	n.a.	n.a.	1.6	2.4	0.6	1.0
1958	n.a.	n.a.	n.a.	n.a.	2.5	11.7	1.1	5.4
1959	n.a.	n.a.	n.a.	n.a.	1.0	3.8	0.4	1.5
1960	n.a.	n.a.	n.a.	n.a.	15.5	5.8	4.9	1.8
1961	n.a.	n.a.	n.a.	n.a.	14.3	9.5	4.1	2.7
1962	0.6	n.a.	0.2	n.a.	5.2	9.0	1.5	2.6
1963	2.1	n.a.	0.3	n.a.	18.1	18.3	4.5	4.6
1964	3.1	n.a.	0.7	n.a.	19.9	15.6	4.1	3.5
1965	10.7	n.a.	2.4	n.a.	41.6	n.a.	6.4	n.a.
1966	5.0	n.a.	0.6	n.a.	29.3	n.a.	4.3	n.a.
1967	12.7	n.a.	1.2	n.a.	57.0	27.9	6.3	3.2
1968	14.7	n.a.	1.0	n.a.	89.9	27.9	8.4	2.6
1969	7.0	n.a.	0.3	n.a.	109.4	51.2	9.1	4.2

(continuing)

Table 13 (continued)

Foreign Direct Investment (FDI) in the Republic of Korea and Taiwan

	KOREA				TAIWAN			
	FDI, realized, official figures	FDI, inflows, B.o.P. figures	FDI, realized, official figures as a share of investment	FDI, inflows, B.o.P. figures as a share of investment	FDI, approved by government a)	FDI, inflows, B.o.P. figures	FDI, approved by government as a share of investment b)	FDI, inflows, B.o.P. figures as a share of investment b)
	in US$ millions (1)	in US$ millions (2)	in % (3)	in % (4)	in US$ millions (5)	in US$ millions (6)	in % (7)	in % (8)
1970	25.3	73.0	1.1	3.2	138.9	61.9	9.6	4.2
1971	36.7	42.1	1.5	1.7	163.0	52.6	9.4	3.0
1972	61.2	64.1	2.6	2.7	126.7	27.1	6.2	1.3
1973	158.4	95.1	4.5	2.7	248.9	61.6	8.0	2.0
1974	162.6	119.1	2.8	2.0	189.4	83.0	3.3	1.5
1975	69.2	57.1	1.2	1.0	118.2	34.0	2.5	0.7
1976	105.6	80.8	1.5	1.1	141.5	71.0	2.5	1.2
1977	102.3	93.4	1.0	1.0	163.9	51.7	2.7	0.8
1978	100.5	88.9	0.6	0.5	212.9	113.9	2.9	1.5
1979	126.0	36.2	0.5	0.1	328.8	126.3	3.1	1.2
1980	96.2	7.8	0.5	0.0	466.0	165.7	3.3	1.2

(continuing)

Table 13 (continued)

Foreign Direct Investment (FDI) in the Republic of Korea, and Taiwan

	KOREA				TAIWAN			
	FDI, realized, official figures	FDI, inflows, B.o.P. figures	FDI, realized, official figures as a share of investment	FDI, inflows, B.o.P. figures as a share of investment	FDI, approved by government a)	FDI, inflows, B.o.P. figures	FDI, approved by government as a share of investment b)	FDI, inflows, B.o.P. figures as a share of investment b)
	in US$ millions	in US$ millions	in %	in %	in US$ millions	in US$ millions	in %	in %
	(1)	(2)	(3)	(4)	(5)	(6)	(7)	(8)
Ø1950	n.a.	n.a.	n.a.	n.a.	2.5	5.6 c)	1.1	2.5 c)
Ø1960	7.0	n.a.	1.1	n.a.	40.0	20.7 c)	5.4	3.2 c)
Ø1970	94.8	75.0	1.6	1.6	183.2	68.3	5.0	1.7

a) Similar to the East European countries, the foreign direct investment projects approved by government are considerably higher than realizations, which are estimated to be 25-40% only. B.o.P. figures, on the other hand, do not take into consideration equity contributions, e.g. in form of machinery. – b) The conversion rate used is the official exchange rate; but as there was no uniform rate until 1961, calculations are somewhat arbitrary up to that year. Figures were calculated from Chang 1984, p. 345, resp. taken over from Menzel 1985, p. 225, and the Taiwan Statistical Data Book 1988, p. 199, for the years 1978-1980. – c) As far as figures were available.

Sources: (1) Menzel 1985, p. 74. – (2) IMF, Balance of Payments Yearbook, various issues, no comparable figures available before 1970. – (3) (1) Divided by gross capital formation, from IMF, Financial Statistics. – (4) (2) Divided by gross capital formation, from IMF, Financial Statistics. – (5) Taiwan Statistical Data Book 1988, p. 268. – (6) 1956-1964: IMF, Balance of Payments Yearbook, various issues (before 1956, no figures for foreign direct investment were available); 1967-1980: Taiwan Statistical Data Book, various issues, balance of payments. – (7) (5) Divided by gross capital formation from Taiwan Statistical Data Book 1988, p. 42. – (8) (6) Divided by gross capital formation from Taiwan Statistical Data Book 1988, p. 42.

Hong Kong, but also in comparison with the further advanced Latin American countries, as has been demonstrated by Göbel, Langhammer, Weiss 1988 for the period 1977-1983.[75]

However, foreign direct investment has been more important in Taiwan than in Korea. Korea's very low share of foreign direct investment in total resource flows is most striking. It stresses the fact that Korea has become much more dependent on foreign loans than Taiwan[76]; but also compared with other highly indebted countries like Mexico and Brazil, foreign direct investment is very low in Korea.

It has been stated, however, that, though relatively small, foreign direct investment has contributed significantly to the economic growth and efficiency of both Korea and Taiwan. The role direct investment played in Korea and Taiwan, different from that played in other developing countries, is even considered a very important reason why the former did not follow the pattern of "dependent development", as did so many other less successful developing countries.

The two main reasons given by Evans 1987 are, that foreign direct investment only came in to a considerable extent when the process of industrialization was already well under way; and that foreign direct investment was concentrated in manufacturing instead of extractive activities, agricultural or mineral (Evans 1987, p. 206 f.). Other reasons mentioned were the below average participation rate of foreign capital and the better infrastructure – including education, due largely to the enormous amounts of economic and military aid that was granted to both countries over a period of more than 15 years. Finally, government politics versus foreign direct investment played a special role.

Table 13 shows that foreign direct investment was negligible in Korea before 1965, and rose to a considerable volume at the beginning of the 1970s only. In Taiwan, the inflow of foreign capital began already in the 1950s, but increased remarkably after 1965. In both countries foreign direct investment thus became important several years after high real growth rates of close to 10% prevailed, and only after two digit growth rates of exports had become quite normal.[77] But foreign direct investment has, beyond doubt, helped to restructure the economy and exports from basic consumer goods, such as food, clothing, simple nondurable consumer goods, to electronics, durable consumer goods, and intermediate products, in providing technology as well as markets. This is indicated by the relatively high share of foreign direct investment in total investment at the beginning of the 1970s in both Korea and Taiwan by the US and Japan, these being the most important sources of foreign direct investment as well as the biggest export markets for both countries.[78] Of course, favorable external conditions as well as rapidly increasing labor costs in the industrialized countries and expanding world markets backed this development, as the decrease of foreign direct investment after the oil crisis in 1973 indicates. The remarkable fact is, however, that local acquisition of know-how, and forward and backward linkages at this stage were already advanced enough, so that the ongoing process of industrialization and economic development did not come to a halt.

Part of the acknowledged positive role of foreign investment in Korea and Taiwan has been attributed to the "strong" state:

Government Policies with Regard to Direct Investment. Though the Korean government has actively promoted a "liberal" image of its foreign investment regime, it has followed a rather restrictive policy in practice. Reviewing the Foreign Capital Inducement Law and its various enforcement decrees during the 1970s, one finds

> that considerations with respect to management control, the balance of payments, technology transfer and employment loom large in the screening process. We find also an emphasis on ensuring the complementarity between foreign direct investment and domestic firms in both export and domestic markets and on ensuring the compatibility of such investments with Korea's development plans. It also transpires, that Korea uses a "positive list system" with respect to foreign direct investment, according to which all sectors are closed to foreign investment unless otherwise specified (Luedde-Neurath 1984, p. 20).[79]

Korea has also been relatively strict in enforcing its policy vis-à-vis foreign investors, especially with respect to local participation.[80]

The government also reserves the right to review and, if need be, to demand changes in agreed contracts. Foreign firms also complain about the high degree of restrictions and interference while they are already operating.

Luedde-Neurath 1984 thus concludes, that Korea has not followed a liberal policy towards foreign direct investment, even if it must be admitted that some types of investment have been granted very generous incentives.

Following the principles of Sun Yat-Sen, foreign direct investment in Taiwan has basically been treated in a more liberal way and was promoted from the very beginning.[81] Since 1960 no special law governs foreign investment, but the "Statute of Encouragement of Investment" applies to domestic as well as foreign investors. By this step foreign direct investment was fused into the government's overall policy of investment incentives.[82] By this statute, export industries were especially promoted, and so was foreign direct investment in the export industries as well. Foreign direct investment in export industries was further promoted by the establishment of Export Processing Zones (EPZ), where imports necessary for exports could be imported tax free.[83] Foreign direct investment, which had been restricted to the manufacturing sector in the beginning, was now also allowed in other sectors (e.g. agriculture, catering and tourism, construction etc.), and in the following years the number of closed sectors kept on shrinking.[84] Yet foreign direct investment needed approval from the Ministry of Economic Affairs, and the screening procedure, as in Korea, took into account national economic requirements (see Gälli 1988, p. 125).

Remittances of profits, royalties, interest, and dividends were in the case of Taiwan treated very generously, due to the favorable development of the balance of payments.

To conclude, both governments, though by different measures, have successfully tried to make foreign direct investment an integral part of their overall economic development programs.

5. Summary and Conclusions

So far, the East European countries battling with the change-over from a centrally planned to a market-driven economy essentially follow classical economic lines and are encouraged by Western experts to do so: free prices, remove subsidies, open your economies to international trade, make your currencies freely convertible, privatize the state-owned companies, invite foreign investment!

However, the East European countries should perhaps not only look to the West, but to Asia as well: because superimposed on their problem of transition is the problem of backwardness in relation to the Western industrialized countries, and as shown in this paper, the path taken by, e.g., Korea and Taiwan, which has most recently enabled them successfully to navigate the course from economic backwardness to world class competitors, differs substantially from that now urged on the East European countries.

Most interesting for the East European countries therefore, Korea and Taiwan present examples of an economic system, different from a pure market economy, that proved very successful in catching up with the advanced industrialized countries. Moreover, the East European countries could learn from the experience of these countries with privatization and the creation of a new entrepreneurial class, as well as of implementation of foreign aid during their first years of economic development. Though certain differences exist between the economic systems of Korea and Taiwan, both are examples of a kind of "mixed economy", but quite different from a social market economy or a welfare state of the Western type. Basically capitalistic, the special features of this system include a strong state, committed to economic growth and development; economic thinking is very much future oriented, which, inter alia, finds its expression in perennial economic plans or rather, economic programs of the government. Extensive use is made of subsidies and other financial and non-financial incentives to implement economic programs, but without putting the market mechanism itself into question. In drawing up the economic programs, frequent consultations and cooperation with the businessmen concerned take place. All told, the rather close relation between government and private business sector is another important characteristic of their economic system. Public enterprises, too, play an important role. The working of the system in general is highly dependent on a well trained and a well functioning bureaucracy.

Although, due to cultural, historical, and above all political differences, the East European countries cannot be expected to copy the economic system outlined above, they could nevertheless take useful hints and draw certain conclusions with regard to their economic policy.

Probably the "pure" market economy approach is a feasible, but not the quickest way to achieve their goals – perhaps they should take a more pragmatic stand in economic policy. After years of disastrous economic planning, the East European countries understandably will eschew all forms of central planning, including Asia's market-directed indicative type; but they might well be hampering their development by the complete absence of future-orientation in economic policy. Economic programs of the right kind, as shown by the example of Korea and Taiwan, serving as a framework for short-term economic policy and as a guideline for long term planning of the private sector, will reduce uncertainty and thus increase the rate of time preference, i.e. the readiness to give up present for future benefits, which is most important for an increase of savings and investments, the cornerstones of capitalistic development.

It is also interesting to see, how in those days US experts were much in favor of economic planning: the Second Five-Year Plan in Korea (1967-1971), for instance, was drawn up with considerable help from experts from the American Agency for International Development, and foreign experts also assisted substantially in the Third Plan; besides, many members of the Economic Planning Board were trained in the US. Obviously, there has been a general shift in the "philosophy" of planning since then. But even in the absence of any kind of longer term economic program, frequent consultation and close cooperation between the bureaucracy and the business sector, as demonstrated in Korea and Taiwan, could be expected to improve efficiency and facilitate implementation of economic policy in the East European countries as well. The "missing link", however, could be a sufficiently qualified bureaucracy.

Certainly, the Confucian tradition, which has obviously been conducive to a qualified and responsible bureaucracy in Korea and Taiwan, cannot be taken over; but the East European countries could perhaps follow the example of the merit based selection system and strict screening procedures, to select from their oversized bureaucracy those, who are really qualified.

As regards subsidies and other financial and non-financial incentives in Korea and Taiwan, they were applied above all in those fields considered of crucial importance for economic growth, as investment(savings) and foreign trade. If looking at the extremely high actual rates of growth of investment(savings) and exports in both countries, there is good reason to suppose that government incentives helped indeed to speed up economic development and growth. As this is very important to note for the East European countries, who are so eager to abolish all kinds of subsidies, the theme deserves more attention.

With regard to foreign trade, both countries, after an initial phase of mere import substitution, from the early 1960s onwards, have followed export oriented growth strategies and have proved very successful indeed. Though international conditions were very favorable, they tried to speed up export by an extensive export promotion scheme. Attention must be paid to the fact, however, that basically, subsidies did not discriminate between different kinds of exports, and thus the structure of exports was determined by the international markets. In order to stimulate the formation of forward and backward linkages between the thriving export sector and the rest of the economy, Korea and Taiwan maintained a large range of import controls for more than 15 years; after this period, they had already become internationally competitive in a broad range of products, including capital goods. The combination of export promotion and import control has in fact proved quite useful in avoiding the danger of continuous inefficiency as a consequence of persistent protection: In order to gain the benefits from export promotion, producers will try to export part of their production as soon as possible. Thus they will deliberately expose their products to international competition, and so reduce the need for protection.

However, in Eastern Europe the need for protection of certain industries could not be derived from the infant industry argument proper: Many industries are mature already, but are not yet internationally competitive, due to the prevailing socialist system. They should therefore be named "infant export industries" rather, and as such they might well be worth being protected for a certain period of time to get a chance to prepare themselves – under new conditions – for the world market. But this kind of protection should be acceptable to the outside world.

It might be of interest to the East European countries, that neither Korea nor Taiwan used undervaluation of their currencies as a means to promote exports: on the contrary, under the given system of import controls, their currencies were rather overvalued. As such a policy will bring down prices for imports relative to exports, it could prove useful to the East European countries as well, if the import content of their exports is high, and if exporters are compensated for their loss in international (price) competitiveness due to the hard-currency policy by other export promoting measures.

As mentioned above, besides export promotion the promotion of investments and savings played an important role in Korea and Taiwan. In both countries the institutional interest rates were set by the government, as banks were either public or under government control. Besides a positive rate of real interest, various tax incentives and measures to facilitate the collection of savings were introduced, special emphasis being laid on the promotion of savings from low income groups. Hence Korea and Taiwan did not rely on market forces only to collect savings necessary for rapid economic growth. To compensate for the negative effect of high real rates of interest on investment, extensive interest subsidies, besides other measures, were applied in both countries. All this seems quite interesting to note for the East European countries ready to prepare for economic growth in a liberal market economy.

Furthermore, when looking at the late 1970s, the danger of a widening gap between domestic savings and investment is clearly demonstrated to the East European countries by the example of Korea as compared with Taiwan: there, from the 1970s onwards, savings on the average surpassed investment; Taiwan had thus become a self-supporting economy. In Korea, though impressive, the increase in savings could not keep pace with the even faster growth of investments; Korea thus remained dependent on foreign capital. Beside her increasing trade deficit, this was an important reason for the dramatic increase of foreign debt in the late 1970s, which made Korea one of the most highly indebted countries in the world. (The failure to match the increase in investments by an adequate increase in savings has been attributed to the overambitious investment programs of the government on the one side, and a considerably lower rate of personal savings in Korea than in Taiwan, due to low or even negative interest rates after 1972, on the other.)

On the average, the share of foreign direct investment in capital formation, though considerably higher in Taiwan than in Korea, was rather small in both countries, as for example compared to Singapore and Hong Kong, but also in comparison with the further advanced Latin American countries. It is generally agreed, however, that foreign direct investment contributed significantly to their economic growth and development. The examples of Taiwan and Korea therefore show to the East European countries, that, though relatively small, foreign direct investment may have an entirely positive effect on the economy as a whole, if concentrated in the "right" branches, and if in harmony with the overall economic development of the host country. With regard to the latter, in both countries foreign direct investment was regulated to a certain extent, but to include foreign direct investment in the overall investment promotion scheme, as in Taiwan, seems superior to the more direct approach of regulating foreign direct investment in Korea.

As indicated above, the East Eurorropean countries could also learn from the experiences of Korea and Taiwan with privatization and the formation of a new entrepreneurial class:

As long as Korea and Taiwan were Japanese colonies, 80 to 90 percent of industrial capital was in Japanese hands. After independence in 1945, the Japanese had to leave. Their property was nationalized and afterwards privatized again. But very similar to the situation in Eastern Europe now, virtually no indigenous class of industrial entrepreneurs did exist. In both countries therefore, privatization of industrial property was connected with an extensive land reform: assets in land were partly exchanged for assets in industrial property. Though under different conditions, certain similarities can be found to the ongoing "voucher experiments" in Eastern Europe. It is thus interesting to see, that in both Korea and Taiwan the secondary market played an important role in the final allocation of industrial property: only very few landowners became industrialists directly, and others, among them technical or managerial employees of former Japanese companies, and mainland refugees (in Taiwan), who had already some industrial experience, took the opportunity to acquire industrial property, often at very low prices, on the secondary market. In both countries it took more than 10 years to reach the desired level of privatization, and thus there was enough time for a new entrepreneurial class to develop – something the governments in Eastern Europe, who want to privatize as fast as possible, should also bear in mind. To note further, though the level of (re)privatization aimed at was quite different between Korea and Taiwan at first, a certain convergence took place after some time: While still somewhat higher in the industry as a whole in Taiwan, the public share in the manufacturing sector found its level at 15% in both countries. While the Korean government was actively increasing the already lower share of public enterprises by founding new ones to foster industrial development, the dynamic private sector in Taiwan simply "outgrew" the public sector up to a certain level. From this, though with great caution, one might draw the conlusion, that perhaps a public share of approximately 15% in manufacturing industry is the level most suitable for a fast growing capitalist economy where private capital and entrepreneurship are yet relatively scarce.

Foreign aid is another field, where Korea and Taiwan have gained experience that could be useful to the East European countries to a certain extent.

Aid given to Taiwan and Korea came mainly from US sources. After Israel, they have received the highest amounts of US aid ever given to a developing country. Behind this stood the strategic interest of the US "to create a bulwark against communism", against North Korea on the one hand and mainland China on the other. Therefore, the first lesson for the East European countries is this: that the strategic interest of the donor is indeed a very good stimulus for granting aid. On the other side this will mean to them, that, if the strategic interest is not very strong, the readiness to help in concrete terms will not be strong either – and this is perhaps the situation most East European countries are facing now. Another lesson to be learned is, that given a certain amount of aid, the way it is managed will play a crucial role: Korea, receiving a much higher amount of aid in absolute terms as well as in per capita terms or as a share of GNP, was obviously less successful in using it. Besides political favoritism, the main reason was, that aid was channeled into non-productive activities, such as commerce first, which is a real danger for the East European countries too. Taiwan, on the other hand, can be considered another successful example for implementing aid according to the principle of a "Marshall Plan." By establishing counterpart funds, aid is multiplied and channeled into productive activities, but can nevertheless be controlled to avoid surplus demand exerting inflationary pressure, which is also important for most East European countries.

Though difficult to quantify, the impact of aid on the economic development of both Korea and Taiwan is considered substantial. The main impact of economic aid was to reduce severe shortages of consumer goods, and inputs necessary for production, to supply the economy with foreign currency for necessary imports, to finance large parts of government expenditures, e.g., for improving the infrastructure (including education) and to launch the process of capital accumulation. It should be noted, however, that besides technical and economic assistance, aid was given in kind rather than money, and money was given in the form of grants mainly; thus they were free from the burden of repayments of debt and interest payments. This contrasts sharply with the high share of loans in Western aid for the East European countries. But this is a point the donors of aid should bear in mind as well as the recipients.

To conclude, I would like to quote from an article by Stanley Katz, who was vice-president of the Asian Development Bank from 1978 to 1990 and became consultant to the European Bank for Reconstruction and Development later on:

> Many cultural, political and social differences seperate east Europe from east Asia, and comparisons should not be pushed too far. But in terms of how to go about transforming a backward economy into an efficient, competitive one, there is much common ground and many lessons to be shared.[85]

Notes

1. In this paper the Republic of Korea is usually referred to as South Korea or simply called Korea. The term "Newly Industrializing Countries" (NICs) has been replaced some time ago by the term "Newly Industrializing Economies" (NIEs) in official OECD language, to avoid difficulties regarding the political status of Taiwan and Hong Kong respectively.

2. Already at the Tokio meeting of the "trilateral committee" (Japan, Europe, USA) in April 1988, Singapore and South Korea were asked to become members of the OECD. On January 24/25, 1989 a first (informal) meeting between representatives of the OECD and the "four little tigers" took place. See Urban 1990, p.413.

3. "Few would have held 'great expectations' for Taiwan, given such a grim beginning" (Chan et al. 1990, p. 112).

4. According to Rostow (1960), "take-off" represents the point at which the "old blocks and the resistance to steady growth are finally overcome" and growth becomes the normal condition of the economy. The economy begins to generate its own investment and technological improvement at sufficiently high rates so as to make growth virtually self-sustaining (quoted after G. Bannoch, *The Penguin Dictionary of Economics*, 2nd ed. 1978, p. 146). The East European countries rather seem to represent a case of suspended development.

5. Myrdal uses the term "strong state" as an antonym to "soft state" (Myrdal 1968, p. 898). He defines a "soft state" as a country where "policies decided on are often not enforced, if they are enacted at all... (and where) the authorities, even when framing policies, are reluctant to place obligations on people. In contrast, he implicitly defines a 'hard state' in arguing that "the success of planning for development requires a readiness to place obligations on people in all social strata to a much greater extent than is now done ... (and it) ... requires, in addition, rigorous enforcement of obligations, in which compulsion plays a strategic role." (Myrdal 1968, pp. 66 und 67, quoted after Jones, Sakong 1980, p. 133).

6. After successful economic modernization, Korea has just recently begun to take the road of political modernization, whereas in Hungary the trends of changing the economic model and transforming the political system simultaneously, parallel with changing the course of economic growth and reallocating economic policy targets, are developing on an ever larger scale (Kim et al. 1990, p. vii).

7. Taiwan was transferred to Japan as a consequence of the first Sino-Japanese War of 1894/95. Korea, although under Japanese protectorate, remained independent, but in the following war between Russia and Japan 1904-1905, Russia accepted Japanese rule in Korea, and in 1910 the last Korean emperor abdicated.

8. Especially Korean workers were also employed in other, further advanced parts of the Japanese empire, as Manchuria, or Japan itself.

9. Though a poor agricultural society, Taiwan's living standards were nevertheless higher than in mainland China when the take-over took place in 1945 (Menzel 1985, p. 158). Mainlanders were accused of exploiting the province after its return.

10. On September 9, 1948 the proclamation of the Peoples Republic of Korea in the North followed suit.

11. See *Sun's Lecture Two on the Principle of Livelihood*, (Sun Yat-Sen, translated by Price 1927, p. 180 f). Sun also recommended a protective tariff policy, to give local industry a chance to develop, referring to the successful examples of the US and Germany in protecting their nascent industries from overwhelming British competition (Sun Yat-Sen, *Lecture Four, op. cit.*, p. 209).

12. These materials were: silk, flax, cotton, wool. Sun himself mentioned 7 methods of increasing agricultural production: use of machinery, use of fertilizers, rotation of crops, eradication of pests, manufacturing, transportation, prevention of natural disasters (Sun Yat-Sen, translation by Price 1927, p. 188).

13. "In human life, economics precedes politics or culture." "In other words, the Asian peoples want to obtain economic equality first and build a more equitable political machinery afterward ... the gem without luster called democracy was meaningless to people suffering from starvation and despair." Park 1970, p. 26 and 1970a, p. 39-40, quoted after Jones, Sakong 1980, p. 43.

14. Transportation, communications, finance and insurance, electricity, water utilization, water works, gas. Jones, Sakong 1980, p. 145.

15. Estimated after Jones, Sakong 1980, p. 149, Table 24.

16. "Private ownership of production should be unconditionally encouraged except in instances where it is necessary to control it to stimulate national development and protect the interests of the people." Park 1970a, p. 218. This has been translated into the 1972 change of the constitution – there Article 116 reads as follows:

> The economic order of the Republic of Korea shall be based on the principle of respect for freedom and creative ideas of the individual in economic affairs. The state shall regulate and coordinate economic affairs within the limits necessary for the realization of social adjustment and for the development of a balanced national economy to fulfill the basic living requirements of all citizens. (Quoted after Jones, Sakong 1980, p. 147).

17. According to this outlook, real GDP per capita is expected to grow at an average of 6.5% (inflation 3.5%) and thus by the Year 2000 per capita income should have reached US$ 13,400 (see Gälli 1988, p. 141).

18. The American Agency for International Development (AID) mission did not hesitate to use its big gun – the threat to withhold aid – when conflict with the government in Taiwan arose.

19. The first plan was drawn up in the framework of the United Nations Korea Reconstruction Agency (UNKRA) in 1954. In 1958, Rhee established the Economic Development Council to draft a plan for the period 1960-1962. It was never implemented because of the overthrow of the Rhee regime in 1960.

20. See Adelman (ed.) 1969.

21. See Gupta, Padula 1977.

22. "It is always open to the doubters to say, echoing Jacques Rueff on French planning, that the policies contributed no more to Taiwan's industrialization than the cock's crow contributes to the dawn" (Wade 1984, p. 70).

23. A frequently used "in-between" measure is "partial mutuality": a desired behavior of the businessman is attained by the threat of witholding a certain privilege or enforcing a certain duty more strictly, for instance, by a rigorous tax audit (see Jones, Sakong 1980, p. 135).

24. The anti-public-ownership ideological bias makes the government less tolerant of public enterprise abuses. There have been numerous cases of divestiture, and though no public enterprise has been actually allowed to die, it has been seriously considered and the threat alone proved effective (see Jones, Sakong 1980, p. 163).

25. In Korea, for instance, the traditional elite of the Yi dynasty (1392-1910) was the "Yangban", holding its status "by virtue of having passed the civil service examinations" (Michell 1984, p. 32). Civil service examinations are still an important screening procedure for government officials at different levels.

26. "It is the Assistant Director (grade 4) who makes most of the day to day decisions in the government. It is openly acknowledged that it is the assistant director who 'really decides policy'. There were about 4200 grade 4 officials in central government in 1974" (Michell 1984, p. 35).

27. Except during the Rhee period in Korea and the first years of National Government in Taiwan.

28. To give an interesting example: only recently an ambitious research project between the International Institute for Applied Systems Analysis in Laxenburg/Austria and the University of Mauritius with the financial support of the United Nations Population Fund has been started on "Population and Sustainable Development", which should provide the basis for scientists as well as politicians for a better understanding of development options for the island of Mauritius (Lutz, Toth 1991).

29. Nationalism coming to the surface after years of suppression did support economic development in Taiwan and Korea ("economic nationalism"). Due to the ethnic heterogeneity of the East European Countries, nationalism so far has only been destructive from the economic perspective, and there is little hope that this could be changed.

30. Hungary was the first East European country to take up diplomatic relations with the Republic of Korea on Februar 11, 1989. But already since 1985 several formal and informal contacts took place, and in 1988 the First Korean-Hungarian Round Table Conference in Budapest was held, followed by a second conference in Seoul, both with the participation of businessman, economists, and political scientists on both sides (Urban 1990, p. 417).

31. In Korea, land owned by the state was sold, too. In Taiwan 7 percent of arable land, used for sugar plantations mainly, and 80 percent of the forests remained with the state.

32. According to Hamilton 1984, p. 39, landlords received compensation to around 15%-20% of their former land assets.

33. 19 percent were merchants, 16 percent factory owners, 6 percent civil servants, 4 percent teachers, and 7 percent professionals.

34. The "Oriental Brewery" beer company was taken over by a Korean minority share holder in the parent Japanese Kirin company; a technician in a Japanese textile firm became acting manager under the Americans, later bought the plant and built it into the Sunkyung Group; a similar sequence was followed by the only Korean employee of a Japanese explosives firm, and it grew into today's Korea Explosives (Jones, Sakong 1980, p. 36).

35. Korean source, quoted after Jones, Sakong 1980, p. 36 and foot-note 49 on p. 397. How the "government estimated price" was determined, is not explained.

36. United Nations Command, "Office of the Economic Coordinator, Fiscal Year 1955, Congressional Presentation" Seoul, March 1954.

37. In Korea, after being divested first, banks were renationalized or came under government control again during the Park regime (Menzel 1985, p. 97).

38. "The million or so refugees who fled to Taiwan made up a good portion of China's capitalists, managers, professionals, and dispossessed landlords" (Hamilton 1983, p. 43).

39. Between 1962 and 1982, average annual growth rates of agricultural production amounted to 3.0 percent in Taiwan and 3.8 percent in Korea. According to the World Bank, average growth rates in agricultural production in "low income developing countries" was slightly less than three percent, and slightly above 3 percent for "middle income developing countries" for the same period. (Between 1952 and 1962, growth rates were considerably higher in Taiwan, namly 4.8 percent; unfortunately no figures were available for Korea before 1962.)

40. Calculated for Taiwan from Menzel 1985, Tables 36, 38, and 65, and for Korea from Menzel 1985, Tables 10, 11, and 20.

41. Chang 1984, p. 155. According to this source, statistical data on military support have not been published officially, but have been collected from "US Overseas Loans and Grants and Assistance, International Organization, Obligations and Loan Authorization", July 1, 1945 – June 30, 1967, *Special Report prepared for the House Foreign Affairs Committee*, p. 63.

42. Menzel 1985, p. 57.

43. See Westphal et al. 1981, p. 10f.

44. "For the larger part of the 1950s and early 1960s fully one half of Korean government revenue came from the USA" (Hamilton 1983, p. 53). 1961 to 1965 transfers from abroad contributed 1/3 to the government revenue – but fell below 10 percent from 1969 onwards; see Menzel 1985, p. 94, Table 17.

45. "The relationship with the United States nonetheless served to augment Korean resources, both directly and indirectly. By far the most important effect appears to have been on the formation of human capital." (Westphal et al. 1981, p. 10, referring to Krueger 1979 and Mason et al. 1980, Ch. 10: Education).

46. "Kyong-Dong Kim has analyzed the development of the chaebol in the 1950s as a process of political favoritism allowing windfall profits on commercial deals connected to foreign aid" (Hamilton 1984, p. 40).

47. In 1938-1940, 20% of total production was exported, 77% of which went to Japan (Kim, Roemer 1981, p. 12, quoted after Serfas 1987, Table 4, p. 19).

48. Up to the beginning of the 1930s, the system of complementary international division of labor, whereunder the developing countries were exporting mainly agrarian goods and raw materials, and the industrialized nations predominantly processed products, was considered advantageous to both sides. However, the world economic crisis initiated a phase of steady change in the world's export structure to the disadvantage of the DCs. This resulted in, int.al., growth-, employment-, and balance-of-payments problems that led to universal rethinking on matters of development policy. Some DCs tried to escape from the handicap of their specialization on primary products by switching to the road of industrialization; import substitution was the guide-mark (see Stecher 1976, p. 1f.).

49. Though empirical evidence to justify the abrupt change-of-mind is still wanting. Even latest extensive empirical studies of the process of industrialization in selected DCs undertaken in the context of an OECD project under the direction of Little, Scitovski, and Scott (1970) cannot satisfactorily settle the so called strategy controversy.

50. Not only did Rhee want to maximize US aid in dollar terms by keeping an overvalued currency, he had also deep resentments against taking up trade links with Japan, the former colonial power.

51. For the empirical relationship between export performance and growth of exports, see e.g. Michaely 1977; Balassa 1978; and Krueger 1978. For the possible reasons see Fransman 1984, who gave a short overview of the neoclassical position (e.g. Little 1982, Balassa 1982); further, the outcome of a conference on the advanced developing countries in the Pacific Basin, the proceedings of which were published in Hong and Krause 1981.

52. In 1950, Taiwan had left Gatt, and tariffs were raised to double and more the level agreed by Gatt.

53. International Cooperation Administration (ICA) and Korean Foreign Exchange (KFX) auctions yielded prices between the free market and official rates, as ICA and KFX dollars were restricted in use, and auctions suffered from certain irregularities (e.g. collusion among bidders). Thus a multiple exchange rate system was established. See Jones, Sakong 1980, p. 87 and Tables 12 and 13 on pp. 88 and 90.

54. Part of the devaluation was only adjustment for the high rate of inflation. Measured by the wholesale price index, inflation in Korea amounted to 10.2% in 1955-1960, 17.2% in 1960-1965, 7.9% in 1965-70 and 18.9% 1970-1975 (source: Westphal 1978, Table 1, p. 349).

55. A noticeable devaluation, and tax rebates on exports were already launched in 1955, when exports suddenly fell from US$ 128.6 mn to US$ 95.9 mn.

56. In August 1959, to comply with the regulations of the IMF, the Bank of Taiwan discontinued the practice of separating the effective exchange rate into the two components of basic rate and the price of exchange certificate (Tsiang 1985, p. 37).

57. For the following, see e.g. Westphal 1978, p. 351, Jones, Sakong 1980, p. 94 f. for Korea, and Chang 1984, p. 164 f., Menzel 1985, p. 225 f. for Taiwan.

58. In Taiwan, instead of tax exemptions, a pay-back system was installed.

59. One extreme example is "Export Day" in Korea: "November 30 is "Export Day" and the highest ranking exporters are, with great fanfare, awarded "industrial merit medals" of gold, silver and bronze pagoda rank." (Jones, Sakong 1980, p. 98). Export Day was established on November 30, 1964, when Korea celebrated the first 100 million dollar export mark in its history.

60. Finally, strong diplomatic efforts on various levels, bilateral trade treaties, as well as very active attachés, who actually performed marketing functions in the early years, gave additional support to exporters.

61. See Fajnzylber 1981, p. 20.

62. Serfas 1987, S 129.

63. The purpose was "to capture the windfall profits that would otherwise accrue to importers receiving import licenses for restricted items" (Jones, Sakong 1980, p. 91).

64. The 1968 tariff law provided "that under certain conditions, emergency duties, countervailing duties, and so called beneficial duties could be levied. A further increase in flexibility was introduced by the 1973 tariff reform that allowed the government to adjust the tariff rates within 100% of the legal rate; the government would also change statutory rates by as much as 50% by administrative decree (Jones, Sakong 1980, p. 91).

65. Nominal protection = percentage excess of the domestic over the world market price, with the latter converted into its domestic currency equivalent at the prevailing exchange rate.

66. See Göbel, Langhammer, Weiss 1988, p. 34. Other factors, considered important as well, are: technical progress and the use of appropriate technology respectively, the formation of human capital, and a sound framework of economic policy.

67. Considerably higher shares were achieved by, e.g., Norway (29.2%), Austria (26.3%), Finland (25.9%), Switzerland (26.0%), Portugal (25.5%), and the Federal Republic of Germany (23.4%). The highest share, of course, was realized in Japan (32.3%) (OECD, *Historical statistics, 1960-1962*, Paris 1984, p.65). In the further advanced Latin American countries, Argentina, Brazil, Chile, Columbia, and Mexico the average share of investment in GDP was 22.2% in the period 1960-1970, 23.6% from 1970-1975, and 24.9% from 1975-1980 (see Göbel, Langhammer, Weiss 1988, p. 44).

68. Tsiang 1985, p. 44. "This surprising quick result happened before the propitious turn of fortune in favor of Taiwan – the resumption of U.S. aid soon after the outbreak of the Korean War on June 27, 1950." (ibidem p.44, 45).

69. Fry 1985, p. 289.

70. E.g. by exempting the interest income from savings and time deposits with maturity terms of two and more years from personal income tax. (Tsiang 1985, p.47).

71. To promote especially longer term savings, the term structure of deposit rates was rather steep in both Korea and Taiwan. In Korea, a special fiscal subsidy is provided for savings of low income workers.

72. Fry 1985, p. 290. Between 1966 and 1971 the real deposit rate of interest averaged about 7.5%, ibidem p. 292.

73. "Hence, the high growth rates ... were the result of considerably higher than average investment rates rather than greater average investment efficiency. Indeed, when investment efficiency was calculated using incremental output/capital ratios as a proxy, the average for Singapore, Taiwan, and South Korea was no better than that for the middle-income developing countries in general" (Fry 1985, p. 317).

74. In the period 1965-1981, the personal savings rates of households (private savings/GNP) was 5.4% in Korea, and 12.1% in Taiwan. The average propensity to consume (private savings/disposable income) was 7.6% in Korea and 17.6% in Taiwan (Scitovsky 1986, pp. 169 and 170).

75. Inter-country comparisons of this kind are of course greatly hampered by limitations in statistics, including differences in coverage and data collections.

76. Taking into account, that total foreign resource inflows in Taiwan were very low due to high domestic savings, the high percentage of foreign direct investment is somewhat misleading as an indicator for its importance.

77. As mentioned above, Japanese investments were confiscated at the end of World War II and did not reappear as an important force until the mid-sixties. The fear of the Japanese dominating the economy again was perhaps the main reason why Korea held a strong attitude against foreign direct investment until the "Normalization Treaty" with Japan in 1965. One year later, a new "Foreign Capital Inducement Law" was issued. Taiwan, following the principles of Sun-Yat-Sen, was from the very beginning in favor of foreign direct investment as a catalyst for economic development, but at first could only attract investments mainly from "Overseas Chinese".

78. In both Korea and Taiwan, electronics (including electrical machinery) and chemicals stand out as major areas of foreign direct investment.

79. A survey by the UN Center on Transnational Cooperations in 1978 on investment regulations in various countries indicates too, that by international standards Korea's legislation towards foreign direct investment does not stand out as particularly liberal (UN 1978, according to Luedde-Neurath 1984, p. 2).

80. In a comparative survey of 187 US multinationals in 66 countries, of those in Korea (as of January 1976), only 29.7% took the form of wholly owned subsidiaries, compared with an average ratio for all countries of 69.1% (Curham, Davidson, Suri 1977, according to Luedde-Neurath 1984, p. 21).

81. E.g. Statute for Investment by Overseas Chinese (1952), and Statute for Investment by Foreign Nationals (1955), Gälli 1988, p. 125; Chang 1984, p. 173.

82. After undergoing several modifications this statute is still valid.

83. The first Export Processing Zone of the world was established in 1966 at Kaoshiung, followed by Nantze and Taichung 1969.

84. In 1990 the "negative list" still comprised government monopolies, public utilities, some strategic industries, and some light manufacturing sectors where local capital is strong, and where there is no great incentive for foreign investors to enter, anyway (OECD 1991, p. 65).

85. S. Katz, "East Europe Should Learn from Asia," *Financial Times*, April 24, 1991.

References

Adelmann, Irma (ed.) (1969), *Practical Approaches to Development Planning: Korea's Second Five-Year Plan*, Baltimore, Johns Hopkins.

Balassa, Bela (ed.) (1982), Development Strategies in Semi-industrial Economies, Baltimore.

Balassa, Bela (1978), "Exports and Economic Growth: Further Evidence," *Journal of Development Economics*, June.

Blumenthal, Tuvia and Lee, Chung, H. (1985), "Development Strategies of Japan and the Republic of Korea: a Comparative Study," *The Developing Economics*, XXIII-3, September.

Brown, Gilbert T. (1973), *Korean Pricing Policies and Economic Development in the 1960s*, Baltimore.

Chan, Steve, Clark, Cal, Davies, David R. (1990), "State Entrepreneurship, Foreign Investment, Export Expansion, and Economic Growth, in: *Journal of Conflict Resolution*, Vol. 34, No. 1, March.

Chang, Sai (1984), *Von der traditionellen Gesellschaft zum Take-off – die Wirtschaftsentwicklung Taiwans*. Saarbrücken/Fort Lauderdale.

Corbo, Vittorio, Krueger Anne O., Ossa, Fernando (eds.) (1985), *Export-Oriented Development Strategies. The Success of Five Newly Industrializing Countries*, Boulder and London.

Corbo, Vittorio, Ossa, Fernando (1985), "Small Open Economies: The Main Issues," in: *Export-Oriented Development Strategies. The Success of Five Newly Industrializing Countries*, Corbo, Krueger, Ossa.

Curhan, J.P., Davidson, W.H., Suri, R. (1977), *Tracing the Multinationals: a Sourcebook on US-based Enterprises*, Cambridge (Mass.).

Evans, Peter B. (1979), *Dependent Development: The Alliance of Multinational State and Local Capital in Brazil*, Princeton, N.J.

Evans, Peter (1987), "Class, State, and Dependence in East Asia: Lessons for Latin Americanists," in: Deyo, Frederic, C. (ed.), *The Political Economy of the New Asian Industrialism*, Ithaca and London.

Fajnzylber, Fernando (1981), "Some Reflections on South-East Asian Export Industrialization," *CEPAL Review*, No. 15, December.

Frank, Charles R., Jr., Kim, Kwang Suk, Westphal, Larry E. (1975), *Foreign Trade Regimes and Economic Development: South Korea*, National Bureau of Economic Research, New York.

Fransman, Martin (1984), "Explaining the Success of the Asian NICs: Incentives and Technology," *IDS Bulletin*, Vol. 15, pp. 50-56.

Fry, Maxwell J. (1985), "Financial Structure, Monetary Policy and Economic Growth in Hong Kong, Singapore, Taiwan and South Korea," 1960-1983, in: *Export-Oriented Development Strategies. The Success of Five Newly Industrializing Countries*, Corbo, Krueger, Ossa, pp. 275-324.

Gabrisch, Hubert, Laski, Kazimierz (1990), "Transition from the Command to Market Economy," *WIIW-Forschungsberichte* No. 163, Vienna, May.

Gälli, Anton, Taiwan, R.O.C. (1988), "Eine chinesische Herausforderung. Von der Handelsmacht zum Technologiezentrum," *IFO Studien zur Entwicklungsforschung*, Special Series: *Informationen und Dokumentation VI*, Munich/Cologne/London.

Galtung, John (1971), "A Structural Theory of Imperialism", *Journal of Peace Research* 13, p. 81-118.

Göbel, Heike, Langhammer Rolf J., Weiss Frank D. (1988), "Wachstum im asiatisch-pazifischen Raum. Implikationen für die internationale Arbeitsteilung," *Kieler Studien 222*, Tübingen.

Gupta, Sen, Padula, Ron (1977), "Alternative Development Strategies of Korea (1976-1990) in an Input-Output Dynamic Simulation Model," *World Bank*, Washington D.C.

Hamilton, Clive (1983), "Capitalist Industrialization in East Asia's Four Little Tigers." *Journal of Contemporary Asia*, Vol. 13.

Hamilton, Clive, Class (1984), "State and Industrialization in South Korea," *IDS Bulletin*, Vol. 15, No. 2.

Hong, Wontack (1979), "Trade Distortions and Employment Growth in Korea," *Korea Development Institute*, Seoul.

Hong, W., Krause, L.B. (eds.) (1981), *Trade and Growth of the Advanced Developing Countries in the Pacific Basin*. Papers and Proceedings of the Eleventh Pacific Trade and Development Conference, Korea Development Institute, Seoul.

Jacoby, Neil, H. (1966), *U.S. Aid to Taiwan. A Study of Foreign Aid, Self Help and Development*, New York.

Jones, Leroy P., Sakong, Il. (1980), *Government, Business, and Entrepreneurship in Economic Development: The Korean Case*, Harvard.

Kim, Dalchoong, Kádár, Béla, Jung, Ku-Hyun, Hámori, Jenö (1990), "Economic Cooperation Between Korea and Hungary." *East and West Studies* Series 10, Institute of East and West Studies, Yonsei University, Seoul.

Kim, Kwang Suk and Roemer, M. (1979), *Growth and Structural Transformation*, Council on East Asian Studies, Harvard University, Cambridge, Mass.

Krueger, Anne O. (1978), *Foreign Trade Regimes and Economic Development: Liberalization Attempts and Consequences*, Cambridge (Mass.).

Krueger, Anne O. (1979), "The Developmental Role of the Foreign Sector and Aid." *Studies in the Modernization of the Republic of Korea, 1945-75*, Harvard University, Cambridge, Mass.

Kuznets, Paul W. (1980), "Accelerated Economic Growth and Structural Change", in: Chang Yunshik (ed.), *Korea: A Decade of Development*, Seoul.

Kuznets, Paul W. (1980), "The Korean Economy: A Contemporary Case of Accelerated Growth," in: D.C. Cole, Lim Youngil, P.W. Kuznets, *The Korean Economy, Issues of Development*, Berkeley.

Lewis, Arthur W. (1966), *Development Planning*, London.

Lim, Linda, Fong, Pang Eng (1991), *Foreign Direct Investment and Industrialization in Malaysia, Singapore, Taiwan and Thailand*, OECD, Development Centre, Paris.

Little, Ian, Scitovsky, Tibor, Scott, Maurice (1970), *Industry and Trade in some Developing Countries: A Comparative Study*. London, New York, Toronto.

Little, I.M.D. (1982), *Economic Development – Theory, Policy and International Relations*, New York.

Luedde-Neurath, Richard (1984), "State Intervention and Foreign Direct Investment in South Korea," *IDS-Bulletin*, Vol. 15, pp. 18-25.

Lutz, Wolfgang, Toth, Ferenc L. (1990), *Population, Economy and Environment in Mauritius*. Proceedings of a Task Force Meeting at the International Institute for Applied Systems Analysis, Sept. 3.-5., 1990, Laxenburg/Austria.

Mason, Edward S. et al. (1980), *The Economic and Social Modernization of the Republic of Korea 1945-1975*. Harvard University, Cambridge, Mass.

Menzel, Ulrich (1985), *In der Nachfolge Europas: Autozentrierte Entwicklung in den ostasiatischen Schwellenländern Südkorea und Taiwan*, München.

Michaely, M. (1977), "Exports and Growth: An Empirical Investigation," *Journal of Development Economics*, March.

Michell, Tony (1984), "Administrative traditions and economic decision-making in South Korea," *IDS-Bulletin*, Vol. 15, no. 2.

Myrdal, Gunnar, (1968), *Asian Drama. An Inquiry into the Poverty of Nations*, New York.

Park, Chung Hee (1970), *The Country, the Revolution and I*. Seoul.

Park, Chung Hee (1970a), *Our Nation's Path*. Seoul.

Rostow, Whitman W. (1960), *The Stages of Economic Growth. A Non-Communist Manifesto*, Cambridge.

Scitovsky, Tibor (1986), "Economic Development in Taiwan and South Korea, 1965-1981," in: Lau, Lawrence J., Klein, Lawrence R. (eds.), *Models of Development. A Comparative Study of Economic Growth in South Korea and Taiwan*, The Institute for Contemporary Studies, San Francisco.

Senghaas, Dieter (1982), *Von Europa lernen. Entwicklungsgeschichtliche Betrachtungen*, Frankfurt.

Serfas, Alexander (1987), *An der Schwelle zum Industrieland: Die wirtschaftliche Entwicklung Südkoreas 1963-1983*, Frankfurt, Bern, New York, Paris.

Simai, Mihaly (1991), *The Emerging New Market Economics and the Evolving New Democracies*, Paper delivered at the International Studies Association, Annual Convention, Vancouver.

Stecher, Bernd (1976), "Erfolgsbedingungen der Importsubstitution und der Exportdiversifizierung im Industrialisierungsprozeß," *Kieler Studien* 136, Tübingen.

Sun, Yat-Sen (1927), San Kim Chu I. (1927), *The Three Principles of the People*, translated into English by Frank W. Price, Taipei.

Tsiang, S.C. (1985), "Foreign Trade and Investment as Boosters for Take-off: The Experience of Taiwan," in: *Export-Oriented Development Strategies. The Success of Five Newly Industrializing Countries*, Corbo, Krueger, Ossa, pp. 27-56.

Urban, Waltraut (1990), "Neue Entwicklungen in den Schwellenländern," *Österreichische Zeitschrift für Politikwissenschaft*, 1990/4, p. 409-419.

Wade, Robert (1984), "Dirigisme in Taiwan-Style," *IDS-Bulletin*, Vol. 15, no. 2.

Wallerstein, Immanuel (1974), *The Modern World System*, New York.

Wallerstein, Immanuel (1979), *The Capitalist World Economy*, Cambridge.

Westphal, Larry E. (1978), "The Republic of Korea's Experience with Export-led Industrial Development," *World Development*, Vol. 6, No. 3, pp. 347-382.

Westphal, Larry E., Rhee, Yung W., Pursell, Garry (1981), "Korean Industrial Competence: Where it Came From." *World Bank Staff Working Paper* No. 469, Juli.

Kazimierz Laski

Kazimierz Laski, born 1921 in Warsaw, studied political economy during 1945-1953 in Warsaw and obtained his M.A. in economics in 1949 and a Ph.D. in economics in 1953.

During the years 1950-1968, Laski held different positions at the Central School of Planning and Statistics in Warsaw: He was Professor Extraordinary and Chairperson of the Political Economy department during 1960-1968; Vice-Rector for Research Affairs during 1960-1963; Chairperson of the Scientific Council of the Advanced Course in National Economic Planning for Economists from Developing Countries during 1961-1968; Visiting Professor at the Institute for Advanced Studies in Vienna in 1964; and Directeur d'Études à titre étranger à la 6-e Section de l'École Pratique des Hautes Études, Sorbonne, Paris during 1966-1967.

Laski left Poland for good in November 1968 for political reasons and settled in Austria. There, he held a position in the Austrian Institute for Economic Research during the years 1969-1971. He was appointed full professor in economics at the University of Linz, where he taught from 1971 until his retirement in 1991. Since 1991 Laski has been Research Director of The Vienna Institute for Comparative Economic Studies. His scholarly work deals mainly with macroeconomics and theory of economic dynamics. He also worked on theory of growth and planning, and his list of publications contains over 100 items.

Laski has published three books, the last of which was written with Wlodzimierz Brus (Oxford) and is entitled *From Marx-Socialism to Market-Socialism* (Oxford University Press, 1989). The German translation appeared in 1990. Laski has also written many contributions to compendia and published papers in *Economista, Journal of Comparative Economics*, and other scientific periodicals. He has participated in a number of international sessions of the Verein für Socialpolitik, of the International Economic Association, the European Economic Association, and other scientific associations.

Latest Publications

1989:

1. Brus, W., Laski, K. (1989), *From Marx to the Market: Socialism in Search of an Economic System,* Oxford: Oxford University Press.

2. Laski, K. (1989), "Polens Wirtschaftskrise als politisch-ökonomisches Strukturproblem," in: Hans-Henning Hahn und Michael G. Müller (Eds.), *Gesellschaft und Staat in Polen. Historische Aspekte der polnischen Krise.* Berlin: Verlag Arno Spitz (64-94).

3. Laski, K., Zieba, J. (1989), "Die Entwicklung Polens und Spaniens in den Jahren 1950 bis 1985," *WIIW-Forschungsberichte,* No. 156, Vienna, May.

4. Laski, K., Brus, W. (1989), "Capital Market and the Problem of Full Employment", *WIIW-Forschungsberichte,* No. 155, Vienna, March.

5. Laski, K., Brus, W. (1989), "Capital Market and the Problem of Full Employment", *European Economic Review* 33 (439-447).

6. Laski, K., Slater, J. (1989), "Summary of the discussion on: The role and functioning of the enterprise", in: Economic Reforms in the European Centrally Planned Economies. Proceedings of a symposium conducted in association with The Vienna Institute for Comparative Economic Studies. United Nations. Economic Commission for Europe. *Economic Studies* No. 1, New York: United Nations (154-157).

7. Laski, K., Zieba, J. (1989), "Jeszcze o Polsce i Hiszpanii," (Again about Poland and Spain), Warsaw, *Zycie gospodarcze*, of Aug. 13.

8. Laski, K., Zieba, J. (1989), "Porownanie gospodarki Polski i Hiszpanii" (Comparison of the economy in Poland and Spain), Warsaw, *Zycie gospodarcze* of Apr. 9.

1990:

1. Brus, W., Laski, K. (1990), *Von Marx zum Markt. Der Sozialismus auf der Suche nach einem neuen Wirtschaftssystem.* Marburg: Metropolis-Verlag (two Editions).

2. Brus, W., Laski, K. (1990), "Product Market and Capital Market in the Light of the Experience of the Hungarian New Economic Mechanism", in O. T. Bogomolov (Ed.), *Market Forces in Planned Economies.* Macmillan in association with the International Economic Association (16-31).

3. Laski, K. (1990), "Note on Some Necessary Changes to Improve Trade of the USSR", in O. T. Bogomolov (Ed.), *Market Forces in Planned Economies.* Macmillan in association with the International Economic Association (217-220).

4. Laski, K. (1990), "O niebezpieczenstwach zwiazanych z planem stabilizacji gospodarki narodowej" (concerning the Dangers of the Stabilization Plan for the Economy), Warsaw, *Gospodarka narodowa,* No. 2/3 (5-9).

5. Laski, K. (1990). "The stabilization plan for Poland", *Wirtschaftspolitische Blätter,* No. 5 (444-458).

6. Laski, K., Podkaminer, L. (1990), "Charemza, W., and Gronicki, M.: Plans and Disequilibria in Centrally Planned Economies. Empirical Investigations for Poland". Review in: *Journal of Economics,*, Vol. 52. No. 2, (199-204).

1991:

1. Brus, W., Laski, K. (1991), *From Marx to the Market: Socialism in Search of an Economic System*, Oxford: Oxford University Press (170 S.) (Hardback reprinted and paperback edition).

2. Gabrisch, H., Laski, K. (1991), "Transition from Command to Market Economies", in P. Havlik (Ed.), *Dismantling the Command Economy in Eastern Europe* (The Vienna Institute for Comparative Economic Studies, Yearbook III), Boulder-San Francisco-Oxford: Westview Press (11-29).

3. Laski, K., Gabrisch, H. (1991), "Transition by Shock in Poland" in: *Dismantling* ..., op.cit. (225-234).

4. Laski, K. (1991), "Die Wirtschaftslage der ehemaligen RGW-Länder im Jahr 1990", Paper read at the General Meeting of Members of The WIIW for the Year 1990, Vienna, April 4, 1991.

5. Laski, K. (1991), "Transition from Command to Market Economies in Central and Eastern Europe: First Experiences and Questions", paper presented at the conference on Medium Term Economic Assessment (MTEA) in Vienna, 14-16, October 1991.

ABOUT THE CONTRIBUTORS

Prof. Dr. Amit Bhaduri, born 1940 in India. Educated in Presidency College, Calcutta, India, at the Massachusetts Institute of Technology, U.S.A., and at the University of Cambridge, England. Wrote books and contributed research papers in diverse areas of economics, including capital and distribution theory, development economics and macroeconomics. Has taught in various Universities in Asia, Europe, North and Latin America, and is currently honorary professor at Nehru University, New Delhi, and professor of economics at the Indian Institute of Management, Calcutta.

Dr. Raimund Dietz, born 1944 in Austria. Study of economics, mathematics and political sciences at the Free University of Berlin; researcher at the Technical University of Berlin. Since 1975 staff member of The Vienna Institute for Comparative Economic Studies (WIIW), specializing in East European economies, energy economics, and theory of comparative economic systems. Jean Monnet Fellow in 1986-1987, and Fellow of the Fritz Thyssen-Stiftung 1990-1992.

Dr. Hubert Gabrisch, born 1950 in the FRG. 1979-1984 researcher at the HWWA Institute for Economic Research, Hamburg. Since 1985 on the research staff of The Vienna Institute for Comparative Economic Studies (WIIW), and since 1992 deputy director. Special fields: Poland's economy; economic reforms of the countries of East Europe, especially of Poland; special forms of East-West trade; energy.

Mag. Ilse Grosser, born 1952 in Austria. Since 1978 active as a researcher on the staff of The Vienna Institute for Comparative Economic Studies (WIIW). Special fields: the Bulgarian economy; East European economic performance; East-West trade, East-South trade.

Dipl.Ing. Peter Havlik, born 1950 in Czechoslovakia. Study of economics and economic statistics in Prague and Vienna. On the staff of The Vienna Institute for Comparative Economic Studies (WIIW) as a researcher since 1983, since 1990 deputy director of the WIIW. Special fields: Soviet economy; East-West comparisons of social product; economic statistics of the CMEA countries; problems of East-West trade and East-West economic relations.

Dr. Gábor Hunya, born 1953 in Hungary. Worked for ten years on the research staff of the Institute for World Economics of the Hungarian Academy of Sciences. Since 1991 on the staff of The Vienna Institute for Comparative Economic Studies (WIIW). Special fields: economy of Romania, privatization in Central and Eastern Europe, regional development in Central and East European Countries.

Prof. Dr. Friedrich Levcik, born 1915 in Czechoslovakia. Active in various functions, between 1946 and 1956, in Czechoslovakia's social security and health administrations, int. al. as Head of Department of Social Policy. 1956-1968 economic research at the Institute for Technical and Economic Information, and at the Economics Institute of the Czechoslovak Academy of Sciences in Prague. 1968-1972 Head of Department of the UNO Economic Commission for Europe. 1972-1978 director of research and deputy director, 1978-1984 and 1990-1991 director, then consultant of The Vienna Institute for Comparative Economic Studies (WIIW). Special fields: economic and social policy, labor economics and labor law, international economic comparisons, problems of transition.

Dipl.Ing. Zdenek Lukas, born 1949 in Czechoslovakia. One year's research in Prague in the field of agriculture. Since 1984 on the staff of The Vienna Institute for Comparative Economic Studies (WIIW) as a researcher. Special fields: the economy of Czechoslovakia; agriculture in the CMEA and Yugoslavia.

Dr. Sándor Richter, born 1953 in Hungary. Study of economics in Budapest. Between 1979 and 1990 worked as researcher of the Economic Information Unit at the Hungarian Academy of Sciences. In 1986-1990 managing director of the ECHO consulting firm. Since 1990 on the research staff of WIIW. Special fields: the economy of Hungary, regional cooperation in Eastern Europe, East-West economic relations.

Dr. Franjo Štiblar, born 1947 in Yugoslavia. Study of economics and law in Ljubljana, Belgrade and Pennsylvania. Since 1970 professor at the University of Ljubljana, 1982-1985 advisor to the Governor of the National Bank of Slovenia. Special fields: economy of Yugoslavia, international economic relations, applied econometrics.

Mag. Waltraut Urban, born in Austria. Study of economics at the University of Vienna. Lecturer at the Technical University of Vienna, then researcher at the Austrian Institute of Economic Research and lecturer at the University of the Witwatersrand (R.S.A.). Since 1984 on the research staff of the Austrian Institute for International Affairs (AIIA). Special fields: International economic relations, international political economy, the Newly Industrializing Countries.

For Product Safety Concerns and Information please contact our EU representative GPSR@taylorandfrancis.com Taylor & Francis Verlag GmbH, Kaufingerstraße 24, 80331 München, Germany

Batch number: 10726013

Printed by Printforce, the Netherlands